Frommer's®

Kauai
2nd Edition

by Jeanette Foster

D0040618

Here's what the critics say about Frommer's:

"Amazingly easy to use. Very portable, very complete."
—*Booklist*

"Detailed, accurate, and easy-to-read information for all price ranges."
—*Glamour Magazine*

"Hotel information is close to encyclopedic."
—*Des Moines Sunday Register*

"Frommer's Guides have a way of giving you a real feel for a place."
—*Knight Ridder Newspapers*

WILEY

Wiley Publishing, Inc.

About the Author

A resident of the Big Island, **Jeanette Foster** has skied the slopes of Mauna Kea—during a Fourth of July ski meet, no less—and gone scuba diving with manta rays off the Kona Coast. A prolific writer widely published in travel, sports, and adventure magazines, she's also a contributing editor to *Hawaii* magazine and the editor of *Zagat's Survey to Hawaii's Top Restaurants*. In addition to this guide, Jeanette is the author of *Frommer's Maui, Frommer's Hawaii, Frommer's Honolulu, Waikiki & Oahu, Frommer's Kauai,* and *Frommer's Hawaii with Kids*.

Published by:

Wiley Publishing, Inc.

111 River St.
Hoboken, NJ 07030-5774

ISBN-13: 978-0-7645-8901-0
ISBN-10: 0-7645-8901-6

Editor: Christina Summers
Production Editor: Katie Robinson
Cartographer: Andrew Dolan
Photo Editor: Richard Fox
Production by Wiley Indianapolis Composition Services

Front cover photo: Allerton Gardens: Woman staring at giant Ficus tree.
Back cover photo: Hanalei, Princeville: Beach scene with overhanging palm fronds.

For information on our other products and services or to obtain technical support, please contact our Customer Care Department within the U.S. at 800-762-2974, outside the U.S. at 317-572-3993 or fax 317-572-4002.

Wiley also publishes its books in a variety of electronic formats. Some content that appears in print may not be available in electronic formats.

Manufactured in the United States of America

5 4 3 2 1

Contents

List of Maps

An Invitation to the Reader

In researching this book, we discovered many wonderful places—hotels, restaurants, shops, and more. We're sure you'll find others. Please tell us about them, so we can share the information with your fellow travelers in upcoming editions. If you were disappointed with a recommendation, we'd love to know that, too. Please write to:

Frommer's Kauai, 2nd Edition
Wiley Publishing, Inc. • 111 River St. • Hoboken, NJ 07030-5774

An Additional Note

Please be advised that travel information is subject to change at any time—and this is especially true of prices. We therefore suggest that you write or call ahead for confirmation when making your travel plans. The authors, editors, and publisher cannot be held responsible for the experiences of readers while traveling. Your safety is important to us, however, so we encourage you to stay alert and be aware of your surroundings. Keep a close eye on cameras, purses, and wallets, all favorite targets of thieves and pickpockets.

Other Great Guides for Your Trip:

Frommer's Hawaii
Frommer's Maui
Frommer's Honolulu, Waikiki & Oahu
Frommer's Hawaii with Kids
Hawaii For Dummies

Frommer's Star Ratings, Icons & Abbreviations

Every hotel, restaurant, and attraction listing in this guide has been ranked for quality, value, service, amenities, and special features using a **star-rating system.** In country, state, and regional guides, we also rate towns and regions to help you narrow down your choices and budget your time accordingly. Hotels and restaurants are rated on a scale of zero (recommended) to three stars (exceptional). Attractions, shopping, nightlife, towns, and regions are rated according to the following scale: zero stars (recommended), one star (highly recommended), two stars (very highly recommended), and three stars (must-see).

In addition to the star-rating system, we also use **seven feature icons** that point you to the great deals, in-the-know advice, and unique experiences that separate travelers from tourists. Throughout the book, look for:

Finds	Special finds—those places only insiders know about
Fun Fact	Fun facts—details that make travelers more informed and their trips more fun
Kids	Best bets for kids and advice for the whole family
Moments	Special moments—those experiences that memories are made of
Overrated	Places or experiences not worth your time or money
Tips	Insider tips—great ways to save time and money
Value	Great values—where to get the best deals

The following **abbreviations** are used for credit cards:

AE	American Express	DISC	Discover	V	Visa
DC	Diners Club	MC	MasterCard		

Frommers.com

Now that you have the guidebook to a great trip, visit our website at **www.frommers.com** for travel information on more than 3,000 destinations. With features updated regularly, we give you instant access to the most current trip-planning information available. At Frommers.com, you'll also find the best prices on airfares, accommodations, and car rentals—and you can even book travel online through our travel booking partners. At Frommers.com, you'll also find the following:

- Online updates to our most popular guidebooks
- Vacation sweepstakes and contest giveaways
- Newsletter highlighting the hottest travel trends
- Online travel message boards with featured travel discussions

What's New in Kauai

The land of endless beaches, majestic, craggy mountains, awe-inspiring canyons, and verdant cliffs, Kauai maybe the oldest Hawaiian island but it is constantly changing. Our second edition comes out when Kauai is among the most popular island destinations in the world. Not as popular (or as crowded) as the island of Maui, not as urban (or as crowded) as Waikiki on Oahu; Kauai attracts a visitor who wants to slow down to a tropical pace, a visitor looking for beauty and serenity in the geographical terrain. Most likely a return visitor, because once you've seen Kauai, you just have to keep coming back.

ACCOMMODATIONS The biggest changes to Kauai in the past year were in accommodations. The **Courtyard by Marriott Kauai–Waipouli Beach** (© 800/760-8555; www.marriott.com) opened after 18 months and more than $23 million in renovations, replacing the old Kauai Coconut Beach Resort. The totally refurbished, 311-room resort sits on 10.5 acres, nestled between a coconut grove and a white sand beach and features a new swimming pool, hot tub, day spa, business center, fitness center, tennis courts, jogging paths, lounge (with nightly entertainment), and restaurant.

The **Hyatt Regency Kauai** (© 800/ 55-HYATT; www.kauai-hyatt.com) has been re-branded as the new **Grand Hyatt Kauai Resort and Spa.** Hard to believe that this luxury hotel (one of Hawaii's best) could get "grander," but the new multi-million dollar renovations of this already "grand" resort have taken casual elegance to a new level.

In the rolling hills behind Kapaa, the **Kauai Country Inn** (© 808/821-0207; www.kauaicountryinn.com) offers visitors on a budget a terrific deal. Each of the four suites (starting at just $95) is uniquely decorated in Hawaiian art deco, complete with hardwood floors, private baths, kitchen or kitchenette, your own computer with high-speed connection, and lots of little amenities that will make you break out into laughter at the hosts' sense of humor.

Closed since Hurricane Iniki slammed into Kauai and nearly destroyed it, the **Coco Palms Resort,** which Elvis Presley made famous when he filmed *Blue Hawaii* in 1961, is now scheduled for renovations and to reopen in 2008. Located on 45 acres in Wailua, Kauai's oldest resort will be developed into a 104-room hotel, with three restaurants and 200 condominium units. Construction is scheduled to begin in 2006.

DINING Several new restaurants have opened on the Garden Isle: In Lihue, **e.b.'s EATS** (3-3142 Kuhio Hwy., Lihue; © 808/632-0328) is a tiny bakery/deli/ cafe, which serves a healthy breakfast and lunch at unbelievably low prices (most of the items are under $9).

Also in Lihue, the chain restaurant **Genki Sushi** (Kukui Grove Shopping Center, 3-2600 Kaumualii Hwy., Lihue; © 808/632-2450) offers families a place to take the kids, who will be fascinated with the conveyor belt carrying plates of sushi around the counter.

Up North, another new restaurant to open is **Kilauea Fish Market** (4270 Kilauea Lighthouse Rd., Kilauea; ℭ **808/ 828-6244**), perfect for a picnic take-out lunch or an easy dinner to go. Most items are under $10.

A couple of restaurants in Kapaa have been so successful that they have moved to bigger quarters: **Blossoming Lotus** (Dragon Building, 4504 Kukui St., Kapaa; ℭ **808/822-7678;** www.blossoming lotus.com) is located just around the corner with the same great organic gourmet vegan cuisine, while the **Olympic Café** has moved to 1354 Kuhio Hwy., Kapaa (ℭ **808/822-5825**), serving the same huge breakfast, filling lunch, and reasonably priced dinners.

Recently the **Sheraton Kauai,** Poipu Beach (ℭ **808/742-8200,** www.sheraton kauai.com) launched the island's only ocean-front luau, the **Surf to Sunset Luau,** held on Monday and Friday, beginning at 6pm, $68 to $80 for adults and $34 for children, ages 6–12 years.

ACTIVITIES   The latest adventure on Kauai is an activity called "zipline." From a high perch, participants (known as "zippers"), outfitted in harnesses and helmets, attach themselves to a cable, which is suspended above the ground from one point to another a hundred or so feet away. Ignoring gravity, the zippers, attached only by a cable, zoom through the air above tree tops at speeds of 35 mph from one end of the cable to another. One of our favorite zipline tours is done by **Outfitters Kauai** (2827A Poipu Rd., Poipu; ℭ **888/742-9887** or 808/742-9667; www.outfitterskauai.com).

SPAS   Two great new spas on Kauai specialize in ayurvedic treatments from India. Once reserved just for royalty, these deep cleaning and rejuvenating treatments consists of two massage therapists using synchronized movements, while pouring warm, soothing oil on your body. Be sure to check out both the **Hanalei Day Spa** (ℭ **808/826-6621;** www.hanaleidayspa. com) and the **Tri Health Ayurveda Spa** (ℭ **800/455-0770;** www.trihealth ayurveda.com), both located on the North Shore.

Best of Kauai

On any list of the world's most spectacular islands, Kauai ranks right up there with Bora Bora, Huahine, and Rarotonga. All the elements are here: moody rainforests, majestic cliffs, jagged peaks, emerald valleys, palm trees swaying in the breeze, daily rainbows, and some of the most spectacular golden beaches you'll find anywhere. Soft tropical air, sunrise bird song, essences of ginger and plumeria, golden sunsets, sparkling waterfalls—you don't just go to Kauai, you absorb it with every sense. It may get more than its fair share of tropical downpours, but that's what makes it so lush and green—and creates an abundance of rainbows.

Kauai is essentially a single large shield volcano that rises 3 miles above the sea floor. The island lies 90 miles across the open ocean from Oahu, but it seems at least a half century removed in time. It's often called "the separate kingdom" because it stood alone and resisted King Kamehameha's efforts to unite Hawaii. In the end, a royal kidnapping was required to take the Garden Isle: After King Kamehameha died, his son, Liholiho, ascended the throne. He gained control of Kauai by luring Kauai's king, Kaumualii, aboard the royal yacht and sailing to Oahu; once there, Kaumualii was forced to marry Kaahumanu, Kamehameha's widow, thereby uniting the islands.

A law on Kauai states that no building may exceed the height of a coconut tree— between three and four stories. As a result, the island itself, not its palatial beach hotels, is the attention-grabber. There's no real nightlife here, no opulent shopping malls. But there is the beauty of the verdant jungle, the endless succession of spectacular beaches, the grandeur of Waimea Canyon, and the drama of the Na Pali Coast. Even Princeville, an opulent marble-and-glass luxury hotel, does little more than frame the natural glory of Hanalei's spectacular 4,000-foot-high Namolokama mountain range.

This is the place for active visitors: There are watersports galore; miles of trails through rainforests and along ocean cliffs for hikers, bikers, and horseback riders; and golf options that range from championship links to funky local courses where chickens roam the greens and balls wind up embedded in coconut trees. But Kauai is also great for those who need to relax and heal jangled nerves. Here you'll find miles of sandy beaches, perfect for just sitting and meditating. There are also quiet spots in the forest where you can listen to the rain dance on the leaves, as well as an endless supply of laid-back, lazy days that end with the sun sinking into the Pacific amid a blaze of glorious tropical color.

1 The Best Beaches

- **Kalapaki Beach:** Kalapaki is the best beach not only in Lihue but also on the entire east coast. Any town would pay a fortune to have a beach like Kalapaki, one of Kauai's best, in its backyard. But little Lihue turns its back on Kalapaki; there's not even a sign pointing the way through the labyrinth of traffic to this graceful half moon of golden sand at the foot of the Kauai Marriott Resort & Beach Club. Fifty yards wide and a quarter mile long, Kalapaki is protected by a jetty, making it very safe for swimmers. The waves are good for surfing when there's a winter swell, and the view from the sand—of the steepled, 2,200-foot peaks of the majestic Haupu Ridge that shield Nawiliwili Bay—is awesome. See p. 154.

- **Poipu Beach Park:** Big, wide Poipu is actually two beaches in one; it's divided by a sandbar, called a tombolo. On the left, a lava-rock jetty protects a sandy-bottomed pool that's perfect for children; on the right, the open bay attracts swimmers, snorkelers, and surfers. You'll find excellent swimming, small tide pools to explore, great reefs for snorkeling and diving, good fishing, nice waves for surfers, and a steady wind for windsurfers. See p. 156.

- **Polihale State Park:** This mini-Sahara on the western end of the island is Hawaii's biggest beach: 17 miles long and as wide as three football fields. This is a wonderful place to get away from it all, but don't forget your flip-flops—the midday sand is hotter than a lava flow. The golden sands wrap around Kauai's northwestern shore from the Kekaha plantation town, just beyond Waimea, to where the ridgebacks of the Na Pali Coast begin. The state park includes ancient Hawaiian *heiau* (temple) and burial sites, a view of the "forbidden" island of Niihau, and the famed **Barking Sands Beach,** where footfalls sound like a barking dog. (Scientists say that the grains of sand are perforated with tiny echo chambers, which emit a "barking" sound when they rub together.) See p. 158.

- **Anini Beach County Park:** Kauai's safest beach for swimming and windsurfing, Anini is also one of the island's most beautiful: It sits on a blue lagoon at the foot of emerald cliffs, looking more like Tahiti than almost any other strand in the islands. This 3-mile-long, gold-sand beach is shielded from the open ocean by the longest, widest fringing reef in Hawaii. With shallow water 4 to 5 feet deep, it's also the very best snorkeling spot on Kauai, even for beginners. On the northwest side, a channel in the reef runs out to the deep blue water with a 60-foot drop that attracts divers. Beachcombers love it, too: Seashells, cowries, and sometimes even rare Niihau shells can be found here. See p. 160.

- **Hanalei Beach:** Gentle waves roll across the face of half-moon Hanalei Bay, running up to the wide, golden sand. Sheer volcanic ridges laced by waterfalls rise to 4,000 feet on the other side, 3 miles inland. Is there any beach with a better location? Celebrated in song and hula and featured on travel posters, this beach owes its natural beauty to its age—it's an ancient sunken valley with post-erosional cliffs. Hanalei Bay indents the coast a full mile inland and runs 2 miles point to point, with coral reefs on either side and a patch of coral in the middle—plus a sunken ship that belonged to a king, so divers love it. Swimming is excellent year-round, especially in summer, when Hanalei Bay becomes a big, placid lake. The aquamarine water is also great for bodyboarding, surfing, fishing, windsurfing, canoe paddling, kayaking, and boating. (There's a boat ramp on the west bank of the Hanalei River.) See p. 160.

- **Haena Beach:** Backed by verdant cliffs, this curvaceous North Shore beach has starred as paradise in many a movie. It's easy to see why Hollywood loves Haena Beach, with its grainy golden sand and translucent turquoise waters. Summer months

Kauai

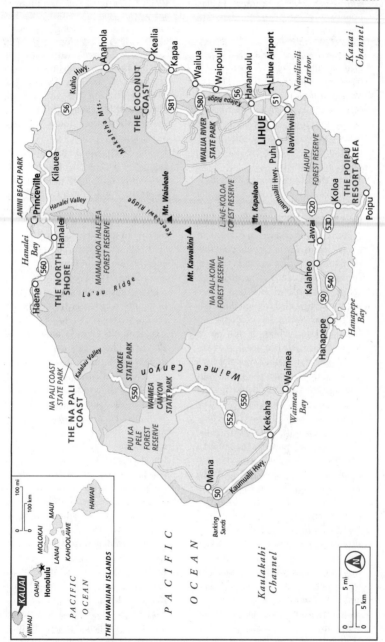

Kauai Channel

Anahola
Kealia
Kapaa
Wailua
Waipouli
Hanamaulu
Lihue Airport
Nawiliwili Harbor

Kuhio Hwy.
THE COCONUT COAST
581
580
Kalepa Ridge
56
51
LIHUE
Nawiliwili
Puhi

Makaleha Mts.

WAILUA RIVER STATE PARK

THE POIPU RESORT AREA

Kilauea
Princeville
ANINI BEACH PARK
Hanalei Valley
Hanalei Bay
Hanalei

HAUPU FOREST RESERVE

Koloa
Poipu

Mt. Waialeale
Keeawai Ridge
Mt. Kapalaoa

LIHUE-KOLOA FOREST RESERVE

Kaumualii Hwy.

520
530

Haena
Haena
THE NORTH SHORE
560

Mt. Kawaikini

MAMALAHOA HALELEA FOREST RESERVE

La'au Ridge

NA PALI-KONA FOREST RESERVE

Lawai
Kalaheo
540
50

Hanapepe Bay

KOKEE STATE PARK

Kalalau Valley

NA PALI COAST STATE PARK

THE NA PALI COAST

Waimea Canyon

WAIMEA CANYON STATE PARK

550

552

550

Waimea
Hanapepe

Kekaha

Waimea Bay

PUU KA PELE FOREST RESERVE

Barking Sands

Mana
50
Kaumualii Hwy.

Kaulakahi Channel

PACIFIC OCEAN

100 mi
100 km

NIIHAU
KAUAI
OAHU
Honolulu
MOLOKAI
MAUI
LANAI
KAHOOLAWE
HAWAII

PACIFIC OCEAN

THE HAWAIIAN ISLANDS

5 mi
5 km

N

bring calm waters for swimming and snorkeling, while winter brings mighty waves for surfers. There are plenty of facilities on hand, including picnic tables, restrooms, and showers. See p. 162.

2 The Best Kauai Experiences

- **Hitting the Beach:** A beach is a beach is a beach, right? Not on Kauai. With 50 miles of beaches, Kauai offers ocean experiences in all shapes and forms. You can go to a different beach every day during your vacations and still not get tired of seeing them. See chapter 7.

- **Taking the Plunge:** Rent a mask, fins, and snorkel, and enter a magical underwater world. Facedown, you'll float like a leaf on a pond, watching brilliant fish dart here and there in water clear as day; a slow-moving turtle may even stop by to check you out. Faceup, you'll contemplate green-velvet cathedral-like cliffs under a blue sky, with long-tailed tropical birds riding the trade winds. See chapter 7.

- **Meeting Local Folks:** If you go to Kauai and see only people like the ones back home, you might as well not have come. Extend yourself—leave your hotel, go out and meet the locals, and learn about Hawaii and its people. Just smile and say "Howzit?"—which means "How is it?" ("It's good," is the usual response—and you may make a new friend.) Hawaii is remarkably cosmopolitan; every ethnic group in the world seems to be represented here. There's a huge diversity of food, culture, language, and customs.

- **Feeling History Come Alive:** It is possible to walk back in history on Kauai. You can see ancient, ancient history, from the times when the *menehune* were around, at the **Menehune Ditch** and **Menehune Fishpond.** Or experience Hawaiian history at the **Kauai Museum,** the archaeological sites at **Wailua River State Park,** and the **Ka**

Ulu O Laka *heiau.* For more recent history, since the arrival of Captain Cook, check out the **Grove Farm Homestead Museum, Kilohana,** and the **Waioli Mission House Museum.** See chapter 8.

- **Going Deep-Sea, Big-Game Fishing:** Don't pass up the opportunity to try your luck in the sportfishing capital of the world, where 1,000-pound marlin are taken from the seas just about every month of the year. Not looking to set a world record? Kauai's charter-boat captains specialize in conservation and will be glad to tag and release any fish you angle, letting it go so someone else can have the fun of fighting a big-game fish tomorrow. See chapter 7.

- **Exploring the Grand Canyon of the Pacific:** The great gaping gulch known as Waimea Canyon is quite a sight. This valley, known for its reddish lava beds, reminds everyone who sees it of the Grand Canyon. Kauai's version is bursting with ever-changing color, just like its namesake, but it's smaller—only a mile wide, 3,567 feet deep, and 12 miles long. A massive earthquake sent streams into the single river that ultimately carved this picturesque canyon. Today, the Waimea River—a silver thread of water in the gorge that's sometimes a trickle, often a torrent, but always there—keeps cutting the canyon deeper and wider, and nobody can say what the result will be 100 million years from now. See chapter 8.

- **Watching the Hula:** The Coconut Marketplace, on Kuhio Highway (Hwy. 56) between mile markers 6 and 7, hosts free shows every day at 5pm. Arrive early to get a good seat for the hour-long performances of both *kahiko* (ancient) and *auwana* (modern) hula. The real show-stoppers are the *keiki* (children) who perform. Don't forget your camera!

- **Bidding the Sun Aloha:** Polihale State Park hugs Kauai's western shore for some 17 miles. It's a great place to bring a picnic dinner, stretch out on the sand, and toast the sun as it sinks into the Pacific, illuminating the island of Niihau in the distance. Queen's Pond has facilities for camping as well as restrooms, showers, picnic tables, and pavilions. See chapter 7.

- **Soaring Over the Na Pali Coast:** This is the only way to see the spectacular, surreal beauty of Kauai. Your helicopter will dip low over razor-thin cliffs, flutter past sparkling waterfalls, and swoop down into the canyons and valleys of the fabled Na Pali Coast. The only problem is that there's too much beauty to absorb, and it all goes by in a rush. See chapter 8.

3 The Best Adventures

- **Take a Helicopter Tour of the Island:** Don't leave Kauai without seeing it from a helicopter. It's expensive but worth the splurge. You can take home memories of the thrilling ride up and over the Kalalau Valley on Kauai's wild North Shore and into the 5,200-foot vertical temple of Mount Waialeale, the most sacred place on the island and the wettest spot on earth. (In some cases, you can even take home a video of your ride.) See p. 197.

- **Explore the Na Pali Coast by Water:** Unless you're willing to make an arduous 22-mile hike (p. 182), there are only two ways to see Na Pali: by helicopter (p. 197) or by boat. Picture yourself cruising the rugged Na Pali coastline in a 42-foot ketch-rigged yacht under full sail, watching the sunset as you enjoy a tropical cocktail, or speeding through the aquamarine water in a 40-foot trimaran as porpoises play off the bow. See p. 182.

- **Kayak Kauai:** You can take the Huleia River into Huleia National Wildlife Refuge (located along the eastern portion of Huleia Stream where it flows into Nawiliwili Bay) It's the last stand for Kauai's endangered birds, and the only way to see it is by kayak. The adventurous can head to the Na Pali Coast, which features majestic cliffs, empty beaches, open-ocean conditions, and monster waves. Or you can just paddle around Hanalei Bay. See p. 165.

- **Duck Underwater:** You haven't really seen Hawaii until you have seen the magical world underwater. Beneath those blue waves is an entire universe in itself. You'll see schools of rainbow-colored fish, dazzling corals, graceful manta rays, lumbering turtles, and quick-moving silvery game fish. If you are really lucky, you may see playful dolphins or the frequent winter visitors to Hawaii, humpback whales. See chapter 7.

- **Hike Until You Drop:** Kauai is made for hiking, from the numerous trails in Waimea Canyon to the high forests of Kokee to the interior trails that give the island its special beauty. See chapter 7.

4 The Best of Natural Hawaii

- **Waterfalls:** Rushing waterfalls thundering downward into sparkling freshwater pools are some of Hawaii's most beautiful natural wonders. Kauai is loaded with waterfalls, especially along the North Shore and in the Wailua area, where you'll find 40-foot **Opaekaa Falls,** probably the best-looking drive-up waterfall on Kauai. With scenic mountain peaks in the background and a restored Hawaiian village on the nearby riverbank, the Opaekaa Falls are what the tourist bureau folks call an eye-popping photo op. See p. 203.

- **Gardens:** The islands are redolent with the sweet scent of flowers. For a glimpse of the full breadth and beauty of Hawaii's spectacular range of tropical flora, we suggest spending an afternoon at a lush garden. **Na Aina Kai Botanical Gardens,** on some 240 acres sprinkled with about 70 life-size (some larger than life-size) whimsical bronze statues, lies hidden off the beaten path of the North Shore. Other great gardens are **Allerton Garden** in Poipu and **Limahuli** outside of Hanalei.

- **National Wildlife Refuges:** Kauai has three wildlife refuges: **Kilauea Point,** which protects seabirds; **Huleia,** which shelters endemic Hawaiian birds and wetlands; and **Hanalei,** which maintains a sheltered area for Hawaiian birds and the watershed. See p. 188.

- **The Grand Canyon of the Pacific— Waimea Canyon:** This valley, known for its reddish lava beds, reminds everyone who sees it of Arizona's Grand Canyon. Kauai's version is bursting with ever-changing color, just like its namesake, but it's smaller—only a mile wide, 3,567 feet deep, and 12 miles long. All this grandeur was caused by a massive earthquake that sent existing streams flowing into a single river, which then carved this picturesque canyon. You can stop by the road to view the canyon, hike down into it, or swoop through it by helicopter. See p. 196.

5 The Best of Underwater Hawaii

- **Caverns:** Located off the Poipu Beach resort area, this site consists of a series of lava tubes interconnected by a chain of archways. A constant parade of fish streams by (even shy lionfish are spotted lurking in crevices), brightly hued Hawaiian lobsters hide in the lava's tiny holes, and turtles swim past. See p. 166.

- **Prince Kuhio Park:** This tiny park, across the street from Ho'ai Bay, marks the birthplace of Prince Jonah Kuhio Kalanianaole. This park is across the street from the ocean, where the rocky drop-off into the water is not very convenient for access (although snorkeling offshore is great). We suggest that you go a bit further east to Keiki (Baby) Beach, a small pocket of sand off Hoona Road, where swimming is generally safe. See p. 157.

- **Hanalei Beach:** Divers love this area because it has an ancient sunken valley with post-erosional cliffs. Hanalei Bay indents the coast a full mile inland and runs 2 miles point to point, with coral reefs on either side and a patch of coral in the middle—plus a sunken ship that belonged to a king, which means excellent diving. See p. 160.

- **Oceanarium:** Northwest of Hanalei Bay you'll find this kaleidoscopic marine world in a horseshoe-shaped cove. From the rare (long-handed spiny lobsters) to the more common (taape, conger eels, and nudibranchs), the resident population is one of the more diverse on the island. The topography, which features pinnacles, ridges, and archways, is covered with cup corals, black-coral trees, and nooks and crannies enough for a dozen dives. See p. 166.

- **Haena Beach Park:** In summer when the water calms down, this golden sand beach becomes a giant aquarium, great for snorkeling amid clouds of tropical fish. See p. 162.

- **Kee Beach:** Where the road ends on the North Shore, you'll find a dandy little reddish-gold-sand beach almost too beautiful to be real. It borders a reef-protected cove at the foot of fluted volcanic cliffs. Swimming and snorkeling are safe inside the reef, where long-nosed butterfly fish flit about and schools of taape (blue stripe snapper) swarm over the coral. See p. 162.

6 The Best Golf Courses

- **Kauai Lagoons Golf Courses** (© **800/634-6400**): Choose between two excellent Jack Nicklaus–designed courses: the **Mokihana Course** (formerly known as the Lagoons Course), for the recreational golfer; or the **Kauai Kiele Championship Course,** for the low handicapper. The 6,942-yard, par-72 Mokihana is a links-style course with a bunker that's a little less severe than Kiele's; emphasis is on the short game. The Kiele is a mixture of tournament-quality challenge and high-traffic playability. It winds up with one of Hawaii's most difficult holes, a 431-yard, par-4 played straightaway to an island green. See p. 183.

- **Puakea Golf Course** (© **866/773-5554**): This former Grove Farm sugar plantation just opened up 18 holes in 2003 to rave reviews. The course was in the middle of construction when Hurricane Iniki slammed into it in 1992, rearranging the greens from golf-course designer Robin Nelson's original plan. The first 9 (actually the first 10) holes finally opened in 1997 to many kudos; *Sports Illustrated* named Puakea one of the 10 best 9-hole golf courses in the U.S. The final 8 holes were finished last year and now give golfers something to think about. See p. 184.

- **Poipu Bay Golf Course** (© **808/742-8711**): This 6,959-yard, par-72 course with a links-style layout is the home of the PGA Grand Slam of Golf. Designed by Robert Trent Jones, Jr., this challenging course features undulating greens and water hazards on 8 of the holes. The par-4 16th hole has the coastline weaving along the entire left side. You can take the safe route to the right and maybe make par (but more likely bogey), or you can try to take it tight against the ocean and possibly make it in two. See p. 186.

- **Kiahuna Golf Club** (© **808/742-9595**): This par-70, 6,353-yard Robert Trent Jones, Jr.–designed course plays around four large archaeological sites, ranging from an ancient Hawaiian temple to the remains of a Portuguese home and crypt built in the early 1800s. This Scottish-style course has rolling terrain, undulating greens, 70 sand bunkers, and near-constant winds. At any given time, about half the players on the course are Kauai residents, the other half visitors. See p. 184.

- **Princeville Golf Club** (☎ **808/ 826-5070**): Here you'll find 45 of the best tropical holes of golf in the world, all the work of Robert Trent Jones, Jr. They range along green bluffs below sharp mountain peaks and offer stunning views in every direction. One of the top three courses in Hawaii, the 18-hole Prince provides a round of golf few ever forget; it winds along 390 acres of scenic tableland bisected by tropical jungles, waterfalls, streams, and ravines. See chapter 7.

7 The Best Luxury Hotels & Resorts

- **Grand Hyatt Kauai Resort & Spa** (☎ **800/55-HYATT**): This Art Deco beach hotel recalls Hawaii in the 1920s—before the Crash—when gentlemen in blue blazers and ladies in summer frocks came to the islands to learn to surf and play the ukulele. The Hyatt's architecture and location on the sunny side of Kauai make this the island's best hotel. The beach is a bit too rough for swimming, but the saltwater swimming pool is the biggest on the island. An old-fashioned reading room by the sea houses club chairs, billiards, and a bar well stocked with cognac and port. Golf, horseback riding, and the shops of Koloa, a plantation town offering numerous boutiques, are nearby diversions. See p. 90.

- **Kauai Marriott Resort & Beach Club** (☎ **800/220-2925**): Water is found everywhere throughout this resort: lagoons, waterfalls, fountains, a 5-acre circular swimming pool (some 26,000 sq. ft., the largest on the island), and a terrific stretch of beach. The lagoons are home to six islands that serve as an exotic mini-zoo, which still lends an air of fantasy to the place and, along with the enormous pool and children's program, makes the resort popular with families. See p. 85.

- **Sheraton Kauai Resort** (☎ **800/ 782-9488**): This modern Sheraton (since 1997) has the feeling of old Hawaii and a dynamite location on one of Kauai's best beaches. It features buildings on both the ocean side and the mountain side of the road. The horseshoe-shaped, Polynesian-style lobby has shell chandeliers dangling from the ceiling. You have a choice of three buildings: one nestled in tropical gardens with koi-filled ponds; one facing the palm-fringed, white-sand beach (our favorite); and one looking across green grass to the ocean, with great sunset views. The rooms overlook either the tropical gardens or the rolling surf. See p. 92.

- **Princeville Resort Kauai** (☎ **800/ 826-4400**): This palace of green marble and sparkling chandeliers recalls Hawaii's monarchy period of the 19th century. It's set in one of the most remarkable locations in the world, on a cliff between the crystal-blue waters of Hanalei Bay and steepled mountains. You arrive on the ninth floor and go down to the beach. Opulent rooms with magnificent views and all the activities of Princeville and Hanalei make this one of Hawaii's finest resorts. See p. 113.

- **Hanalei Bay Resort & Suites** (☎ **800/827-4427**): This 22-acre resort is just up the street from ritzy Princeville Resort (see above), overlooking the fabled Bali Ha'i cliffs and Hanalei Bay. It has the same majestic view, but for as little as half the price. The place recaptures the spirit of old Hawaii, especially in the three-story stucco units that angle down the hill to the gold-sand, palm-fringed beach it shares with its neighbor. Rooms are decorated in island style, with rattan furnishings and lanais overlooking the bay, the lush grounds, and the distant mountains. Shuttle service is available for those who may have problems walking on the steep hillside. See p. 114.

8 The Best Moderately Priced Accommodations

- **Kauai Country Inn** (© 808/821-0207): Fabulous location (nestled in the rolling hills behind Kapaa), terrific prices (from $95 a night), wonderful accommodations (big suites, hardwood floors, kitchen or kitchenette, your own private computer, comfy beds, and great views), and friendly hosts make this a "must-book" place. See p. 109.
- **Hideaway Cove Villas** (© 886/849-2426): Just a block from the beach and next door to an excellent restaurant are these gorgeous condominiums in a plantation setting. Amenities are top-drawer, and no expense was spared in the decor. Living areas are spacious, kitchens come with the best appliances and granite-top counters, and the outdoor lanais are big. You get all of this in a lush, landscaped tropical jungle at an affordable price. See p. 94.
- **Poipu Kapili Resort** (© 800/443-7714): This quiet, upscale oceanfront cluster of condos is outstanding in every area. We like the home-away-from-home comforts and special touches: a video and book library, a spacious pool, several barbecues, tennis courts lit for night play, and an herb garden. (You're welcome to take samples if you're cooking.) A golf course is located nearby. See p. 95.
- **Garden Isle Cottages Oceanfront** (© 800/742-6711): The site is spectacular: a 13-foot cliff overlooking historic Koloa Landing and an ocean inlet (where you can see turtles swimming). Nestled in a tropical garden setting, these one-bedroom apartments have an island feel, with rattan furniture, batiks, and original art on the walls—and great views. This is a quiet, peaceful place to stay in the heart of the Poipu area, within walking distance of beaches, golfing, tennis, shopping, and restaurants. See p. 94.
- **Kauai Cove** (© 800/624-9945): These immaculate cottages, located just 300 feet from Koloa Landing and next to Waikomo Stream, are the perfect private getaway. Each studio has a full kitchen, a private lanai (with barbecue grill), and a big bamboo four-poster bed. The cozy rooms feature beautiful hardwood floors, tropical decor, and cathedral ceilings. The cottages are close enough for walks to sandy beaches, great restaurants, and shopping, yet far enough off the beaten path that privacy and quiet are assured. See p. 97.
- **Waimea Plantation Cottages** (© 800/9-WAIMEA): This beachfront vacation retreat is like no other in the islands: Among groves of towering coco palms sit clusters of restored sugar-plantation cottages, dating from the 1880s to the 1930s and bearing the names of their original plantation-worker dwellers. The lovely cottages have been transformed into cozy, comfortable guest units with period rattan and wicker furniture and fabrics from the 1930s, sugar's heyday on Kauai. Each has a furnished lanai and a fully equipped modern kitchen and bathroom; some units are oceanfront. Facilities include an oceanfront pool, tennis courts, and laundry. The seclusion of the village makes it a nice place for

kids to wander and explore, away from traffic. See p. 104.

- **Wailua Bayview** (© 800/882-9007): Located right on the ocean, these spacious one-bedroom apartments offer excellent value. The bedrooms are roomy, and the sofa bed in the living room allows you to sleep up to four. On-site facilities include a pool and barbecue area. Restaurants, bars, shopping, golfing, and tennis are nearby. See p. 111.

- **Aloha Sunrise Inn/Aloha Sunset Inn** (© 888/828-1008): Hidden on the North Shore, these two unique cottages nestle on a quiet 7-acre farm. They come fully furnished with all the great videos you've been meaning to watch, and an excellent CD library. The cottages are close to activities, restaurants, and shopping, yet isolated enough to offer the peace and quiet of old Hawaii. Rates are $125 to $130. See p. 114.

- **Hanalei Surf Board House** (© 808/ 826-9825): If you are looking for a moderately priced ($150 a night), adorable studio just a block from the beach in Hanalei, get on the phone and book this right now. If you have a great sense of humor and enjoy whimsical little touches in the decor, you will love this place. See p. 117.

9 The Best Inexpensive Accommodations

- **K. K. Bed & Bath** (© 808/822-7348): Attention frugal travelers, this is the place for you. It's not a true B&B, but more just a place to sleep with a private bath. Located just one block from the ocean and one block from "downtown" Kapaa, this Zen-like 300-square-foot room is a steal at $50 double. See p. 112.

- **Garden Island Inn** (© 800/648-0154): Centrally located (a couple of miles from the airport, walking distance to the beach), this small (21 rooms) inn has comfortable accommodations at budget prices (from $85). See p. 88.

- **Kauai Banyan Inn** (© 888/786-3855): Off the beaten path, but still just a 10-minute drive to the beach, this 4-unit inn has the amenities of a much more expensive property (kitchenette, views, in-room massage) at budget prices (from $70). See p. 96.

- **Kalaheo Inn** (© 888/332-6023): What a deal! This boutique inn (15 units), located in the community of Kalaheo (10 minutes to the beach, walking distance to great restaurants) is comfy, clean, and terrific for families. Prices start at $65 (p. 102).

- **Hibiscus Hollow** (© 808/823-0925): One of the best deals in the state, this one-bedroom cottage is just $50 a night. The catch? The hosts are nice people who think $50 a night is a fair deal (and hundreds of happy guests agree with them). See p. 112.

- **Aloha Plantation Kauai** (© 877/ 658-6977): Walk back in history at this old, 1920s plantation home decorated with Hawaiian antiques in Kilauea. Prices start at $69 double. See p. 117.

10 The Best Bed & Breakfasts

- **Victoria Place** (© 808/332-9300): This is our favorite bed-and-breakfast on Kauai. The reason to stay here? One name: Edee Seymour. It's easy to see why she won the Kauai Chamber of Commerce's Aloha Spirit Award. Her motto is, "We pamper!" She lavishes her guests with attention and aloha. Her spacious, sky-lit, U-shaped house wraps around the garden and pool, which are surrounded by flowering walls of bougainvillea, hibiscus, gardenia, and ginger. Edee's breakfasts are truly a big deal: five kinds of fruit, followed by something from the oven such as homemade bread, scones, or muffins. Most of her guests are returnees. As a couple from Germany told us, "Once you stay with Edee, every place else is cold and indifferent." See p. 100.

- **Stonehaven** (© 808/742-2966): In a quiet, country area just a 10-minute drive to Poipu Beach, this 4-unit B&B has beautiful rooms (marble floors, soaking tub, and separate glass shower) and yummy breakfasts. The price is a little high at $135 a night, but the amenities more than make up for it. See p. 95.
- **Hale Kua** (© 800/440-4353): This is for people who love the beach—at a distance, and want to sleep in the quiet and cool climate of the hills of Lawai Valley, away from the maddening crowds. If you want to stay in a forest, wake up to bird song, and see incredible sunsets each night, this is your place. The beach is just a 10-minute drive down the hill. See p. 102.
- **Lani-keha** (© 800/821-4898): Step back in time to the 1940s, when Hawaiian families lived in open, airy, rambling homes on large plots of land

lush with fruit trees and sweet-smelling flowers. This gracious age is still alive and well in Lani-keha, a *kamaaina* (old-timer) home with an open living/game/writing/dining room and oversize picture windows to take in the views. Bedrooms come with private bathrooms. The house is elegant yet casual, with old-style rattan furniture—practicality and comfort outweigh design aesthetics. See p. 110.

- **Rosewood Bed & Breakfast** (© 808/822-5216): This lovingly restored century-old plantation home, set amid tropical flowers, lily ponds, and waterfalls, has accommodations to suit everyone. There's a Laura Ashley–style room in the main house, and two private cottages on the grounds. There's also a bunkhouse with three separate small rooms with a shared shower and toilet. See p. 111.
- **Hale Ho'o Maha** (© 800/851-0291): Kirby Guyer and her husband, Toby, have a spacious four-bedroom, three-bathroom home on 5 acres. It's filled with Hawaiian and South Pacific artifacts and features a fireplace, a library, and a 150-gallon saltwater aquarium more entertaining than TV. The rooms are uniquely decorated and are priced with budget travelers in mind. The home is close to two remarkable white-sand beaches, golf courses, riding stables, restaurants, and markets. See p. 118.

11 The Best Restaurants

- **Duke's Canoe Club** (© 808/246-9599): Tropical atmosphere overlooking the ocean, great fresh fish at attractive prices, and dependably good meals. Don't miss the wallet-pleasing drink prices at happy hour. See p. 123.
- **Casa Blanca at Kiahuna** (© 808/742-2929): This stylish, open-air restaurant overlooking the manicured

grounds of the Kiahuna Swim and Tennis Club is a casual, elegant restaurant serving some of the best cuisine on Kauai, including a gourmet breakfast, a creative lunch, a tapas menu of small items (each one so delicious you could make a meal of them), and probably the best dinner you will eat on Kauai. See p. 131.

- **The Beach House** (© 808/742-1424): All reports are good from this beachfront magnet in Lawai. Though there has been a major cosmetic overhaul, the food is as good as ever. Beach House remains the south shore's premier spot for sunset drinks, appetizers, and dinner—a treat for all the senses. See p. 128.

- **Dondero's** (© 808/742-1234): If you are looking for a romantic dinner either under the stars overlooking the ocean or tucked away at an intimate table surrounded by inlaid marble floors, ornate imported floor tiles, and Franciscan murals, this is your best bet. All this atmosphere comes with the best Italian cuisine on the island, served with efficiency. It's hard to have a bad experience here. Dinners are pricey and worth every penny. See p. 128.

- **Tidepool Restaurant** (© 808/742-1234): An ultra-romantic setting (literally hanging over the water), fabulous creative cuisine, and quick, efficient service with a smile make this restaurant in the Grand Hyatt a stand out. See p. 130.

- **Hanapepe Café** (© 808/335-5011): Now under new management, Hanapepe maintains the same wholesome cuisine in a casual, winning ambience that has drawn foodies for a decade. During lunchtime the place is packed with businesspeople who drive 30 minutes to eat here. On the Friday-night dinner menu, the Italian specialties shine: lasagna quattro formaggio with spinach, mushrooms, and four cheeses; crepes; and other goodies. There's no liquor license, so if you want wine, bring your own. See p. 136.

- **Caffè Coco** (© 808/822-7990): This gets our vote for the most charming ambience on Kauai. Caffè Coco is just off the main road at the edge of a cane field in Wailua, its backyard shaded by fruit trees, with a view of Sleeping Giant Mountain. Gourmet fare is cooked to order—and at cafe prices. The food is excellent, with vegetarian and other healthful delights such as spanakopita, homemade chai, Greek salad, fish wraps, macadamia nut–black sesame ahi with wasabi cream, and an excellent tofu-and-roast-veggie wrap. See p. 140.

- **Blossoming Lotus** (© 808/822-7678): Even if you are not a vegetarian, you will be pleasantly surprised at the creative cuisine in this elegant eatery in Kapaa. Most people can't believe that healthy, non-meat dishes could be this delicious, and even the desserts look sinful (but aren't). See p. 142.

- **La Cascata** (© 808/826-9644): The North Shore's special-occasion restaurant is sumptuous—a Sicilian spree in Eden. Try to get here before dark, so you can enjoy the views of Bali Hai, the persimmon-colored sunset, and the waterfalls of Waialeale, all an integral part of the feast. Click your heels on the terra-cotta floors, take in the *trompe l'oeil* vines, train your eyes through the concertina windows, and pretend you're being served on a terrazzo in Sicily. See p. 145.

- **Kilauea Fish Market** (© 808/828-6244): Perfect for a takeout lunch or dinner on the beach, this tiny deli (with a handful of tables outside) pumps out incredibly delicious meals (even dishes for vegetarians) with fresh, healthy, locally grown and caught ingredients. See p. 151.

12 The Best Shops & Galleries

- **Tropical Flowers by Charles** (© 800/699-7984): Charles is a flower genius who grows a range of tropical flowers, including some very rare and unusual varieties. Prices are extremely reasonable. See p. 214.

- **Banana Patch Studio** (© 808/335-5944): This place has the best prices on the island for anything artsy and cute like tropical plates and cups, hand-painted tiles, artwork, handmade soaps, pillows with tropical designs, and jewelry. Plus, they will pack and ship for you anywhere. See p. 215.

- **Bambulei** (© 808/823-8641): Celebrate the charm and style of 1930s and 1940s collectibles in this treasure trove at the edge of a cane field. Fabulous one-of-a-kind vintage finds—Mandarin dresses with hand-sewn sequins, 1940s *pake* muumuus in mint condition, Peking lacquerware, and Bakelite jewelry—fill this jewel of a boutique, owned by two women with a passion for the past. See p. 216.

- **Kong Lung** (© 808/828-1822): You'll be surprised by what you find inside this 1922 stone building. It's a showcase of design, style, and quality, with items from dinnerware, books, jewelry, and clothing to the finest sake and tea sets on the island. Throw in a lacquer bowl or two, a pair of beaded sandals, and a silk dress from the women's section, and the party's on at "Gump's of the Pacific." See p. 218.

- **Robert Hamada's Studio:** Woodturner Robert Hamada makes works of art for wood purists: museum-quality bowls and large sculptural shapes in kou, milo, kauila, camphor, mango, and native woods he logs himself. He works in his studio at the foot of the Sleeping Giant, quietly producing luminous pieces with unique textures and grains. His skill, his lathe, and his more than 60 years of experience put him in a class of his own. See p. 216.

- **Yellowfish Trading Company** (© 808/826-1227): Surprise yourself at Yellowfish Trading Company, where vintage bark cloth and that one-of-a-kind 1940s rattan sofa are among owner Gritt Benton's short-lived pleasures. The collectibles—1930s lampshades, '40s vases, '50s lunchboxes, antique silk piano shawls—move quickly. See p. 219.

- **Ola's** (© 808/826-6937): Fine crafts from across the country find their way to this temple of good taste: lamps, vases, blown glass, drumsticks, jewelry, hard-to-find books, and the peerless paintings of award-winning artist Doug Britt. See p. 218.

13 The Best Spas

- **ANARA Spa at the Grand Hyatt Kauai** (© 80808/240-6440): This is the place to be to get rid of stress and be soothed and pampered in a Hawaiian atmosphere, where the spirit of aloha reigns. An elegant 25,000-square-foot spa, ANARA (A New Age Restorative Approach) focuses on Hawaiian culture and healing, with some 16 treatment rooms, a lap pool, fitness facilities, lava rock showers that open to the tropical air, outdoor whirlpools, a 24-head Swiss shower, Turkish steam rooms, Finnish saunas, and botanical soaking tubs. Recent renovations make this spa even more serene and relaxing. The new menu of treatments includes a four-handed massage (two therapists at once), which is not be missed. See p. 92.

Pampering in Paradise

Kauai's spas have raised the art of relaxation and healing to a new level. The traditional Greco-Roman–style spas, with lots of marble and big tubs in closed rooms, have evolved into airy, open facilities that embrace the tropics. Spa-goers in Kauai are looking for a sense of place, steeped in the culture. They want to hear the sound of the ocean, smell the salt air, and feel the caress of the warm breeze. They want to experience Hawaiian products and traditional treatments they can get only in the islands.

The spas, once nearly exclusively patronized by women, are now attracting more male clients. There are special massages for children and pregnant women, and some spas have created programs to nurture and relax brides on their big day.

Today's spas offer a wide diversity of treatments. There is no longer plain, ordinary massage, but Hawaiian lomilomi, Swedish, aromatherapy (with sweet-smelling oils), craniosacral (massaging the head), shiatsu (no oil, just deep thumb pressure on acupuncture points), Thai (another oil-less massage involving stretching), and hot stone (with heated, and sometimes cold, rocks). There are even side-by-side massages for couples. The truly decadent might even try a duo massage—not one, but *two* massage therapists working on you at once.

Massages are just the beginning. Body treatments, for the entire body or for just the face, involve a variety of herbal wraps, masks, or scrubs using a range of ingredients from seaweed to salt to mud, with or without accompanying aromatherapy, lights, and music.

After you have been rubbed and scrubbed, most spas offer an array of water treatments—a sort of hydromassage in a tub with jets and an assortment of colored crystals, oils, and scents.

Those are just the traditional treatments. Most spas also offer a range of alternative health care like acupuncture and chiropractic, and more exotic treatments like ayurvedic and siddha from India or reiki from Japan.

Once your body has been pampered, spas also offer a range of fitness facilities (weight-training equipment, racquetball, tennis, golf) and classes (yoga, aerobics, step, spinning, stretch, tai chi, kickboxing, aquacize). Several even offer adventure fitness packages (from bicycling to snorkeling). For the nonadventurous, most spas have salons, dedicated to hair and nail care and makeup.

If all this sounds a bit overwhelming, not to worry, all the spas in Hawaii have individual consultants who will help design you an appropriate treatment program to fit your individual needs.

Of course, all this pampering doesn't come cheap. Massages are generally $95 to $195 for 50 minutes and $150 to $250 for 80 minutes; body treatments are in the $150-to-$250 range; and alternative health-care treatments can be has high as $200 to $300. But you may think it's worth the expense to banish your tension and stress.

- **Princeville Health Club & Spa, Princeville Resort** (© **808/826-5030**): This spa offers good value. Not only are the treatments a full 60 minutes (versus the standard 50 min. in most spas), but prices are also quite a bit lower (hour-long massages and body treatments are way less than what many spas charge). Just a short 7-minute drive (via the free resort shuttle) from the Princeville Hotel, this 10,000-square-foot boutique spa has amenities like a 25m (82 ft.) heated lap pool, outdoor whirlpool, sauna, steam room, five treatment rooms (plus massage cabanas poolside at the hotel), exercise classes, a weight room, a cardio room, and even babysitting services. See p. 113.
- **Hanalei Day Spa** (© **808/826-6621**): Located on the grounds of the Hanalei Colony Resort in Haena, this small but wonderfully effective spa has not only a full menu of massages, body treatments, and body wraps, but specializes in ayurvedic treatments to soothe and comfort your weary body. Spa owner and Ayurveda practitioner Darci Frankel is a recognized expert in the field of ayurvedic treatments. See p. 114.
- **Tri Health Ayurveda Spa** (© **800/455-0770** or 808/822-822-4288): Tucked away on 26 acres is this spa/retreat center specializing in ayurvedic treatments, once reserved for royalty. These are deep-cleansing and rejuvenation massages (with two massage therapists working on you with specialized synchronized movements while continuously bathing your body in warm, calming oil). See p. 16.

2

Planning Your Trip to Kauai

Kauai has so many places to explore, things to do, sights to see—where do you start? That's where we come in. In the pages that follow, we've compiled everything you need to know to plan your ideal trip to Kauai: information on airlines, seasons, a calendar of events, how to make camping reservations, and much more (even how to tie the knot).

If you are thinking about seeing another island in addition to Kauai, we strongly recommend that you **limit your island-hopping to one island per week.** If you decide to go to more than one island in a week, be warned: You could spend much of your precious vacation time in airports, waiting to board flights and for your luggage to arrive, and checking in and out of hotels. Not much fun!

Our second tip is to **fly directly to Kauai;** doing so can save you a 2-hour layover in Honolulu and another plane ride. So let's get on with the process of planning your trip. We fully believe that searching out the best deals and planning your dream vacation to Hawaii should be half the fun.

1 The Island in Brief

Kauai's three main resort areas, where nearly all the island's accommodations are located, are all quite different in climate, price, and type of accommodations offered, but the range is wide and wonderful. On the south shore, dry and sunny **Poipu** is anchored by perfect beaches. This is the place to stay if you like the ocean, watersports, and plenty of sunshine. The **Coconut Coast,** on the east coast of Kauai, has the most condos, shops, and traffic—it's where all the action is. Hanalei, up on the **North Shore,** is rainy, lush, and quiet, with spectacular beaches and deep wilderness. Because of its remote location, the North Shore is a great place to get away from it all—but not a great place from which to explore the rest of the island.

LIHUE & ENVIRONS

Lihue is where most visitors first set foot on the island. This red-dirt farm town,

the county seat, was founded by sugar planters and populated by descendants of Filipino and Japanese cane cutters. It's a plain and simple place, with used-car lots and mom-and-pop shops. It's also the source of bargains: inexpensive lodging, great deals on dining, and some terrific shopping buys. One of the island's most beautiful beaches, **Kalapaki Beach** 𝕽𝕽, is just next door at **Nawiliwili,** by the island's main harbor.

THE POIPU RESORT AREA

POIPU BEACH 𝕽𝕽𝕽 On Kauai's sun-soaked south shore, this is a pleasant if sleepy resort destination of low-rise hotels set on gold-sand pocket beaches. Well-done, master-planned Poipu is Kauai's most popular resort, with the widest variety of accommodations, from luxury hotels to B&Bs and condos. It offers 36 holes of golf, 38 tennis courts, and outstanding restaurants. This is a great place for watersports, and a good base from which to tour the rest of Kauai. The only drawback is that the North Shore is about 1 to 1½ hours away.

KOLOA This tiny old town of gaily painted sugar shacks just inland from Poipu Beach is where the Hawaiian sugar industry was born more than a century and a half ago. The mill is closed, but this showcase plantation town lives on as a tourist attraction, with delightful shops, an old general store, and a vintage Texaco gas station with a 1930s Model A truck in place, just like in the good old days.

KALAHEO/LAWAI Just a short 10- to 15-minute drive inland from the beach at Poipu lie the more residential communities of Lawai and Kalaheo. Quiet subdivisions line the streets, restaurants catering to locals dot the area, and life revolves around family and work. Good bargains on B&Bs, and a handful of reasonably priced restaurants, can be found here.

WESTERN KAUAI

This region, west of Poipu, is more remote than its eastern neighbor and lacks its terrific beaches. But it's home to one of Hawaii's most spectacular natural wonders, **Waimea Canyon** 🌟🌟🌟 (the "Grand Canyon of the Pacific"); and farther upland and inland, one of its best parks, **Kokee State Park** 🌟🌟.

HANAPEPE For a quick trip back in time, turn off Highway 50 at Hanapepe, once one of Kauai's biggest towns. Founded by Chinese rice farmers, it's so picturesque that it was used as a backdrop for the miniseries *The Thornbirds*. Hanapepe makes a good rest stop on the way to or from Waimea Canyon. It has galleries selling antiques as well as local art and crafts, including Georgio's surfboard art and coconut-grams. It's also home to one of the best restaurants on Kauai, the Hanapepe Café (p. 136). Nearby, at **Salt Pond Beach Park** 🌟 (p. 157), Hawaiians

have dried a reddish sea salt in shallow, red-clay pans since the 17th century. This is a great place to swim, snorkel, and maybe even observe an ancient industry still in practice.

WAIMEA This little coastal town, the original capital of Kauai, seems to have quit the march of time. Dogs sleep in the street while old pickups rust in front yards. The ambience is definitely laid-back. A stay in Waimea is peaceful and quiet (especially at the Waimea Plantation Cottages on the beach), but the remote location means this isn't the best base if you want to explore the other regions of Kauai, such as the North Shore, without a lot of driving.

On his search for the Northwest Passage in 1778, British explorer Capt. James Cook dropped anchor at Waimea and discovered a sleepy village of grass shacks. In 1815, the Russians arrived and built a fort here (now a national historic landmark), but they didn't last long: A scoundrel named George Anton Scheffer tried to claim Kauai for Russia, but he was exposed as an impostor and expelled by Kauai's high-ranking *alii,* Kaumualii.

Today, even Waimea's historic relics are spare and simple: a statue of Cook alongside a bas-relief of his ships, the rubble foundation of the Russian fort, and the remains of an ancient aqueduct unlike any other in the Pacific. Except for an overabundance of churches for a town this size, there's no sign that Waimea was selected as the first landing site of missionaries in 1820.

THE COCONUT COAST

The eastern shore of Kauai north of Lihue is a jumble of commerce and condos strung along the coast road named for Prince Kuhio, with several small beaches beyond. Almost anything you need, and a lot of stuff you can live without, can be found along this coast, which is known for its hundreds of coconut trees waving

Niihau: The Forbidden Island

Just 17 miles across the Kaulakahi Channel from Kauai lies the arid island of Niihau, "The Forbidden Island." Visitors are not allowed on this privately owned island, which is a working cattle and sheep ranch with about 200 residents living in the single town of Puuwai.

However, you can spend a couple of hours on the beach in Niihau. **Niihau Helicopter,** the only helicopter company to offer tours of Niihau, has half-day tours, which include a helicopter ride to Niihau, an aerial tour over the island, and landing on the island at a beach. For more information, see chapter 9.

Niihau's history of being forbidden dates back to 1864 when, after an unusually wet winter that turned the dry scrubland of the small island (18 miles by 6 miles) into green pasture, Eliza Sinclair, a Scottish widow, decided to buy Niihau and move her family here. King Kamehameha IV agreed to sell the island for $10,000. The next year, normal weather returned, and the green pastures withered into sparse semi-desert vegetation.

Today, Sinclair's great-great-grandson, Bruce Robinson, continues to run the ranching operation and fiercely protects the privacy of the island residents. From the outside, life on Niihau has not changed much in 140 years: There's no running water, indoor plumbing, or electrically generated power. The Hawaiian language is still spoken. Most of the men work for the ranch when there is work, and fish and hunt where there is no work. The women specialize in gathering and stringing *pupu Niihau,* prized, tiny white seashells (found only on this island), into Niihau's famous leis, which fetch prices in the thousands of dollars.

in the breeze. It's popular with budget travelers because of the myriad B&Bs and affordable hotels and condos to choose from, and it offers great restaurants and the island's major shopping areas.

KAPAA ⚛ The center of commerce on the east coast and the capital of the Coconut Coast condo-and-hotel district, this restored plantation town looks just like an antique. False-fronted wooden stores line both sides of the highway; it looks as though they've been here forever—until you notice the fresh paint and new roofs and realize that everything has been rebuilt since Hurricane Iniki smacked the town flat in 1992. Kapaa has made an amazing comeback without losing its funky charm.

THE NORTH SHORE

Kauai's North Shore may be the most beautiful place in Hawaii. Exotic seabirds, a half-moon bay, jagged peaks soaring into the clouds, and a mighty wilderness lie around the bend from the Coconut Coast, just beyond a series of one-lane bridges traversing the tail ends of waterfalls. There's only one road in and out, and only two towns, Hanalei and Kilauea—the former by the sea, the latter on a lighthouse cliff that's home to a bird preserve. Sun seekers may fret about all the rainy days, but Princeville Resort offers elegant shelter and two golf courses where you can play through rainbows.

KILAUEA ⚛ This village is home to an antique lighthouse, tropical-fruit stands, little stone houses, and Kilauea Point National Wildlife Refuge, a wonderful seabird preserve. The rolling hills and sea cliffs are hideaways for the rich and famous, including Bette Midler and Sylvester Stallone. The village itself has its charms: The 1892 Kong Lung Company, Kauai's oldest general store, sells antiques, art, and crafts; and you can order a jazzy Billie Holiday Pizza to go at Kilauea Bakery and Pau Hana Pizza.

ANINI BEACH 🐟 This little-known residential district on a 2-mile reef (the biggest on Kauai) offers the safest swimming and snorkeling on the island. A great beach park is open to campers and day trippers, and there's a boat ramp where locals launch sampans to fish for tuna. On Sunday, there's polo in the park and the sizzle of barbecue on the green. Several residents host guests in nearby B&Bs.

PRINCEVILLE 🐟 A little overwhelming for Kauai's wild North Shore, Princeville Resort is Kauai's biggest project, an 11,000-acre development set on a high plain overlooking Hanalei Bay. This resort community includes a luxury Sheraton hotel, 10 condo complexes, new timeshare units around two championship golf courses, cliff-side access to pocket beaches, and one B&B right on the golf course.

HANALEI 🐟🐟🐟 Picture-postcard Hanalei is the laid-back center of North Shore life and an escapist's dream; it's also the gateway to the wild Na Pali Coast. Hanalei is the last great place on Kauai yet to face the developer's blade of progress. At **Hanalei Bay,** sloops anchor and surfers play year-round. The 2-mile-long crescent beach, the biggest indentation on Kauai's coast, is ideal for kids in summer, when the wild surf turns placid. Hanalei retains the essence of its original

sleepy, end-of-the-road charm. On either side of two-lane Kuhio Highway, you'll find just enough shops and restaurants to sustain you for a week's visit—unless you're a hiker, surfer, or sailor, or have some other preoccupation that just might keep you here the rest of your life.

HAENA 🐟🐟 Emerald-green Haena isn't a town or a beach but an ancient Hawaiian district, a place of exceptional natural beauty, and the gateway to the Na Pali Coast. It's the perfect tropical escape, and everybody knows it: Old house foundations and temples, now covered by jungle, lie in the shadow of new million-dollar homes of movie stars and musicians like Jeff Bridges and Graham Nash. This idyllic, 4-mile coast has lagoons, bays, great beaches, spectacular snorkeling, a botanical garden, and the only North Shore resort that's right on the sand, the Hanalei Colony Resort.

THE NA PALI COAST 🐟🐟🐟

The road comes to an end, and now it begins: the Hawaii you've been dreaming about. Kauai's Na Pali Coast (*na pali* means "the cliffs") is a place of extreme beauty and Hawaii's last true wilderness. Its majestic splendor will forever remain unspoiled because no road will ever traverse it. You can enter this state park only on foot or by sea. Serious hikers—and we mean very serious—tackle the ancient 11-mile-long trail down the forbidding coast to Kalalau Valley (see "Hiking & Camping," in chapter 7). The lone, thin trail that creases these cliffs isn't for the faint of heart or anyone afraid of heights. Those of us who aren't up to it can explore the wild coast in an inflatable rubber Zodiac, a billowing sailboat, a high-powered catamaran, or a hovering helicopter, which takes you for the ride of your life.

2 Visitor Information

The **Kauai Visitors Bureau** is located on the first floor of the Watumull Plaza, 4334 Rice St., Suite 101, Lihue, HI 96766 (© **808/245-3971;** fax 808/246-9235; www.kauaidiscovery.com). For a free official *Kauai Vacation Planner* or recorded information, call © **800/262-1400.** The **Poipu Beach Resort Association,** P.O. Box 730, Koloa, HI 96756 (© **888/744-0888** or 808/742-7444; poipu-beach.org), will also send you a free guide to accommodations, activities, shopping, and dining in the Poipu Beach area.

If you'd like to learn more about Kauai before you go, contact the **Kauai Historical Society,** 4396 Rice St., Lihue, HI 96766 (© **808/245-3373;** khs@hawaiian. net). The group maintains a video-lending library that includes material on a range of topics, including Hawaiian legends, ghost stories, archaeology, and travelogues on individual areas around Kauai.

Mainland residents can borrow tapes for up to 3 weeks. Rates are $1 for society members, $2.50 for nonmembers; shipping and handling costs $5.

INFORMATION ON KAUAI'S PARKS

STATE PARKS   To find out more about state parks on Kauai and Molokai, contact the **Hawaii State Department of Land and Natural Resources,** P.O. Box 1671, Lihue, HI 96766 (© **808/274-3446;** www.state.hi.us/dlnr/dsp/kauai.html), which provides information on hiking and camping and will send you free topographic trail maps on request.

COUNTY PARKS   For information on Maui County Parks, contact **Kauai County Parks and Recreation,** 4444 Rice St., Lihue, HI 96766 (© **808/241-6670;** www.hawaii.gov/health/dcab/resources/keypdf/recreation.pdf).

3 Money

ATMs

Hawaii pioneered the use of **ATMs** more than 2 decades ago, and now they're everywhere. You'll find them at most banks, in supermarkets, at Long's Drugs, and in most resorts and shopping centers. **Cirrus** (© **800/424-7787;** www.mastercard.com) and **PLUS** (© **800/843-7587;** www.visa. com) are the two most popular networks;

check the back of your ATM card to see which network your bank belongs to (most banks belong to both these days).

TRAVELER'S CHECKS

Traveler's checks are something of an anachronism from the days before the ATM made cash accessible at any time. Traveler's checks used to be the only

---

Tips Dear Visa: I'm Off to Kapaa, Koloa & Kilauea!

Some credit card companies recommend that you notify them of any impending trip so that they don't become suspicious when the card is used numerous times in an exotic destination and your charges are blocked. Even if you don't call your credit card company in advance, you can always call the card's toll-free emergency number (see "Fast Facts: Kauai," later in this chapter) if a charge is refused—a good reason to carry the phone number with you. But perhaps the most important advice is to carry more than one card on your trip; if one card doesn't work for any number of reasons, you'll have a backup card just in case.

sound alternative to traveling with dangerously large amounts of cash. They were as reliable as currency but, unlike cash, they could be replaced if lost or stolen.

These days, traveler's checks are less necessary because most cities have 24-hour ATMs that allow you to withdraw small amounts of cash as needed. However, keep in mind that you will likely be charged an ATM withdrawal fee if the bank is not your own, so if you're withdrawing money every day, you might be better off with traveler's checks—provided that you don't mind showing identification every time you want to cash one.

You can get traveler's checks at almost any bank. **American Express** offers denominations of $20, $50, $100, $500, and (for cardholders only) $1,000. You'll pay a service charge ranging from 1% to 4%. You can also get American Express traveler's checks over the phone by calling © **800/221-7282;** Amex gold and platinum cardholders who use this number are exempt from the 1% fee.

Visa offers traveler's checks at Citibank locations nationwide, as well as at several other banks. The service charge ranges between 1.5% and 2%; checks come in denominations of $20, $50, $100, $500,

and $1,000. Call © **800/732-1322** for information. AAA members can obtain checks without a fee at most AAA offices. **MasterCard** also offers traveler's checks. Call © **800/223-9920** for a location near you.

If you choose to carry traveler's checks, be sure to keep a record of their serial numbers separate from your checks in the event that they are stolen or lost. You'll get a refund faster if you know the numbers.

Credit cards are accepted all over the island. They're a safe way to carry money and they provide a convenient record of all your expenses. You can also withdraw cash advances from your credit cards at banks or ATMs, provided you know your PIN (personal identification number). If you've forgotten yours, or didn't even know you had one, call the phone number on the back of your credit card and ask the bank to send it to you. It usually takes 5 to 7 business days, though some banks will provide the number over the phone if you tell them your mother's maiden name or some other personal information. Still, be sure to keep some cash on hand for that rare occasion when a restaurant or small shop doesn't take plastic.

4 When to Go

Most visitors don't come to Kauai when the weather's best in the islands; rather, they come when it's at its worst everywhere else. Thus, the **high season**—when prices are up and resorts are booked to capacity—generally runs mid-December through March or mid-April. The last 2 weeks of December in particular are the prime time for travel to Kauai; if you're planning a holiday trip, make your reservations as early as possible, count on holiday crowds, and expect to pay top dollar for accommodations, car rentals, and airfare. Whale-watching season begins in January and continues through the rest of winter, sometimes lasting into May.

The **off seasons,** when the best bargain rates are available, are spring (mid-Apr to mid-June) and fall (Sept to mid-Dec)—a paradox, since these are the best seasons in terms of reliably great weather. If you're looking to save money, or if you just want to avoid the crowds, this is the time to visit. Hotel rates tend to be significantly lower during these off seasons. Airfares also tend to be lower—again, sometimes substantially—and good packages and special deals are often available.

Note: If you plan to come to Kauai between the last week in April and the first week in May, be sure to book your

That Long Flight to Hawaii: How to Stay Comfortable

The plane ride probably will not be the most fun part of your trip to Hawaii. Long flights can be trying; stuffy air and cramped seats can make you feel as if you're being sent parcel post in a small box. But with a little advance planning, you can make an otherwise unpleasant experience almost bearable.

- Your choice of airline and airplane will definitely affect your leg room. Find more details at www.seatguru.com, which has extensive details about almost every seat on six major U.S. airlines.

- Emergency exit seats and bulkhead seats typically have the most legroom. Emergency exit seats are usually held back to be assigned the day of a flight (to ensure that the seat is filled by someone able-bodied); it's worth getting to the ticket counter early to snag one of these spots for a long flight. Many passengers find that bulkhead seating (the row facing the wall at the front of the cabin) offers more legroom, but keep in mind that bulkheads are where airlines often put baby bassinets, so you may be sitting next to an infant.

- To have two seats for yourself in a three-seat row, try for an aisle seat in a center section toward the back of coach. If you're traveling with a companion, book an aisle and a window seat. Middle seats are usually booked last, so chances are good you'll end up with three seats to yourselves. And in the event that a third passenger is assigned the middle seat, he or she will probably be more than happy to trade for a window or an aisle.

- To sleep, avoid the last row of any section or a row in front of an emergency exit, as these seats are the least likely to recline. Avoid seats near highly trafficked toilet areas. Avoid seats in the back of many jets—these can be narrower than those in the rest of coach class. You also may want to reserve a window seat so that you can rest your head and avoid being bumped in the aisle.

- Get up, walk around, and stretch every 60 to 90 minutes to keep your blood flowing. This helps avoid **deep vein thrombosis**, or "economy-class syndrome," a potentially deadly condition that can be caused by sitting in cramped conditions for too long. Other preventative measures include drinking lots of water and avoiding alcohol (see next bullet).

- Drink water before, during, and after your flight to combat the lack of humidity in airplane cabins—which can be drier than the Sahara. Bring a big bottle of water (1.5 liter) on board. Avoid alcohol, which will dehydrate you.

- If you're flying with kids, don't forget to carry on toys, books, pacifiers, and chewing gum to help them relieve ear pressure buildup during ascent and descent. Let each child pack his or her own backpack with favorite toys.

accommodations, interisland air reservations, and car rental in advance. In Japan, the last week of April is called **Golden Week,** because three Japanese holidays take place one after the other; the islands are especially busy with Japanese tourists during this time.

Due to the large number of families traveling in **summer** (June–Aug), you won't get the fantastic bargains of spring and fall. However, you'll still do much better on packages, airfare, and accommodations than you will in the winter months.

THE WEATHER

Because Kauai lies at the edge of the tropical zone, it technically has only two seasons, both of them warm. The dry season corresponds to summer, and the rainy season generally runs during the winter from November to March. It rains every day somewhere in the islands at any time of the year, but the rainy season can cause "gray" weather and spoil your tanning opportunities. Fortunately, it seldom rains for more than 3 days straight, and rainy days often just consist of a mix of clouds and sun, with very brief showers.

The **year-round temperature** usually varies no more than 15°F (9°C), from about 70° to 85°, but it depends on where you are. Kauai is like a ship in that it has leeward and windward sides. The **leeward** sides (the west and south) are usually hot and dry, whereas the **windward** sides (east and north) are generally cooler and moist. If you want arid, sun-baked, desertlike weather, go leeward. If you want lush, often wet, junglelike weather, go windward. Your best bet for total year-round sun is the Poipu coast.

Kauai is also full of **microclimates,** thanks to its interior valleys, coastal plains, and mountain peaks. If you travel into the mountains, it can change from summer to winter in a matter of hours, because it's cooler the higher up you go. In other words, if the weather doesn't suit you, go to the other side of the island—or head into the hills.

HOLIDAYS

When Hawaii observes holidays, especially those over a long weekend, travel between the islands increases, interisland airline seats are fully booked, rental cars are at a premium, and hotels and restaurants are busier than usual.

Federal, state, and county government offices are closed on all federal holidays: January 1 (New Year's Day); third Monday in January (Martin Luther King, Jr. Day); third Monday in February (Presidents' Day, Washington's Birthday); last Monday in May (Memorial Day); July 4 (Independence Day); first Monday in September (Labor Day); second Monday in October (Columbus Day); November 11 (Veterans' Day); fourth Thursday in November (Thanksgiving Day); and December 25 (Christmas).

State and county offices also are closed on local holidays, including Prince Kuhio Day (Mar 26), honoring the birthday of Hawaii's first delegate to the U.S. Congress; King Kamehameha Day (June 11), a statewide holiday commemorating Kamehameha the Great, who united the islands and ruled from 1795 to 1819; and Admission Day (third Fri in Aug), which honors Hawaii's admission as the 50th state in the United States on August 21, 1959.

Other special days celebrated by many people in Hawaii but that do not involve the closing of federal, state, or county offices are Chinese New Year (Jan or Feb), Girls' Day (Mar 3), Buddha's Birthday (Apr 8), Father Damien's Day (Apr 15), Boys' Day (May 5), Samoan Flag Day (Aug), Aloha Festivals (Sept or Oct), and Pearl Harbor Day (Dec 7).

KAUAI CALENDAR OF EVENTS

As with any schedule of upcoming events, the following information is subject to change; always confirm details and dates before you plan your schedule around an event.

January

Kauaian Days. "Celebrating our Unity, While Honoring our Diversity" is the theme of this weeklong festival at various locations around the island. Included in the events are entertainment, Hawaiian games for children, sporting events, workshops, dinners, and cultural festivities. Call © **808/338-0111.**

Annual Burns Supper. This is a birthday celebration of Scotland's most acclaimed poet, Robert Burns, on the grounds of Waimea Plantation Cottages. The Burns Supper celebrates this special man with food, Burns's poetry, and music. A fabulous dinner under the palms follows the pipes and drums. Call © **808/338-1427.**

February

Hula Ho'ike. For a traditional hula performance, drop by for this presentation. Call © **808/651-0682** for details.

Eat Dessert First. This annual scholarship fundraiser at the Terrace Restaurant at the Kauai Lagoons Golf Course features desserts, desserts, and more desserts. Call © **808/652-6878.**

Waimea Town Celebration, Waimea, Kauai. This annual party on Kauai's west side celebrates the Hawaiian and multiethnic history of the town where Captain Cook first landed. This is the island's biggest 2-day event, drawing some 10,000 people. Top Hawaiian entertainers, sporting events, rodeo, and lots of food are on tap during the weekend celebration. Call © **808/335-2824.**

Captain Cook Fun Run. The 2, 5, and 10K runs, with a starting time of 7am, go through the old plantation town of Waimea. Call © **808/335-2824.**

Kilohana Long-Distance Canoe Race. Traditional Hawaiian Outrigger Canoe Racing along the Waimea shoreline is the first event of the Kauai canoe-racing season. Starting times for the races Saturday morning are 8am for single-person canoes, 9am for women, and 10:30am for men. The finish is around noon. Call © **808/335-2824.**

March

Annual Family Ocean Fair. Daylong festivities include live entertainment, lectures, games, food, and demonstrations at the Kilauea National Wildlife Refuge. Free admission. Call © **808/246-2860.**

Prince Kuhio Celebration of the Arts. Celebrate the birth of Jonah Kuhio Kalanianaole, who was born on March 26, 1871, and elected to Congress in 1902. Kauai, his birthplace, starts the celebration at the memorial at Prince Kuhio Park in Lawai, and continues it with daylong festivities. Call © **808/240-6369** for details.

April

Daylight Saving Time Begins, on the Mainland but NOT in Hawaii. Be sure to adjust the time. Starting April 2, 2006, Hawaii is 3 hours behind Pacific Time and 6 hours behind the east coast (6pm in New York is only noon in Hawaii).

Garden Isle Artisan Faire. Come browse through the array of handicrafts, products, and art by Kauai's artists at Waioli Town Park in Hanalei. There's Hawaiian music all day, and plenty of food to buy. Call © **808/245-9021.**

Annual Royal Paina. The Kauai Historical Society presents its annual celebration of Hawaii's multi-ethnic heritage, with local entertainment and a great meal at the Kauai Marriott Resort and Beach Club. Call ✆ **808/ 245-3373.**

May

Kauai Museum Lei Day Celebrations. May Day is Lei Day in Hawaii, celebrated with lei-making contests, pageantry, arts, and crafts. Call ✆ **808/ 245-6931** for Kauai events.

Hapa Haole Hula May Day. This festival features daylong activities of Hawaiian music and culture, including solo hula competition at the Radisson Kauai Beach Resort. Call ✆ **808/ 882-2166.**

Annual Visitor Industry Charity Walk. Hawaii's largest single-day fundraiser, which takes place across the state, consists of a 3.2-mile fun walk (with some ambitious runners at the front of the pack). Beginning at the Kukui Grove Pavilion, the walk raises money for local charities. Call ✆ **808/ 923-0404** or visit www.charitywalk.org.

Outrigger Canoe Season. From May to September, nearly every weekend, canoe paddlers across the state participate in outrigger canoe races. Call ✆ **808/ 261-6615,** or go to www.y2kanu.com for this year's schedule of events.

Banana Poka Roundup. This forest education fair features music, workshops, crafts, children's activities, and exhibits on ridding Kauai's native forests of this invasive weed. Call ✆ **808/335-9975.**

Kauai Music Festival. A 4-day celebration of the art of songwriting with seminars, lectures, panel discussions, and concerts. America's top song writers perform and teach. Call ✆ **808/ 634-6237.**

Kauai Polynesian Festival. A 4-day festival with a pageant, dinners, entertainment, crafts, seminars, dance competitions, and more. Call ✆ **808/335-6466.**

June

Annual Taste of Hawaii. The Rotary Club of Kapaa holds its "Ultimate Sunday Brunch" at Smith's Tropical Paradise, where some 60 different chefs will show their culinary skills. Live music all day. Call ✆ **808/246-0857.**

King Kamehameha Celebration Ho'olaule'a. Daylong festivities in Nawiliwili Park will feature entertainment, arts and crafts, and food. Call ✆ **808/821-6895.**

Annual Canoe Surfing Challenge. In front of the Sheraton Kauai and Kiahuna Plantation, teams of four-person canoes compete for prizes. Call ✆ **808/691-5084.**

Annual Hula Exhibition. Na Hula O Kaohikukapulani presents an evening of chants, music, and hula at the Kauai War Memorial Convention Hall. Call ✆ **808/335-6466.**

July

Concert in the Sky. Fourth of July fundraiser for Kauai Hospice at the Vidinha Stadium, Lihue. Concert and fireworks. For more information, call ✆ **808/245-7277.**

Koloa Plantation Days. This is a week-long tribute to Kauai's plantation heritage, with events like the Sunset Ho'olaule'a, Paniolo Rodeo, Plantation Tennis Tournament, Hapa Road Walk, Hawaiian Olympics, Golf Putting Tournament, Craft Faire, ethnic cooking demonstrations, and more. The grand finale on July 31 features a parade and festival in Koloa with entertainment, food, and crafts. Call ✆ **808/822-0734** or go to www.koloaplantationdays.com.

August

Kauai Polynesian Festival. This 2-day event features the dances of Tahiti, New Zealand, and Samoa in a competition, as well as exhibitions and educational cultural workshops plus local foods, arts, and crafts. Call ☎ **808/ 822-9447.** Early August.

Kauai County Farm Bureau Fair. This family-oriented fair, held at the Vidinha Stadium in Lihue, features a petting zoo, a livestock show, floral demonstrations and exhibits, food booths, and arts and crafts, along with amusement park rides. Call ☎ **808/ 639-8432.**

September

Aloha Festivals. Parades and other events celebrate Hawaiian culture and friendliness throughout the island. Call ☎ **800/852-7690,** or visit www. alohafestivals.com for a schedule of events.

Kauai Mokihana Festival. This weeklong festival includes local and ethnic demonstrations, concerts, and competitions, among them a Kauai composers' contest, a hula competition, and a workshop on Kauai's heritage. Call ☎ **808/822-2166.**

All Woman's Koloa Rodeo. The only all-female rodeo in the state features women competing in roping, barrel racing, pole bending, and goat tying. Call ☎ **808/639-6695.**

October

Annual Coconut Festival. Where would Hawaii be without coconuts? This annual event highlights the cultural, social, and historical importance of the coconut, with unusual coconut foods, coconut crafts, games with coconuts, and contests. Call ☎ **808/ 651-3273.**

Hawaiiana Festival. This 3-day event is centered on teaching the customs, crafts, and culture of Hawaii. Held at the Hyatt Regency Kauai Resort & Spa, it includes entertainment and a luau. For information call ☎ **808/ 240-6369.**

Eo E Emalani Festival, Kokee State Park, Kauai. This festival honors Her Majesty Queen Emma, an inveterate gardener and Hawaii's first environmental queen, who made a forest trek to Kokee with 100 friends in 1871. Call ☎ **808/335-9975.**

Daylight Saving Time Ends on the Mainland, but NOT in Hawaii (which does not go on daylight saving time). Be sure to adjust the time, on the last Sunday in October. Hawaii will be 2 hours behind the Pacific coast and 5 hours behind the Atlantic coast (5pm in New York is noon in Hawaii).

November

Hawaiian Slack-Key Guitar Festival. The best of Hawaii's folk music (slack-key guitar) is performed by the best musicians in Hawaii. The show, held at the Kauai Marriott Resort in Lihue, is 5-hours long and absolutely free. For more information call ☎ **808/239-4336** or e-mail kahokuproductions@yahoo.com.

Hawaii International Film Festival. This cinema festival with a cross-cultural spin features filmmakers from Asia, the Pacific Islands, and the United States. Call ☎ **808/528-FILM,** or visit www. hiff.org. First 2 weeks in November.

MasterCard PGA Grand Slam. Top golfers compete for $1 million in prize money at the Poipu Bay Resort Golf Course. Call ☎ **800/PGA-TCKT** or 888/744-0888; or visit www.pga.com. Last weekend in November or first weekend in December.

December

Annual Festival of Lights. The lighting of the Christmas decorations on the grounds of Kauai's historic county building in Lihue is accompanied by local entertainment, Christmas caroling, and a parade down Rice Street, ending at the county building. Call ☎ **808/245-6390.**

Holiday Hula Celebration. A Hawaiian Christmas performance by Na

Tips What to Pack

Kauai is very informal: You'll get by with shorts, T-shirts, and sneakers at most attractions and restaurants; a casual sundress or a polo shirt and khakis is fine even in the most expensive places. Don't forget a long-sleeved coverup (to throw on at the beach when you've had enough sun for the day), rubber water shoes or flip-flops, and hiking shoes and several pairs of good socks if you plan to do any hiking. You might also want to bring binoculars for whale-watching.

Be sure to bring **sun protection:** sunglasses, strong sunscreen, a light hat (like a baseball cap or a sun visor), and a canteen or water bottle if you'll be hiking—you'll easily dehydrate on the trail in the tropic heat. Experts recommend carrying 2 liters of water per person per day on any hike. Campers should bring water purification tablets or devices. Also see "Staying Healthy," below.

Don't bother overstuffing your suitcase with 2 whole weeks' worth of shorts and T-shirts: Kauai has **laundry facilities** everywhere. If your accommodation doesn't have a washer and dryer or laundry service (most do), there will most likely be a laundry nearby. The only exception to this is Kokee Park, so do a load of laundry before you arrive.

One last thing: **It really can get cold on Kauai.** Especially if you are staying in Kokee. It's always a good idea to bring long pants and a windbreaker, sweater, or light jacket. And be sure to bring along rain gear if you'll be in Kauai from November to March.

Hula O Kaohikukapulani includes chants, hula, and Christmas melodies at the Kauai Marriott Resort & Beach Club. Call © **808/335-6466.**

New Year's Eve Fireworks. Come out for the annual aerial fireworks display at Poipu Beach Park. For more information, e-mail info@poipu-beach.org.

5 Travel Insurance

Check your existing insurance policies and credit card coverage before you buy travel insurance. You may already be covered for lost luggage, canceled tickets, or medical expenses. The cost of travel insurance varies widely, depending on the cost and length of your trip, your age, your health, and the type of trip you're taking.

TRIP-CANCELLATION INSURANCE Trip-cancellation insurance helps you get your money back if you have to back out of a trip, if you have to go home early, or if your travel supplier goes bankrupt.

Allowed reasons for cancellation can range from sickness to natural disasters to the State Department declaring your destination unsafe for travel. (Insurers usually won't cover vague fears, though, as many travelers discovered who tried to cancel their trips in Oct 2001 because they were wary of flying.) In this unstable world, trip-cancellation insurance is a good buy if you're getting tickets well in advance—who knows what the state of the world, or of your airline, will be in 9 months? Insurance policy details vary, so read the fine print—and especially make

What to Do if Your Luggage Is Delayed or (Gasp!) Lost

You're standing at the luggage carousel, watching the same baggage go round and round when you realized there are no more bags being unloaded and your bag is not there.

The first thing is not to panic; most bags are delivered to their destination within 24–48 hours. Here are some tips to help you and your bag get reunited as soon as possible.

- **Have your name and destination address both outside and inside your luggage.** At least you'll have a fighting chance of being contacted if your bag is tagged with where your bag is going (not just your home address, but the address of your hotel/condo in Hawaii, with a contact phone number). While you're at it, get rid of all the old airline baggage tags to other destinations.

- **Know where the lost baggage claim counter is for your airline.** While you are waiting for your luggage, make sure you know where you will have to go to file a claim; that way you can be the first in line if your bag did not arrive. If you flew on more than one airline, always go to the last airline you flew on; they are the ones to start processing your claim.

- **To wait or not to wait for the next flight.** The lost luggage claims desk loves to tell people: "Oh, your bag will be in on the next flight." Smile, and politely ask them if they have proof that the bag is in the system and booked on that flight. If they can't guarantee it, you might want to proceed to your destination, rather than wait around the airport in hopes that the suitcase "might" be on the next flight.

- **Before you leave the airport (without your bag),** be sure to get the following: a copy of your lost luggage claim form, the phone number to call to check on your luggage, an estimate on when they will have more information on when your bag will arrive, and what you should do if your bag does not arrive.

- **If your bag is lost,** don't expect the airlines to write you a check for $2,800 on the spot. You will have to make a list of what was in your bags (no exaggerating here—you probably did not have a couple of designer dresses in your bag to Hawaii); be sure to list the cost of the suitcase itself and any money you have had to pay out to replace items in the suitcase. Unfortunately, the airlines will only reimburse you for the depreciated value of your items, *not* the replacement value.

sure that your airline or cruise line is on the list of carriers covered in case of bankruptcy. For information, contact one of the following insurers: **Access America** (© 866/807-3982; www.accessamerica. com); **Travel Guard International** (© 800/826-4919; www.travelguard.com); **Travel Insured International** (© 800/243-3174; www.travelinsured.com); and **Travelex Insurance Services** (© 888/457-4602; www.travelex-insurance.com).

MEDICAL INSURANCE Most health insurance policies cover you if you get sick away from home—but check, particularly if you're insured by an HMO. If you require additional medical insurance, try **MEDEX Assistance** (© 410/453-6300; www.medexassist.com) or **Travel Assistance International** (© 800/821-2828; www.travelassistance.com); for general information on services, call the company's Worldwide Assistance Services, Inc., at © **800/777-8710.**

LOST-LUGGAGE INSURANCE   On domestic flights, checked baggage is covered up to $2,800 per ticketed passenger. On international flights (including U.S. portions of international trips), baggage is limited to approximately $9.07 per pound, up to approximately $635 per checked bag. If you plan to check items more valuable than the standard liability,

see if your valuables are covered by your homeowner's policy, get baggage insurance as part of your comprehensive travel-insurance package, or buy Travel Guard's "BagTrak" product. Don't buy insurance at the airport, as it's usually overpriced. Be sure to take any valuables or irreplaceable items with you in your carry-on luggage because many valuables (including books, money, and electronics) aren't covered by airline policies.

If your luggage is lost, immediately file a lost-luggage claim at the airport, detailing the luggage contents. For most airlines, you must report delayed, damaged, or lost baggage within 4 hours of arrival. The airlines are required to deliver luggage, once found, directly to your house or destination free of charge.

6 Health & Safety

STAYING HEALTHY

If you suffer from a chronic illness, consult your doctor before your departure. For conditions like epilepsy, diabetes, or heart problems, wear a **Medic Alert Identification Tag** (© 888/633-4298; www.medicalert.org), which will immediately alert doctors to your condition and give them access to your records through Medic Alert's 24-hour hot line.

Pack prescription medications in your carry-on luggage. Carry written prescriptions in generic form, not brand name form, and dispense all prescription medications from their original labeled vials. If you wear contact lenses, pack an extra pair in case you lose one.

ON LAND

As in any tropical climate, there are lots of bugs in Kauai. Most of them won't harm you. However, three insects—mosquitoes, centipedes, and scorpions—do sting, and they can cause anything from mild annoyance to severe swelling and pain.

MOSQUITOES   These pesky insects aren't native to Hawaii, but arrived as larvae stowed away in the water barrels on the ship *Wellington* in 1826. There's not a whole lot you can do about them, except apply repellent or burn mosquito punk or citronella candles to keep them out of your area. If they've bitten you, head to the drugstore for sting-stopping ointments (antihistamine creams like

---

Everything You've Always Wanted to Know about Sharks

The Hawaii State Department of Land and Natural Resources has launched a website with more information that you probably wanted to know about sharks: www.hawaiisharks.com. The site has the biology, history, and culture of these carnivores, plus information on safety and data on shark bites in Hawaii.

Benadryl or homeopathic creams like Sting Stop or Florasone); they'll ease the itching and swelling. Most bites disappear in anywhere from a few hours to a few days.

CENTIPEDES   These segmented insects with a jillion legs come in two varieties: 6- to 8-inch brown ones and the smaller 2- to 3-inch blue guys; both can really pack a wallop with their sting. Centipedes are generally found in damp places, like under wood piles or compost heaps. Wearing closed-toe shoes can help prevent stings if you accidentally unearth a centipede. If you're stung, the reaction can range from something similar to a mild bee sting to severe pain; apply ice at once to prevent swelling. See a doctor if you experience extreme pain, swelling, nausea, or any other severe reaction.

SCORPIONS   Rarely seen, scorpions are found in arid, warm regions; their stings can be serious. Campers in dry areas should always check your boots before putting them on, and shake out sleeping bags and bedrolls. Symptoms of a scorpion sting include shortness of breath, hives, swelling, and nausea. In the unlikely event that you're stung, apply diluted household ammonia and cold compresses to the area of the sting and seek medical attention immediately.

Hiking Safety

In addition to taking the appropriate precautions regarding Kauai's bug population (see above), hikers should always let someone know where you're heading, when you're going, and when you plan to return; too many hikers get lost on Kauai because they don't inform others of their basic plans.

Always check weather conditions with the **National Weather Service** (© 808/ 245-6001) before you go. Hike with a pal, never alone. Wear hiking boots, a sun hat, clothes to protect you from the sun and from getting scratches, and high-SPF sunscreen on all exposed areas of skin. Take water. Stay on the trail. Watch your step. It's easy to slip off precipitous trails and into steep canyons, with often disastrous, even fatal, results. Incapacitated hikers are often plucked to safety by fire and rescue squads, who must use helicopters to gain access to remote sites. Many experienced hikers and boaters today pack a cellular phone in case of emergency; just dial © **911.**

Vog

The volcanic haze dubbed "vog" is caused by gases released when molten lava—from the continuous eruption of the volcano on the flank of Kilauea on the Big Island—pours into the ocean. This hazy

---

⸢Tips⸥ A Few Words of Warning about Crime

Although Kauai is generally a safe tourist destination, visitors have been crime victims, so stay alert. The most common crime against tourists is rental-car break-ins. **Never leave any valuables in your car,** not even in your trunk: Thieves can be in and out of your trunk faster than you can open it with your own keys. Be especially leery of high-risk areas, such as beaches, resorts, scenic lookouts, and other visitor attractions. In fact, after you take your suitcases out of the trunk, do not put anything else in it. Buy a fanny pack to carry your keys and wallet when you go to the beach or for a hike. Also, never carry large amounts of cash. Stay in well-lighted areas after dark. Do not display the parking pass from your hotel (look on your windshield or sometimes the parking attendants attach it to your rear view mirror) when you leave the resort property.

air, which looks like urban smog, limits viewing from scenic vistas and wreaks havoc with photographers trying to get clear panoramic shots. Some people claim that long-term exposure to vog has even caused bronchial ailments.

There actually is a vog season in Hawaii: the fall and winter months, when the trade winds that blow the fumes out to sea die down. The vog is felt not only on the Big Island, but also as far away as Maui and Oahu. Kauai generally does not experience vog.

OCEAN SAFETY

Because most people coming to Kauai are unfamiliar with the ocean environment, they're often unaware of the natural hazards it holds. But with just a few precautions, your ocean experience can be a safe and happy one. An excellent book to get is *All Stings Considered: First Aid and Medical Treatment of Hawaii's Marine Injuries* (University of Hawaii Press, 1997), by Craig Thomas (an emergency-medicine doctor) and Susan Scott (a registered nurse). These avid water people have put together the authoritative book on first aid for Hawaii's marine injuries.

SEASICKNESS The waters off Kauai can range from calm as glass to downright frightening (in storm conditions), and they usually fall somewhere in between; in general, expect rougher conditions in winter than in summer.

Some 90% of the population tends toward seasickness. If you've never been out on a boat or if you've gotten seasick in the past, you might want to heed the following suggestions:

- The day before you go out on the boat, avoid alcohol; caffeine; citrus and other acidic juices; and greasy, spicy, or hard-to-digest foods.
- Get a good night's sleep the night before.

- Take or use whatever seasickness prevention works best for you—medication, an acupressure wristband, ginger root tea or capsules, or any combination—*before* you board; once you set sail, it's generally too late.
- Once you're on the water, stay as low and as near the center of the boat as possible. Avoid the fumes (especially if it's a diesel boat); stay out in the fresh air and watch the horizon. Do not read.
- If you start to feel queasy, drink clear fluids like water, and eat something bland, such as a soda cracker.

A bluish-purple floating bubble with a long tail, the **Portuguese man-of-war** causes thousands of stings a year. Stings, although painful and a nuisance, are rarely harmful; fewer than one in a thousand require medical treatment. The best prevention is to watch for these floating bubbles as you snorkel (look for the hanging tentacles below the surface). Get out of the water if anyone near you spots these jellyfish.

Reactions to stings range from mild burning and redness to severe welts and blisters. *All Stings Considered* recommends the following treatment: First, pick off any visible tentacles with a gloved hand, a stick, or anything handy; then rinse the sting with fresh or salt water; and finally apply ice to prevent swelling and to help control pain.

Hawaiian folklore advises using vinegar, meat tenderizer, baking soda, papain, or alcohol, or even urinating on the wound. Studies have shown that these remedies may actually cause further damage. Most Portuguese man-of-war stings will disappear by themselves within 15 to 20 minutes if you do nothing to treat them. Still, be sure to see a doctor if pain persists or if a rash or other symptoms develop.

Tips Don't Get Burned: Smart Tanning Tips

Tanning just ain't what it used to be. Hawaii's Caucasian population has a higher incidence of deadly skin cancer, malignant melanoma, than the population anywhere else in the United States. But none of us are safe from the sun's harmful rays: People of all skin types and races can burn when exposed to the sun too long.

To ensure that your vacation won't be ruined by a painful, throbbing sunburn, here are some helpful tips on how to tan safely and painlessly:

- **Wear a strong sunscreen at all times, and use lots of it.** Use a sunscreen with a sun-protection factor (SPF) of 15 or higher; people with a light complexion should use 30. Apply sunscreen as soon as you get out of the shower in the morning, and at least 30 minutes before you're exposed to the sun. No matter what the label says—even if the sunscreen is waterproof—reapply it every 2 hours and immediately after swimming.
- **Read the labels.** To avoid developing allergies to sunscreens, avoid those that contain para-aminobenzoic acid (PABA). Look for a sunscreen with zinc oxide, talc, or titanium dioxide, which reduce the risk of developing skin allergies. For the best protection from UVA rays (which can cause wrinkles and premature aging), check the label for zinc oxide, benzophenone, oxybenzone, sulisobenzone, titanium dioxide, or avobenzone (also known as Parsol 1789).
- **Wear a hat and sunglasses.** And make sure that your sunglasses have UV filters.

Box jellyfish, transparent, square-shaped bell jellyfish, are nearly impossible to see in the water. Fortunately, they seem to follow a monthly cycle: 8 to 10 days after the full moon, they appear in the waters on the leeward side of the island and hang around for about 3 days. Also, they seem to sting more in the morning hours, when they're on or near the surface. The best prevention is to get out of the water.

Stings range from no visible marks to red, hivelike welts, blisters, and pain (a burning sensation) lasting from 10 minutes to 8 hours. *All Stings Considered* recommends the following course of treatment: First, pour regular household vinegar on the sting; this may not relieve the pain, but it will stop additional burning. Do not rub the area. Pick off any vinegar-soaked tentacles with a stick. For pain, apply an ice pack. Seek additional medical treatment if you experience shortness of breath, weakness, palpitations, muscle cramps, or any other severe symptoms. Again, ignore any folk remedies. Most box jellyfish stings disappear by themselves without treatment.

PUNCTURES Most sea-related punctures come from stepping on or brushing against the needlelike spines of sea urchins (known locally as *wana*). Be careful when you're in the water; don't put your foot down (even if you have booties or fins on) if you cannot clearly see the bottom. Waves can push you into *wana* in a surge zone in shallow water (the *wana*'s spines can even puncture a wet suit).

- **Avoid being in the sun between 9am and 3pm.** Use extra caution during these peak hours. Remember that a beach umbrella is not protection enough from the sun's harmful UV rays; in fact, with the reflection from the water, the sand, and even the sidewalk, some 85% of the ultraviolet rays are still bombarding you.
- **Protect children from the sun, and keep infants out of the sun altogether.** Infants under 6 months should not be in the sun at all. Older babies need zinc oxide to protect their fragile skin, and children should be slathered with sunscreen every hour. The burns that children get today predict what their future with skin cancer will be tomorrow.

If you start to turn red, **get out of the sun.** Contrary to popular belief, you don't have to turn red to tan; if your skin is red, it's burned—and that's serious. The redness from a burn may not show until 2 to 8 hours after you get out of the sun, and the full force of that burn may not appear for 24 to 36 hours. During that time, you can look forward to pain, itching, and peeling. The best **remedy** for a sunburn is to get out of the sun immediately and stay out of the sun until all the redness is gone. Aloe vera (straight from the plant or from a commercial preparation), cool compresses, cold baths, and anesthetic benzocaine may also help ease the pain of sunburn.

If you've decided to get a head start on your tan by using a self-tanning lotion that dyes your skin a darker shade, remember that this will not protect you from the sun. You'll still need to generously apply sunscreen when you go out.

A sea urchin sting can result in burning, aching, swelling, and discoloration (black or purple) around the area where the spines have entered your skin. The best thing to do is to pull out any protruding spines. The body will absorb the spines within 24 hours to 3 weeks, or the remainder of the spines will work themselves out. Again, contrary to popular wisdom, do not urinate or pour vinegar on the embedded spines—this will not help.

CUTS All cuts obtained in the marine environment must be taken seriously because the high level of bacteria present can quickly cause the cut to become infected. The most common cuts are from **coral.** Contrary to popular belief, coral cannot grow inside your body.

However, bacteria can—and very often does—grow inside a cut. The best way to prevent cuts is to wear a wet suit, gloves, and reef shoes. Never, under any circumstances, should you touch a coral head; not only can you get cut, but you can also damage a living organism that took decades to grow.

The symptoms of a coral cut can range from a slight scratch to severe welts and blisters. *All Stings Considered* recommends gently pulling the edges of the skin open and removing any embedded coral or grains of sand with tweezers, or rinsing well with fresh water. Next, scrub the cut well with fresh water. Never use ocean water to clean a cut. If the wound is bleeding, press a clean cloth against it until it stops. If bleeding continues or if

---

> ## *Tips* Enjoying the Ocean & Avoiding Mishaps
>
> The Kauai Visitors Bureau has an excellent website (www.kauaiexplorer.com) to help you enjoy Kauai's beaches and stay safe in the marine environment. The site introduces visitors to the various beaches, pointing out any hazards, surf conditions, whether the beach has a lifeguard, and includes a map.

---

the edges of the injury are jagged or gaping, seek medical treatment.

WHAT TO DO IF YOU GET SICK AWAY FROM HOME

In most cases, your existing health plan will provide the coverage you need. But double-check; you may want to buy **travel medical insurance** instead. (See the section on "Travel Insurance," earlier in this chapter.) Bring your insurance ID card with you when you travel.

7 Specialized Travel Resources

FOR TRAVELERS WITH DISABILITIES

Travelers with disabilities are made to feel very welcome in Kauai. Hotels are usually equipped with wheelchair-accessible rooms, and tour companies provide many special services. The **Hawaii Center for Independent Living,** 414 Kauwili St., Suite 102, Honolulu, HI 96817 (© **808/ 522-5400;** fax 808/586-8129; www. hawaii.gov/health), can provide information and send you a copy of the *Aloha Guide to Accessibility* ($15).

MossRehab ResourceNet (www.moss resourcenet.org) is a great source for information, tips, and resources relating to accessible travel. You'll find links to a number of travel agents who specialize in planning trips for travelers with disabilities here and through **Access-Able Travel Source** (© **303/232-2979;** www.access-able.com), another excellent online source. You'll also find relay and voice numbers for hotels, airlines, and car-rental companies on Access-Able's user-friendly site, as well as links to accessible accommodations, attractions, transportation, tours, local medical resources, equipment repair, and much more.

For travelers with disabilities who wish to do your own driving, hand-controlled cars can be rented from **Avis** (© **800/ 331-1212;** www.avis.com) and **Hertz** (© **800/654-3131;** www.hertz.com). The number of hand-controlled cars in Hawaii is limited, so be sure to book well in advance. For wheelchair-accessible vans, contact **Accessible Vans of Hawaii,** 186 Mehani Circle, Kihei (© **800/303- 3750** or 808/879-5521; fax 808/879-0640; www.accessiblevans.com). Kauai recognizes other states' windshield placards indicating that the driver of the car is disabled, so be sure to bring yours with you.

Vision-impaired travelers who use a Seeing Eye dog can now come to Hawaii without the hassle of quarantine. A recent court decision ruled that visitors with Seeing Eye dogs only need to present documentation that the dog is a trained Seeing Eye dog and has had rabies shots. For more information, contact the **Animal Quarantine Facility** (© **808/483-7171;** www.hawaii.gov).

FOR GAY & LESBIAN TRAVELERS

Known for its acceptance of all groups, Hawaii welcomes gays and lesbians just as it does anybody else.

For information on Kauai's gay community and related events, contact the **Bisexual/Transgender/Gay/Lesbian Community Bulletin Board** (✆ **808/823-6248**).

Pacific Ocean Holidays, P.O. Box 88245, Honolulu, HI 96830 (✆ **800/735-6600** or 808/923-2400; www.gayhawaii.com), offers vacation packages that feature gay-owned and gay-friendly lodgings.

If you want help planning your trip, the **International Gay & Lesbian Travel Association** (IGLTA; ✆ **800/448-8550** or 954/776-2626; www.iglta.org) can link you with the appropriate gay-friendly service organization or tour specialist. With around 1,200 members, it offers quarterly newsletters, marketing mailings, and a membership directory that's updated quarterly. Members are kept informed of gay and gay-friendly hoteliers, tour operators, and airline and cruise-line representatives. **GayWired Travel Services** (www.gaywired.com) is another great trip-planning resource; click on "Travel Services."

Out and About (✆ **800/929-2268** or 415/486-2591; www.outandabout.com) offers a monthly newsletter packed with good information on the global gay and lesbian scene. Its website features links to gay and lesbian tour operators and other gay-themed travel links, plus extensive online travel information for subscribers only. Out and About's guidebooks are available at most major bookstores and through www.adlbooks.com.

FOR SENIORS

Discounts for seniors are available at almost all of Kauai's major attractions, and occasionally at hotels and restaurants. Always inquire when you make hotel reservations, and especially when you buy your airline ticket—most major domestic airlines offer senior discounts.

Members of the **AARP** (formerly the American Association of Retired Persons;

✆ **800/424-3410** or 202/434-2277; www.aarp.org) are usually eligible for such discounts; AARP also puts together organized tour packages at moderate rates.

Some great, low-cost trips to Hawaii are offered to people 55 and older through **Elderhostel,** 75 Federal St., Boston, MA 02110 (✆ **617/426-8056;** www.elderhostel.org), a nonprofit group that arranges travel and study programs around the world. You can obtain a complete catalog of offerings by writing to Elderhostel, P.O. Box 1959, Wakefield, MA 01880-5959.

FOR FAMILIES

Kauai is paradise for children: beaches to frolic on, water to splash in, unusual sights to see, and a host of new foods to taste. Be sure to check out "Family-Friendly Accommodations" in chapter 5, "Family-Friendly Restaurants" in chapter 6, and "Especially for Kids" in chapter 7.

The larger hotels and resorts have supervised programs for children and can refer you to qualified babysitters. You can also contact **People Attentive to Children** (PATCH; ✆ **808/246-0622;** www.patch-hi.org), which will refer you to individuals who have taken their training courses on child care.

Remember that Kauai's sun is probably much stronger than what you're used to at home, so it's important to protect your kids. Keep infants out of the sun; infants under 6 months should not be in the sun at all. Older babies need zinc oxide to protect their fragile skin, and children should be slathered with sunscreen every hour.

Condo rentals are a great option for families; the convenience of having your own kitchen is great for Mom and Dad. See "Types of Accommodations," later in this chapter. Our favorite condo complexes are reviewed throughout that section.

8 Getting Married on Kauai

Whatever your budget, Kauai is a great place for a wedding. Not only does the entire island exude romance and natural beauty, but after the ceremony, you're only a few steps away from the perfect honeymoon. And the members of your wedding party will most likely be delighted, since you've given them the perfect excuse for their own island vacation.

More than 20,000 marriages are performed each year on the islands, and nearly half of the couples married here are from somewhere else. This booming business has spawned dozens of companies that can help you organize a long-distance event and stage an unforgettable wedding, Hawaiian style or your own style.

The easiest way to plan your wedding is to let someone else handle it at the resort or hotel where you'll be staying. All of the major resorts and hotels (and even most of the small ones) have wedding coordinators, whose job is to make sure that your wedding day is everything you've dreamed about. They can plan everything from a simple (relatively) low-cost wedding to an extravaganza that people will remember and talk about for years. Remember that resorts can be pricey—catering, flowers, musicians, and so on may cost more in a resort than outside a resort, but sometimes you can save money because the resort will not charge a room rental fee if they get to do the catering. Be frank with your wedding coordinator if you want to keep costs down. However, you can also plan your own island wedding, even from afar, and not spend a fortune doing it.

THE PAPERWORK

The state of Hawaii has some very minimal procedures for obtaining a marriage license. The first thing you should do is contact the **Marriage License Office,** ✆ **808/241-3498;** www.hawaii.gov/doh

(then click on "Vital Records"). The staff will mail you a brochure, *Getting Married,* and direct you to the marriage licensing agent closest to where you'll be staying on Kauai. The office is open Monday through Friday from 8am to 4pm.

Once on Kauai, the prospective bride and groom must go together to the marriage licensing agent to get a license. A license costs $60 and is good for 30 days; if you don't have the ceremony within the time allotted, you'll have to pay another $60 for another license. The only requirements for a marriage license are that both parties are 15 years of age or older (couples 15–17 years old must have proof of age, written consent of both parents, and the written approval of the judge of the family court) and are not more closely related than first cousins. That's it.

Contrary to some reports from the media, gay couples cannot marry in Hawaii. After a protracted legal battle, and much discussion in the state legislature, in late 1999 the Hawaii Supreme Court ruled that the state will not issue a marriage license to a couple of the same sex.

PLANNING THE WEDDING

DOING IT YOURSELF The marriage licensing agents, which range from the governor's satellite office to private individuals, are usually friendly, helpful people who can steer you to a nondenominational minister or someone who's licensed by the state of Hawaii to perform the ceremony. These marriage performers are great sources of information for budget weddings. They usually know great places to have the ceremony for free or for a nominal fee.

If you don't want to use a wedding planner (see below) but want to make arrangements before you arrive on Kauai, our best advice is to get a copy of the daily newspaper the *Garden Island,* 3137 Kuhio Hwy., Lihue, HI 96766

(© 808/245-3681; www.kauaiworld. com). People willing and qualified to conduct weddings advertise in the classifieds. They're great sources of information, because they know the best places to have the ceremony and can recommend caterers, florists, and everything else you'll need.

USING A WEDDING PLANNER Wedding planners—many of whom are marriage licensing agents as well—can arrange everything for you, from a small, private, outdoor affair to a full-blown formal ceremony in a tropical setting. They charge anywhere from $450 to a small

fortune—it all depends on what you want.

Planners on Kauai include **Coconut Coast Weddings & Honeymoons** (© 800/585-5595 or 808/828-0999; www.kauaiwedding.com); **A Simple Marriage** (© 808/ 742-6115; www. asimplemarriagekauai.com); **A Vow Exchange** (© 800/460-3434 or 808/ 826-1869; www.vowexchange.com); **Island Weddings & Blessings** (© 800/ 998-1548 or 808/828-1548; www. weddings-kauai.com); and **Tropical Dream Wedding** (© 888/615-5656 or 808/332-5664; www.tropicaldream wedding.com).

9 Getting There

If possible, fly directly to Kauai; doing so can save you a 2-hour layover in Honolulu and another plane ride.

The final approach to Lihue Airport is dramatic; be sure to sit on the left side of the aircraft, where passengers are treated to an excellent view of the Haupu Ridge, Nawiliwili Bay, and Kilohana Crater. **United Airlines** (© 800/225-5825; www.ual.com) offers direct service to Kauai, with daily flights from Los Angeles. **American Airlines** (© 800/433-7300; www.aa.com) offers a non-stop, daily flight from Los Angeles. **America West** (© 800/327-7810; www.america west.com) will have direct flights from Phoenix to Lihue starting in 2006. **Sun-Trips** (© 800-SUN-TRIP; www.suntrips. com) offers a charter from San Francisco/Oakland International Airport (OAK) once a week. **Pleasant Hawaiian Holidays** (© 800/742-9244; www. pleasantholidays.com), one of Hawaii's largest travel companies offering low-cost airfare and package deals, has two weekly nonstop flights from Los Angeles and San Francisco using American Trans Air. All other airlines land in Honolulu, where you'll have to connect to a 30-minute

interisland flight to Kauai's Lihue Airport. Between the two interisland carriers, **Aloha Airlines** (© 800/367-5250, 808/ 245-3691, or 808/484-1111; www.aloha air.com) and **Hawaiian Airlines** (© 800/ 367-5320, 808/245-1813, or 808/838-1555; www.hawaiianair.com), there is a flight at least every hour to Lihue.

For information on airlines serving Hawaii from places other than the U.S. mainland, see chapter 3.

FLY FOR LESS: TIPS FOR GETTING THE BEST AIRFARES

- Keep your eye out for periodic **sales.** You'll almost never see a sale during the peak winter vacation months, especially around the holidays. But during the rest of the year, you can find deals. *Note:* The lowest-priced fares are often nonrefundable, require advance purchase of 1 to 3 weeks and a certain length of stay, and carry penalties for changing dates of travel. Make sure you know exactly what the restrictions are before you commit.
- If your schedule is flexible, you can almost always get a cheaper fare by

staying over a Saturday night or by **flying midweek.**

• **Consolidators,** also known as bucket shops, are good places to find low fares, often below even the airlines' discounted rates. There's nothing shady about the reliable ones—basically, they're just big travel agents that get discounts for buying in bulk and pass some of the savings on to you. But be aware that consolidator tickets are usually nonrefundable or come with stiff cancellation penalties.

We've gotten great deals on many occasions from **Cheap Tickets** (© 800/377-1000; www.cheaptickets.com). Other reliable consolidators include **Lowestfare.com** (© 888/278-8830; www.lowestfare.com); **Cheap Seats** (© 800/451-7200; www.cheapseatstravel.com);

and **FlyCheap** (© 800/FLY-CHEAP; www.flycheap.com).

• **Search the Internet for cheap fares,** though it's still best to compare your findings with the research of a dedicated travel agent, if you're lucky enough to have one, especially when you're booking more than just a flight. Three of the best-respected virtual travel agents are **Expedia** (**www.expedia.com**), **Travelocity** (**www.travelocity.com**), and **Yahoo! Travel** (**travel.yahoo.com**).

• Join **frequent-flier clubs.** Accrue enough miles, and you'll be rewarded with free flights and elite status. It's free. You don't need to fly to build frequent-flier miles—**frequent-flier credit cards** can provide thousands of miles for doing your everyday shopping.

Tips Coping with Jet Lag

Jet lag is a pitfall of traveling across time zones. If you're flying north to south and you feel sluggish when you touch down, your symptoms will be caused by dehydration and the general stress of air travel. When you travel east to west, as you do when going to Hawaii, however, your body becomes thoroughly confused about what time it is, and everything from your digestion to your brain gets knocked for a loop. Traveling east, say, from Kauai to Los Angeles, is less difficult on your internal clock than traveling west, say from Atlanta to Hawaii, as most peoples' bodies find it more acceptable to stay up late than to fall asleep early.

Here are some tips for combating jet lag:

• **Reset your watch** to your destination time before you board the plane.
• **Drink lots of water** before, during, and after your flight. Avoid alcohol.
• **Exercise** and **sleep well** for a few days before your trip.
• If you have trouble sleeping on planes, **fly eastward on morning flights.**
• **Daylight** is the key to resetting your body clock. At the website for **Outside In** (www.bodyclock.com), you can get a customized plan of when to seek and avoid light.
• If you need help getting to sleep earlier than you usually would, doctors recommend taking either the hormone **melatonin** or the sleeping pill **Ambien**—but not together. Take 2 to 5 milligrams of melatonin about 2 hours before your planned bedtime.

Flying with Film & Video

Never pack film—developed or undeveloped—in checked bags, as the new, more powerful scanners in U.S. airports can fog film. The film you carry with you can be damaged by scanners as well. X-ray damage is cumulative; the slower the film and the more times you put it through a scanner, the more likely the damage. Film under 800 ASA is usually safe for up to five scans. If you must take your film through additional scans, U.S. regulations permit you to demand hand inspections.

Most photo supply stores sell protective pouches designed to block damaging X-rays. The pouches fit both film and loaded cameras. They should protect your film in checked baggage, but they also may raise alarms and result in a hand inspection.

An organization called **Film Safety for Traveling on Planes** (FSTOP; ℭ **888/ 301-2665;** www.f-stop.org) can provide additional tips for traveling with film and equipment.

Carry-on scanners will not damage **videotape** in video cameras, but the magnetic fields emitted by the walk-through security gateways and hand-held inspection wands will. Always place your loaded camcorder on the screening conveyor belt or have it hand-inspected. Be sure your batteries are charged, as you will probably be required to turn the device on to ensure that it's what it appears to be.

GETTING THROUGH THE AIRPORT

With the federalization of airport security, security procedures at U.S. airports are more stable and consistent than ever. When you leave Kauai, allow 90 minutes before your flight. The airport was not designed for or built with the new security measures in mind, and you have to stand in four different lines before you get to your gate (agricultural inspection, ticketing, baggage inspection, and security), where you will stand in another line for your flight. Believe me, it can take you at least 90 minutes to get through all these lines.

Your airline carrier will tell you when to show up for your flight from your departing city. Some carriers now recommend 90 minutes due to the addition of random vehicle inspections at the airport.

Bring a **current, government-issued photo ID** such as a driver's license or passport. If you have an e-ticket, print out the **official confirmation page;** you'll need to show your confirmation at the security checkpoint, and your ID at the ticket counter or the gate. (Children under 18 do not need photo IDs for domestic flights, but the adults checking in with them do.)

If you want to speed up the security check, **do not wear metal objects** such as big belt buckles or clanky earrings. Most boots and many shoes have steel shafts in them that will set off metal detectors. Save yourself some trouble by taking them off and running them through the X-ray machines along with your carry-on luggage. If you've got metallic body parts, a note from your doctor can prevent a long chat with the security screeners.

Federalization has stabilized **what you can carry on** and **what you can't.** The general rule is that sharp things are out, nail clippers are okay, and food and beverages must be passed through the X-ray machine—but that security screeners can't make you drink from your coffee cup. Bring food in your carry-on rather than checking it, as explosive-detection machines used on checked luggage have been known to mistake food (especially chocolate, for some reason) for bombs. Travelers in the U.S. are allowed one carry-on bag, plus a "personal item" such as a purse, briefcase, or laptop bag. Carry-on hoarders can stuff all sorts of things into a laptop bag; as long as it has a laptop in it, it's still considered a personal item. The Transportation Security Administration (TSA) has issued a list of restricted items; check its website (www.tsa.gov/public/index.jsp) for details.

Passengers with e-tickets and without checked bags can still beat the ticket-counter lines by using **electronic kiosks** or even **online check-in.** Ask your airline which alternatives are available, and if you're using a kiosk, bring the credit card you used to book the ticket. If you're checking bags, you will still be able to use most airlines' kiosks; again, call your airline for up-to-date information. **Curbside check-in** is also a good way to avoid lines, although a few airlines still ban curbside check-in entirely; call before you go.

At press time, the TSA recommends that you **not lock your checked luggage** so screeners can search it by hand if necessary. The agency says to use plastic "zip ties" instead, which can be bought at hardware stores and can be easily cut off.

LANDING AT LIHUE AIRPORT

If there's a long wait at baggage claim, step over to the state-operated **Visitor Information Center.** There you can pick up brochures and the latest issue of *This Week Kauai,* which features great regional maps of the islands, and ask about island activities. After collecting your bags from the pokey, automated carousels, step out, take a deep breath, and cross the street to the rental-car check-in desks. After you check in, the rental-agency shuttle van will take you the half mile to the rental-car checkout desk. (All major rental companies have branches at Lihue; see "Getting Around," later in this chapter.)

Lihue Airport is a couple of miles from downtown Lihue. There is no public transportation and there are no shuttle vans available at the airport, so you must either rent a car or hire a taxi.

INTERISLAND FLIGHTS

Don't expect to jump a ferry between any of the Hawaiian islands. Today, everyone island-hops by plane. Before the September 11, 2001, terrorist attacks, there used to be flights between Honolulu to Kauai

---

Tips **Your Departure: Agricultural Screening at the Airports**

All baggage and passengers bound for the mainland must be screened by agricultural officials before boarding. This takes a little time but isn't a problem unless you happen to be carrying a football-size local avocado home to Aunt Emma. Officials will confiscate fresh avocados, bananas, mangoes, and many other kinds of local produce in the name of fruit-fly control. Pineapples, coconuts, and papayas inspected and certified for export; boxed flowers; leis without seeds; and processed foods (macadamia nuts, coffee, jams, dried fruit, and the like) will pass. Call federal agricultural officials (© **808/877-8757**) before leaving for the airport if you're not sure about your trophy.

The Welcoming Lei

Nothing makes you feel more welcome than a lei. The tropical beauty of the delicate garland, the deliciously sweet fragrance of the blossoms, the sensual way the flowers curl softly around your neck—there's no doubt about it: Getting lei'd in Hawaii is a sensuous experience.

Leis are much more than just a decorative necklace of flowers; they're also one of the nicest ways to say hello, goodbye, congratulations, I salute you, my sympathies are with you, or I love you. The custom of giving leis can be traced back to Hawaii's very roots: According to chants, the first lei was given by Hiiaka, the sister of the volcano goddess, Pele, who presented Pele with a lei of lehua blossoms on a beach in Puna.

During ancient times, leis given to *alii* (royalty) were accompanied by a bow, since it was *kapu* (forbidden) for a commoner to raise his arms higher than the king's head. The presentation of a kiss with a lei didn't come about until World War II; it's generally attributed to an entertainer who kissed an officer on a dare, then quickly presented him with her lei, saying it was an old Hawaiian custom. It wasn't then, but it sure caught on fast.

Lei-making is a tropical art form. All leis are fashioned by hand in a variety of traditional patterns; some are sewn of hundreds of tiny blooms or shells, or bits of ferns and leaves. Some are twisted, some braided, some strung. Every island has its own special flower lei. On Oahu, the choice is *ilima*, a small orange flower. Big Islanders prefer the *lehua*, a large, delicate red puff. Maui likes the *lokelani*, a small rose. On Kauai, it's the *mokihana*, a fragrant green vine and berry. Molokai prefers the *kukui*, the white blossom of a candlenut tree. Lanai's lei is made of *kaunaoa*, a bright yellow moss, while Niihau uses its abundant seashells to make leis that were once prized by royalty and are now worth a small fortune.

Leis are available at the Lihue Airport, from florists, and even at supermarkets.

Leis are the perfect symbol for Hawaii: They're given in the moment, their fragrance and beauty are enjoyed in the moment, but when they fade, their spirit of aloha lives on. Welcome to the islands!

---

almost every 30 minutes of every day from just before sunrise to well after sunset.

Those days are gone. There are fewer and fewer interisland flights, so be sure to book your interisland connection from Honolulu to Kauai in advance.

Aloha Airlines (© **800/367-5250** or 808/244-9071; www.alohaair.com) is the state's largest provider of interisland air transport. It offers 15 regularly scheduled daily jet flights a day from Honolulu to Kauai on its all-jet fleet of Boeing 737 aircraft.

Hawaiian Airlines (© **800/367-5320** or 808/871-6132; www.hawaiianair.com) is Hawaii's other interisland airline featuring jet planes.

Just as we went to press, a new start-up airline was announced, which plans to be in operation in 2006 with flights from Honolulu to Kauai if it can raise enough capital and get the necessary FAA certification. **FlyHawaii Airlines** was still in the planning stages, but proposes to use three 68-seat ATR-72 turboprop aircraft.

For more information, contact © **808/599-5588;** www.flyhi.com.

10 Money-Saving Package Deals

Booking an all-inclusive travel package that includes some combination of airfare, accommodations, rental car, meals, airport and baggage transfers, and sightseeing can be the most cost-effective way to travel to Kauai.

Package tours are not the same as escorted tours. They are simply a way to buy airfare and accommodations (and sometimes extras like sightseeing tours and rental cars) at the same time. When you're visiting Hawaii, a package can be a smart way to go. You can sometimes save so much money by buying all the pieces of your trip through a packager that your transpacific airfare ends up, in effect, being free. That's because packages are sold in bulk to tour operators, who then resell them to the public at a cost that drastically undercuts standard rates.

Packages, however, vary widely. Some offer a better class of hotels than others. Some offer the same hotels for lower prices. With some packagers, your choice of accommodations and travel days may be limited. Which package is right for you depends entirely on what you want.

Start out by **reading this guide.** Do a little homework, and read up on Kauai so that you can be a smart consumer. Compare the rack rates that we've published to the discounted rates being offered by the packagers to see what kinds of deals they're offering: Are you actually being offered a substantial savings, or have they just gussied up the rack rates to make their offer *sound* like a deal? If you're offered a stay in a hotel we haven't recommended, do more research to learn about it, especially if the franchise isn't a reliable one. It's not a deal if you end up at a dump.

Be sure to **read the fine print.** Make sure you know *exactly* what's included in the price you're being quoted, and what's

not. Are hotel taxes and airport transfers included, or will you have to pay extra? Before you commit to a package, make sure you know how much flexibility you have, say, if your kid gets sick or your boss suddenly asks you to adjust your vacation schedule. Some packagers require ironclad commitments, while others will go with the flow, charging only minimal fees for changes or cancellations.

The best place to start looking for a package deal is the travel section of your local Sunday newspaper. Also check the ads in the backs of such national travel magazines as *Arthur Frommer's Budget Travel* and *Travel Holiday.* **Liberty Travel** (© **888/271-1584;** www.libertytravel.com), for instance, one of the biggest packagers in the Northeast, usually boasts a full-page ad in Sunday newspapers. **American Express Travel** (© **800/AXP-6898;** www.americanexpress.com/travel) can also book you a well-priced Hawaiian vacation; it advertises in many Sunday newspaper travel sections.

Other reliable packagers include the airlines themselves, which often package their flights with accommodations. Among the airlines offering good-value package deals to Hawaii are **American Airlines FlyAway Vacations** (© 800/321-2121; www.aa.com), **Continental Airlines Vacations** (© 800/634-5555 or 800/301-3800; www.coolvacations.com), **Delta Dream Vacations** (© 800/872-7786; www.deltavacations.com), and **United Vacations** (© 800/328-6877; www.unitedvacations.com). If you're traveling to the islands from Canada, ask your travel agent about package deals through **Air Canada Vacations** (© 800/776-3000; www.aircanada.ca).

Excellent deals, like a rental car and 6 nights in a Kauai condo starting at $460 per person (based on double occupancy), can be found at **More Hawaii For Less** (© **800/967-6687**; www.hawaii4less.com), a California-based company that specializes in air-condominium packages at unbelievable prices.

GREAT DEALS AT HAWAII'S TOP HOTEL CHAIN

The **ResortQuest Hawaii** chain (© **877/ 997-6667**; www.resortquesthawaii.com)

has hotels, condos, cottages, and vacation homes on Kauai. They range dramatically in price and style, from the elegant Hanalei Bay Resort to the moderate ResortQuest Islander on the Beach. There are plenty of package deals galore, including family plans, discounted senior rates, car, and golf package deals.

11 Planning Your Trip Online

SURFING FOR AIRFARES

The "big three" online travel agencies, **Expedia.com, Travelocity.com,** and **Orbitz.com,** sell most of the air tickets bought on the Internet. (Canadian travelers should try Expedia.ca and Travelocity.ca; U.K. residents can go for Expedia.co.uk and Opodo.co.uk.) Each has different business deals with the airlines and may offer different fares on the same flights, so it's wise to shop around. Expedia and Travelocity will also send you **e-mail notification** when a cheap fare becomes available to your favorite destination. Of the smaller travel agency websites, **SideStep** (www.sidestep.com) has gotten the best reviews from Frommer's authors. It's a browser add-on that purports to "search 140 sites at once" but in reality only beats competitors' fares as often as other sites do.

Also remember to check **airline websites,** especially those for low-fare carriers such as Southwest, JetBlue, AirTran, WestJet, or Ryanair, whose fares are often misreported or simply missing from travel agency websites. Even with major airlines, you can often shave a few bucks from a fare by booking directly through the airline and avoiding a travel agency's transaction fee. But you'll get these discounts only by **booking online:** Most airlines now offer online-only fares that even their phone agents know nothing about. For the websites of airlines that fly

to and from your destination, see "Getting There," later in this chapter.

Great **last-minute deals** are available through free weekly e-mail services provided directly by the airlines. Most of these are announced on Tuesday or Wednesday and must be purchased online. Most are only valid for travel that weekend, but some (such as Southwest's) can be booked weeks or months in advance. Sign up for weekly e-mail alerts at airline websites or check mega-sites that compile comprehensive lists of last-minute specials, such as **Smarter Living** (www.smarterliving.com). For last-minute trips, **www.site59.com** in the U.S. and **www.lastminute.com** in Europe often have better deals than the major-label sites.

If you're willing to give up some control over your flight details, use an **opaque fare service** like **Priceline** (www.priceline.com; www.priceline.co.uk for Europeans) or **Hotwire** (www.hotwire.com). Both offer rock-bottom prices in exchange for travel on a "mystery airline" at a mysterious time of day, often with a mysterious change of planes en route. The mystery airlines are all major, well-known carriers—and the possibility of being sent from Philadelphia to Chicago via Tampa is remote; the airlines' routing computers have gotten a lot better than they used to be. But your chances of getting a 6am or 11pm flight are pretty high.

Frommers.com: The Complete Travel Resource

For an excellent travel-planning resource, we highly recommend **Frommers.com** (www.frommers.com). We're a little biased, of course, but we guarantee that you'll find the travel tips, reviews, monthly vacation giveaways, and online-booking capabilities thoroughly indispensable. Among the special features are our popular **Message Boards,** where Frommer's readers post queries and share advice (sometimes even our authors show up to answer questions); **Frommers.com Newsletter,** for the latest travel bargains and insider travel secrets; and Frommer's **Destinations Section,** where you'll get expert travel tips, hotel and dining recommendations, and advice on the sights to see for more than 2,500 destinations around the globe. When your research is done, the **Online Reservation System** (www.frommers.com/booktravelnow) takes you to Frommer's favorite sites to book your vacation at affordable prices.

Hotwire tells you flight prices before you buy; Priceline usually has better deals than Hotwire, but you have to play their "name our price" game. If you're new at this, the helpful folks at **BiddingFor-Travel** (www.biddingfortravel.com) do a good job of demystifying Priceline's prices. Priceline and Hotwire are great for flights within North America and between the U.S. and Europe. But for flights to other parts of the world, consolidators will almost always beat their fares.

For much more about airfares and savvy air-travel tips and advice, pick up a copy of *Frommer's Fly Safe, Fly Smart* (Wiley Publishing, Inc.).

SURFING FOR HOTELS

Shopping online for hotels on Kauai is easy; nearly every single accommodation in this book has its own website, and most offer online-only discounts through which you can save. Check the hotel or B&B of your choice to see if a deal is offered. If you go to the "big three" sites, they may not list all the smaller hotels and B&Bs we list here, so shop around. **Expedia** may be the best choice, thanks to its long list of special deals. **Travelocity** runs a close second. Hotel specialist sites **www.hotels.com** and **www.hotel discounts.com** are also reliable. An excel-

lent free program, **TravelAxe** (www.travel axe.net), can help you search multiple hotel sites at once, even ones you may never have heard of.

Priceline and Hotwire are even better for hotels than for airfares; with both, you're allowed to pick the neighborhood and quality level of your hotel before paying. *Note:* Hotwire overrates its hotels by one star—what Hotwire calls a four-star is a three-star anywhere else.

SURFING FOR RENTAL CARS

For booking rental cars online, the best deals are usually found at rental-car company websites, although all the major online travel agencies also offer rental-car reservations services. Priceline and Hotwire work well for rental cars, too; the only "mystery" is which major rental company you get, and for most travelers the difference between Hertz, Avis, and Budget is negligible. Don't forget to check package deals. Sometimes you can get an air/car rental package or an air/car/accommodation package in which the rental car is virtually free.

The only caveat we have about car rental agencies is the dozens of letters of complaint about Alamo Car Rental. Apparently during key periods of the day (like when direct flights from the mainland come in) the office on Kauai is not able to process the long line of people wanting to rent a car. Waits of up to 2 hours are not uncommon. So we suggest you book another car rental firm and save yourself the aggravation.

SMART E-SHOPPING

The savvy traveler is armed with insider information. Here are a few tips to help you navigate the Internet successfully and safely.

- **Know when sales start.** Last-minute deals may vanish in minutes. If you have a favorite booking site or airline, find out when last-minute deals are released to the public. (For example, Southwest's specials are posted every Tues at 12:01am Central Standard Time.)

- **Shop around.** If you're looking for bargains, compare prices on different websites, prices at airlines, and travel agents' best fares. Try a range of times and alternative airports before you make a purchase.

- **Stay secure.** Book only through secure sites. (Some airline sites are not secure.) Look for a key icon (Netscape) or a padlock (Internet Explorer) at the bottom of your Web browser before you enter credit card information or other personal data.

- **Avoid online auctions.** Sites that auction airline tickets and frequent-flier miles are the number-one perpetrators of Internet fraud, according to the National Consumers League.

- **Maintain a paper trail.** If you book an e-ticket, print out a confirmation or write down your confirmation number, and keep it safe and accessible—or your trip could be a virtual one!

HAWAII ON THE WEB

Below are some of the best Hawaii-specific websites for planning your trip.

- **Hawaii Visitors & Convention Bureau** (HVCB; **www.gohawaii. com**): An excellent, all-around guide to activities, tours, lodging, and events, plus a huge section on weddings and honeymoons. But keep in mind that only members of the HVCB are listed.

- **Kauai: Island of Discovery** (**www. kauaidiscovery.com**): Extensive listings cover activities, events, recreation, attractions, beaches, and much more. The Vacation Directory includes information on golf, fishing, and island tours; some listings include e-mail addresses and links to websites. You'll also find an interactive map of the Island with listings organized by region.

- **Planet Hawaii** (**www.planet-hawaii. com**): Click on "Island" for an island-by-island guide to activities, lodging, shopping, culture, surf conditions, weather, and more. You'll find mostly short listings with links to companies' own websites. Click on "Hawaiian Eye" for live images from around the islands.

- **Internet Hawaii Radio** (**www. hotspots.hawaii.com**): A great way to get into the mood, this eclectic site features great Hawaiian music, with opportunities to order a CD or cassette. You can also purchase a respectable assortment of Hawaiian historical and cultural books.

- **The Hawaiian Language Web Site** (**hawaiianlanguage.com**): This fabulous site not only has easy lessons on learning the Hawaiian language, but a great cultural calendar, links to other Hawaiian websites, a section on the hula, and lyrics (and translations) to Hawaiian songs.

12. The 21st-Century Traveler

INTERNET ACCESS AWAY FROM HOME

Travelers have any number of ways to check e-mail and access the Internet on the road. Of course, using your own laptop—or a PDA (personal digital assistant) or electronic organizer with a modem—gives you the most flexibility. But even if you don't have a computer, you can still access your e-mail and your office computer from cybercafes.

WITHOUT YOUR OWN COMPUTER

It's hard nowadays to find a city that *doesn't* have a few cybercafes, and Kauai is no exception. Although there's no definitive directory for cybercafes—these are independent businesses, after all—a good place to start is **www.cybercaptive.com**.

You can get Web access at the following places, prices range from a low of $2.50 for 15 minutes to a high of $7.50 for 15 minutes.

In Poipu, the Business Center at the **Grand Hyatt Kauai** (© **808/742-1234**), charges $7.50 for 15 minutes; in Waimea, **Na Pali Explorer,** 9935 Kaumualii Hwy. (© **808/338-9999**), charges 25 cents a minute or $6 an hour.

In Kapaa, try **Business Support Services,** 4-1191 Kuhio Hwy. (© **808/822-5504**), which charges $2.50 every 15 minutes.

In Hanalei, try **Bali Hai Photo,** 5-5190 Kuhio Hwy. (© **808/826-9181**), $3 for 20 minutes.

Aside from formal cybercafes, all **public libraries** on Kauai offer free access if you have a library card, which you can purchase for a $10 fee. For the location of the nearest library, call the Lihue library at © **808/241-3222.** All hotels on Kauai have **in-room dataports** and **business centers,** but the charges can be exorbitant.

To retrieve your e-mail, ask your **Internet Service Provider** (ISP) if it has a Web-based interface tied to your existing e-mail account. If your ISP doesn't have such an interface, you can use the free **mail2web** service (www.mail2web.com) to view (but not reply to) your home e-mail. For more flexibility, you may want to open a free, Web-based e-mail account with **Yahoo! Mail** (mail.yahoo.com). (Microsoft's Hotmail is another popular option, but Hotmail has severe spam problems.) Your home ISP may be able to forward your e-mail to the Web-based account automatically.

WITH YOUR OWN COMPUTER

Major ISPs have **local access numbers** allowing you to go online by simply placing a local call in Kauai. Check your ISP's website or call its toll-free number and ask how you can use your current account away from home, and how much it will cost.

Wherever you go, bring a **connection kit** of the right power, as well as phone adapters, a spare phone cord, and a spare Ethernet network cable.

All hotels on Kauai (and even some of the B&Bs) offer dataports for laptop modems, and a few have high-speed Internet access using an Ethernet network cable. You'll have to bring your own cables either way, so **call your hotel in advance** to find out what the options are.

USING A CELLPHONE

Just because your cellphone works at home doesn't mean it'll work in Kauai (thanks to our nation's fragmented cellphone system). Take a look at your wireless company's coverage map on its website before heading out—T-Mobile, Sprint, and Nextel are particularly weak in Kauai's rural areas. If you need to stay in touch at a destination where you know your phone won't work, **rent** a phone that does from **InTouch USA** (© **800/872-7626;** www.intouchglobal.com) or a rental car location, but be aware that you'll pay $1 a minute or more for airtime.

13 Getting Around

DRIVING AROUND KAUAI

You need a car to see and do everything on Kauai. Luckily, driving here is easy. There are only two major highways, each beginning in Lihue. From Lihue Airport, turn right, and you'll be on Kapule Highway (Hwy. 51), which eventually merges into Kuhio Highway (Hwy. 56) a mile down. This road will take you to the Coconut Coast and through the North Shore before it reaches a dead end at Kee Beach, where the Na Pali Coast begins.

If you turn left from Lihue Airport and follow Kapule Highway (Hwy. 51), you'll pass through Lihue and Nawiliwili. Turning on Nawiliwili Road (Hwy. 58) will bring you to its intersection with Kaumualii Highway (Hwy. 50), which will take you to the south and southwest sections of the island. This road doesn't follow the coast, however, so if you're heading to Poipu (and most people are), take Maluhia Road (Hwy. 520) south.

Kaumualii Highway (Hwy. 50) continues all the way to Waimea, where it then dwindles to a secondary road before reaching a dead end at the other end of the Na Pali Coast.

To get to Waimea Canyon, take either Waimea Canyon Road (Hwy. 550), which follows the western rim of the canyon and affords spectacular views, or Kokee Road (Hwy. 55), which goes up through Waimea Canyon to Kokee State Park (4,000 ft. above sea level); the roads join up about halfway.

CAR RENTALS

Hawaii has some of the lowest car-rental rates in the country. The average non-discounted, unlimited-mileage rate for a 1-day rental for an intermediate-size car in Kauai was $41 in 2005; that's one of the lowest rates in the country, compared with the national average of $54 per day. To rent a car in Hawaii, you must be at least 25 years of age and have a valid driver's license and credit card.

Most of the major car-rental agencies are represented on Kauai. The rental desks are just across the street from Lihue Airport, but you must go by van to collect your car.

The major rental-car agencies at Lihue Airport include: **Avis** (© 800/321-3712; www.avis.com), **Budget** (© 800/935-6878; www.budgetrentacar.com), **Dollar** (© 800/800-4000; www.dollarcar.com), **Hertz** (© 800/654-3011; www.hertz.com), **National** (© 800/227-7368; www.nationalcar.com), and **Thrifty** (© 800/367-2277; www.thrifty.com).

We do not recommend Alamo. As we mentioned above (p. 46), Alamo apparently is not able to process (in a timely manner) the long line of people wanting to rent their cars. Waits of up to 2 hours are not uncommon. Imagine getting off a 5-hour plane ride and having to stand in

---

Tips Traffic Advisory

Believe it or not Kauai has traffic problems. You do NOT want to be on the highways between 7–9am and 4–6pm, Monday through Friday. Your serene vacation will go out the car window as you sit in bumper to bumper traffic. A normal 10- to 15-minute trip from one town to the next can take up to an hour during these times. The problem is that there is only one road that circles the island and connects all the towns. Local people have to get to work, but you are on vacation and plan accordingly. *Another traffic note:* Buckle up your seat belt—Hawaii has stiff fines for noncompliance.

line for a couple of hours. Save yourself the aggravation, and book another car rental agency.

For deep discounts on weekly car-rental rates, call **Hookipa Haven Vacation Services** (⁂ 800/398-6284; www.hookipa.com). Rates in low season (Jan, Apr 16–June, and Aug 21–Dec 18) are $148 a week; they jump to $160 in high season.

Rental cars are usually at a premium and may be sold out on holiday weekends, so be sure to book well ahead.

INSURANCE   Hawaii is a no-fault state, which means that if you don't have collision-damage insurance, you are required to pay for all damages before you leave the state, whether or not the accident was your fault. Your personal car insurance may provide rental-car coverage; read your policy or call your insurer before you leave home. Bring your insurance identification card if you decline the optional insurance, which usually costs from $12 to $20 a day. Obtain the name of your company's local claim representative before you go. Some credit card companies also provide collision-damage insurance for their customers; check with yours before you rent.

DRIVING RULES   Hawaii state law mandates that all car passengers must wear a **seat belt,** and all infants must be strapped into car seats. The fine is enforced with vigilance, so buckle up—you'll pay a $50 fine if you don't. **Pedestrians** always have the right of way, even if they're not in the crosswalk. You can turn **right on red** from the right lane after a full and complete stop, unless there's a sign forbidding you to do so.

ROAD MAPS   The best and most detailed road maps are published by *This Week Magazine,* a free visitor publication. Another good source of maps is *The Ready Mapbook of Kauai,* published by **Odyssey Publishing,** P.O. Box 11173, Hilo, HI 96721 (⁂ 808/935-0092;

www.geckofarms.com/hawaiimaps.htm). The 67-page book not only has detailed maps of the island, but also lists points of interest, parks, beaches, golf courses, campgrounds, shopping centers, and trails. The book retails for $11.

For island maps, check out the University of Hawaii Press maps. Updated periodically, they include a detailed network of island roads, large-scale insets of towns, historical and contemporary points of interest, parks, beaches, and hiking trails. They cost about $3 each, or about $15 for a complete set. If you can't find them in a bookstore near you, contact **University of Hawaii Press,** 2840 Kolowalu St., Honolulu, HI 96822 (⁂ 888/847-7737; www.uhpress.hawaii.edu). For topographic and other maps of the islands, go to the **Hawaii Geographic Society,** 49 S. Hotel St., Honolulu; or contact them at P.O. Box 1698, Honolulu, HI 96806 (⁂ 800/538-3950 or 808/538-3952).

MOTORCYCLE RENTALS

The best place to find a customized, cherried-out Harley is **Two Wheels Rentals,** located near Nawiliwili Harbor in Lihue on Rice Street next to the Kauai Marriott, Anchor Cove shopping center and Harbor Mall shopping center (⁂ 808/246-9457; www.kauaimotorcycle.com), which has Harleys from $60 for 2 hours.

OTHER TRANSPORTATION OPTIONS

Kauai Taxi Company (⁂ 808/246-9554) offers taxi, limousine, and airport shuttle service. **Kauai Bus** (⁂ 808/241-6417) operates a fleet of 15 buses that serve the entire island, but they do not go to the airport. Taking the bus may be practical for day trips if you know your way around the island, but you can't take anything larger than a shopping bag aboard, and the buses don't stop at any of the resort areas. However, they do serve more than a dozen coastal towns from

Kekaha, on the southwest shore, all the way to Hanalei. Buses run more or less hourly from 5:30am to 6pm. The fare is $1, or 50¢ for seniors, students, and passengers with disabilities.

14 Tips on Accommodations

Kauai offers a tremendous variety of accommodations, from ritzy resorts to simple bed-and-breakfasts. Before you book a room, read this section to find out what each option typically offers. We've included tips on how to get the best rates.

TYPES OF ACCOMMODATIONS

HOTELS   In Hawaii, the term *hotel* can indicate a wide range of options, from accommodations with few or no on-site amenities to those with enough extras to qualify as resorts. Generally, a hotel offers daily maid service and has a restaurant, on-site laundry facilities, a pool, and a sundries/convenience-type shop (as opposed to the shopping arcades that most resorts have). Top hotels also provide activities desks, concierge service, business centers, bars and/or lounges, and perhaps a few more shops. The advantages of staying in a hotel are privacy and convenience; the disadvantage is generally noise—due either to thin walls between rooms or to loud music from a lobby lounge late into the night.

RESORTS   In Hawaii, a resort offers everything a hotel offers and more. What you get varies from property to property, of course, but expect facilities, services, and amenities such as direct beach access, with cabanas and chairs; a pool (often more than one) and a Jacuzzi; a spa and fitness center; restaurants, bars, and lounges; a 24-hour front desk; concierge, valet, and bell services; room service (often around the clock); an activities desk; tennis and golf (some of the world's best courses are at Hawaii resorts); ocean activities; a business center; children's programs; and more.

The advantage of staying at a resort is that you have everything you could possibly want in the way of services and things to do; the disadvantage is that the price generally reflects this. Don't be misled by a name—just because a place is called "ABC Resort" doesn't mean it actually *is* a resort. Make sure you're getting what you pay for.

CONDOS   The roominess and convenience of a condo—usually a fully equipped multibedroom apartment—make this a great choice for families. Condominium properties in Hawaii are generally several apartments set in either a single high-rise or a cluster of low-rise units. Condos generally have amenities such as some degree of maid service (ranging from daily to weekly; it may or may not be included in your rate, so be sure to ask), a pool, laundry facilities (either in your unit or in a central location), and an on-site front desk or a live-in property manager. The advantages of a condo are privacy, space, and conveniences—which usually include a fully equipped kitchen, a washer and dryer, a private phone, and perhaps your own lanai or balcony. The downsides include the absence of an on-site restaurant and the density of the units. (The condo may be more private than a B&B or hotel, but not quite as private as your own cottage, villa, or house.)

Condos vary in price according to size, location, and amenities. Many of them are located on or near the beach, and they tend to be clustered in resort areas. While there are some very high-end condos, most tend to be quite affordable, especially if you're traveling in a group that's large enough to require more than one bedroom.

Tips What to Do If Your Dream Hotel Turns Out to Be a Nightmare

To avoid any unpleasant surprises, ask lots of questions when you make your reservation. Find out exactly what the accommodation entails, particularly the cost, minimum stay, and included amenities. Ask if there's a penalty fee for leaving early. Read the small print in the contract—especially the part on cancellation fees. Discuss the cancellation policy ahead of time with the B&B, vacation rental, condominium agent, or booking agency so you'll know what your options are if the accommodation doesn't meet your expectations. Get this in writing so there are no misunderstandings later.

When you arrive, if the room you're given doesn't meet your expectations, notify the front desk, rental agent, or booking agency immediately. Approach the management in a calm, reasonable manner, and suggest a constructive solution (such as moving to another unit). Be reasonable and be willing to compromise. Do not make threats or leave; if you leave, it may be harder to get your deposit returned.

BED-AND-BREAKFASTS Kauai has a wide variety of places that fall into this category: everything from the traditional B&B—several bedrooms in a home (which may or may not share a bathroom), with breakfast served in the morning—to what is essentially a vacation rental on an owner's property that comes with fixings for you to make your own breakfast. Make sure that the B&B you book matches your own mental picture of it. Would you prefer conversation around a big dining-room table as you eat a hearty breakfast, or just a muffin and juice to enjoy in your own private place? Laundry facilities, televisions, and private phones are not always available at B&Bs. We've reviewed lots of wonderful places in this book. If you have to share a bathroom, we've spelled it out in the reviews; otherwise, you can assume that you will have a private bathroom.

There are a few things you should be aware of before you book your first B&B. You do not have the "run" of the house. Generally there is a guest area, which may have a small refrigerator for the guests' use, places to sit and read, and perhaps a television. You are not renting the house of your hosts. And generally they do not allow cooking (especially in their kitchen).

The lower rate at B&Bs can be attributed to **no daily maid service**. You might have to make your own bed, and unless you are staying three or four days, your sheets will not be changed.

Due to Kauai County restrictions, most of the B&Bs do not have certified kitchens, so they can only bake, not cook breakfast. Several hosts are very clever and have recipes for "baked French toast" and "baked" eggs, but generally expect a continental breakfast.

The advantages of a traditional B&B are its individual style and congenial atmosphere. B&Bs are great places to meet other visitors, and the host is generally very happy to act as your private concierge, offering tips on where to go and what to do. In addition, B&Bs are usually an affordable way to go (though fancier ones can run $250 or more a night). The disadvantages are lack of privacy, usually a set time for breakfast, few amenities, generally no maid service, and the fact that you'll have to share the quarters beyond your bedroom with others. In addition, B&B owners usually require a minimum stay of 2 or 3 nights, and it's often a drive to the beach.

VACATION RENTALS This is another great choice for families as well as for long-term stays. The term *vacation rental* usually means there will be no one on the property where you're staying. The actual accommodation can range from an apartment in a condominium building to a two-room cottage on the beach to an entire fully-equipped house. Generally, vacation rentals are the kinds of places you can settle into for a while: They have kitchen facilities (sometimes a full kitchen, sometimes just microwave, minifridge, stovetop, and coffeemaker), on-site laundry facilities, and phone; some have such extras as TV, VCR, and stereo. The advantages of a vacation rental are complete privacy, your own kitchen (which can save you money on meals), and lots of conveniences. The disadvantages are the lack of an on-site property manager, no organized ocean activities, and generally no maid service. Often, a minimum stay is required (sometimes as long as a week). If you book a vacation rental, be sure you have a 24-hour contact so that when the toilet won't flush or you can't figure out how to turn on the air-conditioning, you'll have someone to call.

HOME EXCHANGE If you are interested in trading your home on the mainland for someone's home in Hawaii so that you can both have an inexpensive vacation, the best book to read first is *Home Exchange Guide: How to Find Your Free Home Away from Home,* by M. T. Simon and T. T. Baker, published by Poyee Publishing (2901 Clint Moore, no. 265, Boca Raton, FL 33496; ℂ 561/ 892-0494; www.poyeen.com). This step-by-step guidebook first helps you determine if home exchange is right for you. It then helps you develop a strategy to get the word out. You'll utilize "sure-fire ways" to have a successful home exchange on both sides.

BARGAINING ON PRICES

Rates can sometimes be bargained down, but it depends on the place. In general, each type of accommodation allows a different amount of latitude in bargaining on its rack (or published) rates.

The best bargaining can be had at **hotels** and **resorts.** Hotels and resorts regularly pay travel agents as much as 30% of the rate they get for sending clients their way; if business is slow, some hotels might give you the benefit of at least part of this commission if you book directly instead of go through an airline or travel agent. Most also have *kamaaina* or "local" rates for islanders, which they might extend to visitors during slow periods. It never hurts to ask politely for a discounted or local rate; a host of special rates are also available for the military,

Nickel-&-Dime Charges at High-Priced Hotels

Several upscale resorts in Kauai have begun a practice that we find distasteful and dishonest: charging a so-called "resort fee." This daily fee is added on to your bill for such "complimentary" items as a daily newspaper, local phone calls, use of the fitness facilities, and the like. Amenities that the resort has been happily providing free to its guests for years are now tacked on to your bill under the guise of a "fee." In most cases you do not have an option to decline the resort fee—in other words, this is a sneaky way to further increase the prices without telling you. The only way that this obnoxious fee will ever be rescinded is if you, the consumer, complain, and complain loudly.

seniors, members of the travel industry, families, corporate travelers, and long-term stays.

Ask about package deals, which might include a car rental or free breakfast for the same price as a room. Hotels and resorts offer packages for everyone: golfers, tennis players, families, honeymooners, and more. See "Money-Saving Package Deals," earlier in this chapter.

We've found that it's worth the extra few cents to make a local call to the hotel; sometimes the local reservationists know about package deals that the toll-free operators are unaware of.

If all else fails, try to get the hotel or resort to upgrade you to a better room for the same price as a budget room, or get them to waive the parking fee or the extra fees for children. Persistence and polite inquiries can pay off.

It's harder to bargain at **bed-and-breakfasts.** You may be able to bargain down the minimum stay or negotiate a discount if you're staying a week or longer. But generally, a B&B owner has only a few rooms and has already priced the property at a competitive rate, so expect to pay what's asked.

You have somewhat more leeway to negotiate on **vacation rentals** and **condos.** In addition to asking for a discount on multinight stays, also ask whether the condo or vacation rental can throw in a rental car to sweeten the deal; believe it or not, they often will.

USING A BOOKING AGENCY VERSUS DOING IT YOURSELF

Sometimes you can save money by making arrangements yourself—not only can you bargain on the phone, but some accommodations may also be willing to pass on a percentage of the commission they would normally have to pay a travel agent or a booking agency.

However, if you don't have the time or money to call several places to make sure they offer the amenities you'd like and to bargain for a price you're comfortable with, consider using a booking agency. The time the agency spends on your behalf might well be worth any fees you'll have to pay.

The top reservations service in the state is **Hawaii's Best Bed & Breakfasts,** P.O. Box 758, Volcano, HI 96785 (© **800/ 262-9912** or 808/985-7488; fax 808/ 967-8610; www.bestbnb.com). The fee for this service starts at $20 to book. The staff personally selects the traditional homestays, cottages, and inns, based on each one's hospitality, distinctive charm, and attention to detail.

For vacation rentals, contact **Hawaii Beachfront Vacation Homes** (© **808/ 247-3637** or 808/235-2644; www.hi beach.com). **Hawaii Condo Exchange** (© **800/442-0404;** www.hawaiicondo exchange.com) acts as a consolidator for condo and vacation-rental properties.

15 The Active Vacation Planner

If you want nothing more on your vacation than a fabulous beach and a perfectly mixed mai tai, you're in luck—Kauai has some of the most spectacular beaches (not to mention the best mai tais) in the world. But Kauai's wealth of natural wonders is hard to resist; the year-round tropical climate and spectacular scenery tend to inspire even the most committed desk jockeys and couch potatoes to get outside and explore.

If you have your own snorkel gear or other watersports equipment, bring it. If you can't, don't fret; everything you'll need is available for rent. We list all kinds of places to rent or buy gear in chapter 7.

⌐Tips Safety Tips

Be sure to see "Health & Safety," earlier in this chapter, before setting out on any adventure; it includes useful information on hiking, camping, and ocean safety. Even if you just plan to lie on the beach, check out "Don't Get Burned: Smart Tanning Tips" on p. 34, to learn how to protect yourself against the sun's harmful rays.

When planning sunset activities, be aware that Hawaii, like other places close to the equator, has a very short (5–10 min.) twilight period after the sun sets. After that, it's dark. If you hike out to watch the sunset, be sure you can make it back quickly, or take a flashlight.

SETTING OUT ON YOUR OWN VERSUS USING AN OUTFITTER

There are two ways to go: Plan all the details before you go and schlep your gear 2,500 miles across the Pacific, or go with an outfitter or a guide and let them worry about the details.

Experienced outdoor enthusiasts can follow your noses to coastal campgrounds or even trek into the rainforest on your own, but it's often preferable to go with a local guide who is familiar with the conditions at both sea level and the summit, knows the land and its flora and fauna in detail, and has all the gear you'll need. It's also good to go with a guide if time is an issue. If you really want to see native birds, for instance, an experienced guide will take you directly to the best areas for sightings. And many forests and valleys in the interiors of the islands are either on private property or in wilderness preserves that are accessible only on guided tours. If you go with a guide, plan on spending at least $100 a day per person; we recommend the best local outfitters and tour-guide operators in chapter 8.

But if you have the time, already own the gear, and love doing the research and planning, try exploring on your own. Chapter 8 discusses the best spots to set out for on your own, from the best offshore snorkel and dive spots to great daylong hikes, as well as the federal, state, and county agencies that can help you with hikes on public property; we also list references for spotting birds, plants, and sea life. We recommend that you always use the resources available and inquire about weather, trail, or surf conditions; water availability; and other conditions before you take off on your adventure.

For hikers, a great alternative to hiring a private guide is taking one of the guided hikes offered by the Kauai chapter of the **Sierra Club,** P.O. Box 3412, Lihue, HI 96766 (© **808/246-8748;** www.hi.sierra club.org). The club offers guided hikes on preserves and at special places during the year, as well as 1- to 7-day work trips to restore habitats and trails and root out invasive plants like banana poka, New Zealand flax, nonnative gorse, and wild ginger. This might not sound like a dream vacation to everyone, but it's a chance to see the "real" Kauai—including wilderness areas that are usually off-limits.

The Sierra Club offers four to seven hikes a month on Kauai. Hikes are led by certified Sierra Club volunteers and are classified as easy, moderate, or strenuous. These half-day or all-day affairs cost $1 for Sierra Club members, $5 for nonmembers. (Bring exact change.) For a copy of the newsletter, which lists all outings and trail repair work, send $2 to the address above.

Value **Fun for Less: Don't Leave Home without a Gold Card**

Almost any activity you can think of, from submarine rides to Polynesian luaus, can be purchased at a discount by using the **Activities and Attractions Association of Hawaii Gold Card,** 355 Hukilike St., no. 202, Kahului, HI 96732 (© **800/398-9698** or 808/871-7947; fax 808/877-3104; www.hawaiifun. org). The Gold Card, accepted by members on every island, including Kauai, offers a discount of 10% to 25% off activities and meals for up to four people; it's good for a year from the purchase date and costs $30.

You can save big bucks with the Gold Card. For example, if you have your heart set on taking a helicopter ride that goes for $149, you'll pay only $119 with your Gold Card, saving you nearly $30 per person—almost $120 in savings for a family of four. With just one activity alone, you've gotten the cost of the card back in savings. And there are hundreds of activities to choose from: air tours, attractions, bicycling tours, dinner cruises, fishing, guided tours, helicopter tours, horseback riding, kayaking, luaus, snorkeling, rafting, sailing, scuba diving, submarine rides, and more. It even gets you discounts on rental cars, restaurants, and golf!

Here's how it works: You contact the Activities and Attractions Association via mail, e-mail, fax, phone, or Internet (see above). They issue you the card, good for discounts for 1 year after the date you purchase it. You contact the activity (restaurant, rental car, and so on) directly, give them your Gold Card number, and get discounts ranging from 10% to 25%.

USING ACTIVITIES DESKS TO BOOK YOUR ISLAND FUN

If you're interested in an activity that requires an outfitter or a guide, such as horseback riding, whale-watching, or sportfishing, consider booking through a discount activities center or activities desk. These agents—who act as a clearinghouse for activities, just as a consolidator functions as a discount clearinghouse for airline tickets—can often get you a better price than you'd get by booking an activity directly with the outfitter yourself.

Discount activities centers will, in effect, split their commission with you, giving themselves a smaller commission to get your business—and passing, on average, a 10% discount on to you. In addition to saving you money, good activities centers should be able to help

you find, say, the snorkel cruise that's right for you, or the luau that's most suitable for both you *and* the kids.

But it's in the activity agent's best interest to sign you up with outfitters from which they earn the most commission, and some agents have no qualms about booking you into any old activity if it means an extra buck for them. If an agent tries to push a particular outfitter or activity too hard, be skeptical. Conversely, they'll try to steer you away from outfitters that don't offer big commissions. Another important word of warning: Be careful to avoid those activities centers offering discounts as fronts for timeshare sales presentations. Using a free snorkel cruise or luau tickets as bait, they'll suck you into a 90-minute presentation—and try to get you to buy into a

Kauai timeshare in the process. Not only will they try to sell you a big white elephant you never wanted in the first place, but—since their business is timeshares, not activities—they also won't be as interested, or as knowledgeable, about which activities might be right for you. These shady deals seem to be particularly rampant on Kauai. Just do yourself a favor and avoid them altogether.

We recommend **Tom Barefoot's Cashback Tours** ⚲ (© **888/222-3601;** www.barefoothawaii.com). Tom offers a 10% discount on all tours, activities, and adventures when you pay in cash or with traveler's checks. If you pay with a credit card or personal check, he'll give you a 7% discount. We found Tom's to be very reliable and honest.

OUTDOOR ETIQUETTE

Carry out what you carry in. Find a trash container for all your litter (including cigarette butts). Litterbugs anger the gods.

Observe *kapu* (taboo) and NO TRESPASSING signs. Don't climb on ancient Hawaiian *heiau* (temple) walls or carry home rocks, all of which belong to the Hawaiian volcano goddess, Pele. Some say it's just a silly superstition, but each year the national and state park services get boxes of lava rocks in the mail, sent back to Hawaii by visitors who have experienced unusually bad luck after taking forbidden souvenirs home.

16 Recommended Reading

In addition to the books discussed below, those planning an extended trip to other islands in Hawaii should check out *Frommer's Hawaii; Frommer's Hawaii from $80 a Day; Frommer's Honolulu, Waikiki & Oahu; Frommer's Maui;* and *Frommer's Hawaii with Kids* (Wiley Publishing, Inc.).

FICTION

The first Hawaii-related book people think about is James A. Michener's *Hawaii* (Fawcett Crest, 1974). This epic novel is a fictionalization of Hawaii's history. It manages to put the island's history into chronological order, but remember, it is still fiction, and very sanitized fiction, too. For a more contemporary look at life in Hawaii today, one of the best novels is *Shark Dialogue* by Kiana Davenport (Plume, 1995). The novel tells the story of Pono, the larger-than-life matriarch, and her four daughters of mixed races. Davenport skillfully weaves legends and myths of Hawaii into the "real life" reality that Pono and her family face in the complex Hawaii of today. Lois-Ann Yamanaka, a recent emerging writer from Hawaii, uses a very "local" voice and stark depictions of life in the islands in her fabulous novels *Wild Meat and the Bully Burgers* (Farrar, Straus, Giroux, 1996), *Blu's Hanging* (Avon, 1997), and *Heads by Harry* (Avon, 1999).

NONFICTION

Mark Twain's writing on Hawaii in the 1860s offers a wonderful introduction to Hawaii's history. One of his best books is *Mark Twain in Hawaii: Roughing It in the Sandwich Islands* (Mutual Publishing, 1990). Another great depiction of the Hawaii of 1889 is *Travels in Hawaii* (University of Hawaii Press, 1973) by Robert Louis Stevenson. For contemporary voices on Hawaii's unique culture, one of the best books is *Voices of Wisdom: Hawaiian Elders Speak* by M. J. Harden (Aka Press, 1999), in which some 24 different *kahuna* (experts) in their fields were interviewed about their talent, skill, or artistic practice. These living treasures talk about how Hawaiians of yesteryear viewed nature, spirituality and healing, preservation and history, dance and music, arts and crafts, canoes, and the next generation.

FLORA & FAUNA

Because Hawaii is so lush with nature and blessed with plants, animals, and reef fish seen nowhere else on the planet, a few reference books can help you identify what you're looking at and make your trip more interesting. In the botanical world, Angela Kay Kepler's *Hawaiian Heritage Plants* (A Latitude 20 Book, University of Hawaii Press, 1998) is the standard for plant reference. In a series of essays, Kepler weaves culture, history, geography, botany, and even spirituality into her vivid descriptions of plants. You'll never look at plants the same way. There are great color photos and drawings to help you sort thorough the myriad species. Another great plant book is *Tropicals* (Timber Press, 1988) by Gordon Courtright, which is filled with color photos identifying everything from hibiscus and heliconia to trees and palms. As Courtright puts it, "This book is intended to be a visual plant dictionary."

The other necessary reference guide to have in Hawaii is a book identifying the colorful reef fish you will see snorkeling. The best reference book is John E. Randall's *Shore Fishes of Hawaii* (University of Hawaii Press, 1998). Randall is the expert on everything that swims underwater, and his book is one of the best. Two other books on reef fish identification, with easy-to-use spiral bindings, are *Hawaiian Reef Fish—The Identification Book* (Blue Kirio Publishing, 1993) by Casey Mahaney; and *Hawaiian Reef Fish* (Island Heritage, 1998) by Astrid Witte and Casey Mahaney.

For birders or for those who just wonder about Hawaii's unique birds, H. Douglas Pratt's *A Pocket Guide to Hawaii's Birds* (Mutual Publishing, 1996) gives you everything you need to identify Hawaii's birds.

HISTORY

There are many great books on Hawaii's history, but one of the best places to start is with the formation of the Hawaiian Islands, vividly described in David E. Eyre's *By Wind, By Wave: An Introduction to Hawaii's Natural History* (Bess Press, 2000). In addition to chronicling the natural history of Hawaii, Eyre describes the complex interrelationships among plants, animals, ocean, and people. Eyre points out that Hawaii has become the "extinction capital of the world," but rather than dwell on that fact, he urges readers to do something about it and carefully spells out how.

For history of "precontact" Hawaii (before Westerners arrived), David Malo's *Hawaiian Antiquities* (Bishop Museum Press, 1976) is the preeminent source. Malo, born around 1793, wrote about the Hawaiian lifestyle at that time as well as the beliefs and religion of his people. The book is an excellent reference, but not a fast read. For more readable books on old Hawaii, try *Stories of Old Hawaii* (Bess Press, 1997) by Roy Kakulu Alameide on myths and legends; *Hawaiian Folk Tales* (Mutual Publishing, 1998) by Thomas G. Thrum; and *The Legends and Myths of Hawaii* (Charles E. Tuttle Company, 1992) by His Hawaiian Majesty King David Kalakaua.

The best book on the overthrow of the Hawaiian monarchy in 1898 is told by the woman who experienced it, Queen Liliuokalani, in her book *Hawaii's Story by Hawaii's Queen Liliuokalani* (Mutual Publishing, 1990). When it was written at the turn-of-the-19th century, it was an international plea for justice for her people, but it is a poignant read even today. It's also a "must-read" for people interested in current events and the recent rally in the 50th state for sovereignty. Two contemporary books on the question of Hawaii's sovereignty are Tom Coffman's *Nation Within—The Story of America's Annexation of the Nation of Hawaii* (Epicenter, 1998); and *Hawaiian Sovereignty: Do the Facts Matter?* (Goodale, 2000) by

Thurston Twigg-Smith, which explores the opposite view. Twigg-Smith, former publisher of the statewide newspaper *The Honolulu Advertiser,* is the grandson of Lorrin A. Thurston, one of the architects of the 1893 overthrow of the monarchy. His so-called "politically incorrect" views present a different look on this hotly debated topic.

For more recent history, Lawrence H. Fuchs's *Hawaii Pono* (Bess Press, 1991) is a carefully researched tome on the contributions of each of Hawaii's main immigrant communities (Chinese, Japanese, and Filipino) between 1893 and 1959.

SPECIALTY VACATIONS

If you are looking for a specific type of vacation experience, especially in the areas of health, wellness, or alternative healing, check out *The Call to Hawaii: A Wellness Vacation Guidebook* by Laura and Betsy Crites, published by Aloha Wellness Publishers, 2333 Kapiolani Blvd. no. 2108, Honolulu, HI 96826 (© **808/ 223-2533;** www.alohawellnesstravel. com). This great resource details everything from Hawaiian sacred healing to psychospiritual therapy. Included are practitioners (listed by island) of massage, qigong, holistic medicine, kinesiology, acupuncture, ayurvedic medicine, naturopathy, homeopathy, craniosacral work, energy medicine, sound therapy, yoga, and many other modalities.

For language fans, a couple of books on Pidgin we recommend: *Da Kine Dictionary* and *Pidgin To Da Max,* both published by Bess Press (© **800/910-2377;** www.besspress.com).

FAST FACTS: Kauai

American Express There's no local office on the island.

Area Code All of the islands are in the **808** area code. Note that if you're calling one island from another, you must dial 1-808 first, and you'll be billed at long-distance rates (which can be more expensive than calling the mainland).

Business Hours Most offices are open from 8am to 5pm. The morning commute usually runs from 6 to 8am, and the evening rush is from 4 to 6pm. Bank hours are Monday through Thursday from 8:30am to 3pm, Friday from 8:30am to 6pm; some banks are open on Saturday. Shopping centers are open Monday through Friday from 10am to 9pm, Saturday from 10am to 5:30pm, and Sunday from 10am to 5 or 6pm.

Dentists Emergency dental care is available from **Dr. Mark A. Baird,** 4-9768 Kuhio Hwy., Kapaa (© **808/822-9393**); and **Dr. Michael Furgeson,** 4347 Rice St., Lihue (© **808/246-6960**).

Doctors Walk-ins are accepted at **Kauai Medical Clinic,** 3-3420 Kuhio Hwy., Suite B, Lihue (© **808/245-1500,** or 808/245-1831 after hours). You can also try the **North Shore Clinic,** Kilauea and Oka roads, Kilauea (© **808/828-1418**); **Koloa Clinic,** 5371 Koloa Rd. (© **808/742-1621**); **Eleele Clinic,** 3292 Waialo Rd. (© **808/335-0499**); or **Kapaa Clinic,** 3-1105 Kuhio Hwy. (© **808/822-3431**).

Emergencies Dial © **911** for police, fire, and ambulance service. The **Poison Control Center** can be reached at © **800/362-3585.**

Hospitals **Wilcox Health System,** 3420 Kuhio Hwy., Lihue (© **808/245-1100**), has emergency services available around the clock.

Liquor Laws The legal drinking age in Hawaii is 21. Beer, wine, and liquor are sold in grocery and convenience stores at any hour, 7 days a week. It's illegal (though rarely prosecuted) to have an open container on the beach.

Newspapers The *Honolulu Advertiser* and the *Honolulu Star Bulletin* are circulated statewide. The *Garden Island* is the island's daily paper.

Police For nonemergencies, call ℂ 808/245-9711.

Post Office The main post office is at 4441 Rice St., Lihue. To find the branch office nearest you, call ℂ 800/ASK-USPS.

Radio The most popular stations are KHPR (88.1 or 90.7 FM), the **National Public Radio** station; KONG (570 AM) **news, talk,** and **sports;** KUAI (720 AM) **Hawaiian and contemporary music, surf reports,** and **sports;** KKCR (91.9 and 90.9 FM) **nonprofit community radio** with various formats; KONG (93.5 FM) **contemporary music;** KSRF (95.9 FM) **surf** and **contemporary Hawaiian music;** KFMN (96.9 FM) **adult contemporary;** KITH (98.9 FM) **travel host, island music,** and **commercial travel information;** KTOH (99.9 FM) **oldies music from the 1950s on;** and KSHK (103.3 FM) **classic rock 'n' roll.**

Safety Although Hawaii is generally a safe tourist destination, visitors have been crime victims, so stay alert. The most common crime against tourists is rental car break-ins. Never leave any valuables in your car, not even in your trunk. Thieves can be in and out of your car's trunk faster than you can open it with your own key. Be especially careful at high-risk areas such as beaches and resorts. Never carry large amounts of cash with you. Stay in well-lighted areas after dark. Don't hike on deserted trails alone. See also "Health & Safety," earlier in this chapter, for other safety tips.

Smoking It's against the law to smoke in public buildings, including restaurants, airports, grocery stores, retail shops, movie theaters, banks, and all government buildings and facilities. Hotels have nonsmoking rooms available, bars have nonsmoking sections, and car-rental agencies have smoke-free cars. Most bed-and-breakfasts prohibit smoking indoors.

Taxes Hawaii's sales tax is 4%. Hotel occupancy tax is 7.25%, and hoteliers are allowed by the state to tack on an additional .001666% excise tax. Thus, expect taxes of about 11.42% to be added to every hotel bill.

Time Hawaii Standard Time is in effect year-round. Hawaii is 2 hours behind Pacific Standard Time and 5 hours behind Eastern Standard Time. In other words, when it's noon in Hawaii, it's 2pm in California and 5pm in New York during standard time on the mainland. There's no daylight saving time here, so when daylight saving time is in effect on the mainland, Hawaii is 3 hours behind the West Coast and 6 hours behind the East Coast—so in summer, when it's noon in Hawaii, it's 3pm in California and 6pm in New York.

Hawaii is east of the international date line, putting it in the same day as the U.S. mainland and Canada, and a day behind Australia, New Zealand, and Asia.

Weather For current weather conditions, call ℂ 808/245-6001. For marine conditions, call ℂ 808/245-3564.

3

For International Visitors

Whether it's your first visit or your 10th, a trip to the United States may require additional planning. The pervasiveness of American culture around the world may make the United States feel like familiar territory to foreign visitors, but leaving your own country for the U.S.—especially the unique island of Kauai—still requires some arrangements before you leave home. This chapter will provide you with essential information, helpful tips, and advice for the more common problems that some visitors encounter.

Be advised that no international carrier flies directly to Kauai. You must go to Honolulu to clear Immigration and Customs, then take an interisland carrier from Honolulu to the Lihue Airport in Kauai.

1 Preparing for Your Trip

ENTRY REQUIREMENTS

Check at any U.S. embassy or consulate for current information and requirements. You can also obtain a visa application and other information online at the **U.S. State Department's** website, **www.travel.state.gov**.

VISAS The U.S. State Department has a **Visa Waiver Program** allowing citizens of certain countries to enter the United States without a visa for stays of up to 90 days. At press time, these included Andorra, Australia, Austria, Belgium, Brunei, Denmark, Finland, France, Germany, Iceland, Ireland, Italy, Japan, Liechtenstein, Luxembourg, Monaco, the Netherlands, New Zealand, Norway, Portugal, San Marino, Singapore, Slovenia, Spain, Sweden, Switzerland, the United Kingdom, and Uruguay. Citizens of these countries need only a valid passport and a round-trip air or cruise ticket in your possession upon arrival. If you first enter the United States, you may also visit Mexico, Canada, Bermuda, and/or the Caribbean

islands, and return to the United States without a visa. Further information is available from any U.S. embassy or consulate. Canadian citizens may enter the United States without visas; you need only proof of residence.

Citizens of all other countries must have (1) a valid passport that expires at least 6 months later than the scheduled end of your visit to the United States; and (2) a tourist visa, which may be obtained without charge from any U.S. consulate.

To obtain a visa, the traveler must submit a completed application form (either in person or by mail) with a 1½-inch square photo, and must demonstrate binding ties to a residence abroad. Usually you can obtain a visa at once or within 24 hours, but it may take longer during the summer rush June through August. If you cannot go in person, contact the nearest U.S. embassy or consulate for directions on applying by mail. Your travel agent or airline office may also be able to provide you with visa applications and instructions. The U.S. consulate or embassy that issues your visa will determine whether you will be issued a multiple- or single-entry visa and any restrictions regarding the length of your stay.

British subjects can obtain up-to-date passport and visa information by calling the **U.S. Embassy Visa Information Line** (© 0891/200-290) or the **London Passport Office** (© 0990/210-410 for recorded information), or you can find the visa information on the U.S. Embassy Great Britain website at www.passport. gov.uk.

Irish citizens can obtain up-to-date passport and visa information through the **U.S. Embassy Dublin,** 42 Elgin Rd., Dublin 4, Ireland (© 353/1-668-8777); or check the visa page on the website at http://dublin.usembassy.gov.

Australian citizens can obtain up-to-date passport and visa information by calling the **U.S. Embassy Canberra,** Moonah Place, Yarralumla, ACT 2600 (© 02/6214-5600); or check the website's visa page at http://canberra.usembassy. gov/consular/visas.html.

Citizens of **New Zealand** can obtain up-to-date passport and visa information by calling the **U.S. Embassy New Zealand,** 29 Fitzherbert Terrace, Thorndon, Wellington, New Zealand (© 644/ 472-2068); or get the information directly from the website at http://usembassy. org.nz.

MEDICAL REQUIREMENTS Unless you're arriving from an area known to be suffering from an epidemic (particularly cholera or yellow fever), inoculations or vaccinations are not required for entry into the United States. If you have a medical condition that requires **syringe-administered medications,** carry a valid signed prescription from your physician—the Transportation Security Administration (TSA) no longer allows airline passengers to pack syringes in carry-on baggage without documented proof of medical need. If you have a disease that requires treatment with **narcotics,** you should also carry documented proof with you—smuggling narcotics aboard a plane is a serious offense that carries severe penalties in the U.S.

For **HIV-positive visitors,** requirements for entering the United States are somewhat vague and change frequently. According to the latest publication of *HIV and Immigrants: A Manual for AIDS Service Providers,* the Immigration and Naturalization Service (INS) doesn't require a medical exam for entry into the United States, but INS officials may stop individuals because they look sick or because they are carrying AIDS/HIV medicine.

If an HIV-positive non-citizen applies for a non-immigrant visa, the question on the application regarding communicable diseases is tricky no matter which way it's answered. If the applicant checks "no," INS may deny the visa on the grounds that the applicant committed fraud. If the applicant checks "yes" or if INS suspects the person is HIV-positive, it will deny the visa unless the applicant asks for a special waiver for visitors. This waiver is for people visiting the United States for a short time—for instance, to attend a conference, to visit close relatives, or to receive medical treatment. It can be a confusing situation. For further up-to-the-minute information, contact the Centers for Disease Control and Prevention's **National Center for HIV** (© 404/ 332-4559; http://aidsinfo.nih.gov) or the **Gay Men's Health Crisis** (© 212/367-1000; www.gmhc.org).

DRIVER'S LICENSES Foreign driver's licenses are mostly recognized in the U.S., although you may want to get an international driver's license if your home license is not written in English.

PASSPORT INFORMATION

Safeguard your passport in an inconspicuous, inaccessible place like a money belt.

Make a copy of the critical pages, including the passport number, and store the copy in a safe place, separate from the passport itself. If you lose your passport, visit the nearest consulate of your native country as soon as possible for a replacement. Passport applications are downloadable from the websites listed below.

Note that the International Civil Aviation Organization (ICAO) has recommended a policy requiring that *every* individual who travels by air have your own passport. In response, many countries now require that children must be issued their own passports to travel internationally, whereas before, those under 16 or so may have been allowed to travel on a parent or guardian's passport.

FOR RESIDENTS OF CANADA

You can pick up a passport application at 1 of 28 regional passport offices or at most travel agencies. As of December 11, 2001, Canadian children who travel will need their own passports. However, if you hold a valid Canadian passport issued before December 11, 2001, that bears the name of your child, the passport remains valid for you and your child until it expires. Passports cost C$85 for those 16 years and older (valid 5 years), C$35 for children 3 to 15 (valid 5 years), and C$20 for children under 3 (valid 3 years). Applications, which must be accompanied by two identical passport-size photographs and proof of Canadian citizenship, are available at travel agencies throughout Canada or from the central **Passport Office, Department of Foreign Affairs and International Trade,** Ottawa, ON K1A 0G3 (© **800/567-6868;** www.ppt.gc.ca). Processing takes 5 to 10 days if you apply in person, or about 3 weeks by mail.

FOR RESIDENTS OF THE UNITED KINGDOM

To pick up an application for a regular 10-year passport (the Visitor's Passport has been abolished), visit your nearest passport office, major post office, or travel agency. You can also contact the **London Passport Office** at © **0171/271-3000,** or search its website at www.ukpa.gov.uk. Passports are £21 for adults and £11 for children under 16.

FOR RESIDENTS OF IRELAND

You can apply for a 10-year passport, costing €57, at the **Passport Office,** Setanta Centre, Molesworth Street, Dublin 2 (© **01/671-1633;** http://foreignaffairs.gov.ie). Those under age 18 and over 65 must apply for a €12 3-year passport. You can also apply at 1A South Mall, Cork (© **021/272-525**), or over the counter at most main post offices.

FOR RESIDENTS OF AUSTRALIA

Apply at your local post office or passport office, or search the government website at www.passports.gov.au/Web/index.aspx. Passports for adults are A$126 and for those under 18 A$63.

FOR RESIDENTS OF NEW ZEALAND

You can pick up a passport application at any travel agency or Link Centre. For more info, contact the **Passport Office,** P.O. Box 805, Wellington (© **0800/225-050;** www.passports.govt.nz). Passports for adults are NZ$80; for those under 16 they're NZ$40.

CUSTOMS

WHAT YOU CAN BRING IN   Every visitor over 21 years of age may bring in, free of duty, the following: (1) 1 liter of wine or hard liquor; (2) 200 cigarettes, 150 cigars (but not from Cuba), or 3 pounds of smoking tobacco; and (3) $100 worth of gifts. These exemptions are offered to travelers who spend at least 72 hours in the United States and who have not claimed them within the preceding 6 months. In addition, you cannot bring fresh fruits and vegetables into

Hawaii, even if you're coming from the U.S. mainland and have no need to clear Customs. Every passenger is asked shortly before landing to sign a certificate declaring that you do not have fresh fruits and vegetables in your possession.

Foreign tourists may bring in or take out up to $10,000 in U.S. or foreign currency with no formalities; larger sums must be declared to U.S. Customs upon entering or leaving, which includes filing form CM 4790.

Declare any medicines you are carrying and be prepared to present a letter or prescription from your doctor demonstrating that you need the drugs; you may bring in no more than you would normally use for the duration of your visit.

For many more details on what you can and cannot bring, check the informative U.S. Customs website at **www.customs.ustreas.gov** (click on "Traveler Information"), or call ✆ **202/927-1770.**

WHAT YOU CAN TAKE HOME

U.K. citizens returning from a non-E.U. country have a Customs allowance of 200 cigarettes, or 50 cigars, or 100 cigarillos, or 250 grams of smoking tobacco; 2 liters of wine; and 1 liter of spirits or 2 liters of fortified wine (such as port or sherry). People under 17 cannot have the tobacco or alcohol allowance. For more information, contact HM Customs & Excise at ✆ **0845/010-9000** (from outside the U.K., 020/8929-0152), or consult their website at www.hmce.gov.uk.

For a clear summary of **Canadian** rules, request the booklet *I Declare*, issued by the **Canada Customs and Revenue Agency** (✆ **800/461-9999** in Canada, or 204/983-3500; www.ccra-adrc.gc.ca). Canada allows its citizens a C$750 exemption, and you're allowed to bring back duty-free one carton of cigarettes, one can of tobacco, 40 imperial ounces of liquor, and 50 cigars. In addition, you're allowed to mail gifts to Canada valued at less than C$60 a day, provided they're unsolicited and don't contain alcohol or tobacco. (Write on the package "Unsolicited gift, under $60 value.") All valuables should be declared on the Y-38 form before your departure from Canada, including serial numbers of valuables you already own, such as expensive foreign cameras. *Note:* The $750 exemption can only be used once a year and only after an absence of 7 days.

The duty-free allowance in **Australia** is A$400 or, for those under 18, A$200. Citizens age 18 and over can bring in 250 cigarettes or 250 grams of loose tobacco, and 1,125 milliliters of alcohol. If you're returning with valuables you already own, such as foreign-made cameras, you should file form B263. A helpful brochure available from Australian consulates or Customs offices is *Know Before You Go.* For more information, call the **Australian Customs Service** at ✆ **1300/363-263,** or log on to www.customs.gov.au.

The duty-free allowance for **New Zealand** is NZ$700. Citizens over 17 can bring in 200 cigarettes, 50 cigars, or 250 grams of tobacco (or a mixture of all three if their combined weight doesn't exceed 250g); plus 4.5 liters of wine and beer, or 1.125 liters of liquor. New Zealand currency does not carry import or export restrictions. Fill out a certificate of export listing the valuables you are taking out of the country; that way, you can bring them back without paying duty. Most questions are answered in a free pamphlet available at New Zealand consulates and Customs offices: *New Zealand Customs Guide for Travellers, Notice no. 4.* For more information, contact **New Zealand Customs,** The Customhouse, 17–21 Whitmore St., Box 2218, Wellington (✆ **0800/428-786** or 04/473-6099; www.customs.govt.nz).

HEALTH INSURANCE

Although it's not required of travelers, health insurance is highly recommended.

Unlike many European countries, the United States does not usually offer free or low-cost medical care to its citizens or visitors. Doctors and hospitals are expensive, and in most cases will require advance payment or proof of coverage before they render their services. Insurance policies can cover everything from the loss or theft of your baggage to trip cancellation to the guarantee of bail in case you're arrested. Good policies will also cover the costs of an accident, repatriation, or death. See "Travel Insurance" in chapter 2 for more information. Packages such as **Europ Assistance's "Worldwide Healthcare Plan"** are sold by European automobile clubs and travel agencies at attractive rates. **Worldwide Assistance Services, Inc.** (© 800/821-2828; www.worldwideassistance.com) is the agent for Europ Assistance in the United States.

Though lack of health insurance may prevent you from being admitted to a hospital in non-emergencies, don't worry about being left on a street corner to die: The American way is to fix you now and bill the living daylights out of you later.

INSURANCE FOR BRITISH TRAVELERS Most big travel agents offer their own insurance and will probably try to sell you their package when you book a holiday. Think before you sign. **Britain's Consumers' Association** recommends that you insist on seeing the policy and reading the fine print before you buy travel insurance. **The Association of British Insurers** (© 020/7600-3333; www.abi.org.uk) gives advice by phone and publishes *Holiday Insurance,* a free guide to policy provisions and prices. You might also shop around for better deals: Try **Columbus Direct** (© 020/7375-0011; www.columbusdirect.net).

INSURANCE FOR CANADIAN TRAVELERS Canadians should check with your provincial health plan offices or call **Health Canada** (© 613/957-2991; www.hc-sc.gc.ca) to find out the extent of your coverage and what documentation and receipts you must take home in case you are treated in the United States.

MONEY

CURRENCY The most common **bills** (all ugly) are the $1 (colloquially, a "buck"), $5, $10, and $20 denominations. There are also $2 bills (seldom encountered), $50 bills, and $100 bills. (The last two are usually not welcome as payment for small purchases.) Note that redesigned bills were introduced in the last few years, but the old-style bills are still legal tender.

There are seven denominations of coins: 1¢ (1 cent, or a penny); 5¢ (5 cents, or a nickel); 10¢ (10 cents, or a dime); 25¢ (25 cents, or a quarter); 50¢ (50 cents, or a half dollar); the new gold "Sacagawea" coin worth $1; and, prized by collectors, the rare, older silver dollar.

EXCHANGING CURRENCY There are no direct international flights into Kauai. Exchanging foreign currency for U.S. dollars is usually painless in Honolulu, where you will clear Customs. However, the rate at the currency services at **Honolulu International Airport** isn't fabulous; we suggest just exchanging enough money for a day or so, until you can get to a bank on Kauai. Generally, the best rates of exchange are available through major banks, most of which exchange foreign currency. There are no currency services at the Lihue Airport. Most of the major hotels on Kauai offer currency-exchange services, but generally the rate of exchange is not as good as what you'll get at a bank.

If you plan to stay in Honolulu, you can get reasonably good exchange rates in Waikiki at: **A-1 Foreign Exchange,** which has offices in Waikiki at the Royal Hawaiian Shopping Center, 2301 Kalakaua Ave., and in the Hyatt Regency Waikiki Tower, 2424 Kalakaua Ave. (© 808/922-3327); or at **Pacific Money**

Exchange, 339 Royal Hawaiian Ave. (© **808/924-9318**).

TRAVELER'S CHECKS Though traveler's checks are widely accepted at most hotels, restaurants, and large stores, *make sure that they're denominated in U.S. dollars,* as foreign-currency checks are often difficult to exchange. The three traveler's checks that are most widely recognized—and least likely to be denied—are **Visa, American Express,** and **Thomas Cook/MasterCard.** Be sure to record the numbers of the checks, and keep that information in a separate place in case the checks get lost or stolen. Most businesses are pretty good about taking traveler's checks, but you're better off cashing them at a bank (in small amounts, of course) and paying for purchases with cash. *Remember:* You'll need identification, such as a driver's license or passport, to change a traveler's check. It's generally easier to use ATMs than to bother with traveler's checks.

CREDIT CARDS Credit cards are widely used on Kauai. You can save yourself trouble by using plastic rather than cash or traveler's checks in most hotels, restaurants, retail stores, and a growing number of food and liquor stores. You must have a credit card to rent a car in Hawaii.

SAFETY

GENERAL SAFETY Although tourist areas are generally safe, visitors should always stay alert. It's wise to ask the island tourist office if you're in doubt about which neighborhoods are safe. Avoid deserted areas, especially at night. Generally speaking, you can feel safe in areas where there are many people and open establishments.

Avoid carrying valuables with you on the street, and don't display expensive cameras or electronic equipment. Hold onto your pocketbook, and place your billfold in an inside pocket. In theaters, restaurants, and other public places, keep your possessions in sight.

Remember also that hotels are open to the public and that, in a large hotel, security may not be able to screen everyone entering. Always lock your room door—don't assume that once you're inside your hotel, you're automatically safe.

DRIVING SAFETY Safety while driving is particularly important. Ask your rental agency about personal safety, or request a brochure of traveler safety tips when you pick up your car. Get written directions or a map with your route clearly marked in red showing you how to get to your destination.

Recently, the number of car burglaries in hotel parking structures and at beach parking lots has increased. Park in well-lighted and well-traveled areas if possible. Never leave any packages or valuables visible in the car. If someone attempts to rob you or steal your car, do not try to resist the thief or carjacker—report the incident to the police department immediately.

For more information on driving rules and getting around by car on Kauai, see "Getting Around," in chapter 2.

2 Getting to & around the United States

There are no direct international flights into Kauai. You must go through Honolulu to clear Customs and Immigration if you are flying directly from a foreign country. From Honolulu, take an interisland plane to Lihue, Kauai.

Airlines serving Honolulu, Hawaii, from places other than the U.S. mainland include **Air Canada** (© 800/776-3000; www.aircanada.ca); **Air New Zealand** (© 0800/737-000 in Auckland, 64-3/379-5200 in Christchurch, 800/926-7255 in the U.S.; www.airnewzealand.com), which runs 40 flights per week between Auckland and Hawaii; **Qantas**

(© 008/177-767 in Australia, 800/227-4500 in the U.S.; www.qantas.com.au), which flies between Sydney and Honolulu daily (plus additional flights 4 days a week); **Japan Air Lines** (© 03/5489-1111 in Tokyo, 800/525-3663 in the U.S.; www.japanair.com); **All Nippon Airways** (ANA; © 03/5489-1212 in Tokyo, 800/235-9262 in the U.S.; www.fly-ana.com); **China Airlines** (© 02/715-1212 in Taipei, 800/227-5118 in the U.S.; www.china-airlines.com); **Air Pacific,** serving Fiji, Australia, New Zealand, and the South Pacific (© 800/227-4446; www.airpacific.com); **Korean Airlines** (© 02/656-2000 in Seoul, 800/223-1155 on the U.S. East Coast, 800/421-8200 on the U.S. West Coast, 800/438-5000 from Hawaii; www.koreanair.com); and **Philippine Airlines** (© 631/816-6691 in Manila, 800/435-9725 in the U.S.; www.philippineair.com).

Operated by the European Travel Network, **www.discount-tickets.com** is a great online source for regular and discounted airfares to destinations around the world. You can also use this site to compare rates and book accommodations, car rentals, and tours. Click on "Special Offers" for the latest package deals.

If you're traveling in the United States beyond Hawaii, some large American airlines—such as **American, Delta, Northwest, TWA,** and **United**—offer travelers on transatlantic or transpacific flights special discount tickets under the name **Visit USA,** allowing travel between any U.S. destinations at reduced rates. These tickets must be purchased before you leave your foreign point of departure. This system is the best, easiest, and fastest way to see the United States at low cost. You should obtain information well in advance from your travel agent or the office of the airline concerned, since the conditions attached to these discount tickets can change without advance notice.

Visitors arriving by air should cultivate patience and resignation before setting foot on U.S. soil. Getting through immigration control may take as long as 2 hours on some days, especially summer weekends. Add the time it takes to clear Customs, and you'll see that you should make a very generous allowance for delay in planning connections between international and domestic flights—an average of at least 2 to 3 hours.

After you have cleared Customs in Honolulu, hop a short, 30-minute interisland flight to Lihue, Kauai. For further information about travel to Kauai, see "Getting There," in chapter 2.

FAST FACTS: **For the International Traveler**

Automobile Organizations Auto clubs will supply maps, suggested routes, guidebooks, accident and bail-bond insurance, and emergency road service. The major auto club in the United States, with 955 offices nationwide, is the **American Automobile Association** (AAA; often called "Triple A"). Members of some foreign auto clubs have reciprocal arrangements with AAA and enjoy its services at no charge. If you belong to an auto club, inquire about AAA reciprocity before you leave. The AAA can also provide you with an **International Driving Permit** validating your foreign license. You may be able to join the AAA even if you are not a member of a reciprocal club. To inquire, call © **800/736-2886** or visit www.aaa.com.

Some car-rental agencies now provide automobile club–type services, so inquire about their availability when you rent your car.

Automobile Rentals To rent a car in the United States, you need a valid driver's license, a passport, and a major credit card. The minimum age is usually 25, but some companies will rent to younger people and add a surcharge. It's a good idea to buy maximum insurance coverage unless you're positive your own auto or credit card insurance is sufficient. Rates vary, so it pays to call around.

Business Hours See "Fast Facts: Kauai," in chapter 2.

Climate See "When to Go," in chapter 2.

Electricity Hawaii, like the U.S. mainland and Canada, uses 110–120 volts (60 cycles), compared to the 220–240 volts (50 cycles) used in most of Europe and in other areas of the world, including Australia and New Zealand. Small appliances of non-American manufacture, such as hair dryers or shavers, will require a plug adapter with two flat, parallel pins; larger ones will require a 100-volt transformer.

Embassies & Consulates All embassies are located in Washington, D.C. Some countries have consulates general in major U.S. cities, and most have a mission to the United Nations in New York City. If your country isn't listed below, call for directory information in Washington, D.C. (© 202/555-1212), or point your Web browser to www.embassy.org/embassies for the location and phone number of your national embassy.

The embassy of **Australia** is at 1601 Massachusetts Ave. NW, Washington, DC 20036 (© 202/797-3000; www.austemb.org). There is also an Australian consulate in Hawaii at 1000 Bishop St., Penthouse Suite, Honolulu, HI 96813 (© 808/524-5050).

The embassy of **Canada** is at 501 Pennsylvania Ave. NW, Washington, DC 20001 (© 202/682-1740; www.canadianembassy.org). Canadian consulates are also at 1251 Avenue of the Americas, New York, NY 10020 (© 212/596-1628), and at 550 South Hope St., 9th floor, Los Angeles, CA 90071 (© 213/346-2700).

The embassy of **Japan** is at 2520 Massachusetts Ave. NW, Washington, DC 20008 (© 202/238-6700; www.embjapan.org). The consulate general of Japan is located at 1742 Nuuanu Ave., Honolulu, HI 96817 (© 808/543-3111).

The embassy of **New Zealand** is at 37 Observatory Circle NW, Washington, DC 20008 (© 202/328-4800; www.nzemb.org). The only New Zealand consulate in the United States is at 780 Third Ave., New York, NY 10017 (© 202/328-4800).

The embassy of the **Republic of Ireland** is at 2234 Massachusetts Ave. NW, Washington, DC 20008 (© 202/462-3939; www.irelandemb.org). There's a consulate office in San Francisco at 44 Montgomery St., Suite 3830, San Francisco, CA 94104 (© 415/392-4214).

The embassy of the **United Kingdom** is at 3100 Massachusetts Ave. NW, Washington, DC 20008 (© 202/588-6640; www.fco.gov.uk/directory). British consulates are at 845 Third Ave., New York, NY 10022 (© 212/745-0200); and at 11766 Wilshire Blvd., Suite 400, Los Angeles, CA 90025 (© 310/477-3322).

Emergencies Call © 911 to report a fire, call the police, or get an ambulance.

Gasoline (Petrol) One U.S. gallon equals 3.8 liters, while 1.2 U.S. gallons equal 1 imperial gallon. You'll notice there are several grades (and price levels) of gasoline available at most gas stations. You'll also notice that their names change from company to company. The ones with the highest octane are the most expensive, but most rental cars take the least expensive "regular" gas, with an octane rating of 87.

Holidays See "When to Go," in chapter 2.

Legal Aid The ordinary tourist will probably never become involved with the American legal system. If you're pulled over for a minor infraction (for example, driving faster than the speed limit), never attempt to pay the fine directly to a police officer; you may wind up arrested on the much more serious charge of attempted bribery. Pay fines by mail or directly into the hands of the clerk of the court. If you're accused of a more serious offense, it's wise to say and do nothing before you consult a lawyer. (Under the U.S. Constitution, you have the rights both to remain silent and to consult an attorney.) Under U.S. law, an arrested person is allowed one telephone call to a party of your choice; call your embassy or consulate.

Mail Mailboxes, which are generally found at intersections, are blue with a blue-and-white eagle logo and carry the inscription u.s. postal service. If your mail is addressed to a U.S. destination, don't forget to add the five-digit postal code, or zip code, after the two-letter abbreviation of the state to which the mail is addressed. The abbreviation for Hawaii is HI.

At press time, domestic postage rates are 23¢ for a postcard and 37¢ for a letter. For international mail, a first-class letter of up to 1 ounce costs 80¢ (60¢ to Canada and Mexico); a first-class postcard costs 70¢ (50¢ to Canada and Mexico); and a preprinted postal aerogramme costs 70¢. Point your Web browser to **www.usps.com** for complete U.S. postal information, or call ✆ **800/275-8777** for information on the nearest post office. Most branches are open Monday through Friday from 8am to 5 or 6pm, and Saturday from 9am to noon or 3pm.

Taxes The United States has no VAT (value-added tax) or other indirect tax at a national level. Every state, and every city in it, has the right to levy its own local tax on all purchases, including hotel and restaurant checks, airline tickets, and so on. On Kauai, sales tax is 4%; there's also a 7.25% hotel-room tax and a small excise tax, so the total tax on your hotel bill will be 11.42%.

Telephone & Fax The telephone system in the United States is run by private corporations, so rates, particularly for long-distance service and operator-assisted calls, can vary widely—especially on calls made from public telephones. Local calls—that is, calls to other locations on Kauai—made from public phones cost 50¢.

Generally, hotel surcharges on long-distance and local calls are astronomical. You are usually better off using a **public pay telephone,** which you will find clearly marked in most public buildings and private establishments as well as on the street. Many convenience stores and newsstands sell **prepaid calling cards** in denominations up to $50. Most **long-distance** and **international calls** can be dialed directly from any phone. **For calls within the United States and to**

Canada, dial 1 followed by the area code and the seven-digit number. **For other international calls,** dial 011 followed by the country code, city code, and telephone number of the person you are calling. Some country and city codes are as follows: **Australia** 61, Melbourne 3, Sydney 2; **Ireland** 353, Dublin 1; **New Zealand** 64, Auckland 9, Wellington 4; **United Kingdom** 44, Belfast 232, Birmingham 21, Glasgow 41, London 71 or 81.

If you're calling the **United States from another country,** the country code is 01.

In Hawaii, interisland phone calls are considered long-distance and are often as costly as calls made to the U.S. mainland. The international country code for Hawaii is 1, just as it is for the rest of the United States and Canada.

For **reversed-charge** or **collect calls,** and for **person-to-person calls,** dial 0 (zero, not the letter "O"), followed by the area code and number you want; an operator will then come on the line, and you should specify that you are calling collect, person-to-person, or both. If your operator-assisted call is international, ask for the overseas operator.

Note that all phone numbers with the area codes 800, 888, and 877 are toll-free. However, calls to numbers in area codes 700 and 900 (chat lines, "dating" services, and so on) can be very expensive—usually at charge of 95¢ to $3 or more per minute.

For **local directory assistance** ("information"), dial ⓒ 411. For **long-distance information,** dial 1, then the appropriate area code and ⓒ 555-1212. For **directory assistance for another island,** dial 1, then 808, then ⓒ 555-1212.

Fax facilities are widely available and can be found in most hotels and at many other establishments. Try **The UPS Store** or **Kinko's** (check the local Yellow Pages) or any photocopying shop.

Telephone Directories There are two kinds of telephone directories in the United States. The general directory, the so-called White Pages, lists private and business subscribers in alphabetical order. The inside front cover lists the emergency numbers for police, fire, and ambulance, along with other vital numbers. The first few pages are devoted to community-service numbers, including a guide to long-distance and international calling, complete with country codes and area codes.

The second directory, printed on yellow paper (hence its name, Yellow Pages), lists all local services, businesses, and industries by type of activity, with an index at the front. The listings cover not only such obvious items as automobile repairs and drugstores (pharmacies), but also restaurants by type of cuisine and geographical location, bookstores by special subject and/or language, places of worship by religious denomination, and other information that the visitor might not otherwise readily find. The Yellow Pages also include detailed maps, postal zip codes, and a calendar of events.

Time Zone See "Fast Facts: Kauai," in chapter 2.

Tipping It's part of the American way of life to tip. Many service employees receive little direct salary and must depend on tips for their income. The following are some general rules:

In **hotels,** tip bellhops at least $1 per piece of luggage ($2–$3 if you have a lot of luggage), and tip the housekeeping staff $1 per person, per day. Tip the doorman or concierge only if he or she has provided you with some specific service (for example, calling a cab for you or obtaining difficult-to-get theater tickets). Tip the valet-parking attendant $1 to $2 every time you get your car.

In **restaurants, bars,** and **nightclubs,** tip service staff 15% to 20% of the check, tip bartenders 10% to 15%, and tip valet-parking attendants $1 to $2 per vehicle. Tip the doorman only if he or she has provided you with some specific service (such as calling a cab for you). Tipping is not expected in cafeterias and fast-food restaurants.

Tip **cab drivers** 15% of the fare.

As for **other service personnel,** tip skycaps at airports at least $1 per piece ($2–$3 if you have a lot of luggage), and tip hairdressers and barbers 15% to 20%. Tipping ushers at theaters is not expected.

Toilets Foreign visitors often complain that public toilets are hard to find in most U.S. cities. True, there are none on the streets, but visitors can usually find one in a bar, fast-food outlet, restaurant, hotel, museum, or department store—and it will probably be clean. (The cleanliness of toilets at service stations, parks, and beaches is more open to question.) Note, however, a growing practice in some restaurants and bars of displaying a notice that toilets are for the use of patrons only. You can ignore this sign or, better yet, avoid arguments by paying for a cup of coffee or soft drink, which will qualify you as a patron.

4

Suggested Kauai Itineraries

Your vacation time is precious, you only have so many days, and you don't want to waste one of them. That's where I come in. Below are several suggestions for things to do and how to organize your time. I've included ideas if you have one week or two, are traveling with kids, or want a more active vacation.

The number one thing I would suggest is don't max out your days. This is Hawaii; allow some time to do nothing but relax. Remember that you most likely will arrive jet-lagged. Ease into your vacation. Your first day you most likely will be tired—hitting the pillow at 8 or 9pm will sound good. Don't be surprised if you wake up your first morning in Kauai before the sun comes up. Your internal clock is probably still set 2 to 6 hours earlier than Hawaii.

Finally, think of your first trip as a "scouting" trip. Kauai is too beautiful, too sensual, too enticing to just see just once in a lifetime. You'll be back. You don't need to see and do everything on this trip. In fact, if you find something in the itinerary below and just fall in love with it, go back again. It's your vacation. I've included general, sample itineraries. If you are a golf fan or a scuba diver, check out chapter 1, Best of Kauai (p. 8) to plan your trip around your passion.

One last thing—you will need a car to get around. Kauai does have a local bus system, but it does not go to the resorts . . . so plan to rent a car. But also plan to get out of the car as much as possible. This is Hawaii; don't just view it from your car window. You have to get out to smell the sweet perfume of plumeria, to feel the warm rain on your face, to hear the sound of the wind through a bamboo forest, and to plunge into the gentle waters of the Pacific.

1 One Week on Kauai

I've outlined the highlights for those who just have 7 days and want to see everything. It's a jam-packed 7-day, 6-night itinerary; however, you might want to skip a few suggestions and just veg out on the beach, or substitute your own interests such as sailing, scuba diving, or golf.

Day ❶: Arrive in Kauai; Head for the Beach ✸✸

After you get off the plane, head for the beach closest to your accommodation. Lather up in sunscreen, take sunglasses and a hat, and plop down on the soft sand of the beach. Enjoy a Hawaiian dinner at one of the **luau** offered (see chapter 10) to get into the spirit of your

Hawaiian vacation. Don't be surprised if you find yourself nodding off at 8 or 9pm.

Day ❷: See a Bird's-Eye View of Kauai from a Helicopter ✸✸✸

Since you're probably on mainland time and will be wide awake before the break of dawn, either plan an early morning **helicopter tour** (p. 197) of the island to

One-Week Itinerary

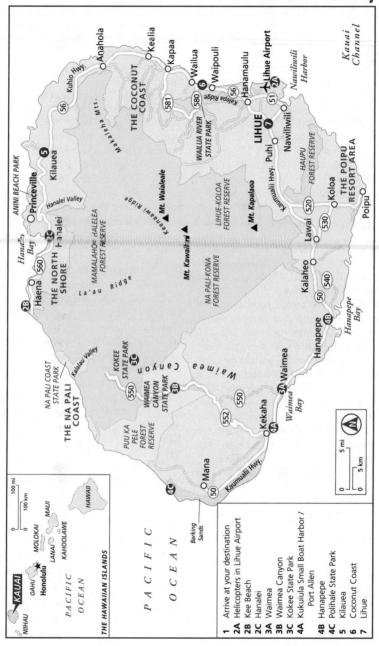

1 Arrive at your destination
2A Helicopters in Lihue Airport
2B Kee Beach
2C Hanalei
3A Waimea
3B Waimea Canyon
3C Kokee State Park
4A Kukuiula Small Boat Harbor /
   Port Allen
4B Hanapepe
4C Polihale State Park
5 Kilauea
6 Coconut Coast
7 Lihue

73

get your bearings, or get up and watch the sunrise from the east shore. If it's not raining, head out to Hanalei Beach to watch the sun make its appearance in the east at 5:30am in summer and 6:30am in winter. Then head into Hanalei for an early breakfast at **Hanalei Wake-up Café** (p. 150).

With the whole day ahead of you, after breakfast drive out to the end of the road at **Kee Beach** (p. 162). Here you can either hike a couple of miles along the **Na Pali Coast** (p. 181) and back (make sure you have good hiking shoes, water, snacks, and sunscreen); or you can venture down the highway to **Tunnels Beach** (p. 162) for an early morning snorkel. After a couple of hours at the beach, continue on to the **Limahuli Garden of the National Tropical Botanical Garden** (p. 206) and step into Eden.

By now you should be hungry. Head back to Hanalei and order takeout at the **Hanalei Gourmet** (p. 146) and head down to Hanalei Beach for a picnic lunch. After lunch, you might want to try kayaking. **Kayak Kauai Outbound** (p. 165) in Hanalei has both guided tours as well as kayak rentals so you can explore by water.

If kayaking is not your preferred activity, then wander through the shops at Hanalei, get a shave ice, and take in the slow pace of life on the North Shore.

Finish the day with a *pau hana*–(quit work) time cocktail at **Tahiti Nui** (p. 223), then enjoy a relaxing dinner in either **Sushi & Blues** in Hanalei (p. 149) or in Princeville at **La Cascata** in the **Princeville Resort** (p. 145).

Day ❸: Hike through Kauai's Grand Canyon ✻✻

Head out west, up to **Waimea Canyon** (p. 196) and **Kokee State Park** (p. 196). Have warm clothes, as it can get cold at 4,000 feet, and be prepared for rain. Get an early start and have breakfast or coffee at the **Kalaheo Coffee Co. & Café** (p. 135). Stop in Waimea town to explore

the **Russian Fort Elizabeth State Historical Park** (p. 195) and the **Menehune Ditch** (p. 195), then plan to spend most of the morning (before the clouds roll in) hiking the various trails in the Waimea Canyon area (see p. 174 for hikes). Then travel another 16 miles and a few thousand feet up the road to Kokee. Stop for lunch at the **Kokee Lodge** (p.175), open from 9am to 3pm. Check in at the **Kokee Natural History Museum** (p. 197) to learn about the forests and surrounding area, locate good hiking trails, and pick up a couple of trail maps. In the afternoon, wander around the park, and stay for sunset. If it's Friday night, eat at the **Hanapepe Café** (p. 136); if it's not, go Italian at **Pomodoro** (p. 134) in Kalaheo.

Day ❹: Winging It on the Water ✻

After a day in the mountains, it's time to head to the beach again. If you like sailing and snorkeling, book a **sail/snorkel tour** out of the Kukuiula Small Boat Harbor or Port Allen (see "Boating," in chapter 7) for the trip of a lifetime—exploring the **Na Pali Coast.**

If you pass on sailing, wander into the old plantation town of **Hanapepe** (p. 19) and browse at the unique shops. Continue west to Kauai's biggest beach at **Polihale State Park** (p. 158). Spend the day here, and be sure to check out the "barking" sands at **Barking Sands Beach** (p. 158). Enjoy the sunset; then head over to **Casa Blanca at Kiahuna** (p. 131) for a fabulous dinner.

Day ❺: Explore Kilauea ✻

Your beach quotient should be filled by now, so spend the day in **Kilauea** (p. 20) area exploring gardens and the **Kilauea Point National Wildlife Refuge** (p. 188). First call **Na Aina Kai Botanical Gardens** (p. 206) to make sure they are open, and book a tour. This incredible, magical garden is for people who shudder at the thought of seeing a botanical garden: The whimsical magic of the place will win over even the most stubborn. Build up an appetite for lunch by checking out the very unusual shops at Kong Kung in Kilauea. Pick up a delicious picnic lunch at **Kilauea Fish Market** (p. 151). Then head down the road to the **Kilauea Point National Wildlife Refuge** (see "Birding," on p. 188), a 200-acre habitat for Hawaii's ocean birds. Eat your picnic on the coast, join a guided hike, or just wander through the fairyland of the wilderness area. Have dinner at the wonderful **Lighthouse Bistro Kilauea** (p. 145).

Day ❻: Casting About on the Coconut Coast ⚘

For those who just can't get enough beach time, make your way to **Wailua Beach** (p. 160) on the **Coconut Coast.** This beach, which features Hawaiian historical and cultural sites, is also a great place to just sit under a palm tree and figure out how you can move here permanently. For those non-beach people, you can visit **Kauai's Children's Discovery Museum** (p. 168) in Kapaa, and then either explore the great shopping along the coast, or head inland and see the sacred Hindu temple, **San Marga Iraivan Temple** (p. 202). Eat lunch in Kapaa at

Mermaids (p. 143) or try something very unusual like **Blossoming Lotus** (p. 142). In the afternoon, consider either hiking up **Sleeping Giant Mountain** (p. 178), bicycling along the shoreline, or renting a kayak from **Water Ski & Surf** (p. 162). By dinnertime, you'll be hungry; head for **Caffè Coco** (p. 140).

Day ❼: Getting the Most Out of Your Last Day

If this is your last day, spend it in the **Lihue** (p. 190) area. It's close to the airport and there are plenty of things to do. You might want to step back in history and visit the **Kauai Museum** (p. 192) in Lihue or take a carriage ride at **Kilohana** (p. 192) in Puhi. Or drive up to the **Wailua Falls** (p. 192), just outside of town. Shoppers may like wandering around the old town of Lihue. Die-hard beachgoers can head to **Kalapaki Beach** (p. 154) for your last few hours of sun. If you are in a casual mode, get some burgers for the beach at **Kalapaki Beach Hut** (p. 127). If you are in the mood for a more filling meal—and you know that it won't get served by the airline—stop at **Aroma** (p. 121) for your last meal on the island.

2 Two Weeks on Kauai

Two weeks on Kauai is perfect. It allows you to see everything at a much slower pace with plenty of relaxation and lazy beach days. I'd suggest adding lots of naps, vegging out on the beach, and stopping to smell all the exotic flowers.

Day ❶: Arrive in Kauai; Go Directly to the Beach ⚘⚘

After you get off the plane, head for the beach closest to your accommodation. Don't forget the sunscreen, sunglasses, and a hat before you leave your hotel. Just like we recommended in the itinerary for 1 week, you might consider a Hawaiian dinner at one of the **luau** offered (see chapter 10) to get into the spirit of your

Hawaiian vacation. Plan on an early bed time, you'll be pooped.

Day ❷: See Kauai from the Sky in a Helicopter ⚘⚘⚘

With the time difference between Kauai and the mainland, most likely you will be wide awake before the break of dawn. We suggest you book an early morning **helicopter tour** (p. 197) of the island to get your bearings. The reason you want to book a tour early in your stay is if weather conditions cancel your flight, you still have plenty of days remaining to rebook a flight. If your flight is canceled, you might as well get up early and watch the sunrise. After your helicopter ride out of Lihue, grab your snorkel gear and head for **Poipu Beach** (p. 156) to see what the fish are up to. Terrific lunches can be had at **Brennecke's Beach Broiler** (p. 131), just across the beach from the park. As the sun sets, stop by the **Beach House** (p. 128) for divine pupu (appetizers) and a liquid libation. Then head for dinner at **Casa Blanca at Kiahuna** (p. 131) for a fabulous dinner.

Day ❸: Dive into the Ocean at the North Shore 🎔🎔🎔

With the whole day ahead of you, after breakfast drive out to the end of the road at **Kee Beach** (p. 162). If you get up early, have breakfast at the **Hanalei Wake-up Café** (p. 150). Head out to the end of the road, park, and hike a couple of miles along the **Na Pali Coast** (p. 181) and back (make sure you have good hiking shoes, water, snacks, and sunscreen); or you can venture down the highway to **Tunnels Beach** (p. 162) for an early morning snorkel. After a couple of hours at the beach, continue on to the **Limahuli Garden of the National Tropical Botanical Garden** (p. 206) and step into Eden.

By now you should be hungry. Head back to Hanalei and grab a bite at the **Hanalei Gourmet** (p. 146); take it down to the beach for a picnic lunch. After lunch, wander through the shops at Hanalei, get a shave ice, and take in the slow pace of life on the North Shore. Finish the day with a *pau hana*–(quit work) time cocktail at **Tahiti Nui** (p. 223), then enjoy a relaxing dinner in either **Sushi & Blues** in Hanalei (p. 149) or in Princeville at **La Cascata** in the **Princeville Resort** (p. 145).

Day ❹: Hike through Kauai's Grand Canyon 🎔🎔

Head out west, up to **Waimea Canyon** (p. 196). Have warm clothes and be prepared for rain. Get an early start and have breakfast or coffee at the **Kalaheo Coffee Co. & Café** (p. 135), where you can pick up a picnic lunch. Stop in Waimea town to explore the **Russian Fort Elizabeth State Historical Park** (p. 195) and the **Menehune Ditch** (p. 195), then plan to spend most of the day hiking the various trails in the Waimea Canyon area (see p. 174 for hikes). All that hiking will work up an appetite, so for dinner go Italian at **Pomodoro** (p. 134) in Kalaheo.

Day ❺: Spend a Day in the Clouds at Kokee 🎔🎔🎔

If you aren't too sore from hiking in Waimea Canyon, head back up the mountain another 16 miles up the hill from the Waimea Canyon, where at 4,000 feet lies the **Kokee State Park** (p. 196). Stop for lunch at the **Kokee Lodge** (p. 175), open from 9am to 3pm. Check in at the **Kokee Natural History Museum** (p. 197) to learn about the forests and surrounding area, locate good hiking trails, and pick up a couple of trail maps. In the afternoon, wander around the park, and stay for sunset. If it's Friday night, plan dinner at the **Hanapepe Café** (p. 136); if it's not, **Toi's Thai Kitchen,** in Eleele (p. 137), has terrific and affordable Thai cuisine; or, **Keoki's Paradise,** in Poipu (p. 131) offers great seafood and steaks in a tropical jungle decor.

Day ❻: Out on the Water 🎔

After a couple of days in the mountains, it's time to head to the beach again. If you are coming from the North Shore or from the Coconut Coast, stop for a yummy breakfast at the **e.b.'s EATS** (p. 126), in Lihue. If you like sailing and snorkeling, book a **sail/snorkel tour** out of the Kukuiula Small Boat Harbor or Port Allen (see "Boating," in chapter 7) for the

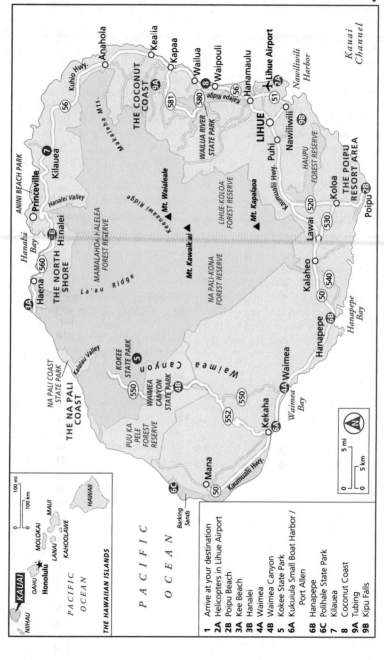

Kauai Channel

Nawiliwili Harbor

Anahola

Kealia

Kapaa

Wailua

Waipouli

Lihue Airport

Hanamaulu

Kuhio Hwy.

56

8

581

580

Kalepa Ridge

56

THE COCONUT COAST

WAILUA RIVER STATE PARK

LIHUE

51

2A

Makaleha Mts.

ANINI BEACH PARK

7

Princeville

Kilauea

Hanalei Valley

Hanalei

Haena

560

3A

Hanalei Bay

THE NORTH SHORE

La'au Ridge

MAMALAHOA-FALELEA FOREST RESERVE

Mt. Waialeale

Mt. Kawaikai

Keanawi Ridge

Nawiliwili

9B

Puhi

HAUPU FOREST RESERVE

Kaumualii Hwy.

LIHUE-KOLOA FOREST RESERVE

Mt. Kapalaoa

NA PALI-KONA FOREST RESERVE

Koloa

THE POIPU RESORT AREA

Lawai

520

530

Poipu

2B

NA PALI COAST STATE PARK

THE NA PALI COAST

Kalalau Valley

PUU KA PELE FOREST RESERVE

KOKEE STATE PARK

550

5

Waimea Canyon

WAIMEA CANYON STATE PARK

4B

Kekaha

6A

552

550

Waimea

4A

Waimea Bay

Kalaheo

540

50

Hanapepe

6B

Hanapepe Bay

Mana

6C

50

Kaumualii Hwy.

Barking Sands

5 mi

5 km

0

0

N

PACIFIC OCEAN

THE HAWAIIAN ISLANDS

NIIHAU

KAUAI

OAHU

Honolulu

MOLOKAI

LANAI

MAUI

KAHOOLAWE

HAWAII

100 mi

100 km

0

0

PACIFIC OCEAN

1   Arrive at your destination
2A Helicopters in Lihue Airport
2B Poipu Beach
3A Kee Beach
3B Hanalei
4A Waimea
4B Waimea Canyon
5   Kokee State Park
6A Kukuiula Small Boat Harbor / Port Allen
6B Hanapepe
6C Polihale State Park
7   Kilauea
8   Coconut Coast
9A Tubing
9B Kipu Falls

trip of a lifetime—exploring the **Na Pali Coast.**

If you pass on sailing, wander into the old plantation town of **Hanapepe** (p. 19) and browse at the unique shops. Continue west to Kauai's biggest beach at **Polihale State Park** (p. 158). Spend the day here, and be sure to checkout the "barking" sands at **Barking Sands Beach** (p. 158). Enjoy the sunset; then head over to **Duke's Canoe Club** (p. 123) in Nawiliwili for dinner on the water.

Day ❼: Explore Kilauea ⋒

Your beach quotient should be filled by now, so spend the day in the **Kilauea** (p. 20) area exploring gardens and the **Kilauea Point National Wildlife Refuge** (p. 188). First call **Na Aina Kai Botanical Gardens** (p. 206) to make sure they are open, and book a tour. This incredible, magical garden is for people who shudder at the thought of seeing a botanical garden: The whimsical magic of the place will win over even the most stubborn. Build up an appetite for lunch by checking out the very unusual shops at Kong Kung in Kilauea. Pick up a delicious picnic lunch at **Kilauea Fish Market** (p. 151). Then head down the road to the **Kilauea Point National Wildlife Refuge** (see "Birding" on p. 188), a 200-acre habitat for Hawaii's ocean birds. Eat your picnic on the coast, join a guided hike, or just wander through the fairyland of the wilderness area. Have dinner at the wonderful **Lighthouse Bistro Kilauea** (p. 145).

Day ❽: Cruise Coconut Coast ⋒

For those who just can't get enough beach time, make your way to **Wailua Beach** (p. 160) on the **Coconut Coast.** This beach, which features Hawaiian historical and cultural sites, is also a great place to just sit under a palm tree and figure out how you can move here permanently. For those non-beach people, you can visit **Kauai's Children's Discovery Museum**

(p. 168) in Kapaa, and then either explore the great shopping along the coast, or head inland and see the sacred Hindu temple, **San Marga Iraivan Temple** (p. 202). Eat lunch in Kapaa at **Mermaids** (p. 143) or try something very unusual like **Blossoming Lotus** (p. 142). In the afternoon, consider either hiking up **Sleeping Giant Mountain** (p. 178), bicycling along the shoreline, or renting a kayak from **Water Ski & Surf** (p. 162). By dinnertime, you'll be hungry; head for **Caffè Coco** (p. 140).

Day ❾: A Day of Adventure ⋒

Try something you have never done before. Sign up for a **Tubing Adventure** with **Kauai Backcountry Adventures** (p. 168), for a chance to float down the former sugar cane irrigation flumes. Or do something zippy like the new **Zipline** adventure; we recommend **Outfitters Kauai's Kipu Falls Zipline Trek** (p. 172) for an adrenaline rush that you won't forget. Plan a quiet afternoon at the beach to relax after your big adventure of the day.

Day ❿: See Kauai from a Different Perspective

See Kauai from the ocean by joining a **kayak tour** (p. 165), where you will skim over the ocean's (or a river's) surface coming eyeball-to-eyeball with turtles, flying fish, and other marine creatures. In the afternoon, book a **horseback riding tour** and see Kauai from the vantage point of sitting on a horse. There are a variety of different types of tours (p. 188), from riding along secluded beaches to trekking back to hidden waterfalls. Plan a quiet dinner and an early bed time.

Day ⓫: Get Pampered—A Day at the Spa

Plan an entire day at a **spa.** In "Best of Kauai," we recommend several top spas (p. 15) which will soothe your aching muscles from your days of adventure. Try something new—maybe a traditional

Hawaiian lomilomi massage or an ayurvedic massage (once given only to royalty for rejuvenation). Do nothing but lie around and relax. Order room service or get takeout for dinner.

Day ⑫: Back to the Beach to Polish Up Your Tan

Now that you've had several days on the beach, either return to your favorite or try a new one. Our list of favorite beaches is in chapter 7 (p. 152). Even if it is raining on one side of the island, frequently you can drive to the other side and it will be bright sunshine. Get a tropical-flavored shave ice (p. 138) and enjoy a taste of the islands.

Day ⑬: Shop Till You Drop

Get out the list of people you must buy gifts for and then turn to chapter 9, "Shopping" (p. 208), for our list of great

places to shop, great buys, and ideas on what to take home.

Day ⑭: Getting the Most Out of Your Last Day

If this is your last day, spend it in the Lihue (p. 190) area. It's close to the airport and there are plenty of things to do. You might want to step back in history and visit the Kauai Museum (p. 192) in Lihue or Kilohana (p. 192) in Puhi. Or drive up to the Wailua Falls (p. 192), just outside of town. Shoppers may like wandering around the old town of Lihue. Die-hard beachgoers can head to Kalapaki Beach (p. 154) for your last few hours of sun. If you are in a casual mode, get some burgers for the beach at Kalapaki Beach Hut (p. 127). If you are in the mood for a more filling meal—and you know that it won't get served by the airline—stop at Aroma (p. 121) for your last meal on the island.

3 Kauai for Families

Your itinerary is going to depend on the ages of your kids. The number one rule is don't plan too much; especially with young children, who will be fighting jet lag, trying to get adjusted to a new bed (and most likely new food), and may be very hyped up and excited to the point of exhaustion. The 7-day itinerary below is a guide to various activities. Pick and choose the ones everyone in your family will enjoy.

Day ❶: Arrive in Kauai; Settle in, and Head for the Swimming Pool 🌟🌟

Even kids suffer from jet lag and need to reset their internal clock. So expose the family to sunlight as soon as you arrive; even an hour or so will help them adjust to the time difference. If you have young kids who are not used to the waves, you might consider taking them to the swimming pool at your accommodation. They'll be happy playing in the water, and you won't have to introduce them to ocean safety after that long plane ride. Plan an early dinner with food your kids are used to; if you're in Poipu take them to Brennecke's Beach Broiler (p. 131).

On the Coconut Coast, try Bubba Burger (p. 142). On the North Shore, head for Hanalei Mixed Plate (p. 150). Go to bed early.

Day ❷: Up, Up, and Away in a Helicopter 🌟🌟🌟

Since you're probably on mainland time, the kids will be wide awake while it's still dark out. If the kids are old enough (8 years or more), plan an early morning helicopter tour (p. 197) so they can see the island from the air. Or if it's not raining, head out to Hanalei Beach to watch the sun make its appearance in the east, at 5:30am in summer, and 6:30am in winter. Then head into Hanalei for an early breakfast at **Hanalei Wake-up Café** (p. 150).

Since you are already at the North Shore, plan a day at the beach with the kids. Gear up with snorkel equipment, lots of floating equipment, and plenty of sunscreen, and plan to spend the morning at **Kee Beach** (p. 162). When the kids start to complain about being hungry, head back to Hanalei and grab a bite at **Tropical Taco** (p. 151); take it down to Hanalei Beach for a picnic lunch.

The kids may be passed out after lunch and all that sunshine. Head back to your hotel (and grab a quick nap yourself). Plan another early dinner.

Day ❸: Wow—Kauai's Own Grand Canyon 🐸🐸

If the kids are 8 or older, head out west, up to **Waimea Canyon** (p. 196) and **Kokee State Park** (p. 196). Have warm clothes along, as it can get cold at 4,000 feet, and be prepared for rain. Get an early start and have breakfast at the **Kalaheo Coffee Co. & Café** (p. 135). Stop in Waimea town to explore the **Russian Fort Elizabeth State Historical Park** (p. 195) and the **Menehune Ditch** (p. 195), then plan to spend most of the morning (before the clouds roll in) either hiking the various trails in the Waimea Canyon area (see p. 174 for hikes) or at least pulling over in the scenic look out areas and view the canyon. Then travel another 16 miles and a few thousand feet up the road to Kokee. Stop for lunch at the **Kokee Lodge** (p. 175), open from 9am to 3pm. Check in at the **Kokee Natural History Museum** (p. 197) to learn about the forests and surrounding area, locate good hiking trails, and pick up a couple of trail maps. In the afternoon, wander around the park, and stay for sunset. Stop for dinner at either the **Brick Oven Pizza** (p. 135) or **Camp House Grill** (p. 135), both in Kalaheo.

Day ❹: Sailing or Swimming in the Ocean 🐸

Head for the ocean. If you think the tykes will like sailing and snorkeling, book a **sail/snorkel tour** out of the Kukuiula Small Boat Harbor or Port Allen (see "Boating," in chapter 7) for the trip of a lifetime—exploring the **Na Pali Coast.**

If your clan is not the boating type, drive west to Kauai's **Poipu Beach Park** (p. 156). Spend the day here, and pick up some Mexican food for lunch at **Taqueria Nortenos** (p. 136). Plan on dinner at **Poipu Beach Broiler** (p. 134), where they kids' menu has all their favorites.

Day ❺: Explore a Magical Garden 🐸

Since the kids might be sunburned by now, take a day off the water and call **Na Aina Kai Botanical Gardens** (p. 206) to make sure they are open, and book a tour. If you have tiny tots, they will love the children's play area. This incredible, magical garden is for people who shudder at the thought of seeing a botanical garden: The whimsical magic of the place will win over even the most stubborn. Drop by **Kilauea Fish Market** (p. 151) to get a picnic lunch to eat down the road at the **Kilauea Point National Wildlife Refuge** (see "Birding" on p. 188), a 200-acre habitat for Hawaii's ocean birds. Eat your picnic on the coast, join a guided hike, or just wander through the fairyland of the wilderness area. Have dinner at the wonderful **Lighthouse Bistro Kilauea** (p. 145).

Day ❻: Discover a Museum or Walk on a Sleeping Giant 🐸

You can visit **Kauai's Children's Discovery Museum** (p. 168) in Kapaa—where the kids can have the time of their lives playing with virtual reality television, playing Hawaiian musical instruments, or hiding out in a "magical" treehouse— or you can join them for hours of interactive activities. Eat lunch just outside of Kapaa at **Duane's Ono-Char Burger**, in

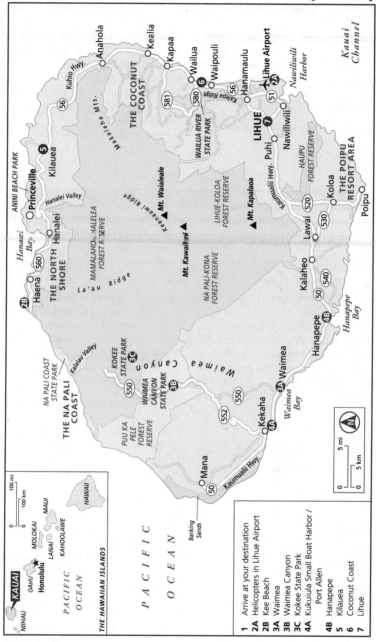

1 Arrive at your destination
2A Helicopters in Lihue Airport
2B Kee Beach
3A Waimea
3B Waimea Canyon
3C Kokee State Park
4A Kukuiula Small Boat Harbor /
    Port Allen
4B Hanapepe
5 Kilauea
6 Coconut Coast
7 Lihue

Anahola (p. 144). In the afternoon, if your kids are teenagers, hike up **Sleeping Giant Mountain** (p. 178). If they are very young, head for Lydgate State Park, where one of the best kid's playgrounds on the island is located. By dinnertime, you'll be hungry; try the **Coconuts Island Style Grill** (p. 140).

Day ❼: Getting the Most Out of Your Last Day

If this is your last day, spend it in the **Lihue** (p. 190) area. It's close to the airport and there are plenty of things to do. Take the family to the **Kauai Museum** (p. 192) in Lihue or take the carriage ride at **Kilohana** (p. 192) in Puhi. Die-hard beachgoers can head to **Kalapaki Beach** (p. 154) for your last few hours of sun. If you are in a casual mode, get some burgers for the beach at **Kalapaki Beach Hut** (p. 127). Start planning your next trip to Kauai.

4 Kauai for the Adventurous

Are you one of those people who hate the thought of laying around at the beach, doing nothing? Is your idea of the perfect vacation to be up, active, and trying new adventures? Then Kauai is the place for you. Our suggested itinerary below covers all the basic things to see on Kauai, with added adventures that active people like you love.

Day ❶: Arrive in Kauai; Head for the Beach ☆☆

I can't say this too often: To readjust your internal clock, get outside and get some sunshine (don't forget the sunscreen). I'd suggest going to the closest beach to your hotel (see my picks on p. 3). Start your adventure by dining on ethnic cuisine that you have never tried; check out our restaurant picks in chapter 6.

Day ❷: Fly through the Sky and Swim through the Water ☆☆☆

One of the best adventures on Kauai is a **helicopter tour** (p. 197) of the island. You most likely will still be on mainland time, so book an early flight (you'll be up long before the sun rises anyway). Plan a day snorkeling for your first adventure. Get snorkel equipment through **Snorkel Bob** (p. 162). If it is summer, and the weather is good, go to the North Shore. In fact, take an island tour and drive all the way to the end of the road at **Kee Beach** (p. 162). If you are up for it, hike a couple of miles along the **Na Pali Coast** (p. 181) and back (make sure you have good hiking shoes, water, snacks, and

sunscreen); or jump into that cool blue water and check out the marine life.

If it is winter, and the waves are up on the North Shore, head south for **Poipu Beach** (p. 156). Snorkel in the morning and then take an easy hike to **Makawehi Point** (p. 172).

Day ❸: Hiking through a Canyon and Up in the Clouds ☆☆

Head out west, up to **Waimea Canyon** (p. 196) and **Kokee State Park** (p. 196). Bring warm clothes along, as it can get cold at 4,000 feet, and be prepared for rain. Get an early start and have breakfast or coffee at the **Kalaheo Coffee Co. & Café** (p. 135). Stop in Waimea town to explore the **Russian Fort Elizabeth State Historical Park** (p. 195) and the **Mene-hune Ditch** (p. 195), then plan to spend most of the morning (before the clouds roll in) hiking the various trails in the Waimea Canyon area (see p. 174 for hikes). Then travel another 16 miles and a few thousand feet up the road to Kokee. Stop for lunch at the **Kokee Lodge** (p. 175), open from 9am to 3pm. Check in at the **Kokee Natural History**

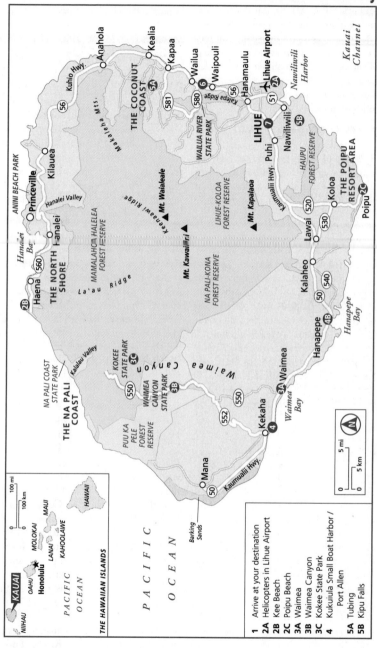

Adventure Itinerary map key:

1 Arrive at your destination
2A Helicopters in Lihue Airport
2B Kee Beach
2C Poipu Beach
3A Waimea
3B Waimea Canyon
3C Kokee State Park
4 Kukuiula Small Boat Harbor / Port Allen
5A Tubing
5B Kipu Falls

Museum (p. 197) to learn about the forests and surrounding area, locate good hiking trails, and pick up a couple of trail maps. In the afternoon, wander around the park, and stay for sunset. If it's Friday night, eat at the **Hanapepe Café** (p. 136); if it's not, go Italian at **Pomodoro** (p. 134) in Kalaheo.

Day ❹: Cruising the Na Pali Coast 🌺🌺

See a side of Kauai that you can only see from the water. Book a **sail/snorkel tour** out of the Kukuiula Small Boat Harbor or Port Allen (see "Boating," in chapter 7) for the trip of a lifetime—exploring the **Na Pali Coast.**

Day ❺: Tubing through the Water, Zipping through the Air 🌺

Try something you have never done before. Sign up for a **Tubing Adventure** with **Kauai Backcountry Adventures** (p. 168), for a chance to float down the former sugar cane irrigation flumes. Or do something zippy like the new **Zipline** adventure, we recommend **Outfitters Kauai's Kipu Falls Zipline Trek** (p. 172) for an adrenaline rush that you won't forget. Plan a quiet afternoon at the beach to relax after your big adventure for the day.

Day ❻: Glide through the Water, and Gallop to Secluded Waterfalls

See Kauai from the ocean by joining a **kayak tour** (p. 165), where you will skim over the ocean's (or a river's) surface coming eyeball-to-eyeball with turtles, flying fish, and other marine creatures. In the afternoon, book a **horseback riding tour** and see Kauai from the vantage point of sitting on a horse. There are a variety of different types of tours (p. 188), from riding along secluded beaches to trekking back to hidden waterfalls. Plan a quiet dinner and an early bed time.

Day ❼: Relax on Your Last Day

Plan your last day at a **spa.** In "The Best of Kauai," we recommend several top spas (p. 15) which will soothe your aching muscles from your days of adventure. Try something new; perhaps a traditional Hawaiian lomilomi massage or an ayurvedic massage (once given only to royalty for rejuvenation). Relax, and start planning your next trip to Kauai.

Where to Stay

Kauai has accommodations to fit every taste and budget, from luxury oceanfront suites to quaint bed-and-breakfast units to reasonably priced condos that will sleep a family of four without requiring that you take out a second mortgage.

Remember to consider *when* you will be traveling to the islands. The high season, during which rooms are always booked and rates are at the top end, runs from mid-December to March. A second high season, when rates are high but reservations are somewhat easier to get, is summer (June–Sept). The low seasons, with fewer tourists and cheaper rates, are April to June and September to mid-December.

Important note: Before you book, be sure to read "The Island in Brief" in chapter 2, which will help you choose your ideal location (you don't want to be stuck with long drives every day), as well as "Tips on Accommodations," also in chapter 2. Also check out the accommodations "bests" in chapter 1 for a quick look at our favorites.

Taxes of 11.42% are added to all hotel bills. Parking is free unless otherwise noted.

1 Lihue & Environs

If you need to stay overnight near the airport, try the **Garden Island Inn** (see below).

VERY EXPENSIVE

Kauai Marriott Resort & Beach Club 𝒦𝒦 *Kids*   The pluses to this luxury resort are Kalapaki (one of the best beaches in Kauai), an enormous swimming pool, a terrific kid's program, and a central location (about an hour's drive to Hanalei and the North Shore in one direction, and about an hour's drive to the Waimea Canyon in the other direction). The minus: the location—Lihue Airport is only a mile away—allows for easy arrival and departure, but it also means you can hear the takeoff and landing of every jet. Fortunately, air traffic stops by 9pm, but it begins again bright and early in the morning.

Once upon a time, this was a glitzy megaresort (the Westin Kauai) with ostentatious fantasy architecture, but then a hurricane (and new owners) toned it down. The result is grand enough to be memorable, but it's now grounded in reality—it looks like a Hawaiian hotel rather than a European palace. Water is everywhere throughout the resort: lagoons, waterfalls, fountains, a 5-acre circular swimming pool (some 26,000 sq. ft., the largest on the island), and a terrific stretch of beach. The lagoons are home to six islands that serve as an exotic mini-zoo, which still lends an air of fantasy to the place and, along with the enormous pool and children's program, makes the resort popular with families.

Guest rooms are comfortable, with fabulous views of gold-sand Kalapaki Beach, verdant gardens, and palm trees; a recent refurbishment has them all looking brand new.

There are also some time-share units in this resort.

Kalapaki Beach, Lihue, HI 96766. ⓒ **800/220-2925** or 808/245-5049. Fax 808/246-5148. www.marriott.com/lihhi. 356 units. $339–$454 double; from $664 suite. Paradise Plus Packages include deluxe accommodations and a choice of car or daily breakfast for 2 starting at $259. Extra person $40. AE, DC, DISC, MC, V. Valet parking $9, self parking $6. Free airport shuttle. **Amenities:** 4 restaurants (see the reviews of Duke's Canoe Club and Whalers Brewpub on p. 123 and 123); 2 bars; the largest pool on the island; 36-hole Jack Nicklaus golf course; 8 tennis courts; state-of-the-art fitness center; 5 Jacuzzis; watersports equipment rentals; children's program; game room; concierge; activities desk; car-rental desk; business center; shopping arcade; salon; room service; massage; babysitting; coin-op washer/dryers; laundry/dry cleaning. *In room:* A/C, TV/VCR, dataport, fridge, coffeemaker, hair dryer, iron, safe.

EXPENSIVE

Kaha Lani Resort   Located on the outskirts of Lihue, almost to the Coconut Coast, this 75-unit condominium project overlooks miles of white sandy beaches. It's a quiet location but not perfect. Conditions can be fair for swimming, but a good percentage of the time it's just too windy and turbulent. The property does have a heated swimming pool, plus barbecue areas, tennis courts, and a putting green. If you are looking for a peaceful, restful vacation this could work for you. The property is bordered by a golf course on one side and the ocean on the other. The units are older, most of them recently renovated, with full kitchens, ceiling fans, and great ocean views from the big lanais.

4460 Nehe Rd., Lihue, HI 96766. ⓒ **800/367-5004** or 808/822-9331. Fax 808/822-2828. www.castleresorts.com. 75 units (28 in rental pool). $210–$315 1-bedroom; $270–$400 2-bedroom; $375–$450 3-bedroom. Check Internet specials, which start at $175. AE, DC, DISC, MC, V. Parking: free. **Amenities:** Outdoor pool; putting green; tennis courts; barbecue area; coin-op washer/dryers; laundry/dry cleaning. *In room:* TV, full kitchen; fridge, coffeemaker, hair dryer, iron, safe.

Radisson Kauai Beach Resort   Radisson took over this oceanfront property in late 2000. They spent $10 million remodeling all guest rooms, creating a new sand pool, and building a health-club facility. The property, located 4 miles north of Lihue, commands a beachfront setting next door to a top-ranked municipal golf course. The location is good, about equidistant from both north- and south-shore activities, and also close to the Wailua River and its kayaking, water-skiing, river tours, historic sites, and drive-by waterfalls. The only downsides here are the windy conditions and the lack of safe swimming on the beautiful white-sand beach.

4331 Kauai Beach Dr., Lihue, HI 96766. ⓒ **888/805-3843** or 808/245-1955. Fax 808/246-9085. www.radisson kauai.com. 347 units. $199–$369 double; from $399 suite. Numerous packages available, including car packages, senior rates, and more. AE, DC, DISC, MC, V. Parking: $6. Free airport shuttle. **Amenities:** Restaurant; bar; 4 outdoor pools; tennis courts; fitness room; Jacuzzi; watersports equipment rentals; concierge; activities desk; car-rental desk; business center; shopping arcade; salon; massage; babysitting; coin-op washer/dryers; laundry/dry cleaning. *In room:* A/C, TV, dataport, fridge, coffeemaker, hair dryer, iron, safe.

MODERATE

Hale Hallelujah *(Kids)*   Perched on the banks of the Huleia Stream, just spitting distance from the Menehune Fishpond, in an upscale residential subdivision is this one-room vacation rental, upstairs in a Frank Lloyd Wright–influenced house. Amenities included a giant swimming pool and spa, and lying within walking distance to the river (take your kayak and take off). A spiral staircase takes you to your room on the second floor (don't overpack; you'll have to schlep it up the stairs) to the private room with a small lanai (great view) and all the amenities you could want (did we mention

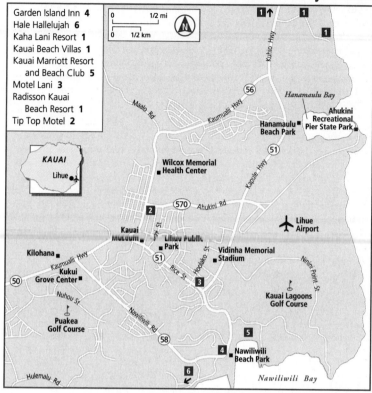

Garden Island Inn **4**
Hale Hallelujah **6**
Kaha Lani Resort **1**
Kauai Beach Villas **1**
Kauai Marriott Resort
   and Beach Club **5**
Motel Lani **3**
Radisson Kauai
   Beach Resort **1**
Tip Top Motel **2**

KAUAI
Lihue

that great mountain/river view?). The owners have three children and welcome families; in fact, they have plenty of toys to keep your bunch entertained. The unusual name came from the owner, who wanted to give thanks to God for the house.

2891 Pua Nani Street, Lihue, HI 96766. (C) 808/652-4578. www.halehallelujah.com. 1 unit. $130 double. 2-night minimum. **Amenities:** Outdoor pool, hot tub, use of washer/dryer. *In room:* TV/DVD, dataport, fridge, coffeemaker, hair dryer, iron.

Kauai Beach Villas   These beachfront condos are a good option for families and others seeking more space and privacy than they'd get elsewhere in Lihue. You get all the space of a condo, plus you get access to the amenities next door at the Radisson (see above) like the spa, charging meals, etc. The only drawback is the unsafe swimming conditions on the beautiful but windy white-sand beach. All units are outfitted with tropical decor and bamboo-style furniture, a fully equipped kitchen, a washer/dryer, and a lanai big enough for two lounge chairs, a table, and four chairs. The two-bedroom units have lanais off each bedroom, too. The immaculately landscaped grounds contain pools, tennis courts, barbecue areas, and a volleyball court. The Wailua Municipal golf course is next door.

4330 Kauai Beach Dr., Lihue, HI 96766. Kauai Vacation Rentals, 3-3311 Kuhio Hwy, Lihue, HI 96766. (C) **800/367-5025** or 808/245-8841. Fax 808/246-1161. www.kauaivacationrentals.com. 150 units. $215–$225 1-bedroom for 4; $119–$350 2-bedroom for 6. 5-night minimum. AE, DISC, MC, V. **Amenities:** 4 outdoor pools; 2 hot tubs; tennis

(Kids Family-Friendly Hotels

Hanalei Colony Resort (p. 114)   These spacious two-bedroom condos come equipped with full kitchens. Management has badminton and croquet sets on hand for the whole family, as well as toys, puzzles, and games for the kids.

Grand Hyatt Kauai Resort and Spa (p. 90)   It's the collection of swimming pools here—freshwater and salt, with slides, waterfalls, and secret lagoons—that makes this oceanfront Hyatt a real kids' paradise. Camp Hyatt (ages 3–12) offers arts and crafts, scavenger hunts, and other special activities for $65 for a full day (9am–4pm), including lunch and a T-shirt. It's $50 for a half day with lunch, and $40 for a half day without lunch. Plus, the Hyatt is one of the few hotels to offer "camp" in the evening, from 6 to 10pm, at $10 an hour. Babysitting and activities on weekend evenings give Mom and Dad some time alone. In summer and during the holiday season, there's Rock Hyatt, an activities room where teens can gather and play electronic games. Also in summer, Family Fun Theatre Nights show some of the more than 400 movies filmed on Kauai.

Kalaheo Inn (p. 102)   Families on a budget will love this budget motel. One-bedroom apartments from $75, 2-bedrooms just $105, and 3-bedrooms only $145, all with kitchenettes. What a deal! Located in the town of Kalaheo, a 12-minute drive from world-famous Poipu Beach, a 5-minute drive from the Kukuiolono Golf Course, and within walking distance of shops and restaurants. Hosts Chet and Tish Hunt love families and have a storeroom full of games to keep the kids entertained. Plus, they happily hand out complimentary beach towels, beach toys, and even golf clubs to guests (links are nearby). This is a must-stay for vacationers on a budget.

Kauai Marriott Resort & Beach Club (p. 85)   This place has Hawaii's largest pool (26,000 sq. ft.), in addition to a new kids' pool—but that's just the beginning. Freshwater lagoons with six islands serve as a mini-zoo with

courts; access to nearby health club; activities desk; laundry/dry cleaning. *In room:* A/C in bedrooms, TV/VCR, dataport, answering machine, kitchen, fridge, coffeemaker, hair dryer, iron, safe, washer/dryer.

INEXPENSIVE

Garden Island Inn (*k* (*Finds*   This bargain-hunter's delight is located 2 miles from the airport, 1 mile from Lihue, and within walking distance of shops and restaurants. The spacious rooms are decorated with island-style furniture, bright prints, and fresh tropical flowers (grown right on the grounds). Each unit contains a fridge, microwave, wet bar, TV, coffeemaker, and ocean view; some have private lanais, and the suites have sitting areas. The grounds are filled with flowers and banana and papaya trees (and you're welcome to help yourself to the fruit at the front desk). Owner Steve Layne offers friendly service, lots of advice on activities (the entire staff happily uses their connections to get you discounts), and even complimentary use of beach gear, golf clubs (a course is nearby, as are tennis courts), and coolers. If they are booked, ask about their two-bedroom condo nearby for $135–$155 per night.

kangaroos, monkeys, llamas, and other exotic creatures; horses lead car-riages through tropical gardens; and a high-energy beach beside Nawiliwili Harbor, Kauai's port of call, provides surfside fun. The informal Kalapaki Kids program (ages 5–12) offers activities ranging from boogie boarding to treasure hunting ($45 for a full day, which includes lunch and a Kalapaki Kids T-shirt).

Kiahuna Plantation Resort (p. 92)   These condominium units feature a chil-dren's program during spring break, summer, and winter for $35 for a full day and $20 for a half day. The activities for children 5 to 12 include every-thing from lagoon fishing to arts and crafts.

Princeville Resort Kauai (p. 113)   The Keiki Aloha Program is centered around children 5 to 12 with activities like snorkeling, lei making, sand cas-tle contests, Hawaiian crafts, and more. Although the program is offered year round, it is not offered on Sunday. Cost is $65 (without lunch) and $55 for each additional child in the same family.

Sheraton Kauai Resort (p. 92)   Open to the public (not just guests of the Sheraton), this daily (Mon–Fri) kids program during the summer (and Mon., Wed., and Fri. during the remainder of the year) offers camp-type activities like bamboo pole fishing, lei making, hula lessons, and tidepool explo-rations from 9am to 4pm (or half days).

Waimea Plantation Cottages (p. 104)   Among groves of towering coco palms are these clusters of meticulously restored plantation cottages that offer families the opportunity to relax off the beaten track. Some people may find Waimea a little too out of the way (it's a 1½-hr. drive to the North Shore), but it is close to Waimea Canyon and Kokee State Park. The re-cre-ated village allows kids plenty of room to wander and play away from traf-fic and crowds. There are also a pool and tennis courts.

3445 Wilcox Rd. (across the street from Kalapaki Beach, near Nawiliwili Harbor), Lihue, HI 96766. © 800/648-0154 or 808/245-7227. Fax 808/245-7603. www.gardenislandinn.com. 21 units (private bathrooms have shower only). $85–$135 double. Extra person $5. AE, DISC MC, V. **Amenities:** Complimentary watersports equipment; activities desk. *In room:* A/C, TV, fridge, coffeemaker, hair dryer, iron.

SUPER-CHEAP SLEEPS

Motel Lani *Value*   For a no-frills bed and shower, this place will do the job. You won't find a little basket of toiletries in the bathroom or a mint on your pillow, but you will get a clean, basic room (no TV) for as little as $34. This small, concrete-block motel mainly serves interisland travelers and a few visitors on a budget. The location, on a busy street right in the heart of Lihue, isn't bad—the airport is just a 5-minute drive away, making this a good rest stop if you have an early-morning flight—but the beach is a significant schlep away. For $50, you can get a room with a kitchenette.

P.O. Box 1836 (4240 Rice St.), Lihue, HI 96766. © 808/245-2965. 9 units (with shower only). $34–$52 double. No credit cards. *In room:* A/C, kitchenette (some rooms), fridge.

Tip Top Motel *(Value)*   The Tip Top is an institution on Kauai. Their motto, "Over 75 years of service on the island of Kauai," lets you know they've been around a while. The two-story concrete tile building, with a cafe on the first floor, provides very basic accommodations: twin beds (with solid, hard mattresses), shower, air-conditioning unit in the window, and a dresser. Don't look for expensive carpeting here—just institutional linoleum tile. But for $45, you get your money's worth. Guests are usually interisland business travelers who like the convenience of the central Lihue location, just 5 minutes from the airport.

3173 Akahi St., Lihue, HI 96766. ℂ 808/245-2333. Fax 808/246-8988. 30 units (with shower only). $45 double. MC, V. From the airport, follow Ahukini Rd.; turn left on Akahi St. **Amenities:** Coffee shop. *In room:* A/C, TV, no phone.

2 The Poipu Resort Area
VERY EXPENSIVE
Gloria's Spouting Horn Bed & Breakfast   As one guest put it, "Staying here makes you want to get married again!" However, the price has been creeping up. Just last year Gloria charged $275, which is expensive but okay for a splurge. The $325 a night she now charges is way too high. True, all three spacious guest rooms are oceanfront, with huge private lanais overlooking the secluded beach. Our favorite is the Punana Aloha ("love nest") room, furnished in willow, including a romantic queen bed with a woven willow canopy overhead. All of the private bathrooms feature Japanese-style deep soaking tubs and separate showers. Each unit also has a wet bar, microwave, toaster, and blender. Breakfasts are elaborate affairs served on linen, crystal, and English china in the dining room (or for those who'd rather stay in bed, on a tray with flowers). The food is five-star quality, and the ambience nothing if not romantic. At sunset, Gloria offers an open bar and a pupu platter. A golf course, tennis courts, and several bars and restaurants are nearby. Still, $325 a night is too pricey for a bed-and-breakfast, even a nice one. For that kind of money you can stay at the Grand Hyatt (see below) and get all the amenities of a resort.

4464 Lawai Beach Rd. (just before Spouting Horn Park), Koloa, HI 96756. ℂ and fax 808/742-6995. www.glorias bedandbreakfast.com. 3 units. $325 double. Rates include full breakfast, afternoon drinks, and pupu. 3-night minimum. No credit cards. **Amenities:** Outdoor pool right next to the ocean. *In room:* TV/VCR, dataport, fridge, coffeemaker, hair dryer, iron, safe.

Grand Hyatt Kauai Resort and Spa ✺✺✺ *(Kids)*   Hard to believe that this luxury hotel (one of Hawaii's best) can get "grander," but the new multi-million dollar renovations have taken the hotel's ambience of casual elegance to a new level. One of Hawaii's best luxury hotels and one of the top-ranked tropical resorts in *Condé Nast Traveller's* annual readers' poll, this four-story resort, built into the oceanside bluffs, spreads over 50 acres that overlook Shipwreck Beach (which is too rough for most swimmers) at the end of the road in Poipu. The $250 million Hyatt uses the island architecture of the mid-1920s to recapture the old Hawaii of the Matson Line steamship era.

The airy atmosphere takes you back to the days of a grand plantation overlooking the sea. This is a comfortable, unostentatious place where you can bring the kids and Grandma. The rooms are large (nearly 600 sq. ft.) and elegantly outfitted. All have marble bathrooms and spacious private lanais; most have ocean views. Club floors have their own concierge and a lounge serving continental breakfast, drinks, and snacks. The hotel is next door to the Robert Trent Jones, Jr.–designed Poipu Golf

Where to Stay in the Poipu Resort Area

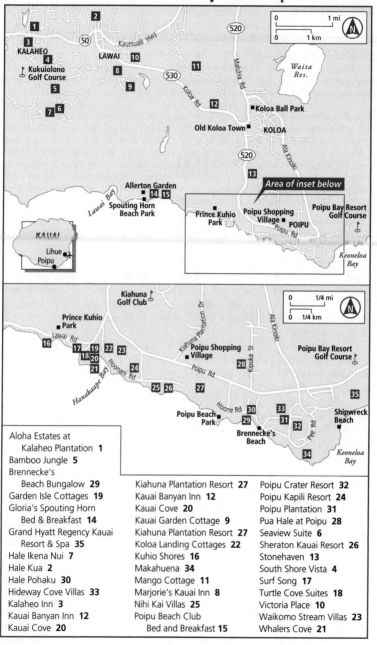

Aloha Estates at
   Kalaheo Plantation **1**
Bamboo Jungle **5**
Brennecke's
   Beach Bungalow **29**
Garden Isle Cottages **19**
Gloria's Spouting Horn
   Bed & Breakfast **14**
Grand Hyatt Regency Kauai
   Resort & Spa **35**
Hale Ikena Nui **7**
Hale Kua **2**
Hale Pohaku **30**
Hideway Cove Villas **33**
Kalaheo Inn **3**
Kauai Banyan Inn **12**
Kauai Cove **20**

Kiahuna Plantation Resort **27**
Kauai Banyan Inn **12**
Kauai Cove **20**
Kauai Garden Cottage **9**
Kiahuna Plantation Resort **27**
Koloa Landing Cottages **22**
Kuhio Shores **16**
Makahuena **34**
Mango Cottage **11**
Marjorie's Kauai Inn **8**
Nihi Kai Villas **25**
Poipu Beach Club
   Bed and Breakfast **15**

Poipu Crater Resort **32**
Poipu Kapili Resort **24**
Poipu Plantation **31**
Pua Hale at Poipu **28**
Seaview Suite **6**
Sheraton Kauai Resort **26**
Stonehaven **13**
South Shore Vista **4**
Surf Song **17**
Turtle Cove Suites **18**
Victoria Place **10**
Waikomo Stream Villas **23**
Whalers Cove **21**

Course. If you stay here, don't leave without a treatment from the **ANARA Spa,** the best spa on Kauai. (Also check out the large selection of classes—some of them free— at the fitness center.) There may be only 23 Grand Hyatt Hotels on the planet, but frankly, I can't image any of them are better than this.

1571 Poipu Rd., Koloa, HI 96756. © 800/55-HYATT or 808/742-1234. Fax 808/240-6596. www.kauai-hyatt.com. 602 units. $455–$785 double; from $1,300 suite. Packages available. Extra person $35. Children 17 and under stay free in parent's room. Resort fee of $15 a day for local calls. AE, DC, MC, V. Self and valet parking, 1 hr. at the tennis court free, fitness access to the ANARA Spa and to classes, and 10% off various shops on property. **Amenities:** 6 restaurants (see review of Dondero's on p. 128); 6 bars (the partially open-air Stevenson's Library has mellow jazz Thurs–Sat nights); an elaborate freshwater fantasy pool complex, plus 2 more pools and 5 acres of saltwater swim- ming lagoons w/islands and a man-made beach; 4 tennis courts; one of the best fitness centers on the island; a 25,000-sq.-ft. ANARA Spa that is reason enough to stay here, w/lava-rock shower gardens, a 10-headed Swedish shower, and indoor-outdoor treatment rooms; 3 Jacuzzis; watersports equipment rentals; bike rental; extensive Camp Hyatt kids program; concierge; activities desk; car-rental desk; business center; shopping arcade; salon; room service; massage; babysitting; complimentary washer/dryers; same-day laundry/dry cleaning; concierge-level rooms. *In room:* A/C, TV/VCR, (DVD players available for rent) dataport (high-speed Internet access), minibar, fridge, coffeemaker, hair dryer, iron, safe.

Sheraton Kauai Resort ☆☆ *(Kids)*   This modern Sheraton (since 1997) has the feel- ing of Old Hawaii and a dynamite location on one of Kauai's best beaches. It features buildings on both the ocean side and the mountain side of the road. The horseshoe- shaped, Polynesian-style lobby has shell chandeliers dangling from the ceiling. You have a choice of three buildings: one nestled in tropical gardens with koi-filled ponds; one facing the palm-fringed, white-sand beach (our favorite); and one looking across green grass to the ocean, with great sunset views. The rooms overlook either the trop- ical gardens or the rolling surf.

The bar is fabulous. Even if you don't stay here, come by to order a cocktail and an appetizer, and take in the view and the Hawaiian music. A golf course is nearby. *Fam- ilies, take note:* Kids eat free with a paying adult at the Shell Restaurant, at both breakfast and dinner.

An obnoxious daily "resort amenities" fee of $25 is tacked on to your bill for the following "free" services: daily buffet breakfast for two, sunset mai tai punch hour with a torch-lighting ceremony, guest library with daily newspapers and three computers with Internet access, use of the fitness center and tennis courts, and shuttle services to Koloa town, the Poipu Shopping Center, and two nearby golf courses.

2440 Hoonani Rd., Koloa, HI 96756. © 800/782-9488 or 808/742-1661. Fax 808/742-4041. www.sheraton-kauai. com. 413 units. $335–$625 double (max. 4 in room); from $675 suite for 4; plus $25 a day "resort amenity" fee. Extra person $50. AE, DC, DISC, MC, V. **Amenities:** 3 restaurants; extraordinary bar; 2 outdoor pools (1 w/water play- ground, 1 for children); 3 tennis courts (2 night-lit); fitness room facing the ocean (one of the most scenic places to work out on Kauai); small massage-and-skin-care center; Jacuzzi; watersports equipment rentals; children's program; concierge; activities desk; shopping arcade; salon; room service; babysitting; coin-op washer/dryers; same-day laun- dry/dry cleaning. *In room:* A/C, TV/VCR, dataport, fridge, coffeemaker, hair dryer, iron, safe.

EXPENSIVE

Kiahuna Plantation Resort ☆☆ *(Kids)*   One of the best condominium develop- ments in the Poipu area, this complex consists of several plantation-style buildings, loaded with Hawaiian style and sprinkled on a 35-acre garden setting with lagoons, lawns, and a gold-sand beach. Golf, shopping, and restaurants are within easy walk- ing distance. Two different management companies handle the rental pool: Outrigger oversees about two-thirds of the units, Castle the remaining third. (Despite any price differences, the units are quite comparable.) Both companies are excellent and have

---

Value The Queen of Condos

_____

One of the easiest ways to find lodging in the Poipu Beach area is to contact **Grantham Resorts**, 3176 Poipu Rd., Koloa, HI 96756 (*©* **800/325-5701** or 808/742-2000; fax 808/742-9093; www.grantham-resorts.com), which handles some 150 rental units for nine different condo developments, plus dozens of vacation homes. Owner Nancy Grantham has high standards for her rental units and offers extremely fair prices. In 2003, Nancy dropped several units and entire condominium projects because they simply did not meet her standards. The condos start at $89 for a basic two-bedroom, garden-view unit in low season and vacation homes start at $185 and go up to $1,140 for exquisite multi-million dollar ocean homes. There's a 5-night minimum for condos and a 7-night minimum for homes.

If you're staying on Kauai for 5 days, ask Grantham Resorts about the "Frommer's Silver Rate," large one- and two-bedroom condos, well-equipped (full kitchen, washer/dryer, wet bar, TV, phone, most with complimentary high-speed Internet service and DVDs), starting as low as $99 a night for one-bedrooms, $129 for two-bedroom Garden Views, or $135 a night for one-bedroom or two-bedroom Ocean View condos. (See "Nihi Kai Villas" and "Waikomo Stream Villas" later in this chapter.) There's not a better deal on Kauai. Kudos to Nancy for these fabulous vacation bargains.

_____

numerous package deals to fit your budget. All condo units are spacious, with full kitchens, daily maid service, and lanais. Kiahuna offers an activities program for children 5 to 12 during spring break, summer, and winter for $35 for a full day and $20 for a half day.

2253 Poipu Rd., Koloa, HI 96756. 333 units. Under 2 different management groups: Outrigger, *©* **800/OUTRIGGER** or 808/742-6411. Fax 808/742-1698. www.outrigger.com. $225–$460 1-bedroom apt (sleeps up to 4); $365–$505 2-bedroom apt (sleeps up to 6). Packages available, including 5th night free, car packages, senior rates, and more. AE, DC, DISC, MC, V. Castle Resorts & Hotels, *©* **800/367-5004** or 808/742-2200. Fax 800/477-2329 or 808/742-1047. www.castleresorts.com. $240–$515 1-bedroom apt; $405–$10500 2-bedroom apt. Ask about packages like 5th night free or free car. AE, DC, DISC, MC, V. **Amenities:** Restaurant (see review of Plantation Gardens on p. 130); bar; outdoor pool; tennis courts; watersports equipment rentals; barbecue areas; children's program; activities desk; shopping arcade nearby; coin-op washer/dryers. *In room:* TV/VCR, kitchen, fridge, coffeemaker, hair dryer, iron, safe.

Whaler Cove *✦✦*   If money is not a worry and you want something really special right on the water, you can't go wrong with these ultra-luxury units. From the koa door at the entry to the ocean view from the master bedroom (and master bathroom), this is first class all the way. The two-bedroom, two-and-a-half bathroom units are in a town house with a two-story configuration, plenty of space (a couple thousand sq. ft.), and plenty of privacy for two couples. These units have it all: a huge deck overlooking the Pacific, top-of-the-line appliances in the kitchen, washer/dryers in the units, and an entertainment center. The property itself features an oceanside infinity pool, a whirlpool, and a barbecue area. Other amenities include an orchid garden, full concierge, and easy access to Koloa Landing (an outcrop of lava where the river and ocean meet, which is great for snorkeling and good for turtle spotting).

2640 Puuholo Rd. Reservations: Grantham Resorts, 3176 Poipu Rd., Koloa, HI 96756. ✆ 800/325-5701 or 808/
742-2000. Fax 808/742-9093. www.grantham-resorts.com. $345–$365 2-bedroom, 2½ bathroom. DC, DISC, MC, V.
Amenities: Outdoor pool; whirlpool; barbecue area; concierge. In room: TV/VCR, kitchen, fridge, coffeemaker, hair
dryer, iron, washer/dryer.

MODERATE

Garden Isle Cottages Oceanfront *Finds*   The site is spectacular: a 13-foot cliff
overlooking historic Koloa Landing and an ocean inlet (where you can see turtles
swimming). Nestled in a tropical garden setting, these one-bedroom apartments have
an island feel, with rattan furniture, batiks, and original art on the walls—and great
views. (Some of the artwork is by owner Robert Flynn, whose work is also on display
at the Honolulu International Airport.) All units, so large that they can easily sleep
four, feature full kitchens and spacious lanais. This is a quiet, peaceful place to stay in
the heart of the Poipu area, within walking distance of beaches, golf, tennis, shopping,
and restaurants.

2666 Puuholo Rd. (overlooking Waikomo Stream), Koloa, HI 96756. ✆ 800/742-6711 or 808/742-6717. www.ocean
cottages.com. 4 units. High season $190 1-bedroom; low season $175 1-bedroom, plus cleaning fee of $45. Extra per-
son $10. 2-night minimum. No credit cards. In room: TV, kitchen, fridge, coffeemaker, washer/dryer.

Hideaway Cove Villas *Value*   Just a block from the beach, and next door to an
excellent restaurant, are these gorgeous condominium units in a plantation setting.
Amenities are top-drawer, and no expense was spared in the interior decorations.
Units have hardwood floors, TV/VCR/DVD, comfy furniture, roomy beds (either
four-poster beds or wood sleigh designs), spacious living areas, kitchenettes with the
best appliances and granite countertops, and big outdoor lanais. You get all of this in
a lush, landscaped tropical jungle at affordable prices. Owner Herb Lee is always on
hand to guide you to Kauai's best spots and loan out his collection of (free) beach toys
and beach cruiser bicycles. A few of the units have Jacuzzis, so ask when you book.

2307 Nalo Rd. Reservations: P.O. Box 1113, Kaloa, HI 96756. ✆ 886/849-2426 or 808/635-6909. www.hideaway
cove.com. 7 units. $135–$150 studio double; $175 1-bedroom double; $220–$255 2-bedroom for 4; $345–$370 3-
bedroom for 4. Plus cleaning fee ranging from $80–$160. Extra person $20. 2-night minimum. AE, DISC, MC, V.
Amenities: Restaurant and bar next door; free beach toys and bicycles; washer/dryers. In room: TV/VCR/DVD, kitchen,
fridge, coffeemaker, hair dryer, iron, phone answering machine.

Kuhio Shores   This older but well-maintained condo is right on the ocean's edge
with a white-sand beach next door. A good deal for families, each one-bedroom unit
has a full kitchen, a pull-out bed for the kids, and a great breeze (from the ocean just
outside your door). We recommend the top floors for great views.

Lawai. Reservations: Grantham Resorts, 3176 Poipu Rd., Suite 1, Koloa, HI 96756. ✆ 800/325-5701 or 808/742-
2000. Fax 808/742-9093. www.grantham-resorts.com. $155–$185 1-bedroom. 5-night minimum. DC, DISC, MC, V.
Amenities: Coin-operated laundry. In room: TV/VCR, full kitchens, fridge, microwave, coffeemaker, hair dryer.

Makahuena *Finds*   The pluses here include: moderately priced two-bedroom
oceanfront and oceanview units ($185–$205), ocean front pool, hydro-spa, complimentary tennis courts, a private lava-rock barbecue area, and some of the most dramatic ocean vistas in Poipu. The units have vaulted ceilings, fully equipped kitchens,
dishwasher, microwave, TV, VCR, CD players, data port in the telephone, air condi-
tioning (in some units), washers/dryers, extra linens, and beach towels. The only
minus we can find here is no maid service. Swimming is just a few blocks away, along
the coast, at Poipu Beach.

1661 Pe'e Rd., Poipu. Reservations: Grantham Resorts, 3176 Poipu Rd., Suite 1, Koloa, HI 96756. **©** **800/325-5701** or 808/742-2000. Fax 808/742-9093. www.grantham-resorts.com. $185–$205 2-bedroom/2-bathroom. 5-night minimum. DC, DISC, MC, V. **Amenities:** Outdoor pool; barbecue area. *In room:* TV/VCR, full kitchen, fridge, microwave, coffeemaker, hair dryer, washer/dryer.

Poipu Beach Club Bed and Breakfast   You can't get much closer to the ocean without getting wet. Located next to a small cove, this waterfront property offers the ocean just outside your door. However, recently they have raised their prices sky high from $135 a night to $185 and from $160 to $225, a bit high for what you get. Chuck and Deb Tomesko have managed the property for nearly a decade and know how to make guests comfortable and happy. They offer a range of units, from a bedroom in their home with a small refrigerator, TV, and view of the water, to a two-bedroom unit in the adjoining house. A hot breakfast is cooked every morning; otherwise, no cooking is allowed. There's an outside shower to wash off the sand and plenty of "ocean toys" you can borrow. The B&B is not appropriate for children.

4560 Lawai Beach Rd., Koloa, HI 96756. **©** 808/742-1639. www.poipubeachclub.com. 3 units. $185–$225. 3-night minimum. No credit cards. *In room:* TV/VCR, fridge, coffeemaker.

Poipu Kapili Resort ✦✦   This quiet, upscale oceanfront cluster of condos is outstanding in every area. We like the home-away-from-home comforts and special touches: a video and book library, a spacious pool, several barbecues, tennis courts lit for night play, and an herb garden. (You're welcome to take samples if you're cooking.) A golf course is also nearby. The apartments are large (1-bedroom/2-bathroom units are 1,150 sq. ft.; 2-bedroom/3-bathroom units are 1,820 sq. ft.) and have fully equipped kitchens, tropical furnishings, ceiling fans, and private lanais. The oceanfront two-story town houses are our favorites because they catch the trade winds. The two-bedroom units also have washer/dryers. (Common laundry facilities are available on the property as well.) Although the Pacific is right outside your window, the nearest sandy beach is a block away (which can be a blessing because it means more privacy).

2221 Kapili Rd., Koloa, HI 96756. **©** **800/443-7714** or 808/742-6449. Fax 808/742-9162. www.poipukapili.com. 62 units. $220–$300 1-bedroom apt (sleeps up to 4); $290–$560 2-bedroom apt (up to 6). Discounts for longer stays; package rates available; 7th night free May 1–Dec 20. Rates include Fri continental breakfast by the pool. MC, V. **Amenities:** Oceanside pool; championship tennis courts lighted for night use; activity desk; washer/dryers. *In room:* TV/VCR, dataport, kitchen, fridge, coffeemaker, loaner hair dryer from front desk, iron.

Stonehaven, an Oasis in Paradise *(Finds)*   On the outskirts of the old plantation community of Koloa, in the quiet country, this luxurious bed-and-breakfast just made its debut. The units face an open court yard, bordered with papaya trees. Each large room has marble floors, a sitting area with a TV, then a curtain of fringe to separate the sitting area from the bedroom (king bed). No expense was spared here, especially in the bathroom where there's a soaking tub and a glass shower. Breakfast is described as "elaborate European style continental" with four different kinds of fruit, a meat and cheese platter, cereal, hard or soft boiled eggs, and toast. Also available is a two-bedroom/two-bathroom manager's house. Everyone also has use of the workout equipment (free weights and machines) in the open-air fitness room.

5465 Wailaau Rd., Koloa, HI 96756. **©** **808/742-2966.** www.stonehavendeluxebnb.com. info@stonehavendeluxe bnb.com. 3 rooms, 1 2-bedroom house. $135 double with breakfast; $175 2-bedroom house without breakfast for 4; $185 house with breakfast for 4. 3-night minimum. No credit cards. **Amenities:** Workout weights. *In room:* TV/VCR, dataport, fridge, coffeemaker, hair dryer, iron, safe.

Turtle Cove Suites ★★ (Value)   What makes this property so incredible is not only the fabulous location (overlooking the stream and ocean) but also the great eye of the interior designer. It also helps that owner Joe Sylvester and his wife own a furniture and fine arts store at which to choose the "perfect" items for their four units. Our favorite unit, located on a quiet street, away from the crowds, is the 1,100-square-foot oceanfront suite with a full kitchen and private Jacuzzi, original art on the walls, and a zillion little touches that make this place seem more like a home than a vacation rental. All units (even the $100 one) come with lanais and use of the swimming pool and Jacuzzi; they feature top-of-the-line materials like slate from India, four-poster beds, and marble bathrooms. At these prices, the units are a deal. Book in advance.

P.O. Box 1899, Poipu Beach, HI 96756. (℃ 866/294-2733. www.kauaibeachrentals.com. 4 units. $135–$240, plus cleaning fees of $70–$85. 5-night minimum. AE, DC, DISC, MC, V. **Amenities:** Outside pool; Jacuzzi; coin-operated washer/dryer. *In room:* TV/VCR, fridge, coffeemaker, microwave. Some units have complete kitchens; some have kitchenettes.

INEXPENSIVE

Brennecke's Beach Bungalow ★ (Finds)   Attention honeymooners (or honeymooner wannabes): This is your place. So close to Poipu Beach that you can see it from your private lanai (about a 45-second walk from the front door to the waves). Tucked into a large two-story house is this private-entrance studio decorated with bamboo floors, maple cabinets, and lots of Hawaiian décor. This studio also has a small kitchenette (microwave, toaster oven, blender, coffee maker and fridge), cozy sitting area and big, and comfortable bed. Outdoors there's a beach shower, barbecue area and big, green lawn. Restaurants, dining, tennis and golf are just minutes away. Book this baby!

2255 Nalo Road, Poipu Beach, Kauai, Hawaii 96756. (℃ 888/393-4646 or 808/742-1116. Fax 808/246-2505. www.poipubeachbungalow.com 1 studio. $125. 6-night minimum. No credit cards. **Amenities:** Barbecue area; golf nearby; tennis courts nearby. *In room:* TV/VCR, free wireless access, fridge, coffeemaker, hair dryer, iron and ironing board.

Hale Pohaku ★ (Finds)   This half-acre tropical compound can be either a great bargain for independent travelers or a terrific find for a big, big family. Just 30 seconds from Poipu Beach, this four-house complex was recently purchased and renovated in 2005, and consists of a five-bedroom manager's house, two restored plantation-era two-bedroom cottages, and a third cottage built in the same plantation style. You can rent everything from a studio to the entire lot (sleeps 22). Each unit features a fully equipped kitchen, washer and dryer, private barbecue area, hardwood floors, and outdoor beach shower. This gated compound has a swimming pool, extra amenities for kids (high chairs, etc.), and plenty of beach toys (boogie boards, snorkeling equipment, etc.). Golf, tennis, restaurants, and shopping are close by.

2231 Pane Rd., Koloa, HI 96756. (℃ 866/742-6462 or 808/742-6462. www.vrbo.com/24157. 5 units. $120 studio double; $200 2-bedroom cottage double; $520 5-bedroom house. 2-night minimum. MC, V. **Amenities:** Pool; golf nearby; tennis courts nearby; *In room:* TV/VCR, free wireless access, kitchen, fridge, coffeemaker, hair dryer, iron and ironing board, washer/dryer, private barbecue area.

Kauai Banyan Inn ★ (Finds)   On a hilltop, overlooking an acre of landscaped property, a stream and of course, an old banyan tree, is this just-opened 4-room inn. Centered around a courtyard with a burbling fountain, this is a place of peace and quiet, great for relaxing and resting. The daughter of owner Lorna is a licensed massage therapist and can give you an in-room massage to relieve jet lag and built up tension. Each room is good sized with a kitchenette (a ¾-size fridge, microwave, two-burner stove, and coffee maker). All the rooms have terrific pastoral views of the rolling country side, lanais, separate private baths, and private entrances. Breakfast is delivered to your room and consists of homemade banana bread, fruit, coffee, and juice. Lorna welcomes kids and can dig up a portable crib and high chair for families. There's a barbecue area outside.

3528-B Mana Hema Pl., Lawai, HI 96765. © 888/786-3855. www.kauaibanyan.com. 4 units. $70–$100 (plus cleaning fee of $30–$45). No credit cards. **Amenities:** Barbecue area; washer/dryer. *In room:* TV/DVD, free wireless access, fridge, coffeemaker, hair dryer, iron and ironing board.

Kauai Cove *Value* These immaculate cottages, located just 300 feet from Koloa Landing, next to Waikomo Stream, are the perfect private getaway. Each studio has a full kitchen, private lanai (with barbecue grill), and big bamboo four-poster bed. The cozy rooms feature beautiful hardwood floors, tropical decor, and cathedral ceilings. Kauai Cove is within walking distance of sandy beaches, great restaurants, and shopping, yet it's far enough off the beaten path that privacy and quiet are assured.

2672 Puuholo Rd., Poipu, HI 96756. ©/fax **800/624-9945** or 808/742-2562. www.kauaicove.com. 3 units. $95–$125 double. 4-night minimum. DISC, MC, V. *In room:* TV, dataport, kitchen, fridge, coffeemaker.

Kauai Garden Cottage *Finds* Hidden in the country is this small but practical one-bedroom cottage just a 10-minute drive to Poipu Beach and a 20-minute drive to the entrance of Waimea Canyon. The well-appointed cottage in Tommy Bahama-type tropical décor has a cozy living room (with TV), a small but very functional kitchen with everything you could possibly need, and a separate bedroom with a comfy pillow-top queen bed. Free high-speed Internet connection, washer and dryer, and lots of beach equipment (cooler, beach chairs, towels, etc.) make this place a bargain.

P.O. Box 746, Kalaheo, HI 96741. © 808/332-0877. Fax 808/332-0878. www.kauaigardencottages.com. 1 cottage. $65–$100 double. 3-night minimum. AE, DC, MC, V. **Amenities:** Barbecue area. *In room:* TV/VCR, free wireless access, (no phone), kitchen, fridge, coffeemaker, hair dryer, iron and ironing board, washer/dryer.

Koloa Landing Cottages *Kids* Most of the return guests at Koloa Landing Cottages have become close friends with former hosts Hans and Sylvia Zeevat, who started this vacation-cottage rental business in 1978. Ellie and Bret Knopf took over the property in 2001 and have restored the five cottages, nestled in tropical landscaping, to their original glory. Located across the street from a beach that offers great snorkeling and diving, the cottages range from a studio to a 1,100-square-foot two-bedroom/two-bathroom home that can sleep up to six. All units have full kitchens; the larger units also have private decks. The units exude comfort and are outfitted with the practical furniture of tropical beach houses—great for flopping down with a good book. Since the Knopfs have four kids, they welcome families.

2704-B Hoonani Rd. (near the Hoonani Rd. Bridge), Koloa, HI 96756. © **800/779-8773** or 808/742-1470. www.koloa-landing.com. 1 studio, 3 cottages, 1 house. $105 studio double; $120 1-bedroom double; $150 2-bedroom for 4; $185 house for 4. 4-night minimum. No credit cards. **Amenities:** Barbecue; washer/dryer facilities. *In room:* TV, kitchen, fridge, coffeemaker.

Mango Cottage *Value* Located in the rolling hills outside of Koloa is this freestanding cottage down a lush, tropical foliage path. The first thing you notice is the skylight in the ceiling illuminating the full kitchen and living room area. The separate bedroom in the 550-square-foot bungalow has a king bed with adjoining bathroom. White tile creates clean lines throughout, and there is a queen sofa bed in the living room for the kids. Owner George Coates spent years in the hotel industry and has thought of every single detail and possible need his guests may want. Very private, very peaceful and great location, just 15 minutes to Poipu Beach, restaurants, shopping, golf, and tennis.

4333 Naulu, Koloa, HI 96756.© **808/742-1216.** Fax 808/742-7344. www.hawaiian.net/~quaylo/bnb.htm. 1 cottage. $95 double. 3-night minimum. No cards. *In room:* TV, kitchen, fridge, coffeemaker, microwave, (no phone).

Marjorie's Kauai Inn ☞ This quiet property, perched on the side of a hill, is just 10 minutes from Poipu Beach and 5 minutes from Old Koloa Town. From its large lanai it offers stunning views over rolling pastures and the Lawai Valley. Every unit has a kitchenette with dining table, ceiling fan, and lanai. The new Sunset View unit has a separate sitting area and a futon sofa for extra guests. On the hillside is a huge, 50-foot swimming pool, perfect for lap swimming. Former owner Marjorie Ketcher has sold her popular inn and will leave in May of 2006, but the new owners, Mike and Alexis, love the inn and promise to keep it the same when they take over. P.S. The inn is not appropriate for families with children.

P.O. Box 866 (off Hailima Rd., adjacent to the National Tropical Botanical Garden), Lawai, HI 96765. © **800/717-8838** or 808/332-8838. Fax 808/332-8838. www.marjorieskauaiinn.com. 3 units. $110–$130 double. Extra person $15. Rates include continental breakfast on 1st day. 2-night minimum. No credit cards. **Amenities:** Outdoor pool; Jacuzzi. *In room:* TV, kitchenette, fridge, coffeemaker, hair dryer, iron.

Nihi Kai Villas ☞ *Value* Nancy Grantham (see "The Queen of Condos," above) is a marketing genius. She offers the deal of the decade on these large, two-bedroom units just 200 yards from the beach. If you stay 7 nights, the rate for these well-equipped oceanview apartments starts at an unbelievable $127 a night (for four, which works out to just $64 a couple). You may not get new carpeting, new furniture, new drapes, or a prime beachfront location, but you *do* get a clean, well-cared-for unit with full kitchen, washer/dryer, and TV/VCR, all at an unbeatable price. The property is a 2-minute walk from world-famous Brennecke's Beach (great for bodysurfing) and a block from Poipu Beach Park. On-site amenities include an oceanfront swimming pool, tennis and paddle courts, and a barbecue and picnic area. Within a 5-minute drive are two great golf courses, several restaurants, and loads of shopping.

1870 Hoone Rd. Reservations: c/o Grantham Resorts, 3176 Poipu Rd., Suite 1, Koloa, HI 96756. © **800/325-5701** or 808/742-2000. Fax 808/742-9093. www.grantham-resorts.com. 70 units. Regular rates: $135–$199 1-bedroom double; $135–$259 2-bedroom for 4 (5-night minimum). Ask about Frommer's "Silver Rate" (5-night minimum). DC, DISC, MC, V. From Poipu Rd., turn toward the ocean on Hoowili Rd., then left on Hoone Rd.; Nihi Kai Villas is just past Nalo Rd. on Hoone Rd. **Amenities:** Outdoor pool; nearby golf course; tennis courts; Jacuzzi; activities desk, concierge. *In room:* TV/VCR, dataport, kitchen, coffeemaker, iron, washer/dryer.

Poipu Crater Resort *Value* Attention, travelers on a budget: two-bedroom garden view units for just $89 a night in low season ($99 mid-season, and a still unbelievable $109 in high season) is a deal you can't pass up. This resort consists of 15 duplexes in a tropical garden setting. Each unit is about 1,500 square feet with living area, kitchen, large lanai, bathroom and guest bedroom downstairs, and master bedroom and bath upstairs. Each has a full kitchen (with microwave), as well as a washer/dryer and VCR. The complex has a swimming pool, tennis and paddle ball courts, sauna, ping-pong tables, and barbecues. Poipu Beach is about a 10-minute walk away, and the entire Poipu Beach resort area (offering everything from restaurants to golf courses) is within a 5-minute drive. The only caveats are no maid service and no air conditioning. Pick up the phone right now and reserve a unit before the rest of the world beats you to it.

2330 Hoohu Rd., Poipu. Reservations: c/o Grantham Resorts, 3176 Poipu Rd., Suite 1, Koloa, HI 96756. © **800/325-5701** or 808/742-2000. Fax 808/742-9093. www.grantham-resorts.com. 30 units. Regular rates: $89–$99 1-bedroom garden view (5-night minimum); ask about Frommer's "Silver Rate" (5-night minimum). DC, DISC, MC, V. From Poipu Rd., turn toward the ocean on Hoowili Rd., then left on Hoone Rd.; continue on Hoone Rd., past the bends, where the road is now called Pee Rd; turn left off Pee Rd onto Hoohu Rd. **Amenities:** Outdoor pool; nearby golf course; tennis courts; sauna; barbecue area. *In room:* TV/VCR, CD, kitchen, coffeemaker, iron, washer/dryer.

Poipu Plantation *(Value)*   This tropical property has three bed-and-breakfast rooms in the main house and separate apartment vacation rentals on the same property. The large rooms in the house are reminiscent of the old plantation days, with shining wooden floors, huge bathrooms, and lots of privacy. Breakfast is served in the dining room; you're also welcome to take yours out on the lanai. The impeccably decorated one- and two-bedroom apartments are huge and come with big lanais, spacious living rooms, large separate bedrooms (with shoji doors), full kitchens, and big bathrooms. Gleaming hardwood floors, air-conditioning, and ocean views add to the value. Located in the heart of Poipu, within walking distance of beach and water activities, golfing, tennis, shops, and restaurants, Poipu Plantation is an excellent choice for budget vacationers.

1792 Pee Rd., Koloa, HI 96756. (C) **800/634-0263** or 808/742-6757. Fax 808/742-8681. www.poipubeach.com. 3 units, 9 apts. $95 double (including continental breakfast); $120–$145 1-bedroom; $175–$190 2-bedroom for 4. Extra person $20. 3-night minimum. MC, V. From Poipu Rd., turn toward the ocean onto Pee Rd. **Amenities:** Hot tub. *In room:* A/C, TV/VCR, kitchen, fridge, coffeemaker.

Pua Hale at Poipu *(Finds)*   Created by an artist and designed by an engineer, Pua Hale is a large (850 sq. ft.) cottage on a quiet dead-end street, just 2 blocks from Poipu Beach. Artist/photographer Carol Ann Davis and her husband, engineer Walter Briant, took an empty space in their yard and created an open, airy cottage with an Asian-influenced interior. The cottage is surrounded by a high fence to ensure privacy; entrance is through a rustic wooden gate draped with colorful bougainvillea. Sliding glass doors run nearly the entire length of the cottage, bringing the outside in. The open-beam ceiling and white-tile floors add to the overall feeling of lightness, and the wood trim, rattan furniture, and colorful throw rugs add to the island feeling. The large main room has a complete kitchen at one end, and living and dining areas (with a queen sofa bed) at the other. The bathroom has a wonderful tiled Japanese *furo* (sunken tub) for soaking as well as a shower. A real bonus is the intimate, curved lanai overlooking Japanese gardens blooming with ginger, heliconia, and plumeria. Other pluses include a barbecue, a stereo, and laundry facilities. Poipu beaches, shopping, and restaurants are just a walk away.

2381 Kipuka St., Koloa, HI 96756. (C) **800/745-7414** or 808/742-1700. Fax 808/742-7392. www.kauai-puahale.com. 1 cottage. $125 double, plus a $60 cleaning fee. Extra person $10. 4-night minimum. DISC, MC, V. From Poipu Rd., turn left on Kipuka St. (just past shopping center). No children under 8. **Amenities:** Washer/dryer. *In room:* A/C, TV/VCR, kitchen, fridge, coffeemaker, iron.

Surf Song *(Value)*   Located in a quiet residential neighborhood among million-dollar oceanfront homes, these three studios and one apartment unit offer excellent value for your vacation dollar. Each unit has a private lanai, queen bed, and sleeper sofa. (Some even have ocean views.) The studios have kitchenettes with microwave, coffeemaker, small refrigerator, and other appliances; the apartment has a full kitchen. All units face a courtyard, landscaped with tropical flowers, with a picnic table and barbecue. The Surf Song is walking distance to the beach, and a 2-minute drive to restaurants and shops in the Poipu Resort area.

5135 Ho'ona Rd., Poipu Beach, HI 96756. (C) **877/373-2331** or 808/742-2331. Fax 808/826-6033. www.surfsong. com. 4 units. $70–$130 double. No credit cards. 3-night minimum. **Amenities:** Washer and dryer. *In room:* TV, kitchenette or kitchen, fridge, coffeemaker.

Victoria Place ✿✿ *(Finds* This is our favorite bed-and-breakfast on Kauai. The reason to stay here? One name: Edee Seymour. It's easy to see why she won the Kauai Chamber of Commerce's Aloha Spirit Award. Her motto is "We pamper!" She lavishes her guests with attention and aloha. Her spacious, skylit, U-shaped house wraps around the swimming pool and garden. Three bedrooms, located in one wing of the home, open onto the pool area, which is surrounded by flowering walls of bougainvillea, hibiscus, gardenia, and ginger. So why is the price so low? Guests share the TV, the phone, and a refrigerator in the common area. Edee also rents a secluded studio apartment (dubbed "Victoria's Other Secret") down a private path; it contains a king bed, shower-only bathroom, kitchen, and TV. Edee's breakfasts are truly a big deal: at least five different tropical fruits, followed by something from the oven, such as homemade bread, scones, or muffins. Most of her guests are returnees. As a couple from Germany told us, "Once you stay with Edee, every place else is cold and indifferent."

3459 Lawai Loa Lane (off Koloa Rd./Hwy. 530), Koloa. c/o P.O. Box 930, Lawai, HI 96765. © **808/332-9300.** Fax 808/332-9465. www.hshawaii.com/kvp/victoria. 4 units. $90 double; $125 studio apt. Rates include yummy breakfast. Extra person $15. No credit cards. No children under 15. **Amenities:** Outdoor pool, beach toys, full breakfast. *In room:* No phone.

Waikomo Stream Villas ✿ *(Value* Nancy Grantham has one more fabulous trick up her sleeve: these 800- to 900-square-foot, one-bedroom apartments which comfortably sleep four, and larger two-bedroom units which sleep six. Tucked into a lush tropical garden setting, the spacious, well-decorated units have everything you could possibly need on your vacation: full kitchen, VCR, washer/dryer, and private lanai. The complex—which has both adults' and children's pools, tennis courts, and a barbecue area—is adjacent to the Kiahuna Golf Club and just a 5-minute walk from restaurants, shopping, and Poipu's beaches and golf courses.

2721 Poipu Rd. (just after entry to Poipu, on ocean side of Poipu Rd.), Poipu. Reservations: c/o Grantham Resorts, 3176 Poipu Rd., Suite 1, Koloa, HI 96756. © **800/325-5701** or 808/742-2000. Fax 808/742-9093. www.grantham-resorts.com. 60 units. Regular rates: $99–$145 1-bedroom for 4, $129–$175 2-bedroom for 6 (5-night minimum). Ask about Frommer's "Silver Rates." DC, DISC, MC, V. **Amenities:** 2 outdoor pools (1 for children and 1 for adults); complimentary tennis courts; Jacuzzi; activities desk, concierge. *In room:* TV/VCR, dataport, kitchen, fridge, coffeemaker, washer/dryer.

ELSEWHERE ON THE SOUTH COAST

Aloha Estates at Kalaheo Plantation *(Value* This is a love story. Part one: A Japanese visitor, LeeAnn, meets stained-glass artist James Hargraves while on vacation on Oahu. They fall in love and marry. Part two: While visiting Kauai, they discover a 1924 plantation house and fall in love with it. They lovingly restore the old house and convert it into a bed-and-breakfast filled with 1920s and 1930s furniture and fabrics, and James's stained-glass work. There's a room to fit every visitor's needs and budget, from a small $55 room with king bed, kitchenette, private entrance, stereo, VCR, and lanai, to a $75 room with full kitchen, private entrance, hot tub, VCR, stereo, and private lanai overlooking the koi pond. Part three: Guests arrive and fall in love with this grand old house themselves . . . and everyone lives happily ever after (at least while they're on Kauai!).

4579 Puuwai Rd. (P.O. Box 872), Kalaheo, HI 96741. © and fax **808/332-7812.** www.kalaheo-plantation.com. 6 units. $45–$75 double. Extra person $10. 2-night minimum. No credit cards. Turn off Hi. 50 toward the mountain onto Puuwai Rd. at Steve's Mini Mart, then turn right immediately again to stay on Puuwai Rd. *In room:* TV, kitchenette, fridge, coffeemaker, iron (on request).

Tips **B&B Etiquette**

In Hawaii, it is traditional and customary to remove your shoes before entering anyone's home. The same is true for most bed-and-breakfast facilities. Most hosts post signs or will politely ask you to remove your shoes before entering the B&B. Not only does this keep the B&B clean, but you'll be amazed how relaxed you feel walking around barefoot. If this custom is unpleasant to you, a B&B may not be for you. Consider a condo or hotel, where no one will be particular about your shoes.

If you have never stayed at a B&B before, here are a few other hints: generally the host lives on property and their part of the house is off limits to guests. (You do not have the run of the house.) Most likely there will be a common area that you can use. Don't expect daily maid service. Your host may tidy up but will not do complete maid service. Also don't expect amenities like little bottles of shampoo and conditioner; this is a B&B, not a resort. Remember that you are sharing your accommodations with other guests; be considerate (that is, quiet) when you come in late at night.

Some hotels, resorts, condos, and vacation rentals may allow smoking in the guest rooms (most also have nonsmoking rooms available), but the majority of bed-and-breakfasts forbid smoking in the rooms. If this matters to you, be sure to check the policy of your accommodation before you book.

Bamboo Jungle ☆ *Finds*   New owners Lucy and Terry Ryan recently took over this property, a jungle of verdant plants, a quaint gazebo, an 82-foot lap pool, and an impeccably decorated old plantation-era house. They are making the much needed repairs and renovations to the rooms, each of which has a private entrance and French doors opening onto a private lanai with an ocean view. The netting over the beds creates a romantic mood and serves a functional purpose (it keeps Hawaii's insects on their side of the sleeping quarters). Accommodations range from a single room with deck to a studio with minikitchen. There are no phones in the units, but you can use the house phone. Breakfast is served in the "great room" inside the house. The next renovation will be to the gardens and yard. Golf and tennis courts are nearby. Note that there is no air-conditioning, which 350 days of the year is fine, but on the few days the trade winds stop blowing, it's not so great.

3829 Waha Rd. Reservations: P.O. Box 737, Kalaheo, HI 96741. ✆ **888/332-5115** or 808/332-5515. www.kauai-bedandbreakfast.com. 3 units. $110–$150 double. 3-night minimum rooms, 5-night minimum suite. MC, V. From Hwy. 50, turn left at the traffic light onto Papalina Rd., then right on Waha Rd. **Amenities:** Outdoor pool; Jacuzzi. *In room:* TV, kitchenette (in 1 room), coffeemaker, no phone.

Hale Ikena Nui *Value*   Patti Pantone opened this 1,000-square-foot, self-contained guest suite on the first floor of her home in 1995 and had instant success. It has a private entrance, a full-size kitchen (with dishwasher), and large dining room and living room areas. With a queen bed and a queen-size sofa bed, the unit easily sleeps four. Outside on the private lanai are a gas barbecue and all the beach and picnic equipment you could possibly need. Throw in a full-size washer/dryer, and you can see why this place is so popular. In 1996 Patti also opened a room upstairs in her house for people looking for less space and a smaller bite out of their budget. The room has a huge walk-in closet, plus gives you run of the house, including the gourmet kitchen.

3957 Ulualii St. (P.O. Box 171), Kalaheo, HI 96741. ☎ **800/550-0778** or 808/332-9005. Fax 808/332-0911. www. kauaivacationhome.com. 1 unit, 1 apt (with shower only). $75 double (includes continental breakfast); $95 double apt (includes continental breakfast on 1st day). Extra person $15. 3-night minimum for apt only. MC, V. At the 11-mile marker on Hi. 50, turn down Papalina Rd. toward the ocean; continue for 1.2 miles; turn right on Waha Rd., then left on Ulualii St. **Amenities:** Washer/dryer. *In apartment:* TV, kitchen, fridge, coffeemaker, iron.

Hale Kua ✿ *Value*   This is for people who love the beach—at a distance—and who want to sleep in the quiet and cool climate of the hills of Lawai Valley, away from the maddening crowds. If you want to stay in a forest, wake up to the sound of birds singing, and see incredible sunsets each night, one of these five units in three different houses may be for you. Hale Kua features a two-story house with a complete three-bedroom home unit with a big kitchen, wraparound dining bar, walk-in closets, washer/dryer, and a view of the bucolic rolling hills. Downstairs are two separate one-bedroom units with a full kitchen, wraparound lanai, washer/dryer, and birds serenading you all day long. Next door, on hosts Bill and Cathy Cowern's 8-acre tree farm, are a one-bedroom separate cottage and a studio apartment in their large home. The beach is just a 10-minute drive down the hill. If you are looking for privacy and all the comforts of a honeymoon or family accommodation, you won't find anything better at this price.

4896-E Kua Rd., Lawai, 96765. ☎ **800/440-4353** or 808/332-8570. www.halekua.com. 5 units. $105 1-bedroom apt for 2; $115 1-bedroom cottage for 2; $125 3-bedroom unit for 2 ($5 extra per person). 5-night minimum in cottage Dec 15–Jan 15. No credit cards. **Amenities:** Barbecue areas. *In room:* TV/VCR and DVD player, kitchen, fridge, microwave, coffeemaker, washer/dryer, phone.

Kalaheo Inn ✿ *Value*   What a deal! Located in the town of Kalaheo, a 12-minute drive from Poipu Beach, a 5-minute drive from the Kukuiolono Golf Course, and within walking distance of shops and restaurants, the inn is a comfortable 1940s motel totally remodeled in 1999 and converted into apartment units with kitchens. Owners Chet and Tish Hunt couldn't be friendlier, handing out complimentary beach towels, beach toys, even golf clubs to guests (links are nearby). They love families and have a storeroom full of games to keep the kids entertained. This is a must-stay for vacationers on a budget. With all the money you save, you won't mind using the phone at the front desk, since there are no phones in the units.

4444 Papalina Rd. (just behind the Kalaheo Steakhouse), Koloa, HI 96756. ☎ **888/332-6023** or 808/332-6023. Fax 808/742-6432. www.kalaheoinn.com. 15 units. $65 double studio with kitchenette; $75–$85 1-bedroom with kitchenette; $105 2-bedroom; $145 3-bedroom with full kitchen. AE, MC, V. **Amenities:** Complimentary watersports equipment; children's games; coin-op washer/dryers. *In room:* TV, kitchen or kitchenette, fridge, coffeemaker, iron, hairdryer, no phone.

Seaview Suite *Value*   Even if you are on a really tight budget, you can still stay in the popular south shore area. Located in a private home in a residential area about a 15-minute drive from the beach is this budget place with two small but affordable rooms. The Seaview Suite, a large studio with separate bedroom area hidden behind sliding shoji doors, contains a full kitchen, big bathroom, walk-in closet, and private lanai with barbecue. Downstairs, owner Monica has added a tiny "ti suite" for those on a very strict budget. The small one-room unit has a tiny kitchenette (microwave, full-size refrigerator), a queen bed, and just enough room for a single bed and TV. Great for the frugal crowd that plans to come home only to sleep. Monica will do one complimentary load of laundry per week for her guests, and she has lots of beach paraphernalia she's happy to loan out.

3913 Ulualii St., Kalaheo, HI 96741. ©/fax **808/332-9744**. www.hshawaii.com/vacplanner/kvp/clients/seaview/index.html. 2 units. $60 small studio; $75 larger studio. 3-night minimum. No credit cards. **Amenities:** Complimentary watersports equipment. *In room:* TV/VCR, full kitchen in 1 unit, kitchenette in other, fridge, coffeemaker.

South Shore Vista ☆ *Kids*   The list of pluses for this one-bedroom apartment, in a residential home, include separate bedroom with queen bed and full bathroom, private entry, big lanai with ocean view, living area with fold-out couch (the unit can sleep up to four), VCR, and fully equipped kitchenette. Your refrigerator is stocked with breakfast provisions like coffee, tea, cereal, and fresh papayas and limes from the garden. Located on a quiet residential street, South Shore Vista is 2 blocks from the Kukuiolono Park and Golf Course (with jogging and walking paths through Hawaiian and Japanese gardens and 9 holes of golf for an unbelievable $9), 10 minutes from Poipu beaches, 40 minutes from Waimea Canyon, and 25 minutes from the airport. You can't go wrong staying here.

4400 Kai Ikena Dr., Kalaheo, HI 96741. © **808/332-9339**. Fax 808/332-7771. www.southshorevista.com. 1 apt. $84 double. Rate includes continental breakfast items stocked in refrigerator. Extra person $10; $5 for children. 3-night minimum. No credit cards. After the 11-mile marker on Hi. 50, turn toward the ocean on Papalina Rd.; continue for nearly a mile to Kai Ikena Dr. *In room:* TV/VCR, kitchen, fridge, coffeemaker, hair dryer, iron.

3 Western Kauai

Inn Waimea *Finds*   The former residence of a church pastor (good karma!), converted into a four-suite inn, this quaint two-story inn occupies an ideal location in Waimea. It is 1 block from the ocean, 1 block from "downtown," and walking distance to restaurants and shops. Each of the suites is uniquely decorated and has a special feature; for example, one room has a Jacuzzi for two, another room has an ADA-compliant shower. All of the rooms have private phones (free local phone calls), bathroom, coffee maker, refrigerator, cable TV, ceiling fans, even free high-speed Internet. The same company also has one- and two-bedroom cottages available in the Waimea area. If you plan to visit the North Shore, this is not a good location, as you will be on the road doing quite a bit of driving.

4469 Halepule Rd., Waimea, HI 96796. © **808/338-0031**. Fax 808/338-1814. www.innwaimea.com. $100–$120 double rooms. $100–$150 double cottages, 3-night minimum for cottages. Extra person $10. *In room:* TV, free high-speed wireless, fridge, coffeemaker. Cottages: TV, kitchen.

Kokee Lodge *Value*   This is an excellent choice, especially if you want to do some hiking in Waimea Canyon and Kokee State Park. There are two types of cabins here: The older ones have dormitory-style sleeping arrangements (and resemble a youth hostel), while the new ones have two separate bedrooms each. Both styles sleep six and come with cooking utensils, bedding, and linens. We recommend the newer units, which have wood floors, cedar walls, and more modern kitchen facilities (some are wheelchair-accessible as well). There are no phones or TVs in the units, but there is a pay phone at the general store. You can purchase firewood for the cabin stove at Kokee Lodge, where a restaurant is open for continental breakfast and lunch every day. The lodge also has a cocktail lounge, a general store, and a gift shop. *Warning for light sleepers:* This area is home to lots of roosters which crow at dawn's first light.

P.O. Box 819, Waimea, HI 96796. © **808/335-6061**. 12 cabins. $35 studio; $45 2-bedroom. 5-night maximum. DC, DISC, MC, V. *In room:* Kitchen, fridge, coffeemaker, no phone.

Ole Kamaole's Beach House *Finds*   You won't find many B&B/vacation rentals in Kekaha, located at the foot of Waimea Canyon and literally the last town on the west side. It's sunny here, but the residential area, coupled with the extreme location on the far end of the island, just doesn't give it much of a draw for visitors. But those looking for a quiet vacation will enjoy the remote setting. There are two houses on this property with two bedrooms each, both have lots of windows, lots of lanais, lots of quiet, and are just across the street from the ocean. The "Ironwoods House," nestled among Ironwoods Pines, is a 700-square-foot cottage, 150 feet from the sea, with open beam ceilings and wood parquet floors. The "Sea Grape House" is about 80 feet from the ocean with huge, huge decks. (Don't get too excited, the ocean here tends to be rough and not great for swimming, but okay for beachcombing and fishing; there are a couple good surfing sites nearby).

8663 Kaumualii Hwy., Kekaha, HI 96752. ℂ **800/528-2465** or 808/337-9113. www.olehawaii.com. 2 houses. $150–$175 double (each house sleeps 6), plus $100 cleaning fee. Extra person $15. Price includes stocked breakfast items. 4-night minimum. No cards. *In room:* TV/VCR, full kitchen, washer, outside shower.

Waimea Plantation Cottages ⚘ (*Kids*) This beachfront vacation retreat is like no other in the islands: Among groves of towering coco palms sit clusters of restored sugar-plantation cottages dating from the 1880s to the 1930s and bearing the names of their original plantation-worker dwellers. The lovely cottages have been transformed into cozy, comfortable guest units with period rattan and wicker furniture and fabrics from the 1930s, sugar's heyday on Kauai. Each has a furnished lanai and a fully equipped modern kitchen and bathroom; some units are oceanfront. Facilities include an oceanfront pool, tennis courts, and laundry. The seclusion of the retreat makes it a nice place for kids to wander and explore away from traffic. The only downsides: the black-sand beach, which is lovely but not conducive to swimming (the water is often murky at the Waimea River mouth); and the location at the foot of Waimea Canyon Drive—its remoteness can be very appealing, but the North Shore is 1½ hours away. Golf courses and tennis courts, however, are much closer.

9400 Kaumualii Hwy. (P.O. Box 367), Waimea, HI 96796. ℂ **800/9-WAIMEA** or 808/338-1625. Fax 808/338-2338. www.waimea-plantation.com. 48 units. $140–$160 hotel room double; $140 studios with kitchenette double; $195–$310 1-bedroom double; $240–$370 2-bedroom (sleeps up to 4); $280–$415 3-bedroom (up to 5); $405–$465 4-bedroom (up to 8); $620–$730 5-bedroom (up to 9). Extra person $20. Children under 18 stay free. AE, DC, DISC, MC, V. **Amenities:** Restaurant; bar; large outdoor pool; activities desk; coin-op washer/dryers; dry cleaning. *In room:* TV, dataport, kitchen, fridge, coffeemaker, iron, safe.

4 The Coconut Coast

This is the land of B&Bs and inexpensive vacation rentals. In addition to those reviewed below, we recommend **Opaeka'a Falls Hale,** which has two exquisite units with pool and hot tub for $90 to $110; reservations are available through **Hawaii's Best Bed & Breakfasts** (ℂ **800/262-9912;** www.bestbnb.com).

EXPENSIVE

Lae Nani Outrigger Resort Condominium ⚘ The Lae Nani ("beautiful promontory point") offers a quiet, relaxing setting right on the beach, next door to restaurants and bars. On the point is the Kukui Heiau, where an ancient temple once stood. The one- and two-bedroom units are roomy with large living rooms, separate dining rooms, complete kitchens, and generous lanais. The two-bedroom/two-bathroom units can easily fit a family of six. Maid service is provided daily. Extras include a swimming pool, lava-rock-protected swimming area, barbecue facilities, tennis courts, and self-service laundry facilities. Next door is the Coconut Marketplace, with shops, restaurants, and nightlife; a golf course is nearby.

Where to Stay in the Coconut Coast

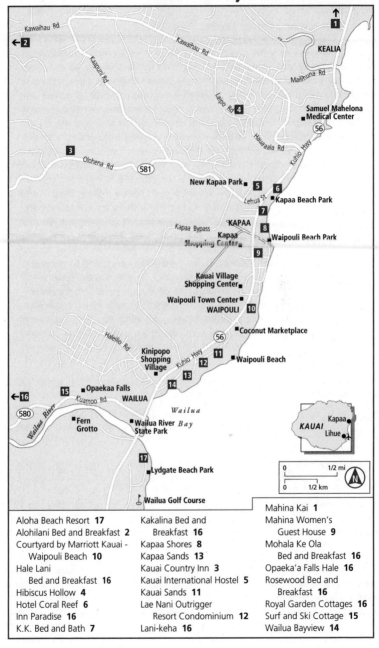

KEALIA

Kawaihau Rd
Kawaihau Rd
Kaapuni Rd
Laipo Rd **4**
Maillhuna Rd

Samuel Mahelona
■ **Medical Center**
(56)

Kuhio Hwy

Haua aala Rd

Olohena Rd
(581)

New Kapaa Park ■ **5** **6**
■ **Kapaa Beach Park**

Lehua St

7

KAPAA

Kapaa Bypass

Kapaa **8**
Shopping Center ■ ■ **Waipouli Beach Park**

9

Kauai Village
Shopping Center ■

Waipouli Town Center ■ **10**
WAIPOULI

(56) ■ **Coconut Marketplace**

Halelilo Rd

Kinipopo
Shopping Kuhio Hwy **11** ■ **Waipouli Beach**
Village **12**
■ **13**

14

15 ■ **Opaekaa Falls**
← **16** Kuamoo Rd **WAILUA**
(580) Kuamoo Rd

Wailua

Kapaa ●
KAUAI
Lihue ●

■ **Fern**
Grotto ■ **Wailua River** *Bay*
State Park

17
■ **Lydgate Beach Park**

| 0 | 1/2 mi |
| 0 | 1/2 km |

⚓ ■ **Wailua Golf Course**

Aloha Beach Resort **17**
Alohilani Bed and Breakfast **2**
Courtyard by Marriott Kauai -
    Waipouli Beach **10**
Hale Lani
    Bed and Breakfast **16**
Hibiscus Hollow **4**
Hotel Coral Reef **6**
Inn Paradise **16**
K.K. Bed and Bath **7**

Kakalina Bed and
    Breakfast **16**
Kapaa Shores **8**
Kapaa Sands **13**
Kauai Country Inn **3**
Kauai International Hostel **5**
Kauai Sands **11**
Lae Nani Outrigger
    Resort Condominium **12**
Lani-keha **16**

Mahina Kai **1**
Mahina Women's
    Guest House **9**
Mohala Ke Ola
    Bed and Breakfast **16**
Opaeka'a Falls Hale **16**
Rosewood Bed and
    Breakfast **16**
Royal Garden Cottages **16**
Surf and Ski Cottage **15**
Wailua Bayview **14**

A Rose by Any Other Name: Timeshares

Timeshares are very big on Kauai, only no one will say that dreaded word. It conjures up slick salesmen from the 1970s hustling people on the beach with promises of nearly free vacations in Hawaii if you just sign on the dotted line. Timeshares denote a condominium project that sells the same unit to several owners, who are allotted a "time" when they can visit the unit. Today, timeshare projects have gone upscale in Hawaii; major resorts like Marriott, Westin, Hilton, and Shell are now building mega-resorts with top-notch units, all furnished with the same top-drawer furniture and equipped with the best electronics and kitchen equipment. But they never, *never,* call them timeshares. The new, politically correct term is "vacation owner-ship"—but the idea is the same: Several owners have a share in the unit and are allotted a certain amount of time every year (from a week to a month) to stay in the unit. These respectable management companies make sure that the unit is well maintained and even rent out the units if none of the owners wishes to stay there. Sometimes you can get "deals" at the various "vacation ownerships" because, quite frankly, they are trying to get you to buy the place (or at least a share in the unit). So guests are offered everything from a free snorkeling trip to a free vacation in Hawaii, if you are willing to sit through a sales pitch. All this is great, as long as you know what you are getting into. The so-called "45-minute" pitch may last all morning, and the sales pressure may not be your idea of a tranquil vacation. So buyer beware; even in paradise there are no free lunches (or breakfasts, or snorkeling trips).

410 Papaloa Rd., Kapaa, HI 96746. ✆ **800/OUTRIGGER** or 808/822-4938. Fax 808/822-1022. www.outrigger.com. 57 units. $215–$295 1-bedroom for 4; $234–$355 2-bedroom for 6. Roll-away bed/crib $15. 2-night minimum. AE, DC, DISC, MC, V. **Amenities:** Oceanfront outdoor pool; complimentary tennis courts; coin-op washer/dryers. *In room:* TV, dataport, kitchen, fridge, coffeemaker, iron.

MODERATE

Aloha Beach Resort *Kids*   Formerly the SunSpree Resorts, a division of Holiday Inn which emphasizes moderate rates and lots of free activities for families, the Aloha Beach is now under new ownership. The result is a family-friendly choice located right next door to Lydgate Beach Park (with Kamalani Playground for the kids) and convenient to nearby golfing. Kids 12 and under eat free when dining with a parent in the restaurant and ordering from the *keiki* (child) menu. The new management is focusing on the ecological and cultural aspects of the resort with activities like free cultural presentations in the lobby, displays by Hawaiian artists, a buffet featuring "local" food, and other events.

3-5920 Kuhio Hwy., Kapaa, HI 96746. ✆ **888/823-5111** or 808/823-6000. Fax 808/823-6666. www.abrkauai.com. 216 units. $198–$231 unit for up to 4; $258 suite for up to 4; 2-room cottages $363 for 4. Roll-away beds/cribs $15. Additional adult $10. Children 18 and under stay free in parent's room. Check the Internet for specials. AE, DC, DISC, MC, V. **Amenities:** 2 restaurants; bar; 2 outdoor pools; complimentary tennis courts; small fitness room; Jacuzzi; snorkel gear ($5/day); activities desk; babysitting; coin-op washer/dryers; laundry/dry cleaning. *In room:* A/C, TV/VCR, dataport, high-speed Internet access in some rooms, fridge, coffeemaker, hair dryer, iron, safe.

Courtyard by Marriott Kauai–Waipouli Beach ⋆ After 18 months and more than $23 million in renovations, the old Kauai Coconut Beach Resort reopened as the Courtyard by Marriott Kauai–Waipouli Beach in 2005. Located just 10 minutes from Lihue Airport in the town of Waipouli, the totally refurbished 311-room resort sits on 10.5 acres, nestled between a coconut grove and a white-sand beach. The convenient location not only is close to shopping and visitor attractions along the Coconut Coast, but also is centrally positioned on the island for easy access to the North Shore and the Poipu Beach area on the south shore.

The remodeled resort features a new swimming pool, hot tub, day spa, business center, fitness center, tennis courts, jogging paths, lounge (with nightly entertainment), and restaurant (Voyager Grille Steak and Seafood). The resort has kept the award-winning Hawaiian luau by Tihati Productions, with dinner and show Tuesday through Sunday evenings. Patrons of the old Kauai Coconut Beach Resort will hardly recognize the new, enlarged lobby and entry way. The large guest rooms have been gutted and redecorated with a Hawaiian theme and include such amenities as hardwood furniture, a 27-inch television, and complimentary wireless Internet access.

1-484 Kuhio Hwy, Kapaa, HI 96746. ☎ 800/760-8555 or 808/822 3455. Fax 808/822-0035. www.marriott.com. 311 units. $229–$449 double. Extra person $25. Children 17 and under stay free in parent's room. AE, DC, DISC, MC, V. **Amenities:** Full-service restaurant and bar; outdoor pool; golf nearby; tennis nearby; Jacuzzi; activities desk; room service; jogging path; coin-op washer/dryers; laundry/dry cleaning. *In room:* A/C, TV/VCR, dataport, complimentary wireless Internet access, voice mail, fridge, coffeemaker, iron, hairdryer, safe.

Mahina Kai *(Finds)* Mahina Kai ("moon over the water") is a traditional Japanese villa (complete with teahouse next door) on 2 landscaped acres just across the road from one of the most picturesque white-sand beaches on Kauai. Three rooms in the main house come complete with shoji screen doors, private bathrooms and lanais, use of the gorgeous living room (with fishpond, vintage Hawaiian furniture, and views of Japanese gardens and Aliomanu Beach), and shared kitchenette. Although this place is undeniably unique, the rooms are tiny and sparsely furnished (no TVs or phones), and the walls are paper-thin. Also available are a large one-bedroom suite with private entrance, and a separate cottage (with kitchenette) next to the saltwater pool. Landscaped into the gardens are a lagoon-style pool and a hot tub. Sitting in the hot tub, listening to the surf across the street, and watching the stars move slowly across the sky, you're pretty darn close to heaven on earth.

4933 Aliomanu Rd. (off Kuhio Hwy. at mile marker 14). c/o P.O. Box 699, Anahola, HI 96703. ☎ 800/337-1134 or 808/822-9451. www.mahinakai.com. 5 units. $165–$295 double. Rates include continental breakfast. 3-night minimum. MC, V. **Amenities:** Saltwater lagoon-like swimming pool; hot tub; massage available. *In room:* No phone.

INEXPENSIVE

Alohilani Bed & Breakfast ⋆ *(Finds)* Owner Sharon Mitchell has furnished her B&B, which sits amid 6 peaceful acres at the very end of a country road, with antiques and other beautiful pieces. The B&B's separate cottage is a large room decorated in country charm with full kitchen, sleeper sofa, and adorable antique bed with its own teddy bear. Our favorite suite is the open, airy Sunshine Atrium, with its floor-to-ceiling windows and arched French glass doors opening onto a lanai that overlooks the entire valley. The white-tiled room has a queen bed, a sleeper sofa, and a microwave.

1470 Wanaao Rd., Kapaa, HI 96746. ☎ 800/533-9316 or 808/823-0128. Fax 808/823-0128. www.hawaiilink.net/~alohila. 3 units. $109–$119 double suite; $119 double cottage. Rates include continental breakfast. Extra person $10. 3-night minimum. MC, V. From Kuhio Hwy. (Hwy. 56), turn left onto Kawaihau Rd.; go about 4 miles, then turn left again on Wanaao Rd. *In room:* TV, kitchenette, fridge, coffeemaker, hair dryer, no phone.

Hale Lani Bed & Breakfast ★★ (Value)   This *hale* is a terrific find that offers great value. The four units (two with their own private hot tubs) all have private entrances, patio, full kitchens, comfy pillow-top queen beds, TV/DVD and stereo, plus complimentary breakfast (hot breakfast, fruit, juice) waiting for you outside your unit (pick it up when you want) every morning, setting this B&B apart from the rest. The units are exquisitely decorated in tropical colors and furniture. The hosts couldn't be nicer or more accommodating.

283 Aina Lani Pl., Kapaa, HI 96746. (C) **877/423-6434** or 808/823-6434. www.halelani.com. 4 units. $105–$150. Rates include continental breakfast. 3-night minimum. AE, DC, MC, V. **Amenities:** Barbecue area, complimentary snorkel equipment, boogie boards, fins, beach chairs and beach towels. *In room:* Hot tub (2 units), TV/VCR/DVD, fridge, coffeemaker, iron, hairdryer.

Hotel Coral Reef (Value)   Here's a budget choice right on the beach. This small, older hotel faces a grassy lawn, coconut trees, and a white-sand beach. Don't expect the Hyatt, but at these prices and this location it's a great way for frugal travelers to enjoy the beach. It offers economical rooms and friendly service in an ideal location, within walking distance of shops, restaurants, golf, and tennis, and just 50 yards away from good swimming and snorkeling. There's even an 8-mile bike path that starts right on the grounds. Of the two wings in the hotel, we prefer the oceanfront one which has big rooms that overlook the beach through sliding-glass lanai doors. Each two-room unit has a separate bedroom and a living room with a sofa bed—perfect for families. Some of the rooms are well used (and some a bit worn). Linda Warriner, owner and gracious hostess of this hotel, is always happy to give you pointers on how to stretch your budget and still have a good time on Kauai.

1516 Kuhio Hwy. (at the northern end of Kapaa, between mile markers 8 and 9), Kapaa, HI 96746. (C) **800/843-4659** or 808/822-4481. Fax 808/822-7705. www.hotelcoralreef.com. 21 units. $89–$149 double; from $159 suite. Extra person $25. Children 12 and under stay free in parent's room. Room/car packages available. AE, DC, MC, V. **Amenities:** Activities desk; coin-op washer/dryers. *In room:* A/C, TV, fridge, coffeemakers, safes (in oceanfront rooms).

Inn Paradise (Finds)   Out in the country, about a 10- to 15-minute drive from the beach, Inn Paradise is a plantation-style building with a wraparound lanai that houses three guest units on 3½ landscaped acres. The units range from the one-room "Prince," with a tiny kitchenette tucked away in a closet; to the large, two-bedroom "King," which has a full kitchen. Carefully decorated rooms with sparkling tile floors and a quiet, relaxing ambience come together to make this property a good budget choice. The large deck overlooks the flower-filled grounds and a valley dotted with fruit trees beyond. A bonus is the hot tub for soaking after a long day of sightseeing.

Makana Rd., Kapaa. Reservations: c/o Hawaii's Best Bed-and-Breakfasts, P.O. Box 563, Kamuela, HI 96743. (C) **800/ 262-9912** or 808/885-4550. Fax 808/885-9912. www.bestbnb.com. 3 units. $70–$95 double. Rates include welcome basket with fruit, juice, cereal, bread, or muffins. Extra person $10. 2-night minimum. No credit cards. **Amenities:** Hot tub; washer and dryer. *In room:* TV, kitchen, fridge, coffeemaker.

Kakalina's Bed and Breakfast (Finds)   Nestled in the foothills of Mount Waialeale, about a 10-minute drive from the beach, is this 3-acre flower farm and bed-and-breakfast. You can just imagine the view: flowers, flowers, and more flowers. The most popular unit is Hale Akahi, a two-room unit located beneath Kathy and Bob Offley's round home, on the ground floor. You enter through an enclosed wooden porch, which has a spectacular view of the verdant valley; the apartment is decorated in white wicker furniture with brilliant tropical flowers splashing color throughout. The views are breathtaking and the king bed is comfortable, but the draw here is the bathroom:

A huge, blue-tiled tub, big enough to soak in and surrounded by green plants, makes this unit one of a kind. Also on the property, in a separate cottage, is Hale Elua, a studio with a queen bed, a full kitchen, and a breakfast nook with a view of the flower gardens, a mountain lake, and the ocean in the distance; a queen-size futon can accommodate extra guests. A third unit with a separate bedroom has a full kitchen, so breakfast is not included.

6781 Kawaihau Rd., Kapaa, HI 96746. ⓒ 800/662-4330 or 808/822-2328. Fax 808/823-6833. www.kakalina.com. 3 units. $90–$155 double. Rates include continental breakfast in 2 units. Extra person $15. 2-night minimum. MC, V (with 5% processing fee). Turn left off Kuhio Hwy. (Hi. 56) onto Kawaihau Rd. and go 4½ miles. **Amenities:** Activity desk; car-rental desk; laundry service. *In room:* TV/VCR, kitchen, fridge, coffeemaker, hair dryer, iron, no phone.

Kapaa Sands ⓡ *Finds* This boutique establishment (just 24 units) offers condo units right on the ocean with all the comforts of home at bargain prices. Each unit is decorated by its owners, but they are all comfortable (some studio units have pull-down beds to take advantage of the living space) and have everything you need for a vacation. The bathrooms tend to be tiny, but the kitchens are roomy enough. Ask for a unit on the ocean; they cost a bit more but are worth it. On-site amenities include a freshwater swimming pool, laundry facilities, maid service, and a very friendly staff happy to advise on where to eat and what to do.

380 Papaloa Rd., Kapaa, 96746. ⓒ **800/222-4901** or 808/822-4901. Fax 808/822-1556. www.kapaasands.com. 24 units. $110–$128 studio double; $147–$168 2-bedroom units for 4. Extra person $10. 3-night minimum Dec. 15–March 15. MC, V. **Amenities:** Swimming pool, barbecue area, laundry facilities, maid service. *In room:* TV, kitchens, fridge, microwave, coffeemaker, dishwasher.

Kapaa Shores ⓡ These apartments are located right on the beach in the heart of Kapaa. Even the budget units have partial views of the ocean, but oceanfront units are available for a bit more money. The one-bedrooms can comfortably sleep four, while the two-bedrooms can sleep as many as six (the sofa in each unit pulls out into a queen-size bed). All units are in excellent shape and come with fully equipped modern kitchens and large lanais where you can enjoy a sunrise breakfast or sunset cocktails. On-site amenities include a large pool, a tennis court, a family-size hot tub, a shuffleboard court, laundry facilities, and barbecues. Golf courses, restaurants, and bars are nearby.

900 Kuhio Hwy. (between mile markers 7 and 8). Reservations: c/o Garden Island Properties, 4–928 Kuhio Hwy., Kapaa, HI 96746. ⓒ **800/801-0378** or 808/822-4871. Fax 808/822-7984. www.kauaiproperties.com. 84 units. $115–$125 1-bedroom; $140–$163 2-bedroom. 5-night minimum. MC, V. **Amenities:** Outdoor pool; complimentary tennis courts; Jacuzzi; salon; coin-op washer/dryers. *In room:* TV/VCR or TV/DVD, dataport (some rooms), kitchen, fridge, coffeemaker, iron.

Kauai Country Inn ⓡⓡ *Finds* Run to the phone right now and book this place! Hard to believe that nestled in the rolling hills behind Kapaa, this old fashioned country inn exists. Not only does it exist, but hosts Mike and Martina Hough, refugees from the fast life of running an international advertising agency in Los Angeles, have taken their considerable creative talents and produced a slice of paradise on 2 acres. Each of the four suites is uniquely decorated in Hawaiian Art Deco with a touch of humor, complete with hardwood floors, private baths, kitchen or kitchenette, your own computer with high speed connection, and lots of little amenities that will make you break out into laughter at the Hough's sense of humor. Everything is top drawer from the furniture to the subzero refrigerator. They recently added a two-bedroom country cottage for families with young children. The grounds are immaculate, and you can pick as much organic fruit as you want from the abundance of mango, guava, lilikoi, starfruit, oranges, and lemons. Beatles fans take note: Mike has been collecting memorabilia for decades and has the only private Beatles Museum in the state (including a Mini Cooper S car owned by Brian Epstein, the Beatles manager; original paintings by John Lennon; and a host of books, records, movies, tapes, T-shirts, and other interesting and unusual rare items). And for those missing the family pooch, Annie, the staff golden retriever personally greets each guest like her long lost friend.

6440 Olohena Rd., Kapaa, HI 96746. © 808/821-0207. www.kauaicountryinn.com. 4 units and 1 2-bedroom cottage. $95–$145 1- and 2-bedroom suites double; $245 2-bedroom cottage for 6. $15 extra person in suites. 3-night minimum suites; 5-night minimum cottage. Discount car rentals available. AE, MC, V. In room: TV/VCR/DVD, computer with high-speed Internet connection, kitchen or kitchenette, fridge, coffeemaker, iron, hair dryer.

Kauai Sands These modest motel-style accommodations will do just fine for budget travelers who want a basic, clean room with a central location. Right on the ocean, next door to the Coconut Marketplace, the Kauai Sands is located near tennis courts and a golf course. The small rooms have simple furniture (two doubles or twin beds), ceiling fans, and small refrigerators; most have tiny lanais.

420 Papaloa Rd., Kapaa, HI 96746. © 800/560-5553 or 808/822-4951. Fax 808/882-0978. www.sand-seaside.com. 200 units. $125–$160 double. Packages available including car and room for 2 are just $99. MC, V. **Amenities:** Restaurant; bar; 2 small outdoor pools; exercise room; coin-op washer/dryers. In room: A/C, TV, kitchenette (some units), fridge.

Lani-keha ★ (Finds) Step back in time to the 1940s, when old Hawaiian families lived in open, airy, rambling homes on large plots of land lush with fruit trees and sweet-smelling flowers. This gracious age is still alive and well in Lani-keha, a *kamaaina* (old-timer) home with an open living/game/writing/dining room, with oversize picture windows to take in the views, and bedrooms with private bathrooms. The house is elegant yet casual, with old-style rattan furniture—practicality and comfort outweigh design aesthetics. The large communal kitchen has everything a cook could want, even a dishwasher. All the guests share the TV/VCR and single phone in the living area.

848 Kamalu Rd. (Hwy. 581), Kapaa, HI 96746. © 800/821-4898 or 808/822-1605. Fax 808/822-2429. www. lanikeha.com. 3 units. $65 double. Rates include continental breakfast. Extra person $15. 3-night minimum. No credit cards. From Kuhio Hwy. (Hwy. 56), turn left at the stoplight at Coco Palms onto Hwy. 580 (Kuamoo Rd.); go 3 miles; turn right at Hwy. 581 (Kamalu Rd.) and go 1 mile. **Amenities:** Washer/dryer. In room: No phone.

Mahina's Women's Guest House (Finds) Hostess Sharon Gonsalves has transformed this old plantation house into a warm, friendly place for women (only). The guests in the four bedrooms share the kitchen (no breakfast), living areas, and three bathrooms. The rooms are clean and functional, and Sharon adds fresh tropical flowers on your arrival. There is no phone or television in the house, but the beach is a 2-minute walk, and shops and restaurants are just 5 minutes away.

4433 Panihi Rd., Kapaa, HI 96746. © 808/823-9364. www.mahinas.com. 4 units. $75–$110 double. MC, V. **Amenities:** Shared kitchen. In room: No phone.

Mohala Ke Ola Bed & Breakfast Looking for a healthy, relaxing, rejuvenating vacation at frugal prices? Here's the place. Acupuncturist and massage therapist Ed Stumpf hosts this three-room B&B in a luxurious house with spectacular views of waterfalls and mountains in the residential area of Kapaa. He offers his services of various healing techniques that include acupuncture and Hawaiian lomilomi massage. The rooms are all light and airy with private baths. Complimentary breakfast (pastry, fruit, cereal, coffee, tea, and juice), a big swimming pool, and a Jacuzzi are the extras that make this place well worth the money.

5663 Ohelo Rd., Kapaa, HI 96746. (C) 888/GO-KAUAI or 808/823-6398. Fax 808/823-6398. www.waterfallbnb.com. 3 rooms. $100–$125 double. Rates include continental breakfast. Extra person $15. 3-night minimum. No cards. **Amenities:** Pool, Jacuzzi, washer and dryer (fee). *In room:* A/C (just 1 room), TV/VCR/DVD, free wireless connection, shared use of kitchen.

Rosewood Bed & Breakfast ✦ (Finds

This lovingly restored century-old plantation home, set amid tropical flowers, lily ponds, and waterfalls, has accommodations to suit everyone. There's a Laura Ashley–style room in the main house along with two private cottages: one a miniature of the main house, with oak floors and the same Laura Ashley decor; the other a little grass shack set in a tropical garden, with an authentic thatched roof and an outside shower. There's also a bunkhouse with three separate small rooms with a shared shower and toilet. Hostess Rosemary Smith also has a list of other properties she manages. *Note:* Smoking is not permitted on the property.

872 Kamalu Rd., Kapaa, HI 96746. (C) 808/822-5216. Fax 808/822-5478. www.rosewoodkauai.com. 7 units (3 with shared bathroom). $85 double in main house (includes continental breakfast); $45–$55 double in bunkhouse; $115–$150 cottage double (sleeps up to 4); $135 2-bedroom cottage (sleeps 4); $200 3-bedroom home (sleeps 6) Extra person $15. 3-night minimum. No credit cards. From Kuhio Hwy. (Hwy. 56), turn left at the stoplight at Coco Palms onto Hwy. 580 (Kuamoo Rd.); go 3 miles; at junction of Hwy. 581 (Kamalu Rd.), turn right; go 1 mile and look for the yellow house on the right with the long picket fence in front. *In room:* No phone. *In cottages:* TV, kitchen, fridge, coffeemaker, hair dryer, iron, no phone. *In bunkhouse:* Kitchenette, fridge, coffeemaker, no phone.

Royal Garden Cottages (Finds

Down a quiet private road in beautiful Wailua (just minutes from the beaches and the Wailua River) lies a little bit of paradise: three cozy, comfortable houses surrounded by lush gardens and flowering fruit trees. The two cottages have twin beds that can be combined into one king, well-equipped kitchenettes, ceiling fans, and garden views. One cottage has a TV and phone; the other is for those looking to get away from the distractions of the outside world. There's also a unit in the main house with two bedrooms and two bathrooms. Guests are encouraged to pick all the bananas, avocados, breadfruit, pomelos, and lemons they can eat.

147 Royal Dr. (off Hi. 580), Kapaa, HI 96746. (C) 808/245-5758. Fax 303/444-5931. www.royaldrive.com. 3 units (2 with shower only). $85 double cottage; $110 2-bedroom house for 2, $125 for 4, $140 for 6. Children 15 and younger stay free. Additional cleaning fee: $50 cottage, $75 house. 3-night minimum in cottage, 4-night in house. No credit cards. From Kuhio Hwy. (Hi. 56), turn left at the stoplight at Coco Palms on to Hi. 580 (Kuamoo Rd.); go 2.8 miles and turn left on Royal Drive. **Amenities:** Complimentary use of laundry facilities. *In room:* TV/VCR, kitchen, fridge, coffeemaker, iron.

Wailua Bayview ✦ (Value

Located right on the ocean, these spacious one-bedroom apartments offer excellent value. All units have ceiling fans, full kitchens (including microwave and dishwasher), washer/dryers, and large lanais. Some have air-conditioning as well. The bedrooms are roomy, and the sofa bed in the living room allows you to sleep up to four. Several of the units were renovated in 1998 with new carpet and reupholstered furniture. Some of the $110 garden units are close to the road and can be noisy; ask for one with air-conditioning, which generally drowns out the street sounds. The oceanview units are more expensive but still a great deal. On-site facilities include a pool and barbecue area. Restaurants, bars, shopping, golf, and tennis are nearby.

320 Papaloa Rd., Kapaa, HI 96746. (C) 800/882-9007. Fax 425/391-9121. www.wailuabay.com. 45 units. $125–$150 double. Cleaning fee $85. Apr 15–June 14 and Sept 1–Dec 16, 7th night free. Discount car rentals available. MC, V. **Amenities:** Small outdoor pool; barbecue area. washer/dryers. *In room:* A/C (most units), TV/VCR, dataport, kitchen, fridge, coffeemaker, iron.

SUPER-CHEAP SLEEPS

Hibiscus Hollow ★ *Value*   Yes, Virginia, the price is $50. And no—there's nothing wrong with this place. It's the best budget buy not just in Kauai, but in the entire state of Hawaii. Book this place.

A one-bedroom unit attached to the main house in a residential area, Hibiscus Hollow has a living room (with queen-size sleeper couch); a separate bedroom; a kitchenette with refrigerator, coffeemaker, microwave, and everything you need to make and serve a meal; and a large lanai with picnic table and chairs, barbecue, and chaise lounge. The only drawback that we could find was the street noise—but at $50 a day, you'll be able to afford earplugs.

So what's the deal? Greg and Sue Liddle are nice people who think $50 is a fair price (and hundreds of happy guests agree with them). They moved to Kauai in 1990 and wanted a place where their customers could stay. (They're in the surfboard and dog-grooming businesses.) One thing led to another, and now they offer their cute cottage as a vacation rental. The Kapaa location is perfect: close to beaches, restaurants, trails, and shopping. If you stay for a week, the price drops—believe it or not—to $44 a night!

4906 Laipo Rd., Kapaa, HI 96746. ✆ 808/823-0925. www.hawaiian.net/~hollow. 1 unit (with shower only). $50 double. Extra person $10. 3-night minimum. No credit cards. From Kuhio Hwy. (Hi. 56), take the 1st left after Kapaa Fish and Chowder House (Hauaala St.), then go left again on Laipo Rd. *In room:* TV/VCR, kitchen, fridge, coffeemaker.

K. K. Bed & Bath *Value*   Attention, bargain hunters: If you are looking for an economical, no frills room close to the beach (just 1 block away), yet close to restaurants and shops in Kapaa, this is your place. This one-room unit, simple, yet functional, dates back to 1919, when Richard Kawamura's grandfather used it as the family warehouse for the general store around the corner. Richard's grandfather always dreamed of having a lodging house on his property. Richard made this dream come true with this practical 300-square-foot room, with a queen bed, small refrigerator, microwave, phone, TV, and fan. The separate bathroom is ADA compliant. Richard also is very active in the Kapaa Historical Society and leads weekly walking tours of this quaint old town. Reserve early because the word is out on this fabulous deal.

Kauwila St., Kapaa, HI 96746. ✆ 808/822-7348. www.kkbedbath.com. 1 unit. $40 single, $50 double, $60 triple. 3-night minimum. No credit cards. **Amenities:** Outdoor shower, free use of beach chairs, beach mats, beach towels. *In room:* TV, fan, refrigerator, microwave, coffee maker.

Kauai International Hostel *Value*   Located in the heart of Kapaa, a block from the beach, this hostel provides clean rooms in a friendly atmosphere. Guests are generally European backpackers. The low-rise building has a very clean kitchen and laundry facilities, a TV, a pool table, and a barbecue area; just 1 block from the highway, it's within walking distance of shops and restaurants. In addition to the bunk-bed dorm rooms, there are private rooms for two (with shared bathrooms). Airport pick-up is available ($10 for two, $15 for three). Long-term (a week or more) rates make this bargain hostel even more affordable.

4532 Lehua St. (off Kuhio Hwy.), Kapaa, HI 96746. ✆ 808/823-6142. www.hostels.com/kauaihostel. 30 bunk beds, 5 private rooms (shared bathrooms with showers only). $20 dorm single; $50 private double. MC, V. **Amenities:** Coin-op laundry facilities; community kitchen w/fridge and coffeemaker; community TV. *In room:* No phone.

Surf & Ski Cottage ★ *Value*   Even if you aren't a kayaking/water-skiing/watersports enthusiast, this is a fantastic place to stay. Right on the Wailua River, surrounded by fruit trees and tropical plants, Surf & Ski Cottage is an adorable 22-square-foot self-contained guesthouse. Essentially one large room (with a separate bathroom), the open, airy, high-ceilinged cottage has a complete kitchen, a TV, and a queen bed. Located close to the old Coco Palms Resort, the cottage is within walking distance of Kapaa's shops, restaurants, and beaches. Kenny and Kathy Terheggen, the owners of Kauai Water Ski & Surf (who also live on the property), are a wealth of information on nearly everything to do on Kauai. If you plan to play in the water, this is the place to stay—cottage guests get a 20% discount on all outdoor equipment and activities at Kauai Water Ski & Surf Co. (including water-skiing, kayaking, and surfing lessons, plus boogie board and snorkel rentals, and much more), which could really save you a lot of dough.

Ohana St. (in Wailua River Lots), off Hi. 580 (Kuamoo Rd.), Kapaa. Reservations: c/o Kauai Water Ski & Surf Co., 4-356 Kuhio Hwy., Kapaa, HI 96746. 🕐 800/344-7915 or 808/822-3574. Fax 808/822-3574. surfski@aloha.net. 1 cottage (with shower only). $65 double. 4-night minimum. AE, DC, DISC, MC, V. *In room:* TV, kitchenette, fridge, coffeemaker, hair dryer, iron.

5 The North Shore

Want to rent a rock star's treehouse? How about coochy-coochy entertainer Charo's beachfront estate? **Hanalei North Shore Properties** (🕐 **800/488-3336** or 808/826-9622; fax 808/826-1188; www.kauai-vacation-rentals.com) handles all kinds of weekly rentals—from beachfront cottages and condos to romantic hideaways and ranch houses—along the North Shore. Renting a home is a great way to enjoy the area's awesome nature, especially for those who like to avoid resorts and fend for themselves. Shopping, restaurants, and nightlife are abundant in nearby Hanalei. The company does not accept credit cards.

VERY EXPENSIVE

Princeville Resort Kauai *☆☆☆* *(Kids)* This resort is the jewel in the Sheraton crown, a palace full of marble and chandeliers. It enjoys one of the world's finest settings, between Hanalei Bay and Kauai's steepled mountains. Nearby are outstanding surfing and windsurfing areas, as well as a wonderful reef for snorkeling. The panoramic view from the lobby has to be the most dramatic vista from any hotel in the state. The Princeville is Kauai's most popular setting for weddings; more than 300 a year are performed outdoors by the pool.

This grand hotel steps down a cliff; the entrance is actually on the 9th floor, and you take elevators down to your room and the beach. Each opulent room has such extras as a door chime, dimmer switches, bedside control panels, a safe, original oil paintings, an oversize bathtub, and a "magic" bathroom window: a liquid-crystal shower window that you can switch in an instant from clear to opaque. There are no lanais, but oversize windows allow you to admire the awesome view from your bed.

In addition to a great children's program, this property has oodles of activities not only for children but for the entire family, from horseback riding to adventures exploring the island. The hotel grounds are a fantasy land for children (and some adults) with a huge swimming pool next to a sandy beach.

Other great amenities here: twice-daily fresh towels, daily newspaper, complimentary resort shuttle, comprehensive Hawaiiana program, riding stables, in-house cinema, arts program (from photography to painting), and a wealth of outdoor activities. Golfers may choose from two courses, both designed by Robert Trent Jones, Jr.; the whirlpools, steam baths, 35m (115 foot) lap pool, and multitude of treatments will delight spa-goers.

P.O. Box 3069 (5520 Kahaku Rd.), Princeville, HI 96722-3069. © **800/826-4400** or 808/826-9644. Fax 808/826-1166. www.princeville.com. 252 units. $465–$695 double; from $820 suite. Extra person $75. Children under 18 stay free in parent's room. AE, DC, DISC, MC, V. Parking $15. **Amenities:** 3 restaurants (1 w/excellent nightly entertainment; also see the review for La Cascata on p. 145); 3 bars; huge ocean-side outdoor pool; outstanding golf on 2 courses; 25 tennis courts; first-rate health club and spa; 3 outdoor Jacuzzis (including a really palatial one); watersports equipment rentals; bike rental; children's program; concierge; activities desk; car-rental desk; business center; shopping arcade; salon; 24-hr. room service; massage; babysitting; 24 hr. return laundry/dry cleaning. *In room:* A/C, TV, VCR available for rent, CD, dataport, minibar, fridge, coffeemaker, hair dryer, iron, safe.

EXPENSIVE

Hanalei Bay Resort & Suites 🌺🌺   This 22-acre resort is just up the street from ritzy Princeville Resort (see above), overlooking the fabled Bali Hai cliffs and Hanalei Bay. It has the same majestic view but for as little as half the price. The place recaptures the spirit of old Hawaii, especially in the three-story stucco units that angle down the hill to the gold-sand, palm-fringed beach it shares with its neighbor. Rooms are decorated in island style with rattan furnishings and lanais overlooking the bay, the lush grounds, and the distant mountains. Shuttle service is available for those who may have problems walking on the steep hillside.

The Happy Talk Lounge is one of our favorite places on Kauai for sunset cocktails, while the open-air restaurant, Bali Hai, has a view so distractingly gorgeous that you can hardly concentrate on the food.

P.O. Box 220 (5380 Honoiki St.), Princeville, HI 96722. © **800/827-4427** or 808/826-6522. Fax 808/826-6680. www.hanaleibayresort.com. 236 units. $185–$275 double; $240 studio with kitchenette (up to 4); $350–$390 1-bedroom apt (up to 4). Suites include full breakfast and afternoon cocktails. AE, DC, DISC, MC, V. **Amenities:** Restaurant; bar; 2 inviting outdoor freshwater pools; complimentary shuttle to Princeville Resort's top-ranked golf courses; 8 tennis courts, pro shop, and tennis school; Jacuzzi; concierge; activities desk; massage; babysitting; coin-op washer/dryers; laundry/dry cleaning. *In room:* A/C, TV, dataport, kitchenette, fridge, coffeemaker, hair dryer, iron, safe.

MODERATE

Aloha Sunrise Inn/Aloha Sunset Inn 🌺🌺 *Finds*   Hidden on the North Shore are these two unique cottages nestled on a quiet 7-acre farm with horses, fruit trees, flowers, and organic vegetables. We highly recommend both of these darling bungalows. Each is fully furnished with hardwood floors, top-of-the-line bedding, tropical island–style decor, complete kitchen, washer/dryer, and everything you can think of to make your stay heavenly (from all the great videos you have been meaning to watch to an excellent CD library). It's close to activities, restaurants, and shopping, yet far enough away to have the peace and quiet of the Hawaii of yesteryear. Hosts Allan and Catherine Rietow, who have lived their entire lives on the islands, can help you plan your stay, give you money-saving tips, and even hand out complimentary masks, snorkels, boogie boards, and other beach toys while pointing you to their favorite beaches. ***Note to parents:*** These cottages are not appropriate for children.

P.O. Box 79, Kilauea, HI 96754. © **888/828-1008** or 808/828-1100. Fax 808/828-2199. www.kauaisunrise.com. 2 1-bedroom cottages. $145–$170 double (plus a 1-time $60 cleaning fee). 3-night minimum. No credit cards. **Amenities:** Washer and dryer. *In room:* TV/VCR in 1 cottage, cable TV in other cottage, kitchen, fridge, coffeemaker, hair dryer, iron.

Hanalei Colony Resort 🌺 *Kids*   Picture this: A perfect white-sand beach just steps from your door, with lush tropical gardens, jagged mountain peaks, and fertile jungle serving as your backdrop. Welcome to Haena, Kauai's northernmost town and gateway to the famous Na Pali Coast, with miles of hiking trails, fabulous sunset views, and great beaches. This 5-acre resort is the place to stay if you're looking to experience

Where to Stay on Kauai's North Shore

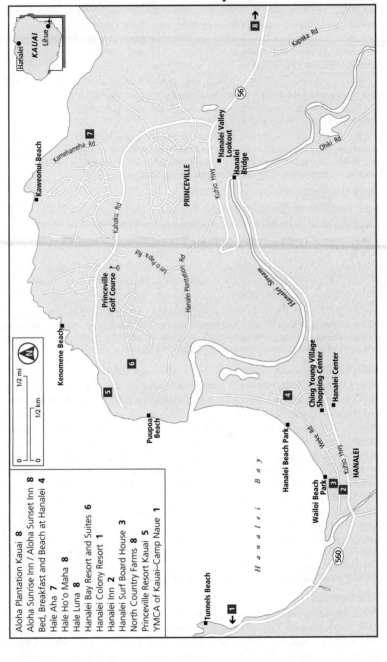

Aloha Plantation Kauai **8**
Aloha Sunrise Inn / Aloha Sunset Inn **8**
Bed, Breakfast and Beach at Hanalei **4**
Hale Aha **7**
Hale Ho'o Maha **8**
Hale Luna **8**
Hanalei Bay Resort and Suites **6**
Hanalei Colony Resort **1**
Hanalei Inn **2**
Hanalei Surf Board House **3**
North Country Farms **8**
Princeville Resort Kauai **5**
YMCA of Kauai–Camp Naue **1**

the magic of the enchanting North Shore. The units are unbelievably spacious—six people could sleep here comfortably—making them great for families. Each has a private lanai (the less-expensive budget units face the garden), a full kitchen, a dining area, a living room, and ceiling fans. (The area is blessed with cooling trade winds, so air-conditioning isn't necessary.) The atmosphere is quiet and relaxing: no TVs, stereos, or phones. The property has a large pool, laundry facilities, and a barbecue and picnic area. Guests have access to complimentary beach mats and towels, a lending library, and children's toys, puzzles, and games (plus badminton and croquet for the entire family). A spa and deli are next door.

5-7130 Kuhio Hwy. c/o P.O. Box 206, Hanalei, HI 96714. © 800/628-3004 or 808/826-6235. Fax 808/826-9893. www.hcr.com. 48 units. $210–$375 2-bedroom apt for 4. Rate includes continental breakfast once a week. 7th night free. Minimum 5 nights June 1–Sept 8 and Dec 20–Jan 4. Extra person $15. AE, MC, V. **Amenities:** Good-size outdoor pool; Jacuzzi; coin-op washer/dryers. *In room:* kitchen, fridge, coffeemaker, no phone.

INEXPENSIVE

Bed, Breakfast & Beach at Hanalei Bay *Finds*   On a quiet street in a residential area just 150 yards from Hanalei Bay lies one of the best deals on the North Shore. The three guest rooms in Carolyn Barnes's three-story house range from a 700-square-foot suite with a 360-degree view to a mini-apartment on the ground floor with a kitchenette and an outdoor shower. The location couldn't be better (some guests don't even bother to rent a car). It's a 4-minute walk to Hanalei Bay's 2-mile-long beach, and a 10-minute walk to the shops and restaurants of Hanalei. For families, Carolyn also has a cozy two-bedroom, one-bathroom house a couple of blocks away.

P.O. Box 748, Hanalei, HI 96714. © 808/826-6111. www.bestofhawaii.com/hanalei. 4 units. $85–$135 double room (includes continental breakfast); extra person $15. $1,000 a week for cottage (for 2); extra person $100 a week. 2- to 3-night minimum for rooms, 7-night minimum in cottage. No credit cards. *In room:* TV, no phone.

Hale 'Aha *Finds*   Golfers take note: This large home, which looks like something out of *Architectural Digest*, fronts 480 feet of the fairway and the 6th hole of the Makai Golf Course at Princeville. In addition to discounts on greens fees at both the Prince and the Makai courses, Hale 'Aha ("House of Gathering") offers luxury accommodations in a beautiful Princeville setting. The B&B is the dream of Herb and Ruth Bockleman. They've thought out every detail, even designing their guest rooms so that none have adjoining walls, thereby ensuring all their visitors peace and privacy. The four rooms range from the well-priced Bali Hai Room, with an ocean view, a private entrance, and a refrigerator; to the Penthouse Suite, where you can splurge in the 1,000-square-foot suite with a whirlpool tub in the bathroom, a private lanai, its own washer/dryer, and 360-degree panoramic views of the golf course, mountains, and ocean. Not appropriate for children.

3875 Kamehameha Dr. (the 3rd street on the right past the entrance to Princeville), P.O. Box 3370, Princeville, HI 96722. © 800/826-6733 or 808/826-6733. Fax 808/826-9052. www.kauai-bandb.com. 4 units. $135–$145 double; $205–$300 suite. Extra person $25. Rates include continental breakfast. 3-night minimum. DISC, MC, V. **Amenities:** Laundry service. *In room:* A/C, TV/VCR, kitchenette (in suite), fridge, coffeemaker (in suite), hair dryer, iron.

Hale Luana *Finds*   Tucked into the hills of Kilauea is this 5-acre property, with two B&B rooms available inside an architect-designed home, as well as a five-bedroom vacation rental. The light and airy rooms have several great conveniences like a microwave, refrigerator, coffee maker, huge TV/VCR, and ocean views. Breakfast (banana/macadamia nut pancakes, tarragon baked eggs, or pecan waffles) is served outside on the lanai overlooking the 50-foot-long swimming pool. Tropical foliage landscapes the area around the home as well as acres of the working fruit farm (avocado, banana, papaya, and grapefruit). Guests are welcome to the plentiful supply of beach toys (snorkel, masks, fins, boogie boards). Also on the property is a five-bedroom vacation rental, which sleeps 14 for $2,300 a week.

4680 Kapuna Rd., Kilauea, HI 96754. ✆ **808/828-6784.** Fax 808/828-1564. www.haleluana.com. 2 rooms. $99 double, includes breakfast. 3-night minimum. MC, V. **Amenities:** Pool, complimentary beach toys, barbecue, washer/dryer. *In room:* TV/VCR, microwave, fridge, coffeemaker, hair dryer, iron.

Hanalei Surf Board House 🂁🂁 *(Finds*   Book now, because this place is so fabulous it will go fast! Just a block from the beach, these two incredibly decorated studio units are a steal at $150. Host Simon Potts is a former record company executive from England who thinks he has retired to Hawaii. He's the hardest working retired guy we have ever met. The first thing he did was ask the kids he coaches in soccer if they had any old surfboards; he even offered them a few bucks. Potts got enough surfboards to line them all standing up next to each other, to create the most unusual fenced-in yard in Hawaii. Next, Potts turned to decorating: one studio is filled with whimsical "cowgirl" decor, and the other in pure Elvis Presley memorabilia. Both units have kitchenettes, 300-channel televisions, free high-speed Internet access, DVD, barbecues, and backyard lanais. But the best reason to stay here (besides the 2-minute walk to either the beach or downtown Hanalei) is Simon himself; his stories about the record industry will keep you howling with laughter for hours.

5459 Weke Rd., Hanalei, HI 96714. ✆ **808/826-9825.** simon.potts@verizon.net. 2 units. $150 double. 2-night minimum. No cards. *In room:* TV, DVD, kitchenette, fridge, coffeemaker, free high-speed Internet connection.

North Country Farms 🂁 *(Kids*   In the rolling green hills outside of Kilauea, on a 4-acre organic vegetable, fruit, and flower farm, Lee Roversi and her family have a private, handcrafted redwood cottage for rent. This restful spot is an excellent choice, both in terms of comfort and value, especially for a family. The cottage has hardwood floors, a large lanai with garden views, a compact kitchenette for cooking (Lee stocks fruit, juice, muffins, croissants, fresh eggs, coffee, and tea for breakfast), and a separate bedroom with a beautiful Hawaiian quilt on the queen bed. The couch in the living room turns into two separate beds, so the cottage can easily sleep four. (Children are welcome.) Outside is another shower for washing off sand from the beach. The only thing the cottage lacks is a TV, but since it's so close to beaches, hiking, shopping, and restaurants, you're likely to find yourself too tired at the end of the day to watch the tube anyway.

Kahlili Makai St. (P.O. Box 723, off Kuhio Hwy. at mile marker 22), Kilauea, HI 96754. ✆ **808/828-1513.** Fax 808/828-0805. 1 cottage. $120 double. Rate includes fixings for breakfast, plus fruits and veggies from organic farm. Extra person $5. Children under 16 stay free in parent's room. No credit cards. *In room:* Kitchen, fridge, coffeemaker, hair dryer, iron.

SUPER-CHEAP SLEEPS

Aloha Plantation Kauai *(Finds*   Step back in history at this 1920's plantation home (the oldest in Kilauea Village), where hosts Paul and Laurie have decorated it in impeccable old Hawaiian antiques. There are three units, ranging from an old garage converted into a 500-square-foot studio to two rooms in the main house. The rooms, both with very comfortable wrought-iron beds and ceiling fans, share a screen porch, with a coffee pot and an old 7-Up machine used as a refrigerator. One room has a half bath and shares a shower with the owner; the other room has its own full bathroom. In the courtyard is a cooking area with gas burner stove, barbecue, microwave, rice cooker, and refrigerator. The studio has air-conditioning, TV, phone, and CD, plus a private bath. The plantation is located just off the highway (some highway noise, but not much), about 15 minutes from Princeville and 20 minutes from Hanalei.

4481 Malulani St., Kilauea, HI 96754. © **877/658-6977** or 808/828-1693. www.garden-isle.com/aloha. 3 units. $69–$79 rooms double. $99 studio double. 2-night minimum. No cards. **Amenities:** Cooking area w/gas burner stove, barbecue, microwave, rice cooker, and refrigerator. In room: Studio only: A/C, TV, phone, CD.

Hale Ho'o Maha *(Finds)* Kirby Guyer and her husband, Toby, have a spacious four-bedroom, three-bathroom home on 5 acres. It's filled with Hawaiian and South Pacific artifacts and features a fireplace, library, and a 150-gallon saltwater aquarium (more entertaining than TV). The rooms are uniquely decorated and priced with budget travelers in mind. We recommend the Pineapple Room with its 7-foot round bed (with custom quilted pineapple spread and matching handmade area rug) and an ocean view from the large picture window. The landscaped grounds feature a stream and pond, and there's a waterfall across the street. Kirby has everything you need, from beach chairs to surfboards; you also have access to a complete kitchen. Within spitting distance are two remarkable white-sand beaches; also close by are golf courses, riding stables, restaurants, and markets. *Warning:* The property is next to the main highway; light sleepers may be bothered by traffic noise.

P.O. Box 422 (on Kalihiwai Rd., off Kuhio Hwy. at mile marker 24), Kilauea, HI 96754. © **800/851-0291** or 808/826-7083. Fax 808/826-7084. www.aloha.net/~hoomaha. 4 units (2 with shared bathroom). $75–$95 double. Rates include continental breakfast. Extra person $15. AE, DC, MC, V. **Amenities:** Complimentary use of laundry facilities. In room: TV, hair dryer.

Hanalei Inn Despite its very romantic-sounding name, the Hanalei Inn is an attempt at frugal accommodations in this very "high-end" neighborhood. Located on the sometimes noisy main highway, the "inn" is a series of old, very basic rooms (picture the spartan look of a youth hostel). The majority of rooms are small studios with a bed, small kitchenette, tiny bathroom, and TV—period. The rooms are clean, but unless you insist on staying in Hanalei and are unable to secure accommodations elsewhere, this would not be our first choice of accommodations. For those on a shoestring budget looking for stripped down accommodations, the Hanalei Inn has a few rooms which offer bed and bath only (no cooking facilities); they are even tinier than the already small units.

5-5468 Kuhio Hwy., Hanalei 96714. © **808/826-9333.** www.hanaleiinn.com. 4 units. $99 studio with kitchenette; $89 bed and bathroom only. MC, V. **Amenities:** Barbecue; pavilion; hammocks; coin-operated laundry facilities; pay phone. In room: TV, kitchenette, fridge, no phone.

YMCA of Kauai–Camp Naue *(Value)* Attention, campers, hikers, and backpackers: This is the ideal spot to stay before or after conquering the Na Pali Trail, or if you just want to spend a few days lounging on fabulous Haena Beach. This Y camp site sits right on the ocean, on 4 grassy acres ringed with ironwood and kamani trees and bordered by a sandy beach that offers excellent swimming and snorkeling in the summer (the ocean here turns really rough in the winter). Camp Naue has two bunkhouses overlooking the beach; each has four rooms with 10 to 12 beds. The facilities are coed, with separate bathrooms for men and women. There's no bedding here, so bring your sleeping bag and towels. Large groups frequently book the camp, but if there's room, the Y will squeeze you into the bunkhouse or offer tent space. Also on the grounds are a beachfront pavilion, and a campfire area with picnic tables. You can pick up basic supplies in Haena, but it's best to stock up on groceries and other necessities in Lihue or

Hanalei. Remember, this is the Y, not the Ritz: they only have one employee who handles all the bookings, plus everything else related to the Y activities. The best way to find out if they have space available is to call (*do not* e-mail, *do not* send a letter). The Y simply is not set up to answer mail. Instead, a few months before your trip, call and they will let you know if there is space in the camp site or if the bunk house will be available.

YMCA, P.O. Box 1786, Lihue, HI 96766. (✆) **808/246-9090**. On Kuhio Hwy., 4 miles west of Hanalei and 2 miles from the end of the road, Haena. 50 bunk beds (with shared bathroom), 1 cabin, tent camping. $12 per bunk; $12 tent camping. No credit cards.

6

Where to Dine

Dining in Kauai is an activity unto itself. Dining is not just eating (although you will find scrumptious meals created from locally grown, raised, or caught products), but an entire feast for the senses.

Dining on Kauai begins with views and decor. Resort areas will feast your eyes with romantic settings and panoramic ocean views. In Poipu, the Beach House and the restaurants at the Grand Hyatt Kauai Resort and Spa offer spectacular settings right on the beach that will linger in your memory long after you return home. In Hanalei, the restaurants at Princeville Resort look out onto an awe-inspiring vista of Hanalei Bay with cloud-shrouded, majestic peaks in the background.

Next on Kauai's sensuous dining experiences are the enticing aromas, especially at ethnic restaurants. Even if the cuisine is unfamiliar to you, your taste buds will be standing up to applaud at just the wonderful scents wafting out from the kitchen. Kauai offers a rainbow of different ethnic cuisines, from Asian and Polynesian to Mexican/Central American, European, and eclectic mixes.

Dining also means soothing sounds, from the strumming of a ukulele to the gentle rhythm of tumbling waves in the sand. In our reviews we note which restaurants feature live music, which is so important not only to the digestion, but also to the relaxing atmosphere that seems to calm the soul and makes the entire dining experience a banquet for the senses.

Best of all, dining on Kauai is a divine experience in tasting. Taste the familiar, the new, the exotic, and even the adventurous. I urge you to try at least one restaurant featuring cuisine you are totally unfamiliar with. Who knows, you may become enamored with it.

Don't pass up the small mom-and-pop places, the takeouts, the hole-in-the-wall eateries; some very fine food at very budget-pleasing prices comes out of these tiny places.

On your jaunt across the island, you'll find affordable choices in every town, from hamburger joints to *saimin* (noodles in broth topped with scrambled eggs, onions, and sometimes pork) stands to busy neighborhood diners. As long as you don't expect filet mignon on a fish-and-chips budget, it shouldn't be difficult to please both your palate and your pocketbook. But if you're looking for lobster, rack of lamb, or risotto to write home about, you'll find those pleasures, too.

For condo dwellers preparing your own meals, chapter 9 features a variety of markets and shops around Kauai—including some wonderful green markets and fruit stands—where you can pick up the island's best foodstuffs.

Restaurants listed in this chapter do not require reservations unless otherwise noted.

My, what an inefficient way to fish.

Ring toss, good. Horseshoes, bad.

Faster! Faster! Faster!

We take care of the fiddly bits, from providing over 43,000 customer reviews of hotels, to helping you find our best fares, to giving you 24/7 customer service. So you can focus on the only thing that matters. Goofing off.

* travelocity
You'll never roam alone.™

Where to Dine in Lihue

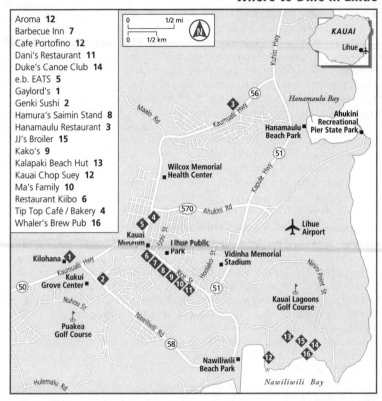

Aroma **12**
Barbecue Inn **7**
Cafe Portofino **12**
Dani's Restaurant **11**
Duke's Canoe Club **14**
e.b. EATS **5**
Gaylord's **1**
Genki Sushi **2**
Hamura's Saimin Stand **8**
Hanamaulu Restaurant **3**
JJ's Broiler **15**
Kako's **9**
Kalapaki Beach Hut **13**
Kauai Chop Suey **12**
Ma's Family **10**
Restaurant Kiibo **6**
Tip Top Café / Bakery **4**
Whaler's Brew Pub **16**

1 Lihue & Environs

You'll find the restaurants in this section on the "Where to Dine in Lihue" map above.

EXPENSIVE

Aroma 🎌🎌 *(Kids)* ECLECTIC/PACIFIC RIM   Chef/owner Robert Moler spent a considerable amount of time cooking for an interisland cruise ship and picked up a variety of cooking styles that he displays in his second-floor restaurant across the street from the ocean in the Harbor Mall. Open for mouthwatering breakfast (try the Cherry Hill French toast, which is French bread stuffed with dried cherries and cream cheese), hearty lunches (make reservations, as the local residents flock here during lunchtime), and dinner. Aroma has something for everyone on the menu, from pork osso buco to a vegetarian seared tofu tower to fresh island fish in a coconut-mint-orange beurre blanc sauce. The open-aired restaurant has a kids' menu (hamburgers, hot dogs, grilled barbecue chicken, and grilled cheese sandwiches). Don't be disappointed; make reservations for lunch and dinner.

Harbor Mall, 3501 Rice St. (across from the entrance to the Kauai Marriott), 2nd floor, Nawiliwili. ✆ **808/245-9192.** Reservations recommended. Main courses $3.75–$9.75 breakfast; $5.95–$11 lunch; $16–$24 dinner. AE, DC, DISC, MC, V. Thurs–Sun 8am–11am; Tues–Sun 11:30am–3pm; daily 5–9pm.

Gaylord's *&* CONTINENTAL/PACIFIC RIM   One of Kauai's most splendid examples of *kamaaina* architecture, Gaylord's is the anchor of a 1930s plantation manager's estate on a 1,700-acre sugar plantation. You'll enter a complex of shops, galleries, and a living room of Hawaiian artifacts and period furniture. The private dining room has a lavish table, always elegantly set as if Queen Liliuokalani were expected at any minute; another room accommodates private parties. The main dining room, which winds around a flagstone courtyard overlooking rolling lawns and purple mountains, serves American classics (New York steak, rack of lamb, prime rib) along with pasta, fresh seafood, and lavish desserts. The ambience, historic surroundings, and soothing views from the terrace make Gaylord's a special spot for lunch—salads, soups, fresh fish, Oliver Shagnasty's signature baby back ribs, burgers, sandwiches, and lighter fare predominate. Daily specials include international dishes such as kalua pork and Mexican fajitas, and fresh island fish in various cross-cultural preparations.

At Kilohana, 3-2087 Kaumualii Hwy., Lihue. © **808/245-9593.** www.gaylordskauai.com. Reservations recommended. Main courses $9–$12 lunch, $19–$30 dinner. AE, DC, DISC, MC, V. Mon–Sat breakfast buffet 7:45–9:45am and lunch 11am–3pm. Dinner daily 5:30–9pm; Brunch Sun 9:30am–3pm.

JJ's Broiler *&* AMERICAN   Famous for its Slavonic steak (tenderloin in butter, wine, and garlic), herb-crusted ahi, and the lazy Susan of salad greens that's brought to your table, JJ's is a lively spot on Kalapaki Bay with open-air dining and a menu that covers more than the usual surf-and-turf. We have found the service to be both laudable and lamentable, but the quality of the food is consistent. The coconut shrimp and Manila clams are big sellers, and the Mauna Kea scallops (which look like a mountain on a heap of rice with nori) are an imaginative twist on seafood. Lunchtime appetizers include potato skins, calamari rings, quesadillas, and wontons—the United Nations of pupu! The high ceilings, two-story dining, Kenwood Cup posters, and nautically designed rooms are enhanced by stellar views of the bay.

3416 Rice St., Nawiliwili. © **808/246-4422.** Reservations recommended for dinner. Lunch sandwiches $10–$15; dinner main courses $20–$30. DISC, MC, V. Daily 11am–10pm.

MODERATE

Barbecue Inn *&* AMERICAN/JAPANESE/PACIFIC RIM   Watch for the specials at this 65-year-old family restaurant, where everything from soup to dessert is made in the Sasakis' kitchen. You can get an inexpensive hamburger for lunch, but there are fancier specials on the wide-ranging menu. Complete dinners go for $9 to $24; entrees include grilled fresh ahi or ono and macadamia-nut chicken. The familiar favorites remain as well (oxtail soup, Japanese-style dinners, chow mein, and roast turkey). Locally grown organic greens are a big hit, and specialty salads are a welcome addition. Several-course dinner combinations of Japanese and American favorites draw long lines.

2982 Kress St. (off Rice St.), Lihue. © **808/245-2921.** Main courses $7–$13 lunch, $8–$24 dinner. MC, V. Mon–Thurs 7:30am–1:30pm and 5–8:30pm; Fri–Sat 7:30am–1:30pm and 4:30–8:45pm.

Café Portofino *&&* ITALIAN   For a romantic dinner with a harpist or classical guitarist strumming softly in the background, this candlelit restaurant offers authentic Italian cuisine at reasonable prices in a relaxing atmosphere. Owner Giuseppe Avocadi personally greets every guest and then checks again when you leave to make sure that your dining experience was impeccable. The menu lists appetizers ranging from ahi (or beef) carpaccio to the house special antipasto (with five different daily choices). But it's the pasta that will bring you back here a second time: These homemade dishes are so light you'd swear you could keep on eating all night. There's a dozen different dishes to choose from, plus the chef usually has a few new creations to make your decision all the harder. Also on the menu are fresh fish, a variety of chicken dishes, veal and beef dishes (from the traditional osso buco to scaloppini a la Marsala to chicken cacciatore), and a few items for vegetarians. Live music is featured every night.

Harbor Mall, 3501 Rice St. (across from the entrance to the Kauai Marriott), 2nd floor, Nawiliwili. ℂ 808/245-2121. Main courses $14–$26. Reservations recommended. MC, V. Daily 5–9pm.

Duke's Canoe Club ⚑ STEAK/SEAFOOD   It's hard to go wrong at Duke's. Part of a highly successful restaurant chain (including Duke's Canoe Club in Waikiki, and three similar restaurants on Maui), this oceanfront oasis is the hippest spot in town, with a winning combination of great view, affordable menu, attractive salad bar, popular music, and a very happy happy hour. The noontime bestseller is stir-fried cashew chicken, but the fresh mahi burger and the grilled chicken quesadilla are front-runners, too. The inexpensive fish tacos are a major attraction. The five or six varieties of fresh catch each night are a highlight and a great value. Hawaiian musicians serenade diners nightly, while downstairs in the Barefoot Bar traditional and contemporary Hawaiian music adds to the cheerful atmosphere. On Tropical Friday, tropical drinks go for under $5 from 4 to 6pm and live music stirs up the joint.

In the Kauai Marriott Resort & Beach Club, 3610 Rice St., Nawiliwili. ℂ 808/246-9599. Reservations recommended for dinner. Lunch $4–$11; dinner $8–$28. Taco Tuesdays 4–6pm, with $2.50 fish tacos and $2.50 draft beer. AE, DISC, MC, V. Barefoot Bar daily 11am–11pm; main dining room daily 5–10pm.

Whalers Brewpub ⚑ SEAFOOD   The brewpub, located where the road in to the Marriott ends at Ninini Point, opens to a view of Kalapaki Bay and the Kauai Lagoons golf course. The yellow-and-white wooden building hangs on a perch over the harbor, with gazebo-like decks that are a good place to be at sunset. (Check out the whales during the winter season.) The environment and the fare are both surf-and-turf, and appetizers rule: fried flowering onion with ranch dip, egg rolls, chicken skewers, and nachos. At lunch and dinner, diners gasp when the 20-ounce Whale of a Burger comes to the table with its giant bun, lettuce, sautéed onions, mushrooms, and cheeses, enough for two whale-size appetites. Fish and chips in beer batter are accompanied by Cajun coleslaw, and the house fresh fish comes with a choice of soy-ginger, fruit salsa, and lemon-thyme beurre blanc sauces. Steamed whole local snapper with shoyu and ginger, baby back ribs, fresh catch, and vegetarian lasagna are also available. On Sunday the beer brunch is a beer fest (all you can drink), with omelets, smoked salmon, and more seafood pub fare than you can shake a stick at. With live Hawaiian music on Tuesday, Friday, Saturday, and Sunday nights, it's a lively place all week.

In the Kauai Marriott Resort & Beach Club, 3132 Ninini Point. ℂ 808/245-2000. Reservations recommended. Main courses $15–$25 lunch, $17–$25 dinner. AE, DC, DISC, MC, V. Daily 11am–9pm.

INEXPENSIVE

Dani's Restaurant AMERICAN/HAWAIIAN   Formica all the way and always packed for breakfast, Dani's is the pancake palace of Lihue. Pancakes include banana, pineapple, papaya, and buttermilk, plus there are sweet-bread French toast and kalua-pig omelets. Regulars know that fried rice is offered on Thursday only and that the papaya hot cakes are always a deal. At lunch, Hawaiian specials—laulau, kalua pig, lomi salmon, and beef stew in various combinations—dominate the otherwise standard American menu of fried foods and sandwiches.

4201 Rice St., Lihue. ℂ 808/245-4991. Main courses $3.30–$8.50. MC, V. Mon–Fri 5am–1pm; Sat 5am–noon

Plate Lunch Palaces

If you haven't yet come face-to-face with the local phenomenon called *plate lunch,* Kauai is a good place to start. Like saimin, the plate lunch is more than a gastronomic experience—it's part of the local culture. Lihue is peppered with affordable plate-lunch counters that serve this basic dish: two scoops of rice, potato or macaroni salad, and a beef, chicken, fish, or pork entree—all on a single plate. Although heavy gravies are usually *de rigueur,* some of the less traditional purveyors have streamlined their offerings to include healthier touches, such as lean grilled fresh fish. Pork cutlets and chicken or beef soaked in teriyaki sauce, however, remain staples, as does the breaded and crisply fried method called *katsu,* as in chicken katsu. Most of the time, *fried* is the operative word; that's why it's best to be ravenously hungry when you approach a plate lunch, or it can overpower you. At its best, a plate lunch can be a marvel of flavors, a saving grace after a long hike; at its worst, it's a plate-sized grease bomb.

The following are the best plate-lunch counters on Kauai. How fortunate that each is in a different part of the island!

The **Koloa Fish Market,** 5482 Koloa Rd. (© **808/742-6199**), is in southern Kauai on Koloa's main street. A tiny corner stand with plate lunches, prepared foods, and two stools on a closet-sized veranda, it sells excellent fresh fish poke, Hawaiian-food specials, and seared ahi to go. It's gourmet fare masquerading as takeout. Daily specials may include sautéed ahi or fresh opakapaka with capers, and regular treats include crisp-on-the-outside, chewy-on-the-inside poi dumplings (when poi is available), one of life's consummate pleasures. For a picnic or outing on the south shore, this is a good place to start.

On the Hanamaulu side of Lihue, across the street from Wal-Mart, look for the prim, gray building that reads **Fish Express,** 3343 Kuhio Hwy. (© **808/ 245-9918**). It's astonishing what you'll find here for the price of a movie: Cajun-style grilled ahi with guava basil, fresh fish grilled in a passion-orange-tarragon sauce, fresh fish tacos in garlic and herbs, and many other delectables, all served with rice, salad, and vegetables. The Hawaiian plate lunch (laulau or kalua pork, lomi salmon, ahi poke, rice, or poi) is a top seller, as are the several varieties of smoked fish, everything from ahi to swordfish. The owners marinate the fish in soy sauce, sugar, ginger, and garlic (no preservatives), and smoke it with kiawe wood. The fresh fish specials, at $6.95, come in six preparations and are flavored to perfection. At the chilled counter you can choose freshly sliced sashimi and many styles of poke, from scallop, ahi, and octopus to exotic marinated crab. This is a potluck bonanza that engages even newcomers, who point and order while regulars pick up sweeping assortments of seafood appetizers on large platters. They're all fresh and at good prices, especially for Friday-afternoon *pau hana* (after-work) parties.

In east Kauai's Kapaa town, the indispensable **Pono Market,** 4–1300 Kuhio Hwy. (© **808/822-4581**), has similarly enticing counters of sashimi, poke, Hawaiian food, sushi, and a diverse assortment of take-out fare. It's known for its flaky *manju* (sweet potato and other fillings in baked crust), apple turnovers, sandwiches, excellent boiled peanuts, pork and chicken laulau, and plate lunches—shoyu chicken, sweet-and-sour spareribs, pineapple-glazed chicken, teriyaki fish, and so on. The potato-macaroni salad (regulars buy it by the pound for barbecues and potlucks) and roast pork are top sellers. Pono Market is as good as they come. If they're available, pick up some Taro Ko taro chips; they're made in Hanapepe, hard to find, and definitely worth hand-carrying home.

At **Mark's Place,** 1610 Haleukana St. in Puhi Industrial Park (© **808/245-2722**), just southwest of Lihue, island standards (Korean-style chicken, teriyaki beef, beef stew, chicken katsu) come with brown rice (or white) and salad for $5 or $5.50. The selection, which changes daily, always includes two salad and three entree choices as well as hot sandwiches (chicken, beef, and hamburgers) and the ever-popular bentos. Mark's is a take-out and catering operation, so don't expect table seating.

Lihue, the island's county and business seat, is full of ethnic eateries serving inexpensive plate lunches, everything from *bento* (rice with beef, chicken, or fish, arranged in a lidded box) to Hawaiian, Korean, and Chinese food. **Local Boy's Restaurant & Deli,** 3204 Kuhio Hwy (© **808/246-8898**), is a budget bonanza and a popular stop for jumbo-sized appetites. They offer generous servings of noodles (ramen, several types of chow mein, vegetarian fried noodles); barbecued chicken, beef, and spare ribs by the pound; sandwiches; mini- and regular- (big) sized plate lunches, and local favorites such as chili and beef stew. The Korean plate, a heroic serving of short ribs, chicken, and teriyaki beef, and kim chee for a mere $6.75, is very popular. The $4 mini-plate of teriyaki chicken is actually very large, and although the chicken is not boneless or skinless, it's quite tasty. **Po's Kitchen,** 4100 Rice St. (© **808/246-8617**), offers Japanese specials: cone sushi, chicken katsu, teriyaki beef plates, and bentos. One block away, **Garden Island BBQ,** 4252–A Rice St. (© **808/245-8868**), is the place for Chinese plate lunches and local staples such as barbecued or lemon chicken and teriyaki steak, as well as soups and tofu dishes.

In the Kukui Grove Center, at Kaumualii Highway (Hwy. 50) and Old Nawiliwili Road, **Joni-Hana** (© **808/245-5213**) is famous for its specials—nearly 20 a day! The tiny counter serves fried noodles, lemon-shoyu *ono* (wahoo), teriyaki everything, and many other local dishes. It's arguably the busiest place on the mall.

e.b.'s EATS ⚔ *Finds* AMERICAN/BAKERY   If you are on your way to the other side of the island and need a quick bite to eat or a cup of java to get you going, stop by this tiny bakery/deli/cafe which serves up a healthy breakfast and lunch at unbelievably low prices. The breakfast menu has an assortment of muffins, scones, bagels, and a quiche of the day. The offerings for lunch range from salads and sandwiches to entrees like pesto-crusted salmon, meatloaf, chicken cutlets, and lasagna. The local residents tend to take out, but there are a handful of tables to eat in. Save room for fruit tarts, chocolate bread pudding, or one of the other tasty desserts.

3-3142 Kuhio Hwy., Lihue. ℭ **808/632-0328.** All items under $9. No cards. Mon–Sat 7am–3pm.

Genki Sushi SUSHI   This affordable chain is a great place to take the kids: the sushi is inexpensive, and it's fun to select as it circulates the counter on a conveyor belt. Prices are based on the color of the plate containing the sushi: gold plates (which have items like tamago, a green salad, miso soup, and tofu) are $1.40, green (ahi poke, spicy tuna, mochi ice cream) $2, red (hamachi, ahi, ebi sushi) $3, silver (dragon roll) $3.75, and black (ahi sashimi, ikura, rainbow roll) $4.60. The sushi is continually made fresh and added to the conveyor belt.

Kukui Grove Shopping Center, 3-2600 Kaumualii Hwy., Lihue. ℭ **808/632-2450.** Sushi plates $1.40–$4.60. MC, V. Sun–Thurs 11am–9pm, Fri–Sat 10:30am–10pm.

Hamura's Saimin Stand ⚔ *Finds* SAIMIN   If there were a saimin hall of fame, Hamura's would be in it. It's a cultural experience, a renowned saimin stand where fans line up to take their places over steaming bowls of this island specialty at a few U-shaped counters that haven't changed in decades. The saimin and teriyaki barbecue sticks attract an all-day, late-night, pre- and post-movie crowd. The noodles come heaped with vegetables, wontons, hard-boiled eggs, sweetened pork, vegetables, and condiments. We love the casualness of Hamura's and the simple pleasures it consistently delivers.

2956 Kress St., Lihue. ℭ **808/245-3271.** Most items less than $5. No credit cards. Mon–Thurs 10am–11pm; Fri–Sat 10am–midnight; Sun 10am–9pm.

Hanamaulu Restaurant *Kids* CHINESE/JAPANESE/SUSHI   When passing this restaurant, you'd never know that serene Japanese gardens with stone pathways and tatami-floored teahouses are hidden within. You can dine at the sushi bar, American style, or in the teahouse for lunch or dinner (the teahouse requires reservations). At lunch enter a world of chop suey, wontons, teriyaki chicken, and sukiyaki (less verve than value), with many other choices in budget-friendly Japanese and Chinese plate lunches. Special Japanese and Chinese menus can be planned ahead for groups of up to 60 people, who can dine at low tables on tatami floors in a Japanese-garden setting. Old-timers love this place, and those who came here in diapers now stop in for after-golf pupu and beer.

3-4291 Kuhio Hwy., Hanamaulu. ℭ **808/245-2511.** Reservations recommended. Main courses $6–$15. MC, V. Tues–Fri 10am–1pm; daily 4:30–8:30pm.

Kako's ⚔ *Finds* SAIMIN   Wonderful home-cooked broth and noodles are Kako's signature. Kako's saimin was a west-side phenomenon for years until Hurricane Iniki turned out the lights, so saimin aficionados are ecstatic that this former Hanapepe fixture has reopened, this time in Lihue. After a long absence, the new installation—just as tiny and just as good as the original—is cause for applause. Owner Dorothea

Hayashi uses a secret recipe to make her broth from scratch, and the noodles, also house-made and fresh, are the perfect accompaniment. When teamed with her teriyaki chicken sticks, the saimin and wonton mein are pure heaven for noodle lovers. The saimin comes with a choice of toppings, such as barbecued chicken, cabbage, sliced eggs, and green onions. Old-fashioned, home-style hamburgers like Mom used to make, flavored with onions mixed into the patties, fly out the door at a miraculous $1.75.

2980 Ewalu St. ℂ 808/246-0404. Saimin $3–$5.50. No credit cards or checks. Mon–Sat 10:30am–2pm.

Kalapaki Beach Hut (Kids) AMERICAN   Tricky to find, but what a savings for your wallet! (*Hint:* Look for an anchor chain in front of a blue building.) Opened in 1990 by Steve and Sharon Gerald as Kalapaki Beach Burgers, the tiny eatery started adding more items and then evolved into serving breakfast. This "hut" has window service, a few tables downstairs, and more tables upstairs (with an ocean view out the screen windows). The basic fare is served on paper plates with plastic cutlery at cheap, cheap prices. Breakfasts are hearty omelets, pancakes, and numerous egg dishes. Lunches are heavy on the hamburgers (prepared 10 different ways), lots of sandwiches, a few healthy salads, and fish and chips. Kids get their own menu in a smaller portion size. This casual restaurant welcomes people in their bathing suits and slippers.

3474 Rice St., Nawiliwili. ℂ 808/246-6330. Breakfast $3.75–$6.50; lunch $3.95–$6.25. No cards. Daily 7am–7pm.

Kauai Chop Suey CANTONESE   This long-time Kauai favorite recently closed and then re-opened under new management. The huge menu has something for everyone: chow mein, Cantonese shrimp, roast duck, lemon chicken, and hundreds of choices of Cantonese noodles, soups, sweet-and-sours, foo-yongs, and stir-fries.

In the Harbor Mall, 3501 Rice St., Nawiliwili. ℂ 808/245-8790. Most dishes $6–$9. No credit cards. Tues–Sat 11am–2pm and 4:30–9pm; Sun 4:30–9pm.

Ma's Family (Finds) LOCAL/HAWAIIAN   This is a family affair, not only for the clients, but also for Ma, aka Akiyo Honjo, who works alongside her kids and grandkids in this tiny, off-the-beaten-track restaurant. The place is packed with local residents lining up for Ma's filling breakfast at super-cheap prices—coffee is free (something you don't see anymore in Hawaii). Ma's lunches include everything from hamburgers to local favorites (teriyaki beef, loco moco, and noodle dishes) to Hawaiian dishes like kalua pork and lomi salmon.

4277 Haleani St., Lihue. ℂ 808/245-3142. Most dishes under $6. No cards. Mon–Fri 5am–1:30pm, Sat–Sun 5–11:30 am.

Restaurant Kiibo (Finds) JAPANESE   Neither a sleek sushi bar nor a plate-lunch canteen, Kiibo is a neighborhood staple with inexpensive, unpretentious, tasty, home-style Japanese food served in a pleasant room accented with Japanese folk art. You can dine on sushi, ramen, sukiyaki, tempura, teriyaki, or the steamed egg-rice-vegetable marvel called *oyako donburi.* There are satisfying, affordable lunch specials and teishoku specials of mackerel, salmon, soup, dessert, and condiments.

299 Umi St., Lihue. ℂ 808/245-2650. Main courses $5–$19. No cards. Mon–Fri 11am–1:30pm; Mon–Sat 5:30–9pm.

Tip Top Café/Bakery (Kids) LOCAL   This small cafe/bakery (also the lobby for the Tip Top Motel) has been serving local customers since 1916. The best deal is their breakfast: Most items are $5 or under, and their macadamia pancakes are known throughout Kauai. Lunch ranges from pork chops to teriyaki chicken, but their specialty is oxtail

Lamperts Ice Crem
Koloa Fish Market

soup. For a real treat, stop by the bakery (where you pay your bill) and take something home (we recommend the freshly baked *malasadas*).

3173 Akahi St., Lihue. © **808/245-2333**. Breakfast items under $5; lunch entrees under $6. MC, V. Tues–Sun 6:30am–2pm.

2 The Poipu Resort Area

EXPENSIVE

The Beach House ★★★ HAWAII REGIONAL   The Beach House remains the south shore's premier spot for sunset drinks, appetizers, and dinner—a treat for all the senses. The oceanfront room is large, accented with oversize sliding-glass doors, with old Hawaii Regional favorites on the menu. Come for cocktails or early dinner, when you can still see the sunset and perhaps a turtle or two bobbing in the waves. The appetizer menu is enough to make a meal on. The menu changes daily and includes Kauai asparagus salad, seared crusted macadamia-nut mahimahi with miso sauce, sea scallops with lemon grass and kaffir lime, and the Beach House crab cake with mint sambal butter sauce and grilled tomato compote. "Local boy paella" features fresh seafood with home-style fried rice and seafood saffron broth. Desserts shine, too, like the molten chocolate desire—a hot chocolate tart served warm and wonderful; and the Kahlúa taro cheesecake—tangy, with lilikoi crème fraîche.

5022 Lawai Rd., Poipu. © **808/742-1424**. Reservations recommended. Main courses $19–$32. AE, DC, MC, V. Daily 5:30–9pm.

Casa di Amici ★★ ITALIAN/INTERNATIONAL   It was hard to see terrific Italian food leave the North Shore for the south, but hey, risotto happens. Chef Randall Yates and his wife, Joanna, took over a free-standing wood-and-stone building in Poipu and turned it into a storybook restaurant with fairy lights, high ceilings, beveled glass, and a generous open deck where you can dine among palms and heliotropes. (There's live classical music Fri and Sat 6:30 to 9:30pm on the baby grand piano.)

The memorable Italian food has strong Mediterranean and cross-cultural influences. You'll find organic greens from Kilauea, several risotto choices (quattro formaggio and smoked salmon are outstanding), black tiger prawns with ravioli of lobster thermidor, chicken Angelica (a favorite, served on farfalle), and surprises such as Thai lobster bisque and duck Kahlúa carbonara. Among the nearly two dozen pasta selections is a classic fettuccine Alfredo for which Yates is deservedly famous. While the set menu is Italian, the specials showcase international influences, such as soy-sauce reductions, furikake (seaweed sprinkle), and the assertive touches of jalapeño tequila aioli on salmon and grilled tiger prawns. This is flamboyant, joyful Italian fare. Casa di Amici is located in an enclave of condos and vacation rentals; to get there, take the third left turn past Brennecke's Beach, not more than 2 minutes from Poipu Beach Park.

2301 Nalo Rd., Poipu. © **808/742-1555**. Reservations recommended. Main courses $15–$20 for "light" size and $22–$25 for regular size. DC, MC, V. Daily 6pm–closing.

Dondero's ★★★ ITALIAN   If you are looking for a romantic dinner either under the stars overlooking the ocean or tucked away at an intimate table surrounded by inlaid marble floors, ornate imported floor tiles, and Franciscan murals, this is the place for you. You get all this atmosphere at Dondero's, plus the best Italian cuisine on the island, served with efficiency. It's hard to have a bad experience here. Our recommendations for a meal to remember: Start with either the fresh mozzarella cheese with tomatoes and roasted peppers, or the warm goat cheese, roasted eggplant, cannellini

Where to Dine in the Poipu Resort Area

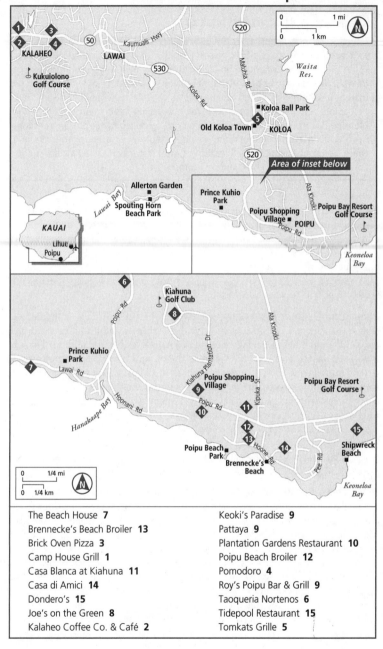

The Beach House **7**
Brennecke's Beach Broiler **13**
Brick Oven Pizza **3**
Camp House Grill **1**
Casa Blanca at Kiahuna **11**
Casa di Amici **14**
Dondero's **15**
Joe's on the Green **8**
Kalaheo Coffee Co. & Café **2**

Keoki's Paradise **9**
Pattaya **9**
Plantation Gardens Restaurant **10**
Poipu Beach Broiler **12**
Pomodoro **4**
Roy's Poipu Bar & Grill **9**
Taoqueria Nortenos **6**
Tidepool Restaurant **15**
Tomkats Grille **5**

⌒Moments A Taste of the Islands

Hawaii's Meadow Gold Dairies has just released a new product line of premium ice cream. This creamier, richer dessert is not for those counting calories but for those ice cream aficionados who are looking for a melt-in-your-mouth taste of Hawaii. We recommended the Kona coffee, macadamia nut, or honeydew melon. Traditionalists will go for the vanilla, chocolate, Neapolitan, rocky road, or cookies and cream. People who can't make up their minds will love the blended flavors like mint chocolate chip or the espresso fudge pie. Sherbet fans have two flavors to choose from: rainbow rapture or orange. You can find these ice creams in the frozen section of most supermarkets across the island. For more information: www.lanimoo.com.

---

beans, and fried basil leaves. Then move on to the black-ink linguine with scallops, shrimp, mussels, salmon, clams, and lobster; the risotto with porcini mushrooms and taleggio cheese; or the grilled snapper with roasted vegetables and balsamic glaze. Save room for dessert, especially the chocolate crème brûlée with fresh berries. Dinners are pricey but worth every penny.

Grand Hyatt Kauai Resort and Spa, 1571 Poipu Rd., Poipu. ℭ **808/742-1234.** Reservations a must. Main courses $18–$36. AE, DC, DISC, MC, V. Tues–Sat 6–10pm.

Plantation Gardens Restaurant ℱ HAWAII REGIONAL   The Plantation Gardens Restaurant is a mix of irresistible garden ambience and a well-executed menu fashioned around fresh local ingredients and a respect for island traditions. The fish is from local waters, and many of the fruits, herbs, and vegetables are grown on the restaurant premises. You can make a meal out of the baby back barbecue ribs appetizer. The historic architecture includes a generous veranda, koa trim, and Brazilian cherry floors, with the gracious details of a 1930s estate that belonged to the manager of Hawaii's first sugar plantation. Come before sunset to properly view this sprawling horticultural marvel; the property includes koi ponds, shade-giving coconut and kou trees, orchids, bromeliads, and a cactus and succulent garden.

In Kiahuna Plantation Resort, 2253 Poipu Rd. ℭ **808/742-2216.** Reservations recommended. Main courses $14–$26. AE, DC, MC, V. Daily 5:30–10pm dinner (open at 4pm for pupu and cocktails).

 Roy's Poipu Bar & Grill ℱℱℱ EURO-ASIAN   This is a loud, lively room with ceiling fans, marble tables, works by local artists, and a menu tailor-made for foodies. The signature touches of Roy Yamaguchi (of Roy's restaurants in Oahu, the Big Island, Maui, Tokyo, Guam, and the U.S. mainland) are abundantly present: an excellent, progressive, and affordable wine selection; fresh local ingredients prepared with a nod to Europe, Asia, and the Pacific; and service so efficient it can be overbearing. Because appetizers (such as nori-seared ahi with black-bean sauce, spinach-shiitake ravioli, and crisp shrimp cakes with butter sauce) are a major part of the menu, you can sample Roy's legendary fare without breaking the bank. The three dozen nightly specials invariably include eight fresh fish dishes prepared at least five or six different ways.

In Poipu Shopping Village, 2360 Kiahuna Plantation Dr. ℭ **808/742-5000.** www.roysrestaurant.com. Reservations recommended. Main courses $19–$29. AE, DC, DISC, MC, V. Daily 5:30–9:30pm.

Tidepool Restaurant ℱℱℱ SEAFOOD   Here's another ultra-romantic restaurant at the Grand Hyatt: A cluster of Polynesian-style thatched bungalows overlook the lagoon in a dreamy, open-aired restaurant with tiki torches flickering in the moonlight. The atmosphere would be enough to make you book a table, but the cuisine is outstanding, a definite "do not miss." Their specialty is fresh fish, which they prepare in a number of ways (the signature dish is macadamia nut–crusted mahimahi with a Kahlúa, lime, and ginger butter sauce), but they also have juicy steaks and ribs, as well as entrees for vegetarians. Service is quick and efficient. Book early, and ask for a table overlooking the water.

Grand Hyatt Kauai Resort and Spa, 1571 Poipu Rd., Poipu. ☎ 808/742-1234. Reservations a must. Main courses $23–$43. AE, DC, DISC, MC, V. Daily 5:30–10pm.

MODERATE

Brennecke's Beach Broiler ⚐ *(Kids)* AMERICAN/SEAFOOD   Cheerful petunias in window boxes and second-floor views of Poipu Beach are pleasing touches at this seafood-burger house, a longtime favorite for more than 15 years. The view alone is worth the price of a drink and pupu, but it helps that the best hamburgers on the south shore are served here, as well as excellent vegetarian selections. Quality is consistent in the kiawe-broiled steak, fresh fish, and vegetarian gourmet burger. The place is so casual that you can drop in before or after you go to the beach and dine on nachos and peppers, fresh fish sandwiches, kiawe-broiled fish and kebabs, prime rib, pasta, build-your-own gourmet burgers, and the salad bar. Look for the early dinner (4–6pm), the happy-hour daily specials, and the Alaskan king crab and prime rib nights.

2100 Hoone Rd. (across from Poipu Beach Park). ☎ 808/742-7588. www.brenneckes.com. Main courses $9–$30. AE, DC, DISC, MC, V. Daily 11am–10pm (street-side deli takeout daily 8am–9pm).

Casa Blanca at Kiahuna ⚐⚐⚐ MEDITERRANEAN   Elizabeth "Liz" Foley is the creative force behind this stylish, open-air restaurant overlooking the manicured grounds at the Kiahuna Swim and Tennis Club. Liz makes sure that every detail is taken care of, from polished slate floors to fresh flowers. This casual sophistication makes for a wonderful setting, but the real reason to visit Casa Blanca is the food. As the sun rises across the horizon, Liz serves a gourmet breakfast with everything from Basque piperrada (Spanish scrambled eggs) and fruit crepes to a variety of eggs (lots of manifestations of eggs Benedict) and old-fashioned waffles. Lunch is a creative selection of sandwiches, salads, soups, and brochettes; among the offerings are Greek lamb, prawn and scallop skewers, Algerian chicken skewers, and Moroccan vegetables with couscous. There's even a kid's menu with such classics as PB&J and grilled cheese. Liz also offers a tapas menu of small items, each one so delicious you could make a meal of it: Moroccan chicken crepe, Italian shrimp, and their signature "must-try" lobster ceviche. But it's at dinnertime that the stars come out, and Liz's famous culinary talents really stand out. Try her North African lamb with fennel and harissa, *maiale con ginepro* (pork with juniper and gin sauce), *zarzuela* (Spanish stew with lobster, shrimp, mussels, tomato, and saffron), and *pollo limone* (roasted chicken with lemon and wine). Whatever you order, do not miss the light and creamy chocolate mousse with orange. Even non-chocolate fans will be licking the bowl.

2290 Poipu Rd. (in the Kiahuna Swim and Tennis Club), Poipu. ☎ 808/742-2929. Reservations recommended for dinner. Breakfast $6–$9; lunch $6–$12; tapas $5–$16; dinner entrees $14–$32. DISC, MC, V. Mon–Thurs 7:30am–10pm; Fri–Sat 7:30am–11pm; Sun 8:30am–3pm.

Keoki's Paradise STEAK/SEAFOOD   Keoki's Paradise is a sprawling and lively restaurant that has improved over the years. Lunch favorites include a fresh ahi sandwich, fresh-fish tacos, Thai shrimp sticks, and chicken Caesar salad—all good and

Family-Friendly Restaurants

In addition to the plate-lunch eateries, where children are welcome, the following restaurants not only tolerate kids but make them feel right at home:

LIHUE

Hanamaulu Restaurant (3–4291 Kuhio Hwy., Hanamaulu; ✆ 808/245-2511). Generations of local families have grown up dining at this Japanese/Chinese eatery. Prices are so reasonable you can feed a family of four for less than $10 each and still leave food on the plate. Stop by for lunch; the kids will get a kick out of dining at low tables on tatami floors in a Japanese-garden setting.

Kalapaki Beach Hut (3474 Rice St., Nawiliwili; ✆ 808/246-6330). This tiny "hut" is a great place for burgers (prepared 10 different ways). After a day at the beach, heck, you and the kids can show up in your bathing suits and slippers. Burgers for four, plus drinks, will only set you back $20.

Kauai Chop Suey (in the Harbor Mall, 3501 Rice St., Nawiliwili; ✆ 808/245-8790). One look at the crowded tables filled with families will let you know that you can't go wrong here. The huge menu has something for everyone: chow mein, Cantonese shrimp, roast duck, lemon chicken, and hundreds of choices of Cantonese noodles, soups, sweet-and-sours, foo-yongs, and stir-fries.

Tip Top Café/Bakery (3173 Akahi St., Lihue; ✆ 808/245-2333). This is a great place to take the entire family to breakfast. Most items are $5 or under, and the kids will love the macadamia-nut pancakes. On the way out, stop by the bakery and get the freshly baked *malasadas.*

POIPU RESORT AREA

Brennecke's Beach Broiler (2100 Hoone Rd., across from Poipu Beach Park; ✆ 808/742-7588). After a morning at Brennecke's Beach, just walk across the street to this casual eatery and chow down on their famous hamburgers. They also have "kid" items like nachos and peppers, fresh fish sandwiches, build-your-own gourmet burgers, and desserts. Look for the early dinner (4–6pm) to save even more money.

Poipu Beach Broiler (1941 Poipu Rd., Poipu; ✆ 808/742-6433). The kids' menu at this steak-and-seafood restaurant features pasta ($5), baby back ribs ($8), grilled chicken ($7), cheeseburgers ($6), and the standard grilled cheese sandwich ($5). Come early and take in the sunset.

Brick Oven Pizza (2-2555 Kaumualii Hwy. [Hwy. 50], Kalaheo, inland from Poipu; ✆ 808/332-8561). Kids and pizza just go together, especially at this old-fashioned stone-oven pizzeria featuring more pizza toppings than you can count. There will be something here to please every member of the family, including Mom and Dad when they get the bill. A 15-inch pizza will feed four and cost less than $7 a person.

Camp House Grill (Kaumualii Hwy., across the street from the Menehune Foodmart, Kalaheo; ✆ 808/332-9755). If your kids turn up their noses at gourmet food and just want plain ol' American, here's the answer. For just $3.95 you can get a burger, fries, and a small soft drink. For the same price you can substitute macaroni and cheese or a grilled cheese sandwich. (Hey, for a buck more they can chow down on popcorn chicken.)

COCONUT COAST

Wailua Family Restaurant (4361 Kuhio Hwy., across from Kinipopo Shopping Village; ✆ 808/822-3325). Seniors and kids get discounts on the huge menu, and Mom and Dad save on the all-you-can-eat buffet (soup, salad, pasta, taco, and desserts), a steal at $12. This family-friendly eatery serves breakfast, lunch, and dinner.

Bubba Burgers (4-1421 Kuhio Hwy., Kapaa; ✆ 808/823-0069; also Hanalei Center, Hanalei; ✆ 808/826-7839). Here at the house of Bubba they dish out humor, great T-shirts, and old-fashioned hamburgers. They also serve up the Slopper (open-faced with chili), the half-pound Big Bubba (three patties), the Hubba Bubba (with rice, hot dog, and chili—a Bubba's plate lunch), chicken burgers, Bubba's famous Budweiser chili, and a daily trio of fresh-fish specials, fish burgers, and fish and chips.

Ono Family Restaurant (4-1292 Kuhio Hwy., Kapaa; ✆ 808/822-1710). Most items on the breakfast/lunch menu are less than $8 and the portions are huge. (You may want to split an order with the kids, and you'll still walk away full.) Breakfast is a big deal here, with many egg dishes; banana, coconut, and macadamia-nut pancakes; and a few dozen other choices. The lunch menu lets you choose from fish, veggie, steak, tuna, and turkey sandwiches. Beef or buffalo burgers with various toppings highlight the menu.

Duane's Ono-Char Burger (on Kuhio Hwy., Anahola; ✆ 808/822-9181). If you're on your way to or from the beaches on the North Shore and the kids are starvin,' stop at this hamburger stand for Duane's huge selection of burgers: teriyaki, mushroom, cheddar, barbecue, and the Special, with grilled onions, sprouts, and two cheeses. (Even Boca burgers are offered for vegetarians.) These one-of-a-kind burgers will set you back $3.90 to $6.20, with plenty of money left over for the marionberry ice-cream shake.

NORTH SHORE

Hanalei Mixed Plate (5-5190 Kuhio Hwy. (next to Ching Young Village), Hanalei; ✆ 808/826-7888). If you are looking for a quick lunch or want to get takeout for a picnic on the beach, this low-priced lunch counter serves up plate lunches, sandwiches, burgers, and hot dogs. A family of four can eat a great lunch for under $25.

affordable. In the evenings, regulars tout the fresh fish crusted in lemon grass, basil, and bread crumbs. When it's time for dessert, the original Hula pie from Kimo's in Lahaina is sinfully good. The cafe in the bar area serves lighter fare and features live Hawaiian music on Thursday and Friday nights and Sunday afternoon.

In Poipu Shopping Village, 2360 Kiahuna Plantation Dr. ℂ **808/742-7534**. Reservations recommended. Main courses $6–$12 lunch, $16–$27 dinner. AE, DC, DISC, MC, V. Daily 5–10pm in the main dining room and cafe menu daily 11am–11pm.

Pattaya THAI   This moderately priced cafe, centrally located in the middle of the Poipu Shopping Village, offers a great selection of authentic Thai cuisine in an indoor/outdoor setting. The atmosphere is casual, with Thai mahogany tables and chairs over a flagstone flooring. Most of the dishes can be ordered mild, medium, or spicy, and can be made vegetarian or with chicken, pork, beef, shrimp, or seafood. We recommend the spicy lemon grass soup (a traditional *tom-yum* soup) with kaffir lime leaves, Thai parsley, and home-grown Thai herbs simmered in a broth; or try the chef's special noodles: stir-fried Thai rice noodles tossed with vegetables or one of their homemade curries.

Poipu Shopping Village, Poipu. ℂ **808/742-8818**. Entrees $9.95–$17. MC, V. Mon–Sat 11:30am–2:30pm; Mon–Sun 5–9:30pm.

Poipu Beach Broiler *Kids* STEAK/SEAFOOD   Located in the former House of Seafood, this new casual eatery has a relaxing atmosphere, like an old beach house. We love their large appetizer menu. In fact, we recommend that you drop by at sunset, have a drink, and chow down on the great variety of pupu—like vegetable summer rolls, sea scallops, seared ahi sashimi, or tender calamari. You can easily make a meal of these appetizers. Lunch is burgers, sandwiches, and salads; dinner entrees include fresh fish, prime rib, grilled sirloin, and baby back ribs. There's also a menu for the kids.

1941 Poipu Rd., Poipu. ℂ **808/742-6433**. Lunch $6–$8; dinner $15–$19. MC. V. Daily, 11am–3pm lunch, 2–5pm happy hour, 5–10pm dinner.

Pomodoro *⌘* ITALIAN   Pomodoro is the Italian magnet of the west side, a small, casual, and intimate second-floor dining room with a bar, potted plants, soft lighting, and pleasing Italian music. It's a warm, welcoming place where Hawaiian hospitality meets European flavors: homemade garlic focaccia, homemade mozzarella, chicken saltimbocca, and homemade pastas (cannelloni, manicotti, and excellent lasagna, the house specialty). Whether you order the veal, chicken, scampi, calamari, or very fresh organic green salads, you'll appreciate the wonderful home-style flavor and the polite, efficient servers.

In Rainbow Plaza, Kaumualii Hwy. (Hwy. 50), Kalaheo (inland from Poipu). ℂ **808/332-5945**. Reservations recommended. Main courses $12–$22. MC, V. Mon–Sat 5:30–9:30pm.

Tomkats Grille AMERICAN/GRILL   Fried appetizers, inexpensive New York steak, rotisserie chicken, seafood salad with fresh catch, sandwiches, and burgers are served at this serene garden setting in Old Koloa Town. Old-fashioned brews are big here—everything from Watney's and Samuel Adams to Guinness Stout, plus two dozen others, all the better for washing down the spicy jalapeños stuffed with cream cheese. For the reckless: the Cats' Combo, a heart-stopping basket of fried jumbo onion rings, mozzarella sticks, zucchini, and mushrooms.

5404 Koloa Rd., Old Koloa Town. ℂ **808/742-8887**. Main courses $11–$37. MC, V. Daily 7am–10pm. Happy hour daily 3–6pm; bar daily until midnight.

INEXPENSIVE

Brick Oven Pizza *(Kids)* PIZZA A Kalaheo fixture for nearly 25 years, Brick Oven Pizza is the quintessential mom-and-pop business. This is the real thing! The pizza is cooked directly on the brick hearth, brushed with garlic butter, and topped with cheeses and long-simmering sauces. You have a choice of whole-wheat or white crust, plus many toppings: house-made Italian sausage, Portuguese sausage, bay shrimp, anchovies, smoked ham, vegetarian combos, and more. The result: very popular pizza, particularly when topped with fresh garlic and served with Gordon Biersch beer. The seafood-style pizza-bread sandwiches are big at lunch, and the "super pizza" with everything on it—that's *amore.*

2-2555 Kaumualii Hwy. (Hwy. 50), Kalaheo (inland from Poipu). © 808/332-8561. Sandwiches less than $7.40; pizzas $10–$31. MC, V. Tues–Sun 11am–10pm.

Camp House Grill *(Kids)* AMERICAN Nick Morrison has been cooking up burgers, chicken, barbecue ribs, and spectacular breakfasts since he opened Camp House Grill in 1988. This down-home country place is "the" place for breakfast, with everything from pancakes, biscuits and gravy, and sweet-bread French toast to dozens of omelets. If you get here before 8am, enjoy low-priced specials such as scrambled eggs, bacon, and toast for $3. Lunch and dinner range from burgers and deep-fried chicken to fresh fish. (Prices are the same for lunch or dinner.) A kids' menu is available.

Kaumualii Hwy. (across the street from the Menehune Foodmart), Kalaheo. © 808/332-9755. Breakfast $3.50–$7.95. Lunch and dinner $3.95–$16. Daily 6am–9pm.

Joe's on the Green *(Finds)* AMERICAN Psst! We'll let you in on a secret. This "hidden" eatery is mainly known to local residents who flock here for breakfast or for lunch after a round of golf. This is the place to go for breakfast; not only do you have a great setting—outdoors overlooking the golf course—but the menu has everything you could possibly want, from fluffy pancakes (banana-macadamia nut are the best) to biscuits-'n'-gravy to healthy tofu scramble. Breakfasts are a bargain, especially if you go before 9am and get the early bird special for $4.99, and the coffee keeps coming so your cup is never empty. At lunch time Joe's serves a variety of sandwiches (from fresh fish and Joe's Mama Burger, to "a dog named Joe," a quarter-pounder with sauerkraut and Cleveland stadium mustard), salads (build your own), and desserts. (Don't pass up the large, warm chocolate chip cookie.) Joe recently added dinner on Wednesday and Thursday nights with live Hawaiian music.

2545 Kiahuna Plantation Dr., at the Kiahuna Golf Club Clubhouse, Poipu. © 808/742-9696. Breakfast $4.95–$9.50, lunch $5.50–$9.50, dinner $6.95–$18. MC, V. Daily, breakfast 7–11:30am, lunch 11:30am–2:30pm, and happy hour 3–5:30pm; Wed–Thurs, dinner 5:30–8:30pm.

Kalaheo Coffee Co. & Cafe COFFEEHOUSE/CAFE John Ferguson has long been one of our favorite Kauai chefs, and his cafe is a coffee lover's fantasy: Kauai Estate Peaberry, Kona Dark Roast, Maui's Kaanapali Estate, Molokai Estate, Guatemalan French Roast, Colombian, Costa Rican, Sumatran, and African coffees—you can visit the world on a coffee bean! The coffeehouse also serves masterful breakfasts: Bonzo Breakfast Burritos (sautéed ham, peppers, mushrooms, onions, and olives scrambled with cheese and served with salsa and sour cream); veggie omelets with sun-dried tomatoes and mushrooms; Belgian waffles; and bagels. At lunch, the fabulous grilled-turkey burger (heaped with grilled onions and mushrooms on a sourdough bun) is the headliner on a list of winners. Fresh-from-the-garden salads brighten up the day. The tasty, inexpensive soup changes daily. The cinnamon "knuckles" (baked fresh daily), lilikoi cheesecake, fresh apple pie, and carrot cake are more reasons to stop by.

2-2436 Kaumualii Hwy. (Hwy. 50), Kalaheo (inland from Poipu). ✆ 808/332-5858. Most items less than $7.95. DISC, MC, V. Mon–Fri 6am–3pm; Sat 6:30am–3pm; Sun 6:30am–2pm.

Taqueria Nortenos _Value_ MEXICAN   This hole-in-the-wall (literally a takeout counter with a window) is the perfect place to stop by on your way to or from Poipu Beach to pick up some authentic Mexican food to go. There always seems to be a line at this unpretentious place that draws the locals in with tasty food and budget prices. In addition to the usual south-of-the-border fare (tacos, burritos, tostadas, nachos) they have daily specials (an enchiladas colorados, with two cheese enchiladas topped with Colorado sauce and beans and rice for $4.50, was the special one day) and a local style plate lunch (beef or chicken with salad, beans, and rice for $4.50).

Poipu Plaza, 2827 Poipu Rd. (a small five-shop strip mall before the road forks to the Poipu/Spouting Horn turn off). Poipu. No phone. All items under $4.50. No cards. Thurs–Tues 11am–9pm.

3 Western Kauai

MODERATE

Hanapepe Café ✦✦ GOURMET VEGETARIAN/ITALIAN   Andrea Pisciotta, a former waitress in the restaurant, is now the manager. The first thing she did was upgrade the facilities, repaint the walls, put in new artwork, introduce fish on the menu, and add dinners on Friday nights with live entertainment. Lunch is packed; people come for the several varieties of garden burger, a modest staple elevated to gourmet status. You can top yours with sautéed mushrooms, grilled onions, pesto, fresh-grated Parmesan, and other ingredients. Other lunch notables include fresh rosemary home fries, a heroic grilled vegetable sandwich, and whole roasted garlic heads. On the Friday-night dinner menu, Italian specialties shine: Southwestern-style lasagna (with green chiles, polenta, and sun-dried tomatoes); lasagna quattro formaggio with spinach, mushrooms, and four cheeses; crepes; and the nightly special with the cafe's famous marinara sauce—terrific choices all. There's no liquor license, so if you want wine, bring your own.

3830 Hanapepe Rd., Hanapepe. ✆ 808/335-5011. Reservations recommended for dinner. Lunch main courses $6.50–$10; dinner main courses $16–$24. MC, V. Mon–Thurs 11am–3pm; Fri 11am–2pm; Fri 6–9pm.

Waimea Brewing Company ECLECTIC   This popular brewery in the Waimea Plantation Cottages is a welcome addition to the dry west side, serving pub fare with a multi-ethnic twist. "Small plates" for grazing are composed of ale-steamed shrimp, taro leaf, and goat cheese dip with warm pita bread; or try the ahi-roasted corn chowder. "Big plates" come with roasted chicken, steak, short ribs, or kalua pork. Between plates are soups, salads, and sandwiches, including fresh catch. The beer is brewed on the premises. This is a pleasant stop, one of the top two places in Waimea for dinner.

In Waimea Plantation Cottages, 9400 Kaumualii Hwy., Waimea. ✆ 808/338-9733. Main courses $10–$30. AE, DC, DISC, MC, V. Daily 11am–9pm.

Wrangler's Steakhouse STEAK   Good service and pleasant veranda seating are among the pluses of this family-run operation. Western touches abound: a wagon in the loft, log-framed booths with gas lanterns, and lauhala _paniolo_ hats in the made-in-Hawaii gift shop. A combination of cowboy, plantation, and island traditions, Wrangler's serves lots of steak—big, hand-selected cuts—and adds some island touches, from vegetable tempura to grilled steak to ahi with penne pasta. Families like Wrangler's because its multicourse dinners won't break the bank.

9852 Kaumualii Hwy., Waimea. ℂ 808/338-1218. Lunch $8–$12; dinner main courses $17–$30. AE, DISC, MC, V. Mon–Thurs 11am–8:30pm; Fri 11am–9pm; Sat 5–9pm.

INEXPENSIVE

Barefoot Burgers BURGERS/SANDWICHES   This roadside burger joint along the highway to Waimea Canyon is a throwback to the 1950's, with everything except the car hop to come out and take your order. Burgers galore from the "bare-foot" quarter pounder to burgers with onions, barbecue, even teriyaki sauce. Sandwiches (tuna, BLT, chicken, even hot dogs) come either a la carte or with fries. After you order and pick up your burger you have the choice of eating inside or out. If you're still hungry, try one of their ice cream desserts from a cup or cone, to sundaes and banana-splits. Oddly enough they also serve great espresso, even espresso smoothies.

9643 Kaumualii Hwy., Waimea. ℂ 808/338-2082. Burgers and sandwiches $2–$5.50. No cards. Mon–Fri 10am–5pm, Sat–Sun 8am–5pm.

Green Garden AMERICAN/ISLAND   This Hanapepe landmark continues a decades-old tradition of offering local fare amid layers of foliage inside and out. A riot of fishing balls suspended in nets, plants everywhere, and a labyrinthine dining room make for a unique environment. The Green Garden is known for its inexpensive fresh fish sandwiches, lilikoi cream pies, and, at dinner, the kiawe-grilled fresh-fish specials (onaga, opakapaka, and ehu) that come with soup and salad.

Hwy. 50, Hanapepe. ℂ 808/335-5422. Reservations recommended for 4 or more. Entrees $15–$30. AE, MC, V. Wed–Mon 5–9pm.

Shrimp Station SHRIMP   Looking for a picnic lunch to take up to Waimea Canyon? Stop at this roadside eatery, which is nothing more than a kitchen with a few picnic tables outside. But the shrimp cooking up inside will make up for the lack of ambience. The shrimp is prepared a variety of ways, from shrimp taco to a shrimp burger, but the star attraction is their shrimp plates (choice of garlic shrimp, Cajun, Thai, or sweet chile garlic). If you take out, make sure you have plenty of dry-wipes to clean up with after munching these tasty but messy dishes. (They offer a sink with soap for those who eat in.)

9652 Kaumualii Hwy., Waimea. ℂ 808/338-1242. Shrimp platters $11–$12. MC, V. Daily 11am–5pm.

Toi's Thai Kitchen THAI/AMERICAN   A west Kauai staple, Toi's has gained a following for its affordable, authentic Thai food and a casual atmosphere. Tucked into the corner of a small shopping complex (look for the McDonald's on the highway), Toi's serves savory dishes utilizing fresh herbs and local ingredients, many of them from the owner's garden. Popular items include the house specialty, Toi's Temptation (home-grown herbs, coconut milk, lemon grass, and your choice of seafood, meat, or tofu); the vegetable curries; shrimp satay; and ginger-sauce *nua* (your choice of seafood, meat, or tofu in a fresh ginger stir-fry). Most of the rice, noodle, soup, curry, and main-course selections can be made with pork, chicken, seafood, beef, or vegetarian. Buttered garlic *nua,* peanut-rich satays, and stir-fried Basil Delight are among Toi's many tasty preparations. All dishes come with green-papaya salad, dessert, and a choice of jasmine, sticky, or brown rice.

In the Eleele Shopping Center, Eleele. ℂ 808/335-3111. Main courses $9–$17. DC, MC, V. Mon–Sat 10:30am–2pm and 5:30–9:30pm.

Icy-Cold Dessert

Maybe it's because Hawaii can be hot. Maybe it's because the local population loves sweets. Maybe it's because it's just downright refreshing and delicious, but don't leave Kauai until you have tried "shave ice." The mainland has "snow cones," which are made from crushed ice with sweet flavorings poured over the top. Shave ice (not "shaved" ice) is made by shaving a block of ice with an ultra-sharp blade, which results in ice as thin as frozen powder. The shave ice is then saturated with a sweet syrup. (Flavors can range from old-fashioned strawberry to such local treats as *li hing mui*.) You can also ask for shave ice on top of ice cream. (Try it with sweet Japanese azuki beans for a special treat.) Shave ice can be found all over the island, from small, hole-in-the-wall stores to vans alongside the road. A few to look for are: **Shave Ice Paradise,** in the Hanalei Center (© 808/826-6659); **Hawaiian Blizzard,** a small stand in front of Big Save, in the Kapaa Shopping Center, 4-1105 Kuhio Hwy., no phone; **Halo Halo Shave Ice,** 2956 Kress St., Lihue (© 808/245-5094); **Hawaiian Hut Delights** (which features sugar-free shave ice), 3805 Hanapepe Rd., Hanapepe (© 808/335-3781); and **Jo-Jo's Clubhouse,** mile marker 23, Kaumualii Highway (Hwy. 50), Waimea (© 808/635-7615).

Wong's Restaurant CHINESE/JAPANESE/DELI/BAKERY   "Eat at Wong's, you can't go Wrong," proclaims the menu of this longtime island institution. Wong's has all the bases covered for breakfast, lunch, and dinner: They feature both Japanese and Chinese dishes, and have one of the best delis and bakeries (Omoide's Deli and Bakery—great for picking up picnic fixings and sandwiches for the beach). Wong's also has one of the world's best homemade lilikoi (passion fruit) chiffon pies—it's worth the drive just to sample this piece of heaven. Wong's is not known for its ambience; in fact, it looks like a typical Chinese restaurant, one big giant cafeteria-size room. If you go at the wrong time, you'll find that the tour buses love this place and it can be crowded. But the portions are huge, the prices right, and the service smiling. Takeout is available.

1-3543 Kaumualii Hwy., Hanapepe. © **808/335-5066.** Main courses under $8. Tues–Sun 6am–9pm.

4 The Coconut Coast

EXPENSIVE

The Bull Shed STEAK/SEAFOOD   The informality and oceanfront location are big pluses, but Kauai regulars also tout the steaks and chops—prime rib, Australian rack of lamb, garlic tenderloin—and the fresh catch. The seafood selection includes broiled shrimp, Alaskan king crab, and Parmesan-drenched scallops. Dinner orders include rice and the salad bar. Combination dinners target the ambivalent, with chicken, steak, seafood, and lobster pairings. The salad bar alone is a value, and the entrees are so big they're often shared.

796 Kuhio Hwy., Waipouli. © **808/822-3791.** Reservations recommended for parties of 6 or more. Main courses $12–$38. AE, DC, DISC, MC, V. Daily 5:30–10pm.

Where to Dine in the Coconut Coast

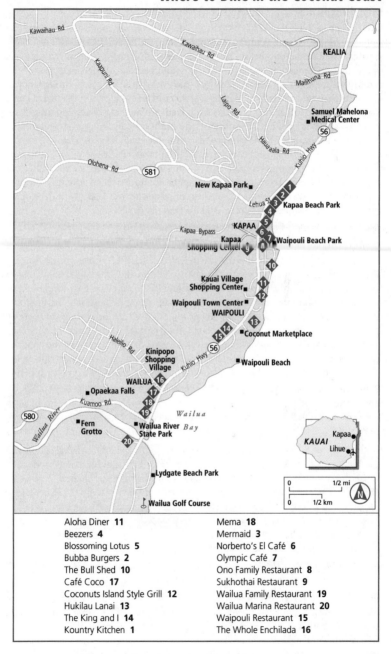

Aloha Diner **11**
Beezers **4**
Blossoming Lotus **5**
Bubba Burgers **2**
The Bull Shed **10**
Café Coco **17**
Coconuts Island Style Grill **12**
Hukilau Lanai **13**
The King and I **14**
Kountry Kitchen **1**

Mema **18**
Mermaid **3**
Norberto's El Café **6**
Olympic Café **7**
Ono Family Restaurant **8**
Sukhothai Restaurant **9**
Wailua Family Restaurant **19**
Wailua Marina Restaurant **20**
Waipouli Restaurant **15**
The Whole Enchilada **16**

MODERATE

Caffè Coco 🌺🌺 GOURMET BISTRO   This gets our vote for the most charming ambience on Kauai, with gourmet fare cooked to order, and at cafe prices. Food gets a lot of individual attention here. Caffè Coco is just off the main road at the edge of a cane field in Wailua, its backyard shaded by pomelo, avocado, mango, tangerine, litchi, and banana trees, with a view of Sleeping Giant Mountain. The trees provide many of the ingredients for the muffins, chutneys, salsas, and fresh-squeezed juices that Ginger Carlson whips up in her kitchen. Seats are indoors (beyond the black-light art gallery) or on the gravel-floored back courtyard where tiki torches flicker at night. From interior design to cooking, this is clearly a showcase for Carlson's creativity. The food is excellent, with vegetarian and other healthful delights such as spanakopita, homemade chai, Greek salad, fish wraps, macadamia nut–black sesame ahi with wasabi cream, and an excellent tofu-and-roast-veggie wrap. Although the regular menu is limited, there are many impressive specials. Service can be, to say the least, laid-back. Next door, Carlson's sister runs **Bambulei,** a vintage shop of treasures (p. 216).

4-369 Kuhio Hwy., Wailua. 🕐 808/822-7990. Reservations recommended for 4 or more. Main courses $7–$21; specials usually less than $20. MC, V. Tues–Fri 11am–9pm, Sat–Sun 5–9pm.

Coconuts Island Style Grill 🌺 AMERICAN/ECLECTIC   One of Kauai's newer eateries—where fans line up for the happy-hour pupu and affordable, tasty fare—is right on the highway, next to Taco Bell. Coconuts is upbeat and busy, with a cheerfully tropical dining room of bamboo ceilings and coconut everything: bar floor, fixtures, furniture, and lights. There are many wines served by the glass, good beers on tap, and a diverse menu including the best-selling teriyaki-dipped fresh salmon, fresh catch (oven roasted, with kaffir lime broth and wasabi mashed potatoes), and an excellent seafood chowder. Grilled polenta with herb pesto and braised spinach, the burger with house-made potato chips, and shrimp cakes are also popular. The appetizer menu—nine items, from baby back ribs to lobster ravioli—is a hit from the time the doors open at 4pm.

4-919 Kuhio Hwy. 🕐 808/823-8777. Reservations accepted only for 5 or more. Main courses $11–$27. AE, DC, MC, V. Daily 4–10pm.

Hukilau Lanai STEAK/SEAFOOD   The owners of Gaylord's in Kilohana opened this restaurant in the Kauai Coast Resort featuring local products and produce of Kauai; they promise that the dishes "are made from scratch in our kitchen." The menu offers a wide selection of appetizers, from spinach and laulau leaf dip (a creamy cheese dip with luau leaf, spinach, and tomato relish served in a homemade bread bowl) to prosciutto, basil, and prawns (jumbo shrimp wrapped with thinly sliced Italian ham and fresh basil). Entrees include fresh fish, beef, chicken, and pork dishes. Save room for dessert, especially the goat cheese tart.

Kauai Coast Resort, Kapaa. 🕐 808/822-0600. Main course $14–$23. MC, V. Tues–Sun 5–9pm. Live music Wed and Fri 6:30–9:30pm. Comedy show Thurs 7pm.

Mema THAI/CHINESE   If you're looking for a casual dining experience with something exotic but priced reasonably, this is your place. This family-run restaurant is decorated with a profusion of plants and flowers, and the waitstaff wear traditional Thai costumes. The large menu offers some 50 different appetizers, a range of curries (we recommend the house curry, a Siam-style *panans* curry with lime leaves, lemon grass, and coconut milk), and a host of traditional Thai and Chinese specialties. Most of the dishes can be ordered mild, medium, or spicy, with either vegetables, tofu, chicken, pork, beef, shrimp, or seafood.

4-369 Kuhio Hwy., Kapaa. (②) **808/823-0899**. Main Courses $8.95–$18. Mon–Fri 11am–2pm. Daily 5–9pm.

Wailua Family Restaurant AMERICAN/LOCAL   The salad bars, efficient service, and family-friendly feeling here are legendary. Seniors and kids get discounts on the huge menu and cross-cultural salad bar that includes a Mexican bar, pasta bar, sushi section, homemade soups, and ethnic samplings from Korean, Japanese, Filipino, and Hawaiian cuisines. Everything here is done big and generous, from the menu and serving sizes to the budget-friendly prices. The papaya is always freshly sliced at breakfast (there's a breakfast buffet Sat–Sun), the cornbread is good, and the eggs Benedict comes with a choice of ham or turkey. You can also order mahimahi or ono with the eggs for a high-protein start. The all-you-can-eat buffet (soup, salad, pasta, taco, and desserts) is a steal for $12. The menu features American and ethnic classics like sandwiches, stir-fries, teriyaki steak, and a seafood combo. There is outdoor seating, too.

4361 Kuhio Hwy, across from Kinipopo Shopping Village. (②) **808/822-3325**. Reservations recommended for dinner. Breakfast $6–$8; lunch most items under $10; dinner main courses $11–$16. MC, V. Sun–Thurs 6:30am–9:30pm; Fri–Sat 6:30am–10pm.

Wailua Marina Restaurant *(Kids)* AMERICAN   This is a strange but loveable place, anti-nouvelle to the end. We recommend the open-air seating along the Wailua River where you can linger over sandwiches (mahimahi is a favorite) and salads as you watch riverboats heading for the Fern Grotto. The interior is cavernous, with a high ceiling and stuffed fish adorning the upper walls—bordering on weird, but we love it anyway. The salad bar makes the place friendly for dieters and vegetarians. Otherwise, you'll find the 40-plus down-home items heavy on the sauces and gravies; they include Alaskan king crab legs with filet mignon (or filet paired with lobster tail), stuffed prawns, the famous hot lobster salad, steamed mullet, and teriyaki spareribs. Although the open salad bar is a meal in itself, the more reckless can try the mayo-laden mini-lobster salad appetizer, the crab-stuffed mushrooms, or the baked stuffed Island chicken. *Money-saving tip:* The early bird specials (5–6pm) start at $9 for spaghetti dinner and go up to $11 for a mixed plate of shrimp tempura, chicken yakitori, and teriyaki top sirloin.

5971 Kuhio Hwy., Wailua. (②) **808/822-4311**. Reservations recommended. Lunch $7–$10; dinner main courses $9–$29. AE, MC, V. Tues–Sun 10:30am–2pm and 5–8:30pm.

INEXPENSIVE

Aloha Diner HAWAIIAN   It's funky and quirky and claims legions of fans for its authentic Hawaiian plates. Lunch and dinner specials include kalua pig, laulau, lomi salmon, fried whole *akule* (big-eyed scad, hooked, not netted), and other Hawaiian dishes. Saimin and wonton mein are the other favorites at this tiny diner, where steaming dishes and perspiring faces are cooled by electric fans whirring over Formica tables. Although the Aloha Diner may intimidate the uninitiated, it's pure comfort for lovers of Hawaiian food.

971-F Kuhio Hwy., Waipouli. (②) **808/822-3851**. Most items less than $7.50. No credit cards. Tues–Sat 10:30am–2:30pm and 5:30–8:30pm.

Beezers SODA FOUNTAIN   If you can remember American Bandstand on TV, when ice cream sundaes were served in real sundae glasses, when malts were thick and the extra amount that didn't fit into your glass was put in front of you (at no extra charge), and when root beer floats had lots of ice cream that floated—then put on your saddle shoes and drop by this genuine, old-fashioned, 1950s soda fountain. Owner and "chief soda jerk" Kriss Erickson spent years researching this soda-fountain idea before he put all the ingredients together. He found a real soda fountain and added a black-and-white tile floor, red vinyl stools, and a 16-foot mahogany mirrored bar. Bring your date to share a soda, shake, malt, or banana split. He also serves sandwiches, desserts, and sloppy Joes. Bring quarters for the jukebox.

Kapaa Trade Center, 1380 Kuhio Hwy., Kapaa. (C) 808/822-4411. Most items under $10. No credit cards. Daily 11am–10pm.

Blossoming Lotus 𝒜𝒜 VEGETARIAN   This vegetarian restaurant has become so popular that they had to move into larger quarters just around the corner. In a tranquil atmosphere with plenty of light from the two-story dining room, stone lining the floors, wooden tables, and muted music, this organic gourmet vegan restaurant even has carnivores raving about the incredible food. Appetizers include spring rolls filled with fresh garden veggies with a Thai dipping sauce, and a cosmic corn bread packed with cilantro and chiles. Entrees range from a coconut curry to the daily pizza. Lots of salads, wraps/sandwiches, and sinful-looking (but healthy) desserts round out the always-changing menu. There's live entertainment every night and a terrific vegan brunch on Saturday and Sunday. If you want a quick drink or snack, the **Lotus Root,** 4-1384 Kuhio Hwy. (the previous location for this restaurant), offers just-baked goods, ice cream, juices, and smoothies. Once a month Blossoming Lotus presents a "Vegan Luau," an all-you-can-eat vegan buffet plus Polynesian music and dancing for just $25 per person.

Dragon Building, 4504 Kukui St., Kapaa. (C) 808/822-7678. www.blossominglotus.com. Lunch $7–$15, dinner entrees $14–$17, brunch $7–$15. MC, V. Daily 11am–3pm and 5:30–9:30pm.

Bubba Burgers 𝘒𝘪𝘥𝘴 AMERICAN   At Bubba the burger is king, attitude reigns, and lettuce and tomato cost extra. They dish out humor, great T-shirts, and burgers nonpareil, along with tempeh burgers for vegetarians. Grilled fresh fish sandwiches cater to the sensible, fish and chips to the carefree, and fish burgers to the undecided. But old-fashioned hamburgers are the main attraction. You can order the Slopper (open-faced with chili), the half-pound Big Bubba (three patties), or the Hubba Bubba (with rice, hot dog, and chili—a Bubba's plate lunch), among others. Chicken burgers, Bubba's famous Budweiser chili, and other American standards are also served here. For a burger joint, it's big on fish, too, with a daily trio of fresh-fish specials, fish burgers, and fish and chips.

4-1421 Kuhio Hwy., Kapaa. (C) 808/823-0069. All items less than $6.95. MC, V. Daily 10:30am–8pm.

The King and I THAI   This medium-size restaurant, in a small and nondescript roadside complex, serves reasonably priced specials and vegetarian selections, including spring rolls, salads, curries, and stir-fries. The owners grow their own herbs for the menu's savory curries and seasonings. At dinner, the pad Thai noodles with shrimp have a special touch and are a popular counterpoint to the red, green, and yellow curries. The vegetarian menu is generous—everything from noodles to spring rolls to curries and eggplant/tofu—but most diners come back for the Evil Jungle Prince: your choice of veggies, chicken, or fish in a sauce of coconut milk, spices, and kaffir-lime leaves.

In Waipouli Plaza, 4-901 Kuhio Hwy. ⓒ **808/822-1642.** Reservations recommended. Main courses $6–$13. AE, DC, DISC, MC, V. Daily 4:30–9:30pm.

Kountry Kitchen AMERICAN   Forget counting calories when you sit down to the brawny omelets here. Choose your own fillings from several possibilities, among them kimchi with cream cheese and several vegetable, meat, and cheese combinations. Sandwiches and American dinners (steak, fish, and chicken) are standard coffeehouse fare, but sometimes fresh-fish specials stand out. *Warning:* Sit as far away from the grill as possible; the smell of grease travels—and clings to your clothes.

1485 Kuhio Hwy., Kapaa. ⓒ **808/822-3511.** Main courses $6–$9. MC, V. Daily 6am–1:30pm.

Mermaids Cafe ⓕ HEALTHFUL/ISLAND STYLE   Don't you love these places that use fresh local ingredients, make everything to order, and barely charge anything for all that trouble? A tiny sidewalk cafe with brisk takeout and a handful of tables on Kapaa's main drag, Mermaids takes kaffir lime, lemon grass, local lemons (Meyers when available), and organic herbs when possible, to make the sauces and beverages that go with their toothsome dishes. Sauces are lively and healthful, such as the peanut satay made with lemon juice instead of fish sauce. The sauce is used in the tofu and chicken satays, the chicken coconut curry plate, and the chicken satay wrap. The seared ahi wrap is made with the chef's special blend of garlic, jalapeño, lemon grass, kaffir lime, basil, and cilantro, then wrapped in a spinach tortilla—fabulous. The fresh-squeezed lemonade is made daily, and you can choose white or organic brown rice. These special touches elevate the simple classics to dreamy taste sensations; if you don't believe us, try the coconut custard French toast, made with Hawaiian guava-taro bread and served with fresh local fruit—divine.

1384 Kuhio Hwy., Kapaa. ⓒ **808/821-2026.** Main courses $7.95–$9.95. DC, MC, V. Daily 11am–9pm.

Norberto's El Cafe MEXICAN   The lard-free, home-style Mexican fare here includes top-notch chiles rellenos with homemade everything, vegetarian selections by request and, if you're lucky, fresh fish enchiladas. All of the sauces are made from scratch, and the salsa comes red-hot with homegrown chile peppers fresh from the chef's garden. Norberto's signature is the spinachy Hawaiian taro-leaf enchiladas, a Mexican version of laulau, served with cheese and taro or with chicken.

4-1373 Kuhio Hwy., Kapaa. ⓒ **808/822-3362.** Reservations recommended for parties of 6 or more. Main courses $4.75–$9.45; complete dinners $14–$18. AE, DISC, MC, V. Mon–Sat 5–9pm.

Olympic Café AMERICAN   This casual eatery became so successful that it had to move—and it moved up, upstairs that is. It's worth hunting around for this second floor restaurant, which now has views of the ocean and historic downtown Kapaa. The breakfasts are huge, lunches filling, and dinners reasonably priced. In fact, the Olympic is known for big portions and small prices. Breakfast features a range of espresso drinks, pancakes, omelets, and egg dishes. Lunch includes sandwiches, burgers, salads, and a range of wraps. Dinner includes something for everyone, from burgers to fresh fish and steaks. Stop by for a drink; they have smoothies, juice, Italian sodas, specialty teas, and a menu of specialty coffee drinks.

1354 Kuhio Hwy., Kapaa. ⓒ **808/822-5825.** Breakfast under $8; lunch $6–$11. Dinner entrees $8–$23. Mon–Thurs and Sun, 7am–9pm; Fri–Sat, 7 am–10 pm.

Ono Family Restaurant 🄺ids AMERICAN   Breakfast is a big deal here, with eggs Florentine (two poached eggs, blanched spinach, and hollandaise sauce) leading the pack, and eggs Canterbury (much like eggs Benedict, but with more ingredients) following close behind. The Garden Patch, a dollop of fried rice topped with fresh steamed vegetables, scrambled eggs, and hollandaise sauce, is a real conscience-buster. Steak and eggs; banana, coconut, and macadamia-nut pancakes; and dozens of omelet choices also attract throngs of loyalists. Lunch is no slouch either, with scads of fish, veggie, steak, tuna, and turkey sandwiches to choose from. Ono beef or buffalo burgers with various toppings highlight the menu. The gourmet hamburger with fries and soup demands an after-lunch siesta.

4-1292 Kuhio Hwy., Kapaa. ✆ **808/822-1710.** Most items less than $9. AE, DC, DISC, MC, V. Daily 7am–1:30pm.

Sukhothai Restaurant THAI/VIETNAMESE/CHINESE Curries, saimin, Chinese soups, satays, Vietnamese pho, and a substantial vegetarian menu are a few of the features of this unobtrusive—but extremely popular—Thai restaurant. Menu items appeal to many tastes and include 85 Vietnamese, Chinese, and Thai choices, along with much-loved curries and the best-selling pad Thai noodles. The coconut/lemon grass/kaffir lime soups (eight choices) are the Sukhothai's highlights, along with the red and green curries.

In the Kapaa Shopping Center (next to Kapaa's Big Save Market), 4-1105 Kuhio Hwy., Kapaa. ✆ **808/821-1224.** Main courses $8–$17. AE, DC, DISC, MC, V. Daily 10:30am–3pm and 5–9pm.

Waipouli Restaurant AMERICAN/JAPANESE Modest home-style cooking at low, low prices attracts throngs of local folks who love the saimin, pancakes, and $3 "rice bowls" with chili, teriyaki beef, chicken katsu, or "anything," says the owner. The saimin is great here, especially the miso saimin special, a hefty bowl of steaming noodles with tofu, vegetables, and a boiled egg (but hold the Spam, please!). There are always inexpensive dinner specials, ranging from sukiyaki to roast chicken. This place is crowded from breakfast till closing.

In Waipouli Town Center, Waipouli. ✆ **808/822-9311.** Most lunch items less than $7; dinner less than $10. No credit cards. Daily 7am–2pm; Tues–Sat 5–8:30pm.

The Whole Enchilada MEXICAN Tucked away in a small shopping center, just after the Wailua River Bridge, this tiny cafe has all the Mex favorites from nachos to burritos, including a few "super-sized" dishes like the "macho nachos" (corn tortilla chips covered with cheese, chiles, onion, black beans, guacamole, salsa, sour cream, and choice of meat or shrimp) for just $9, or the "two-hander burrito" (10-inch tortilla with beans, cheese, rice, meat, salsa, guacamole, and sour cream) for $6. If you are looking for a great takeout plate for a party on the beach, order up the "whole enchilada" (a shrimp taco, pork taco, chicken enchilada, mini-macho nacho, mini–cheese quesadilla, and a salad) for $18.

Kinipopo Shopping Village, 4-356 Kuhio Hwy., Kapaa. ✆ **808/822-4993.** Most items under $10. No credit cards. Mon–Sat 11am–3 pm, 5–8 pm.

EN ROUTE TO THE NORTH SHORE

Duane's Ono-Char Burger *Kids* HAMBURGER STAND We can't imagine Anahola without this roadside burger stand; it's been serving up hefty, all-beef burgers for generations. (And now they offer Boca burgers for vegetarians.) The teriyaki sauce and blue cheese are only part of the secret of Duane's beefy, smoky, and legendary ono char-burgers served several ways: teriyaki, mushroom, cheddar, barbecue, and the Special, with grilled onions, sprouts, and two cheeses. The broiled fish sandwich (another marvel of the seasoned old grill) and the marionberry ice-cream shake, a three-berry combo, are popular as well.

On Kuhio Hwy., Anahola. © **808/822-9181.** Hamburgers $4.15–$6.45. MC, V. Mon–Sat 10am–6pm; Sun 11am–6pm.

5 The North Shore

EXPENSIVE

La Cascata ✿✿✿ MEDITERRANEAN/SOUTHERN ITALIAN   The North Shore's special-occasion restaurant is sumptuous—a Sicilian spree in Eden. Try to get here before dark so you can enjoy the views of Bali Hai, the persimmon-colored sunset, and the waterfalls of Waialeale, all an integral part of the feast. Click your heels on the terra-cotta floors, take in the *trompe l'oeil* vines, train your eyes through the concertina windows, and pretend you're being served on a terrazzo in Sicily. The menu dazzles quietly with its Mediterranean-inspired offerings and fresh local ingredients. Polenta, charred peppers, Kauai asparagus, organic Kauai vegetables, risottos, ragouts, grilled fresh fish, and vegetable napoleons are colorful and tasty, and beautifully presented.

In the Princeville Resort, 5520 Ka Haku Rd. © **808/826-9044.** Reservations recommended for dinner. Main courses $24–$38; 3-course prix-fixe dinner $56. AE, DC, DISC, MC, V. Daily 6–9:30pm.

Lighthouse Bistro Kilauea ✿ CONTINENTAL/PACIFIC RIM/ITALIAN   Even if you're not on your way to the legendary Kilauea Lighthouse, this bistro is so good it's worth a special trip. The charming green-and-white wooden building next to Kong Lung Store has open sides, old-fashioned plantation architecture, open-air seating, trellises, and high ceilings. The ambience is wonderful, with a retro feeling. The food is excellent, an eclectic selection that highlights local ingredients in everything from fresh fish tacos and fresh fish burgers to macadamia nut–crusted ahi and four preparations of fresh catch. The mango-cherry chicken in light lilikoi sauce is a tropical delight. The ahi quesadilla comes beautifully presented with rice, black beans, and spicy condiments on a plate painted with purple cabbage shavings and herbs—much more elegant than the usual lunchtime fare.

In Kong Lung Center, Kilauea Rd. (off Hwy. 56 on the way to the Kilauea Lighthouse), Kilauea. © **808/828-0481.** Reservations recommended for 6 or more. Lunch $5–$11; dinner main courses $18–$39. MC, V. Daily 11am–2pm and 5:30–9:30pm.

MODERATE

Bamboo Bamboo SEAFOOD/PASTA/PIZZA   This elegant, open-air eatery in the Hanalei Center offers a range of fresh fish, pastas, filet mignon, lamb, pizza, and light dinners (fish sandwich or fish and chips). Interesting fish preparations include the sesame-crusted ahi and the potato-crusted mahimahi. On weekends (Fri–Sun) the brick oven is fired up for a range of interesting pizza pies like white pizza with garlic, tomatoes, basil, and cheeses; or pesto and chicken. You can also build your own. Live music is featured on weekend evenings.

Hanalei Center, Hanalei. © **808/826-1177.** www.bamboobamboohanalei.com. Reservations recommended. Main courses $16–$26. AE, DC, MC, V. Tues–Sun 11am–2:30pm; daily 5:30–9pm.

Hanalei Dolphin Restaurant & Fish Market ✿ SEAFOOD   Hidden behind a gallery called Ola's are this fish market and adjoining steak-and-seafood restaurant, on the banks of the Hanalei River. Particularly inviting are the fresh fish sandwiches, served under umbrellas at river's edge. Most appealing (besides the river view) are the appetizers: artichokes steamed or stuffed with garlic, butter, and cheese; buttery stuffed mushrooms; and ceviche fresh from the fish market, with a jaunty dash of green olives. From fresh catch to baked shrimp to Alaskan king crab and chicken marinated in soy sauce, the Dolphin has stayed with the tried-and-true.

5144 Kuhio Hwy., Hanalei. (C) 808/826-6113. Main courses $16–$36. MC, V. Daily 11am–10pm. (Fish market daily 10am–7pm in the winter and until 8pm in the summer.)

Hanalei Gourmet AMERICAN   The wood floors, wooden benches, and blackboards of the old Hanalei School, built in 1926, are a haven for today's Hanalei hipsters noshing on the Tu Tu Tuna (far-from-prosaic tuna salad with green beans, potatoes, niçoise olives, and hard-boiled eggs); fresh grilled ahi sandwiches; roasted eggplant sandwiches; chicken-salad boats (in papaya or avocado, with macadamia nuts and sans mayonnaise); and other selections. This is an informal cross-cultural tasting, from stir-fried veggies over udon to Oriental ahi-pasta salad to artichoke hearts fried in beer batter. Big Tim's burger is, unsurprisingly, big, and the sandwiches served on fresh-baked bread represent timeless deli faves, from roast beef and pastrami to smoked turkey and chicken salad. The TV over the bar competes with the breathtaking view of the Hanalei mountains and waterfalls, and the wooden floors keep the noise level high. (The music on the sound system can be almost deafening.) Nightly live music adds to the fun.

In the Old Hanalei Schoolhouse, 5-5161 Kuhio Hwy., Hanalei. (C) 808/826-2524. Main courses $7–$23. DC, DISC, MC, V. Sun–Thurs 8am–10:30pm; Fri–Sat 8am–11:30pm.

Kilauea Bakery & Pau Hana Pizza (☆) PIZZA/BAKERY   When owner, baker, and avid diver Tom Pickett spears an ono and smokes it himself, his catch appears on the Billie Holiday pizza, guaranteed to obliterate the blues with its brilliant notes of Swiss chard, roasted onions, Gorgonzola-rosemary sauce, and mozzarella. And the much-loved bakery puts out guava sourdough; Hanalei poi sourdough; fresh chive, goat-cheese, and sun-dried-tomato bread; blackberry and white chocolate scones; and other fine baked goods. The breads go well with the soups and hot lunch specials, and the pastries with the new full-service espresso bar, which serves not only the best of the bean, but also blended frozen drinks and such up-to-the-minute voguish things as iced chai and Mexican chocolate smoothies (with cinnamon). We also love the fresh vegetables in olive oil and herbs, baked in a baguette; the olive tapenade; and the classic scampi pizza with tiger prawns, roasted garlic, capers, and cheeses. The Picketts have added a small dining room, and the few outdoor picnic tables under umbrellas are as inviting as ever. The macadamia nut–butter cookies and lilikoi-fruit Danishes are sublime.

In Kong Lung Center, Kilauea Rd. (off Hwy. 56 on the way to the Kilauea Lighthouse), Kilauea. (C) 808/828-2020. Pizzas $11–$30. MC, V. Daily 6:30am–9pm.

Neide's Salsa and Samba BRAZILIAN/MEXICAN   Tucked away in the very back of the Hanalei Center is a "hot" eatery dishing up Brazilian cuisine like *muqueca* (fresh fish with coconut sauce), *ensopado* (baked chicken and vegetables), or *bife acebolado* (beef steak with onions), plus the usual popular Mexican dishes like enchiladas and burritos. Big portions, friendly service, and reasonable prices make this a good bet.

Hanalei Center, Hanalei. (C) 808/826-1851. Entrees $9–$15. MC, V. Daily noon–2:30pm and 5–9:30pm.

Postcards Cafe (☆☆) GOURMET SEAFOOD/NATURAL FOODS   The charming plantation-style building that used to be the Hanalei Museum is now Hanalei's gourmet central. Postcards is known for its use of healthful ingredients, island-fresh

Where to Dine on Kauai's North Shore

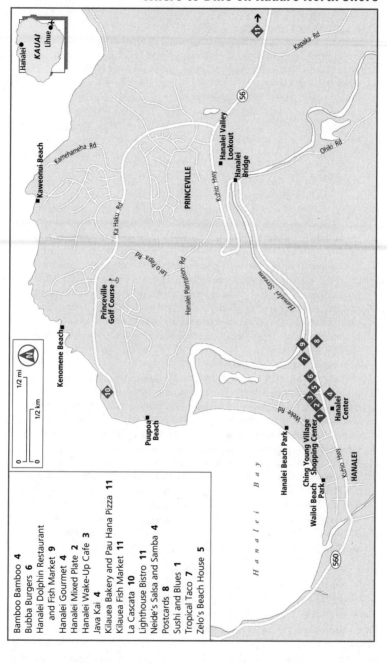

Bamboo Bamboo **4**
Bubba Burgers **6**
Hanalei Dolphin Restaurant
    and Fish Market **9**
Hanalei Gourmet **4**
Hanalei Mixed Plate **2**
Hanalei Wake-Up Cafe **3**
Java Kai **4**
Kilauea Bakery and Pau Hana Pizza **11**
Kilauea Fish Market **11**
La Cascata **10**
Lighthouse Bistro **11**
Neide's Salsa and Samba **4**
Postcards **8**
Sushi and Blues **1**
Tropical Taco **7**
Zelo's Beach House **5**

A Hawaiian Feast: The Luau

Originally, an ancient Hawaiian feast was called a *pa'ina* or *'aha'aina*, but in 1856, the *Pacific Commercial Advertiser* (the newspaper of the day) started referring to the feast as a "luau," a name referring to the young taro tops always served at the feast. Try to take in a luau while you're on Kauai. A luau today can range from a backyard affair to a commercial production at a major resort. The best ones are put on by local churches, schools, or hula *halau*. However, most visitors won't have the opportunity to see these truly authentic feasts. Several commercial luau listed below will provide a taste and a feel for them.

Most luau are fixed in price, generally $58 to $80 for adults, less for children. A variety of traditional foods and entertainment is provided. The luau usually begins at sunset and features Polynesian and Hawaiian entertainment, which can range from lavish affairs with flaming knives or torches being juggled, to performances of ancient hula, missionary-era hula, and modern hula, as well as narration of the stories and legends portrayed by the dances. The food always includes imu-roasted kalua pig, lomi salmon, dried fish, poke (raw fish cut into small pieces), poi (made from taro), laulau (meat, fish, and vegetables wrapped in ti leaves), Hawaiian sweet potato, sautéed vegetables, salad, and the ultimate taste treat, a coconut dessert called haupia. Don't worry; if you've never heard of these items (and can't pronounce them either), most luau will also have more common preparations of fish, chicken, and roast beef, as well as easily recognizable salads and standard desserts like cake.

The mainstay of the feast is the imu, a hot earthen pit in which the pig and other items are cooked. The preparations for the feast actually begin in the morning, when the luau master layers hot stones and banana stalks in the pit to get the temperature up to 400°F. The pig, vegetables, and other items are lowered into the pit and cooked all day. The water in the leaves steams the pig and roasts the meat to a tender texture.

One of the larger commercial luau in the island is **Smith's Tropical Paradise Garden Lu'au,** in the Tropical Paradise Gardens on the Wailua River (© **808/821-6895** or 808/821-6896; www.smithskauai.com), every Monday, Wednesday, and Friday at 5pm (during the popular summer months it is 5 days a week Mon–Fri). Luau prices are $65 for adults, $30 for children 7 to 13, and $19 for children 3 to 6; or you can come for just the entertainment at 7:30pm and pay $15 for adults, $7.50 for children under 12.

and creatively presented dishes (like fresh fish, grilled or blackened, with macadamia-nut butter, honey Dijon, or peppered-pineapple sage), and for its imaginative use of local ingredients (as in taro fritters served with papaya salsa). Other choices include Thai summer rolls, sautéed prawns, nori rolls (filled with rice, vegetables, and tempeh), and ever-popular laulau-style fish tacos and seafood specials. Omelets, bagels, eggs Florentine, hot cakes, and muffins are some of the day's starters. In the front yard,

Recently the **Sheraton Kauai,** Poipu Beach (✆ **808/742-8200,** www. sheratonkauai.com), launched the island's only ocean-front luau. The Surf to Sunset Luau is held on Monday and Friday, beginning at 6pm with a shell lei greeting and a mai tai. Photos with Poipu Beach serving as the background are offered, and guests can wander among the local artisans who teach lei making, lauhala weaving, and coconut frond weaving. After the feast, and before Pilah's Royal Polynesian Revue begins the entertainment, there is a pareu (sarong) fashion show that teaches visitors several techniques for tying this island cloth into a variety of different types of clothing. Cost for adults range from $68 for the buffet dinner and entertainment to $80 for premier seating, table service, and professional photos. Children, ages 6 to 12 years, are $34.

Tihati's Hiva Pasefica puts on the luau at the **Courtyard by Marriott Kauai-Waipouli Beach,** Kapaa (✆ 808/823-0311; Tuesday to Sunday) beginning at 6pm with an imu ceremony where the pig is removed from the pit. Their entertainment is among the best on the island, with ancient and modern hula performances. The cost is $62 for adults, $57 for seniors, $40 for teenagers 13 to 18, $30 for children 3 to 12, and free for children 2 and under.

Every Tuesday and Thursday, **Reflections of Paradise,** at the Kilohana Carriage House (where Gaylord's Restaurant is located), 3-2087 Kaumualii Hwy., Lihue (✆ **808/245-9593;** www.kilohana.com), gets underway at 6:15pm with a full buffet, followed by the music and dances of Polynesia. The cost is $58 for adults, $54 for seniors and teens 13 to 19, $30 for children 4 to 12, and free for children under 4.

The Princeville Resort puts on a beachside luau called **Pa'ina O' Hanalei,** 5520 Kahaku Rd., Princeville (✆ **800/826-4400** or 808/826-9644; www. princeville.com), Monday and Thursday at 6pm. Under a canopy of stars, a full feast is served and a Polynesian revue performs. The cost is $69 for adults, $60 for seniors, $35 for children 6 to 12.

On the south coast, check out **Drums of Paradise,** in the Grand Hyatt Kauai Resort & Spa, 1571 Poipu Rd., Poipu (✆ **800/55-HYATT** or 808/742-1234; www.kauai-hyatt.com), every Sunday, Tuesday, and Thursday during summer (Sunday and Thursday only during the rest of the year). Not only do they have an elaborate buffet but a very professional Polynesian show. The cost is $75 for adults, $65 for teens 13 to 19, and $38 for children 6 to 12.

an immense, mossy, hollowed-out stone serves as a free-standing lily pond and road-side landmark. Great menu, presentation, and ambience—a winner.

On Kuhio Hwy. (at the entrance to Hanalei town). ✆ 808/826-1191. Reservations recommended for dinner. Main courses $15–$28. AE, DC, MC, V. Daily 6–9pm.

Sushi & Blues ✦ SUSHI/PACIFIC RIM This second-floor oasis has copper tables and a copper-topped bar, large picture windows for gazing at the Hanalei waterfalls and, most importantly, chefs who know their sushi. Traditional sushi, fusion sushi, and hot Pacific Rim dishes for those who aren't sushi lovers please diners of every stripe. Big hits: the temaki hand rolls; the Las Vegas roll, a heroic composition of ahi, hamachi, and avocado, dipped in tempura batter and quickly fried so it's hot on the outside and chilled on the inside; the Rainbow Roll, a super-duper California roll with eight different types of fish; and fresh fish prepared several ways, in fusion flavorings involving mango, garlic, sake, sesame, coconut, passion fruit, and other Pacific Rim ingredients. The action fires up Wednesday, Thursday, Saturday, and Sunday from 8:30pm on, with live music, from Hawaiian to blues, jazz to rock 'n' roll.

In Ching Young Village, Hanalei. ✆ 808/826-9701. www.sushiandblues.com. Reservations recommended for parties of 6 or more. Main courses $18–$23; sushi rolls $4 and up. MC, V. Daily 6–10pm. Live music from 8:30pm on.

Zelo's Beach House ⊛ STEAK/SEAFOOD Good food, concrete floors, window tables with flower boxes, seating on the deck with mountain views—what's not to like? Along with Sushi & Blues, Zelo's is the hippest, most popular spot in Hanalei, a "beach house" spiced up with South Pacific kitsch, a wide variety of coffee drinks, excellent mai tais, and sliding doors all around. The congenial bar area has a tin roof and ironwood poles, and a one-person canoe hangs overhead. Gourmet burgers, pastas, steaks, 50 different microbrews and 30 tropical drinks, a wonderful salad in a large clam-shaped bowl, warm bread, seafood chimichangas, and a good seafood chowder are some of the attractions. Zelo's is always packed, and when happy hour rolls around (3:30–5:30pm), the inexpensive tap beers and tacos start flowing. A children's menu, appetizers and entrees in all price ranges, and the new Martini Madness menu make Zelo's a Hanalei must, especially if you can snag a table on the deck.

Kuhio Hwy. and Aku Rd., Hanalei. ✆ 808/826-9700. Reservations recommended for parties of 6 or more. Main courses $8–$12 lunch, $9–$25 dinner. MC, V. Winter daily 11am–9:30pm; summer daily 11am–10pm.

INEXPENSIVE

Bubba Burgers AMERICAN Green picnic tables and umbrellas thatched with coconut leaves stand out against the yellow walls of Bubba's, the burger joint with attitude. The burgers are as flamboyant as the exterior. This North Shore version of the Kapaa fixture (p. 142) has the same menu, same ownership, and same high-quality, all-beef burgers that have made the original such a smashing success.

In Hanalei Center (on the town's main road), Hanalei. ✆ 808/826-7839. All items less than $7. MC, V. Daily 10:30am–8pm.

Hanalei Mixed Plate (Kids PLATE LUNCH/SANDWICHES If you are looking for a quick lunch or want to get takeout for a picnic on the beach, this low-priced lunch counter serves up plate lunches that include one to three entrees (plus rice): kalua pork, vegetable stir-fry, or shoyu ginger chicken. They also serve sandwiches (teriyaki chicken, sautéed mahimahi), burgers (beef, Kauai buffalo, garden, or tempeh), salads, and hot dogs. There is a small counter with a few stools if you want to eat here, but we suggest walking over a couple blocks to the beach.

5-5190 Kuhio Hwy. (next to Ching Young Village), Hanalei. ✆ 808/826-7888. Plate lunch $5.95-$7.95, sandwiches $6.95–$11. No cards. Daily 10:30am–9pm.

Hanalei Wake-up Café (Finds BREAKFAST This is where the surfers go to get fueled up for a day on the waves. In fact, breakfast—make that a big, huge, monstrous breakfast—is all they serve in this tiny eatery that truly defines "hole-in-the-wall." Not

---

Moments **A Piece of Heaven: Kauai Tropical Fudge**

Even if you just get a tiny piece, don't miss the mouthwatering, made-from-scratch, rich, creamy fudge coming out of Mindy Jergens' **Kauai Tropical Fudge,** 5-5080 Kuhio Highway (© **808/826-5504**). On the menu are five different "handmade gourmet" selections: choc-mac (milk chocolate and macadamia nut), hula (milk chocolate, coconut, and macadamia nuts), Kona coffee & cream (yummy white chocolate and mocha coffee), lava java (dark chocolate and coffee), and mahalo mint (a combination of dark chocolate and refreshing mint). If you fall in love with this sinful treat, you'll be relieved to learn that they ship it anywhere.

---

a lot of atmosphere, not a lot of tables, but cowabunga, dude! The portions are big, the prices small, and the staff surprisingly cheery at 6am.

5144 Kuhio Hwy. (at Aku Rd.) © **808/826-5551**. Most items less than $8. No credit cards. Daily 6am–11:30am.

Java Kai COFFEEHOUSE   In 1997, 5 years after Hurricane Iniki, Kauai was still recovering economically when Jennifer and Bruce Hickman took over the Old Hanalei Coffee Company. This was the first of three Java Kai coffeehouses on Kauai (there's also one in Honolulu, plus one in California, and more to come) featuring coffee grown in Hawaii, a gourmet bakery, and a juice bar. They also serve a few breakfast and lunch items (waffles, quiche, and sandwiches).

55183-C Kuhio Hwy., Hanalei. © **808/826-6717**. Also at 4-1384 Kuhio Hwy., Kapaa (© 808/823-6887); and at 4302 Rice St., Lihue (© 808/245-6704). Most items under $6. MC, V. Daily 6:30am–6pm.

Kilauea Fish Market ☞ HEALTHY PLATE LUNCH   This is the perfect place to get a picnic take-out lunch or an easy dinner to go to take back and watch the sunset. Coriena Rogers not only has healthy, yummy meals made with just-caught fish, but she also has a deli section with fresh fish for those looking to cook it themselves. Located just off the road to the Kilauea Lighthouse, this tiny hole-in-the-wall has a few tables outside in a garden setting, but generally people pick up and go. Vegetarians will be happy with the daily specials. She has options of brown or white rice and insists on using organic greens in her salads. These are some of the best prices on the north shore.

4270 Kilauea Lighthouse Rd., Kilauea. © **808/828-6244**. Most items under $10. MC, V. Mon–Sat 11am–8pm.

Tropical Taco ☞ MEXICAN   For more than a quarter of a century Roger Kennedy has been making tacos and burritos in Hanalei. For years, you could find him working out of his green "taco wagon" parked along the road. But recently Roger has come up in the world. He now has a permanent "regular" restaurant (with wood floors and seating along the outside lanai, where you can people watch) in the Hanalei Building, but he's still serving his tasty assortment of tacos and burritos, plus his signature "fat Jack" (a 10-inch tortilla deep fried with cheese, beans, and beef or fish). Roger does warn everyone that his tasty treats are "not to be consumed 1 hour before surfing!" Just like his taco wagon, Roger still offers "anything you want to drink, as long as it's lemonade."

Hanalei Building, 5-5088 Kuhio Hwy., Hanalei. © **827-TACO**. www.tropicaltaco.com. Most items under $8. No cards. Mon–Sat 11am–5pm.

7

Fun in the Surf & Sun

This is the part of your vacation you've dreamed about—the sun, the sand, and the surf. In this chapter we'll tell you about the best beaches on Kauai, from where to soak up the rays to where to plunge beneath the waves for a fish-eye-view of the underwater world. Plus, we've scoured the island to find the best ocean activities on the Garden Isle. We'll tell you our favorites, and give you a list of the best marine outfitters. Also in this chapter is a range of activities to do on dry land, from hiking and camping to the best golfing on the island.

1 Beaches

Eons of wind and rain have created this geological masterpiece of an island, with its fabulous beaches. In fact, Kauai, the oldest of the major Hawaiian Islands, has more sand beaches per mile of shoreline than any of the other seven islands. Gorgeous white-sand beaches make up about 50 miles of Kauai's 113 miles of shoreline. That works out to some 44% of the shoreline, far greater than the shoreline percentage of any other island. (Oahu has only half that amount.)

The most popular beaches are on the island's north and south coasts. They can be crowded, especially on weekends. But there are plenty of beaches, white sand, and surf for everyone. Be sure to read "Safety in the Surf" (p. 156) to learn how to avoid potential dangers in Kauai's ocean environment.

Hawaii's beaches belong to the people. All beaches (even those in front of exclusive resorts) are public property and you are welcome to visit them. Hawaii state law requires that all resorts and hotels offer public right-of-way access (across their private property) to the beach, along with public parking. So just because a beach fronts a hotel doesn't mean that you can't enjoy the water. It does mean that the hotel may restrict certain areas on private property for hotel guests' use only. Generally, hotels welcome nonguests to their facilities. They frown on nonguests using the beach chairs reserved for guests, but if a nonguest has money and wants to rent gear, buy a drink, or eat a sandwich, well, money is money, and they will gladly accept it from anyone. However, that does not mean that you can willy-nilly cross private property to get to a beach. Look for BEACH ACCESS signs; don't trespass.

Note: Despite what you may have heard, nudity is against the law in Hawaii. You can be prosecuted. (Yes, the police do arrest people for being bare on the beach.)

For beach toys and equipment, head to **Activity Warehouse,** 788 Kuhio Hwy. (across from McDonald's), Kapaa (© **800/688-0580** or 808/822-4000; www.travel hawaii.com).

Kauai Beaches

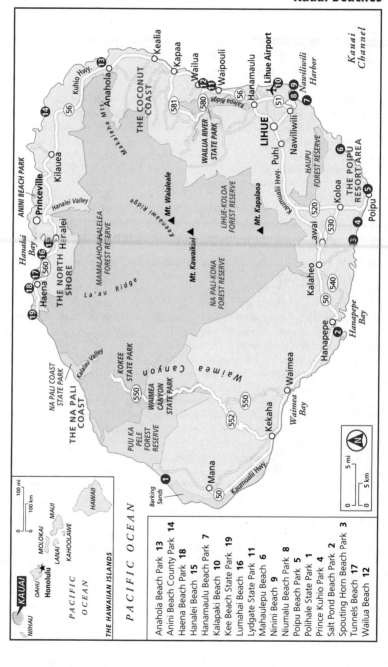

Anahola Beach Park **13**
Anini Beach County Park **14**
Haena Beach Park **18**
Hanalei Beach **15**
Hanamaulu Beach Park **7**
Kalapaki Beach **10**
Kee Beach State Park **19**
Lumahai Beach **16**
Lydgate State Park **11**
Mahaulepu Beach **6**
Ninini Beach **9**
Niumalu Beach Park **8**
Poipu Beach Park **5**
Polihale State Park **1**
Prince Kuhio Park **4**
Salt Pond Beach Park **2**
Spouting Horn Beach Park **3**
Tunnels Beach **17**
Wailua Beach **12**

LIHUE

KALAPAKI BEACH 𝒜

Any town would pay a fortune to have a beach like Kalapaki, one of Kauai's best, in its backyard. But little Lihue turns its back on Kalapaki; there's not even a sign pointing the way through the labyrinth of traffic to this graceful half moon of golden sand at the foot of the Marriott Resort & Beach Club. Fifty yards wide and a quarter mile long, Kalapaki is protected by a jetty, making it very safe for swimmers. The waves are good for surfing when there's a winter swell, and the view from the sand—of the steepled, 2,200-foot peaks of the majestic Haupu Ridge that shield Nawiliwili Bay—is awesome. Kalapaki is the best beach not only in Lihue but also on the entire east coast. During certain times of the year there are strong currents and dangerous shorebreaks. From Lihue Airport, turn left onto Kapule Highway (Hwy. 51) to Rice Street; turn left and go to the entrance of the Marriott; pass the hotel's porte-cochere and turn right at the SHORELINE ACCESS sign. Facilities include free parking, restrooms, and showers; food and drink are available nearby at Kalapaki Beach Hut (p. 127). There is no lifeguard.

NININI BEACH

If you are looking for a good snorkeling/swimming beach off the beaten track, this small beach, consisting of two sandy coves separated by lava, is a great place to get away from the crowds. Some local residents call this Running Waters Beach due to the former irrigation runoff when sugar was in production here. Located at the northern end of Nawiliwili Harbor and hidden behind some cliffs, this beach is generally protected from the wind and currents. However, high surf can kick up and southern storms can charge in suddenly. The small northern sandy cove has good snorkeling and swimming most of the year. Follow the trail down from the dirt road to the beach. Occasionally a few nudists show up here, but remember—nudity is against the law in Hawaii and you can be prosecuted (for lewd and lascivious behavior—how would you like that on your record?). We prefer the larger beach because of the gentle sandy slope (great for sunbathing) and because the sandy bottom makes for great snorkeling. When the surf does roll in here, the bodysurfers will be in the water. To get here, take Ahukini Road toward the airport; when the road appears to end, veer left (still on Ahukini Rd.) and head for the ocean. When the road meets the ocean, turn right on the dirt road that circumnavigates the airport with the ocean on your left. Travel about 2½ miles on this dirt road to the Nawiliwili Lighthouse. Look for the two trails down to the ocean. Ninini Beach has no facilities and no lifeguard.

NIUMALU BEACH PARK

This is a great place at which to stop in the middle of the day for a picnic. It's located close to Lihue; you can pick up lunch and wander down to this 3-acre quiet area, which has campgrounds. Bordered by Nawiliwili Harbor on one end and the small boat ramp on the other, Niumalu sits next to a very profound archaeological area—the Menehune Fishpond. The pond (also called Alekoko) on the Huleia River was an aquaculture feat built hundreds of years ago. The builders of this 2,700-foot-long stone wall (that cuts off a bend in the river) were believed to be the mythical people who inhabited Kauai before the Polynesians came here (see "Discovering the Legendary 'Little People'" on p. 193). The fishpond is located in the Huleia National Wildlife Refuge, 238 acres of river valley that is a habitat for endangered Hawaiian water birds (ae'o, or Hawaiian stilt; 'alae Ke'oke'o, or Hawaiian coot; 'alae 'ula, or

Hawaiian Monk Seals & Turtles: Look, but Don't Get Too Close

If you are lucky, you will get to see one of Hawaii's rare Hawaiian monk seals or endangered Hawaii green sea turtles when they lumber up on a sunny beach. One of the most endangered species on earth, about 25 seals *(Monachus schauinslandi)* call Kauai home. These 400- to 600-pound seals (stretching out 4 ft.–6 ft.) are protected by very strict laws, and it is illegal to approach a seal (or a turtle for that matter) closer than 100 feet. It's exciting when you spot a seal (or turtle), and you'll want to rush up and get a photo. Remember that this is not Disneyland or a zoo, and that the beach is their native habitat. Stay back 100 feet, and do not use your flash when photographing. (Hey, how would you like cameras flashing when you're trying to get a little snooze in?) Be sure to instruct your children to stay back and not throw anything at the seals or turtles. The endangered-species laws are strictly enforced on Kauai, and the fines are very steep. For more information, go to www.kauaimonkseal.com.

Hawaiian gallinule; and Koloa maoli, or Hawaiian duck). Although you can see the fishpond and the refuge from the road, the area is not open to the public. Various small boats, kayaks, jet skis, windsurfers, and water-skiers use the river. You can spend the day watching them ply their crafts up and down. From Lihue, take Rice Street to Nawiliwili Harbor. Turn left on Niumalu Road and follow it to the beach park. The beach does not have a lifeguard, but it does have picnic tables, showers, and restrooms.

HANAMAULU BEACH PARK

If you are looking for a great picnic beach, this large bay is not only close to Lihue but is protected from the open ocean. However, it is not a great swimming beach due to the dirt (mainly silt) in the water entering the bay from Hanamaulu stream. The waters outside the bay are cleaner. This area is very popular with scuba divers and with fishermen, who flock here when akule and other migratory fish are schooling in the bay. Camping is allowed in this 6½-acre park; see "Hiking & Camping" (p. 169) for details. From Lihue, take the Kapule Highway (Hwy. 51) north, and turn right on Hehi Road to the beach park. Hanamaulu has no lifeguard but it does have free parking, restrooms, showers, and a pavilion.

THE POIPU RESORT AREA
MAHAULEPU BEACH 🐾🐾

Mahaulepu is the best-looking unspoiled beach in Kauai and possibly in the whole state. Its 2 miles of reddish-gold, grainy sand line the southeastern shore at the foot of 1,500-foot-high Haupu Ridge, just beyond the Hyatt Regency Poipu and the McBryde sugar cane fields, which end in sand dunes and a forest of casuarina trees. Almost untouched by modern life, Mahaulepu is a great escape from the real world. It's ideal for beachcombing and shell hunting, but swimming can be risky, except in the reef-sheltered shallows 200 yards west of the sandy parking lot. There's no lifeguard, no facilities—just great natural beauty everywhere you look. (This beach is where George C. Scott portrayed Ernest Hemingway in the movie *Islands in the Stream*.) While you're here, see if you can find the Hawaiian petroglyph of a voyaging canoe carved in the beach rock.

Safety in the Surf

Before you even think about packing your bathing suit, get a copy of the free brochure *Kauai Beach Safety Guide.* It could save your life. This color brochure explains how to avoid potential dangers in Kauai's ocean environment. The power of the ocean is nothing to fool around with. The surf can increase in size in a short period of time, or an offshore rip current can carry you out to sea. Even a walk alone on the beach without paying attention to the ocean can have potentially dangerous results (like being swept out to sea).

The number-one advice given by this brochure (put out by the Kauai Ocean Rescue Council) is to swim at beaches where there are lifeguards and to talk to the lifeguards before entering the ocean. The brochure lists all beaches on Kauai and whether a lifeguard is on duty. It also lists each beach's potential hazards, like strong currents, dangerous shorebreaks, high surf conditions, slippery rocks, sharp coral, sudden drop-offs, and waves on ledges.

In general, the north and west shores are hazardous in winter (Sept–May), with big surf. In summer, the opposite is true, and the big waves occur along the south and east shores. But hazardous conditions can occur on any beach at any time of the year. The brochure stresses the following points:

- **Swim in lifeguard areas** and check with lifeguards on ocean conditions before you go into the water.
- **Watch the ocean at least 20 minutes** before you go in. Lifeguards can show you what potential hazards to look for.
- **Always (always, always, always) swim (or snorkel) with a buddy.**
- **Always keep a close watch over young children.**

You can get this free brochure by contacting the **Kauai Visitors Bureau,** 4334 Rice St., Suite 101, Lihue, HI 96766 (© **808/245-3971**), or download it from www.kauaiexplorer.com.

To get here, drive past the Hyatt Regency Poipu 3 miles east on a red-dirt road, passing the golf course and stables. Turn right at the T-intersection; go 1 mile to the big sand dune, turn left, and drive a half mile to a small lot under the trees.

POIPU BEACH PARK ⭐

Big, wide Poipu is actually two beaches in one; it's divided by a sandbar, called a tombolo. On the left, a lava-rock jetty protects a sandy-bottomed pool that's perfect for children; on the right, the open bay attracts swimmers, snorkelers, and surfers. And everyone likes to picnic on the grassy lawn graced by coconut trees. You'll find excellent swimming, small tide pools for exploring, great reefs for snorkeling and diving, good fishing, nice waves for surfers, and a steady wind for windsurfers. Poipu attracts a daily crowd, but the density seldom approaches Waikiki levels except on holidays. Facilities include a lifeguard, restrooms, showers, picnic areas, Brennecke's

Beach Broiler nearby (p. 131), and free parking in the red-dirt lot. To get here, turn onto Poipu Beach Road, then turn right at Hoowili Road.

PRINCE KUHIO PARK

This tiny park, across the street from Ho'ai Bay, marks the birthplace of Prince Jonah Kuhio Kalanianaole, who was born March 26 (a state holiday), 1871. Kuhio's mother died shortly after his birth; he was adopted by his mother's sister, Kapiolani, and her husband, Kalakaua. When Kalakaua became king in 1874, Kuhio became prince. However, he did not become king because his aunt, Liliuokalani, ascended to the throne upon Kalakaua's death. In 1893, her reign was overthrown by the U.S. government. However, in 1902 Kuhio was elected as Hawaii's delegate (nonvoting member) to Congress, where he served until his death in 1922. This park is across the street from the ocean, where the rocky drop-off into the water is not very convenient for access (although snorkeling offshore is great). We suggest that you go a bit further east to Keiki (Baby) Beach, a small pocket of sand off Hoona Road, where swimming is generally safe. To get to Prince Kuhio Park, take Poipu Road toward the ocean and veer right at the fork in the road onto Lawai Beach Road. To get to Baby Beach, turn onto Hoona Road.

SPOUTING HORN BEACH PARK

According to ancient Hawaiian legend, a *mo'o* (lizard) was returning to Kauai from Niihau, where he had just been to a funeral for his two sisters. With tears streaming down his face, he missed landfall on the south shore and got stuck in the blowhole here, where you can still hear his voice during high surf. One of Hawaii's most famous blowholes, Spouting Horn gets its name from the loud roar created when the surf rushes to the lava shoreline and gets funneled up in the narrow chimney, which then spits out the water. Don't be so distracted by this intense display of Mother Nature that you get too close to the blowhole; not only are the rocks slippery, but also people have been killed here when large waves swept them into the ocean or into the blowhole. The main attraction here is the blowhole, as the shoreline is mainly rocks. There is a small sandy beach (most of the year) to the west, which does have good swimming when the waters are calm. However, when the surf comes up, the sandy beach disappears. If you look offshore, you can see several boats bobbing in the water; commercial dive and snorkel tour operators frequently bring their tour groups to this area. Facilities include a paved parking lot, restrooms, and vendors. Take Poipu Road toward the ocean, and veer right at the fork in the road onto Lawai Beach Road. Follow the road for about a couple of miles to the beach park.

WESTERN KAUAI
SALT POND BEACH PARK

Hawaii's only salt ponds still in production are at Salt Pond Beach, just outside Hanapepe. Generations of locals have come here to swim, fish, and collect salt crystals that are dried in sun beds. The tangy salt is used for health purposes and to cure fish and season food. The curved reddish-gold beach lies between two rocky points and features a protected reef, tide pools, and gentle waves. Swimming here is excellent, even for children; this beach is also good for diving, windsurfing, and fishing. Amenities include a lifeguard, showers, restrooms, a camping area, a picnic area, a pavilion, and a parking lot. To get here, take Highway 50 past Hanapepe and turn onto Lokokai Road.

Frommer's Favorite Kauai Experiences

Snorkeling Kee Beach. Rent a mask, fins, and snorkel and enter a magical underwater world. Facedown, you'll float like a leaf on a pond, watching brilliant fish dart here and there in water clear as day; a slow-moving turtle may even stop to check you out. Face-up, you'll contemplate green-velvet cathedral-like cliffs under a blue sky, where long-tailed tropical birds ride the trade winds. See p. 162.

Hiking Waimea Canyon, the Grand Canyon of the Pacific. Ansel Adams would have loved this ageless desert canyon, carved by an ancient river. Sunlight plays against its rustic red cliffs, burnt-orange pinnacles, and blue-green valleys. There's nothing else like it in the islands. See p. 174.

Wandering Around a High Mountain Forest. Kokee State Park, through Waimea Canyon at the end of Highway 550, is a combination rainforest and bog up around 4,000 feet. The park's 45 miles of trails offer everything from casual nature strolls to hardy camping and hiking adventures among the redwoods. See p. 174.

Strolling Through Hawaiian History. Old Waimea Town looks so unassuming that you'd never guess it stood witness to a great many key events in Hawaii's history. This is the place where Capt. James Cook "discovered" the Hawaiian Islands, where Russians once built a fort, and where New England missionaries arrived in 1820 to "save the heathens." A self-guided walking tour is available at **Waimea Public Library,** Kaumualii Highway (© **808/338-6848**). See "Waimea Town," in chapter 8.

Taking a Long Walk on a Short (but Historic) Pier. First built in 1910, Hanalei's Pier was once a major shipping port for local farmers. Today, the rebuilt pier makes a great platform for swimming, fishing, and diving. It's at Black Pot Beach where, in the olden days, local families would camp out all summer and always have something cooking in a "black pot" on the shore.

POLIHALE STATE PARK ★

This mini-Sahara on the western end of the island is Hawaii's biggest beach: 17 miles long and as wide as three football fields. This is a wonderful place to get away from it all, but don't forget your flip-flops—the midday sand is hotter than a lava flow. The golden sands wrap around Kauai's northwestern shore from Kekaha plantation town, just beyond Waimea, to where the ridgebacks of the Na Pali Coast begin. The state park includes ancient Hawaiian *heiau* (temple) and burial sites, a view of the "forbidden" island of Niihau, and the famed **Barking Sands Beach,** where footfalls sound like a barking dog. (Scientists say that the grains of sand are perforated with tiny echo chambers, which emit a "barking" sound when they rub together.) Polihale also takes in the Pacific Missile Range Facility, a U.S. surveillance center that snooped on Russian subs during the Cold War; and Nohili Dune, which is nearly 3-miles long and 100-feet high in some places.

Be careful in winter, when high surf and rip currents make swimming dangerous. The safest place to swim is **Queen's Pond,** a small, shallow, sandy-bottomed inlet

Black Pot—and all of Hanalei Beach—is great for swimming, snorkeling, and surfing. See p. 180.

Watching for Whales. Mahaulepu Beach, in the Poipu area, offers excellent land-based viewing conditions for spotting whales that cruise by December through April. See p. 155.

Journeying into Eden. For a glimpse of the spectacularly remote Na Pali Coast, all you need to do is hike the first 2 miles along the well-maintained Kalalau Trail into the first tropical valley, Hanakapiai. Hardier hikers can venture another 2 miles to the Hanakapiai waterfalls and pools. *Warning:* Na Pali's natural beauty is so enticing that you may want to keep going—but the trail turns rugged and extremely challenging after the 2-mile mark. Contact the State Division of Parks for a permit if you want to camp along the trail. See "Hiking & Camping," later in this chapter.

Catching a Poipu Wave. Vividly turquoise, curling, and totally tubular, big enough to hang ten yet small enough to bodysurf, the waves at Poipu are endless in their attraction. Grab a boogie board—you can rent one for just dollars a day—or simply jump in and go with the flow. See p. 156.

Watching the Hula. The Coconut Marketplace, on Kuhio Highway (Hwy. 56) between mile markers 6 and 7, hosts free shows every day at 5pm. Arrive early to get a good seat for the hour-long performances of both *kahiko* (ancient) and *auwana* (modern) hula. The real showstoppers are the *keiki* (children) who perform. Don't forget your camera!

Bidding the Sun Aloha. Polihale State Park hugs Kauai's western shore for some 17 miles. It's a great place to bring a picnic dinner, stretch out on the sand, and toast the sun as it sinks into the Pacific, illuminating the island of Niihau in the distance. Queen's Pond has facilities for camping as well as restrooms, showers, picnic tables, and pavilions. See p. 158.

protected from waves and shore currents. It has facilities for camping, as well as restrooms, showers, picnic tables, and pavilions. There is no lifeguard. To get here, take Highway 50 past Barking Sands Missile Range and follow the signs through the sugar cane fields to Polihale. Local kids have been known to burglarize rental cars out here, so don't leave tempting valuables in your car.

THE COCONUT COAST
LYDGATE STATE PARK 🤿

This coastal park has a rock-walled fishpond that blunts the open ocean waves and provides the only safe swimming and the best snorkeling on the eastern shore. The 1-acre beach park, near the mouth of the Wailua River, is named for the Rev. J. M. Lydgate (1854–1922), founder and first pastor of Lihue English Union Church, who likely would be shocked by the public display of flesh here. This popular park is a great place for a picnic or for kite flying on the green. It's 5 miles north of Lihue on Kuhio Highway (Hwy. 56); look for the turnoff just before the Kauai Resort Hotel. Facilities include a pavilion, restrooms, outdoor showers, picnic tables, barbecue grills, a life-guard, and parking.

WAILUA BEACH

This popular beach includes Wailua River State Park and Wailua Bay. The draw here is the 100-foot-wide beach that runs for about a half mile from the Wailua River to a rocky area north. Surfers (board, body, and bodyboard) love this area for its generally good surfing conditions. However, when the high surf kicks up in winter and into spring, the conditions can become dangerous, with strong rip currents, sharp shore-breaks, sudden drop-offs, and high surf. At the Wailea River end of the beach you can see boats being launched into the river for water-skiing, jet skiing, kayaking, and out-rigger canoeing. Located where the river meets the ocean is one of the best archaeo-logical sites in the state. At the mouth of the river are a series of Hawaiian *heiau* (temples) and other sacred sites, identified with markers within the state park. Wailua Beach is located just past the intersection of Kuhio Highway (Hwy. 56) and Kuamoo Road (Hwy. 580), across the street from the now-closed Coco Palms Resort. There is a part-time lifeguard, but no public facilities.

ANAHOLA BEACH PARK

Local residents, who love this park and are here almost every day, say this is the safest year-round swimming beach and great for small children. Tucked behind Kala Point, the narrow park has a shallow offshore reef that protects the sandy shoreline from the area's high surf. Another plus is that board surfing is prohibited in this area. Surfers have to head to the north end of the beach to the sandbar where surfing is allowed. To get here, take Kuhio Highway (Hwy. 56 north) to Anahola. Turn right onto Ana-hola Road and right on Manai Road. There are no facilities, but there is a part-time lifeguard.

THE NORTH SHORE

ANINI BEACH COUNTY PARK 🏕🏕

Anini is Kauai's safest beach for swimming and windsurfing. It's also one of the island's most beautiful. It sits on a blue lagoon at the foot of emerald cliffs, looking more like Tahiti than almost any other strand in the islands. This 3-mile-long, gold-sand beach is shielded from the open ocean by the longest, widest fringing reef in Hawaii. With shallow water 4 to 5 feet deep, it's also the very best snorkeling spot on Kauai, even for beginners. On the northwest side, a channel in the reef runs out to the deep blue water with a 60-foot drop that attracts divers. Beachcombers love it, too; seashells, cowries, and sometimes even rare Niihau shells can be found here. Anini has a park, a campground, picnic and barbecue facilities, and a boat-launch ramp; several B&Bs and vacation rentals are nearby. Follow Kuhio Highway (Hwy. 56) to Kilauea; take the second exit, called Kalihiwai Road (the first dead-ends at Kalihiwai Beach), and drive a half mile toward the sea; turn left on Anini Beach Road.

HANALEI BEACH 🏕

Gentle waves roll across the face of half-moon Hanalei Bay, running up to the wide, golden sand; sheer volcanic ridges laced by waterfalls rise to 4,000 feet on the other side, 3 miles inland. Is there any beach with a better location? Celebrated in song and hula and featured on travel posters, this beach owes its natural beauty to its age—it's an ancient sunken valley with eroded cliffs. Hanalei Bay indents the coast a full mile inland and runs 2 miles point to point, with coral reefs on either side and a patch of coral in the middle—plus a sunken ship that belonged to a king, so divers love it. Swimming is excellent year-round, especially in summer, when Hanalei Bay becomes a big, placid lake. The aquamarine water is also great for bodyboarding, surfing, fishing, windsurfing, canoe paddling, kayaking, and boating. (There's a boat ramp on the west bank of the Hanalei River.) The area known as **Black Pot,** near the pier, is particularly good for swimming, snorkeling, and surfing. Facilities include a lifeguard, a pavilion, restrooms, picnic tables, and parking. This beach is always packed with both locals and visitors, but you can usually find your own place in the sun by strolling down the shore; the bay is big enough for everyone.

To get here, take Kuhio Highway (Hwy. 56), which becomes Highway 560 after Princeville. In Hanalei town, make a right onto Aku Road just after Tahiti Nui, then turn right again on Weke Road, which dead-ends at the parking lot for the Black Pot section of the beach; the easiest beach access is on your left.

LUMAHAI BEACH

One of the most photographed beaches in Kauai (it's where Mitzi Gaynor "washed that man right out of her hair" in *South Pacific,* filmed here in 1957), this is a great beach for a picnic or for sitting and watching the waves. It is *not* a good swimming beach. The scenic beach is almost a mile long and extremely wide; the far eastern end occasionally is calm enough for swimming in the summer, but it can be very, very dangerous during the rest of the year. (The best reason to go to this beach is to picnic, inland, under the trees—chow down on lunch and watch the waves roll in.) *The reason for caution:* Unlike other beaches on Kauai, Lumahai has no protective reef offshore, so the open ocean waves come rolling in—full force. The force is so strong that the waves reshape the beach every year, moving the sand from one end to the other. When the surf is up there is a strong rip current and a powerful backwash, along with a dangerous shorebreak. There have been drownings here, so if the surf is up, do not go near the ocean (high surf has swept people out to sea).

Summer is the best time to enjoy this beach. On the eastern side (technically Kahalahala Beach), the surf is only calm enough for swimming on the few days when there are no waves—even small ones. The western end appeals more to body and board surfers. To get here, take Kuhio Highway (Hwy. 560); just after Hanalei, look for the wide turnoff for the scenic lookout, park here, and take the trail from the highway that leads to the beach below. Keep heading east for Kahalahala Beach. There is also a parking area at the western end of the beach, off the highway, just before you get to Lumahai River. Lumahai Beach has no facilities and no lifeguard.

Moments Stargazing

Any Kauai beach is great for stargazing, almost any night of the year. Once a month, on the Saturday nearest the new moon, when the skies are darkest, the **Kauai Educational Association for the Study of Astronomy** sponsors a star watch at Waimea Plantation Cottages. For information on the next star watch, contact KEASA, P.O. Box 161, Waimea, HI 96796 (© **808/332-STAR (7827);** www. keasa.org). Video presentations start at 6pm, with star gazing on the ocean side of the resort to follow.

TUNNELS BEACH & HAENA BEACH PARK ☆☆

Postcard-perfect, gold-sand Tunnels Beach is one of Hawaii's most beautiful. When the sun sinks into the Pacific along the fabled peaks of Bali Hai, there's no better-looking beach in the islands: You're bathed in golden rays that butter the blue sky, bounce off the steepled ridges, and tint the pale clouds hot pink. Catch the sunset from the pebbly sand beach or while swimming in the emerald-green waters, but do catch it. Tunnels is excellent for swimming almost year-round and is safe for snorkeling because it's protected by a fringed coral reef. (However, the waters can get rough in winter.) The long, curving beach is sheltered by a forest of ironwoods that provides welcome shade from the tropical heat.

Around the corner is grainy-gold-sand Haena Beach Park, which offers excellent swimming in summer and great snorkeling amid clouds of tropical fish. But stay out of the water in winter, when the big waves are dangerous. Haena also has a popular grassy park for camping. Noise-phobes will prefer Tunnels.

Take Kuhio Highway (Hwy. 56), which becomes Highway 560 after Princeville. Tunnels is about 6 miles past Hanalei town, after mile marker 8 on the highway. (Look for the alley with the big wood gate at the end.) Haena is just down the road. Tunnels has no facilities, but Haena has restrooms, outdoor showers, barbecue grills, picnic tables, and free parking (no lifeguard, though).

KEE BEACH STATE PARK ☆☆

Where the road ends on the North Shore, you'll find a dandy little reddish-gold beach almost too beautiful to be real. Don't be surprised if it looks familiar; it was featured in *The Thornbirds*. Kee (*kay*-ay) is on a reef-protected cove at the foot of fluted volcanic cliffs. Swimming and snorkeling are safe inside the reef but dangerous outside; those North Shore waves and currents can be killers. This park has restrooms, showers, and parking—but no lifeguard. To get here, take Kuhio Highway (Hwy. 56), which becomes Highway 560 after Princeville; Kee is about 7½ miles past Hanalei.

2 Watersports

Several outfitters on Kauai offer not only equipment rentals and tours, but also expert information on weather forecasts, sea and trail conditions, and other important matters for hikers, kayakers, sailors, and all backcountry adventurers. For watersports questions and equipment rental, contact **Kayak Kauai Outbound,** 1 mile past Hanalei Bridge on Highway 560, in Hanalei (© **800/437-3507** or 808/826-9844; www.kayakkauai.com), the outfitters' center in Hanalei. They have a private dock (the only one on Kauai) for launching kayaks and canoes. In Kapaa, contact **Kauai Water Ski & Surf Co.,** Kinipopo Shopping Village, 4-356 Kuhio Hwy. (on the ocean side of the highway), Kapaa (© **808/822-3574**). In Kapaa and Koloa areas, go with **Snorkel Bob's Kauai** at 4-734 Kuhio Hwy. (just north of Coconut Plantation Marketplace), Kapaa (© **800/262-7725** or 808/823-9433; www.snorkelbob.com); in Koloa, Snorkel Bob's is at 3236 Poipu Rd. (just south of Poipu Shopping Village), near Poipu Beach (© **808/742-2206**).

For general advice on the activities listed below, see "The Active Vacation Planner," in chapter 2.

BODYBOARDING (BOOGIE BOARDING) & BODYSURFING

The best places for bodysurfing and boogie boarding are **Kalapaki Beach** (near Lihue) and **Poipu Beach.** In addition to the rental shops listed above, one of the most inexpensive places to rent boogie boards is the **Activity Warehouse,** 788 Kuhio Hwy. (across from McDonald's), Kapaa (© **800/343-2087** or 808/822-4000; www.travel hawaii.com), where they go for $2 to $6 a day. **Snorkel Bob's** (see above) rents boogie boards for just $15 a week.

BOATING

One of Hawaii's most spectacular natural attractions is Kauai's **Na Pali Coast.** Unless you're willing to make an arduous 22-mile hike (p. 182), there are only two ways to see it: by helicopter (see "Helicopter Rides over Waimea Canyon & the Na Pali Coast," p. 197) or by boat. Picture yourself cruising the rugged Na Pali coastline in a 42-foot ketch-rigged yacht under full sail, watching the sunset as you enjoy a tropical cocktail, or speeding through the aquamarine water in a 40-foot trimaran as porpoises play off the bow.

When the Pacific humpback whales make their annual visit to Hawaii from December to March, they swim right by Kauai. In season, most boats on Kauai—including sail and powerboats—combine **whale-watching** with their regular adventures.

Kauai has many freshwater areas that are accessible only by boat, including the Fern Grotto, Wailua State Park, Huleia and Hanalei national wildlife refuges, Menehune Fishpond, and numerous waterfalls. If you want to strike out on your own, **Paradise Outdoor Adventures,** 4-1596 Kuhio Hwy., Kapaa (© **800/66-BOATS** or 808/822-0016; www.kayakers.com), has 40 different rental boats to choose from, like the popular Boston whaler (six-person capacity) for $295 for a half a day and $590 for a full day, plus kayaks and sea cycles. Included are all the amenities, such as safety equipment, coolers, dry bags (for cameras, wallets, towels), and a comprehensive orientation on where to go. The staff will even deliver the boat to the Wailua River at no extra charge.

For sportfishing charters, see "Fishing," below. For tours of the Fern Grotto, see p. 201.

Captain Andy's Sailing Adventures ⊛ Captain Andy operates a 55-foot, 49-passenger catamaran out of two locations on the south shore. The **snorkel/picnic cruise,** a 5½-hour cruise to the **Na Pali Coast,** from May to October, costs $129 for adults and $89 for children 2 to 12, and includes a deli-style lunch, snorkeling, and drinks. There's also a 4-hour Na Pali Coast **dinner sunset cruise** that sets sail for $95 for adults and $70 for children, and a 2-hour pupu **cocktail sunset sail** with drinks and pupu for $59 adults and $40 children. They also offer a 6-hour Na Pali Zodiac cruise on inflatable boats for $129–$159 adults and $89–$106 children 5–12 years old.

Kukuiula Small Boat Harbor, Poipu; and Port Allen, Eleele. © 800/535-0830 or 808/335-6833. www.capt-andys.com. Prices vary depending on trip.

Holoholo Charters This outfitter has taken over several boats and features both swimming/snorkeling sailing charters as well as powerboat charters to the Na Pali Coast. The 5½-hour sailing trips take place on a 48-foot catamaran called *Leila,* and are offered both in the morning (with a continental breakfast and lunch) and afternoon (big buffet lunch) for $119 adults and $85 children. The 7-hour power-boat trip is on the 61-foot vessel *Holoholo,* and not only cruises the Na Pali Coast but then crosses the channel to the forbidden island of Niihau, where they stop to snorkel. A continental breakfast, buffet lunch, and snorkel equipment is included in the price: $169 adults, $119 children. They've recently added a 42-foot sailboat that does a 5½ hour cruise of the Na Pali Coast with snorkeling for $99 adults and $69 kids ages 2–12. They also provide complimentary shuttle service to and from your hotel.

Port Allen, Eleele. ✆ **800/848-6130** or 808/335-0815. www.holoholocharters.com. Prices and departure points vary depending on trip.

Liko Kauai Cruises ☆ (Kids)   Liko offers more than just a typical whale-watching cruise; this is a 4-hour combination **Na Pali Coast tour**–deep-sea fishing–historical lecture–whale-watching extravaganza with lunch. It all happens on a 49-foot power catamaran (with only 24 passengers). In addition to viewing the whales, you'll glimpse sea caves, waterfalls, lush valleys, and miles of white-sand beaches; you'll also make stops along the way for snorkeling.

Kekaha Small Boat Harbor, Waimea. ✆ **888/SEA-LIKO** or 808/338-0333. Fax 808/338-1327. www.liko-kauai.com. Na Pali Trips $110 adults, $75 children 4–12 (lunch included).

FISHING

DEEP-SEA FISHING   Kauai's fishing fleet is smaller and less well recognized than others in the islands, but the fish are still out there. All you need to bring are your lunch and your luck. The best way to book a sportfishing charter is through the experts; the best booking desk in the state is **Sportfish Hawaii** ☆ (✆ **877/388-1376** or 808/396-2607; www.sportfishhawaii.com), which books boats not only on Kauai, but on all islands. These fishing vessels have been inspected and must meet rigorous criteria to guarantee that you will have a great time. Prices are $1,050 for a full-day exclusive charter (you and five of your closest friends get the entire boat to yourself), $850 for a three-quarter day exclusive, and $650 for a half-day exclusive.

FRESHWATER FISHING   Freshwater fishing is big on Kauai, thanks to its dozens of "lakes," which are really man-made reservoirs. Regardless, they're full of large-mouth, small-mouth, and peacock bass (also known as *tucunare*). The **Puu Lua Reservoir,** in Kokee State Park, also has rainbow trout and is stocked by the state every year. Fishing for rainbow trout in the reservoir has a limited season: It begins on the first Saturday in August and lasts for 16 days, after which you can only fish on week-ends and holidays through the last Sunday in September.

Before you rush out and get a fishing pole, you have to have a **Hawaii Freshwater Fishing License,** available through the **State Department of Land and Natural Resources,** Division of Aquatic Resources, P.O. Box 1671, Lihue, HI 96766 (✆ **808/ 241-3400**). The license is also available through any fishing-supply store, like **Lihue Fishing Supply,** 2985 Kalena St., Lihue (✆ **808/245-4930**); **Rainbow Paint and Fishing Supplies,** Hanapepe (✆ **808/335-6412**); or **Waipouli Variety,** 4-901 Kuhio Hwy., Kapaa (✆ **808/822-1014**). A 1-month license costs $3.75; a 1-year license is $7.50. When you get your license, pick up a copy of the booklet *State of Hawaii Freshwater Fishing Regulations.* Another great little book to get is *The Kauai Guide to Freshwater*

(Tips) Not So Close! They Hardly Know You

In your excitement at seeing a whale or a school of dolphins, don't get too close—both are protected under the Marine Mammals Protection Act. Swimmers, kayakers, and windsurfers must stay at least 100 yards away from all whales, dolphins, and other marine mammals. And yes, visitors have been prosecuted for swimming with dolphins! If you have any questions, call the **National Marine Fisheries Service** (✆ **808/541-2727**) or the **Hawaiian Islands Humpback Whale National Marine Sanctuary** (✆ **800/831-4888**).

Sport Fishing by Glenn Ikemoto, available for $2.50 plus postage from **Magic Fishes Press,** P.O. Box 3243, Lihue, HI 96766. If you would like a guide, **Sportfish Hawaii** ☞ ((✆ 877/388-1376 or 808/396-2607; www.sportfishhawaii.com) has guided bass fishing trips starting at $265 per person for a half day and $375 for a full day.

KAYAKING

Kauai is made for kayaking. You can take the Huleia River into **Huleia National Wildlife Refuge** (located along the eastern portion of Huleia Stream, where it flows into Nawiliwili Bay). It's the last stand for Kauai's endangered birds, and the only way to see it is by kayak. The adventurous can head to the Na Pali Coast, featuring majestic cliffs, empty beaches, open-ocean conditions, and monster waves. Or you can just paddle around Hanalei Bay.

Kayak Kauai Outbound ☞, a mile past Hanalei Bridge on Highway 560, in Hanalei ((✆ 800/437-3507 or 808/826-9844; www.kayakkauai.com), has a range of tours for independent souls. The shop's experts will be happy to take you on a guided kayaking trip or to tell you where to go on your own. Equipment rental starts at $28 for a one-person kayak and $52 for a two-person ocean kayak per day. Kayak lessons are $50 per person per hour. Tours (some including snacks) start at $115 per person and include transportation and lunch for the all-day excursion. Kayak Kauai also has its own private dock (the only one on Kauai) for launching kayaks and canoes.

Rick Haviland, who gained fame after he was mentioned in Paul Theroux's book *The Happy Isles of Oceania,* is the owner of **Outfitters Kauai** ☞, 2827A Poipu Rd. (at Poipu Plaza, a small five-shop mall before the road forks to Poipu/Spouting Horn), Poipu ((✆ 888/742-9887 or 808/742-9667; www.outfitterskauai.com), which offers several kayaking tours. A full-day trip along the entire Na Pali Coast (summer only) costs $185 per person and includes a guide, lunch, drinks, and equipment. Another kayak tour takes you up a jungle stream and involves a short hike to waterfalls and a swimming hole; it's $94 (children, ages 5–14, $72) including lunch, snacks, and drinks. Outfitters Kauai also rents river kayaks by the day ($40).

In the winter, mid-September to mid-May, **Outfitters Kauai** ☞ has launched a new **South Shore Sea Kayak Tour.** This 8-mile tour, from Poipu to Port Allen, lets you explore secluded bays and beaches that you can only get to by the sea. Along the way, the guided tour stops for coffee and snacks and later for lunch. This fabulous tour is not for everyone; if you get seasick, you might want to reconsider. Also, the paddling is moderately strenuous and not appropriate for kids under 12. But those adventurous souls, who are somewhat fit and love exploring, will be talking about this tour for a long time. Cost is $129 for adults and $105 for kids ages 12 to 14.

The cheapest place to rent kayaks is the **Activity Warehouse,** 788 Kuhio Hwy. (across from McDonald's), Kapaa ((✆ 808/822-4000), where a one-person kayak goes for $10 a day and a two-person kayak is $15. You can also rent from **Kauai Water Ski & Surf Co.,** Kinipopo Shopping Village, 4-356 Kuhio Hwy. (on the ocean side), Kapaa ((✆ 808/822-3574); or **Pedal 'n Paddle,** Ching Young Village Shopping Center, Hanalei ((✆ 808/826-9069; pedalnpaddle.com).

PADDLING INTO HULEIA NATIONAL WILDLIFE REFUGE Ride the Huleia River through Kauai's 240-acre Huleia National Wildlife Refuge, the last stand of Kauai's endangered birds, with **True Blue,** Nawiliwili Harbor ((✆ 888/245-1707 or 808/245-9662; www.kauaifun.com). You paddle up the picturesque Huleia (which appeared in *Raiders of the Lost Ark* and the remake of *King Kong*) under sheer pinnacles that open into valleys full of lush tropical plants, bright flowers, and hanging vines. Look for great blue herons and Hawaiian gallinules taking wing. The 4½-hour voyage, which starts at Nawiliwili Harbor, is a great trip for all—but especially for movie buffs, birders, and great adventurers under 12. It's even safe for nonswimmers. Wear a swimsuit, T-shirt, and boat shoes. The cost is $89 for adults, $36 for children 8 to 12. The prices include a picnic snack, juice, kayak, life vest, and guide services.

SCUBA DIVING

Diving on Kauai is dictated by the weather. In winter, when heavy swells and high winds hit the island, diving is generally limited to the more protected south shore. Probably the best-known site along the south shore is **Caverns,** located off the Poipu Beach resort area. This site consists of a series of lava tubes interconnected by a chain of archways. A constant parade of fish streams by (even shy lionfish are spotted lurking in crevices), brightly hued Hawaiian lobsters hide in the lava's tiny holes, and turtles swim past.

In summer, when the north Pacific storms subside, the magnificent North Shore opens up. You can take a boat dive locally known as the **Oceanarium,** northwest of Hanalei Bay, where you'll find a kaleidoscopic marine world in a horseshoe-shaped cove. From the rare (long-handed spiny lobsters) to the more common (taape, conger eels, and nudibranchs), the resident population is one of the more diverse on the island. The topography, which features pinnacles, ridges, and archways, is covered with cup corals, black-coral trees, and nooks and crannies enough for a dozen dives.

Because the best dives on Kauai are offshore, we recommend booking a two-tank dive off a dive boat. **Bubbles Below Scuba Charters,** 6251 Hauaala Rd., Kapaa (© **808/822-3483;** www.aloha.net/~kaimanu), specializes in highly personalized, small-group dives, with an emphasis on marine biology. The 35-foot dive boat, *Kaimanu,* is a custom-built Radon that comes complete with a hot shower. Two-tank boat dives cost $110 ($25 more if you need gear); nondivers can come along for the ride for $50. In summer (May–Sept) Bubbles Below offers a three-tank trip for experienced divers only to the "forbidden" island of Niihau, 90 minutes by boat from Kauai. You should be comfortable with vertical drop-offs, huge underwater caverns, possibly choppy surface conditions, and significant currents. You should also be willing to share water space with the resident sharks. The all-day, three-tank trip costs $260, including tanks, weights, dive computer, lunch, drinks, and marine guide (if you need gear, it's $25 more).

On the south side, call **Fathom Five Adventures,** 3450 Poipu Rd. (next to the Chevron), Koloa (© **808/742-6991**).

GREAT SHORE DIVES FROM KAUAI If you want to rent your own equipment for shore dives, it will probably cost around $25 to $40 a day. Try **Dive Kauai,** 4-976 Kuhio Hwy., Kapaa (© **808/822-0452**); or **Fathom Five Adventures,** 3450 Poipu Rd. (next to the Chevron), Koloa (© **808/742-6991**).

Spectacular shoreline dive sites on the North Shore include **Kee Beach/Haena Beach Park** (where the road ends), one of the most picturesque beaches on the island. On a calm summer day, the drop-off near the reef begs for underwater exploration. Another good bet is **Tunnels Beach,** also known as Makua Beach. It's off Highway 560, just past mile marker 8; look for the short dirt road (less than a half mile) to the beach. The wide reef here makes for some fabulous snorkeling and diving, but again, only during the calm summer months. **Cannons Beach,** east of Haena Beach Park (use the parking area for Haena, located across the street from the Dry Cave near mile marker 9 on Hwy. 560), has lots of vibrant marine life in its sloping offshore reef.

On the south shore, if you want to catch a glimpse of sea turtles, head to **Tortugas** (located directly in front of Poipu Beach Park). **Koloa Landing** has a horseshoe-shaped reef teeming with tropical fish. **Sheraton Caverns** (located off the Sheraton Kauai) is also popular, due to its three large underwater lava tubes, which are usually filled with marine life.

SNORKELING

See the intro to this section for locations of **Snorkel Bob's.**

For great shoreline snorkeling, try the reef off **Kee Beach/Haena Beach Park,** located at the end of Highway 560. **Tunnels Beach,** about a mile before the end of Highway 560 in Haena, has a wide reef that's great for poking around in search of tropical fish. Be sure to check ocean conditions—don't go if the surf is up or if there's a strong current. **Anini Beach,** located off the northern end of Kalihiwai Road (between mile markers 25 and 26 on Kuhio Hwy., or Hwy. 56), just before the Princeville Airport, has a safe, shallow area with excellent snorkeling. **Poipu Beach Park** has some good snorkeling to the right side of Nukumoi Point—the tombolo area, where the narrow strip of sand divides the ocean, is best. If this spot is too crowded, wander down the beach in front of the old Waiohai resort; if there are no waves, this place is also hopping with marine life. **Salt Pond Beach Park,** off Highway 50 near Hanapepe, has good snorkeling around the two rocky points, home to hundreds of tropical fish.

SURFING

Hanalei Bay's winter surf is the most popular on the island, but it's for experts only. **Poipu Beach** is an excellent spot at which to learn to surf; the waves are small and—best of all—nobody laughs when you wipe out. Check with the local surf shops or call the **Weather Service** (☎ 808/245-3564) to find out where surf's up.

Surf lessons are available for $60 for a 1½-hour session, including all-day use of equipment (board, wet suit top, and carrying rack for your car), from **Windsurf Kauai,** in Hanalei (☎ 808/828-6838). Poipu is also the site of numerous surfing schools; the oldest and best is **Margo Oberg's School of Surfing,** at the Nukumoi Surf Shop, across from Brennecke's Beach (☎ 808/742-8019). Margo charges $50 for 2 hours of group instruction, including surfboard and leash; she guarantees that by the end of the lesson, you'll be standing and catching a wave.

Equipment is available for rent (ranging from $5 an hour or $20 a day for "soft" beginner boards to $7.50 an hour or $30 a day for hard boards) from **Nukumoi Surf Shop,** across from Brennecke's Beach, Poipu Beach Park (☎ 888/384-8810 or 808/742-8019); **Hanalei Surf Co.,** 5-5161 Kuhio Hwy. (across from Zelo's Beach House Restaurant in Hanalei Center), Hanalei (☎ 808/826-9000); and **Pedal 'n Paddle,** Ching Young Village Shopping Center, Hanalei (☎ 808/826-9069). The cheapest place to rent a board is the **Activity Warehouse,** 788 Kuhio Hwy. (across from McDonald's), Kapaa (☎ 808/822-4000), where they start at $5 a day.

TUBING

Back in the days of the sugar plantations, on really hot days, if no one was looking, local kids would grab inner tubes and jump in the irrigation ditches crisscrossing the cane fields for an exciting ride. Today you can enjoy this (formerly illegal) activity by

(Kids) Especially for Kids

Surfing with an Expert (p. 167)   If seven-time world champ Margo Oberg, a member of the Surfing Hall of Fame, can't get your kid—or you—up on a board riding a wave, nobody can. She promises same-day results even for klutzes.

Paddling up the•Huleia River (p. 165)   Indiana Jones ran for his life up this river to his seaplane in *Raiders of the Lost Ark*. You and the kids can venture down it yourself in a kayak. The picturesque Huleia winds through tropically lush Huleia National Wildlife Refuge, where endangered species like great blue herons and Hawaiian gallinules take wing. It's ideal for everyone.

Climbing the Wooden Jungle Gyms at Kamalani Playground   Located in Lydgate State Park, Wailua, this unique playground has a maze of jungle gyms for children of all ages. You can whip down slides, explore caves, hang from bars, and climb all over. It's a great place to spend the afternoon.

Cooling Off with a Shave Ice (p. 131)   On a hot, hot day, stop by **Brennecke's Beach Broiler**, across from Poipu Beach Park (© **808/742-1582**), and order a traditional Hawaiian shave ice. This local treat consists of crushed ice stuffed into a paper cone and topped with a tropical-flavored syrup. If you can't decide on a flavor, go for the "rainbow"—three different flavors in one cone.

Exploring a Magical World (p. 206)   **Na Aina Kai Botanical Gardens,** located on about 240 acres sprinkled with some 70 life-size (some larger than life-size) whimsical bronze statues, and hidden off the beaten path of the North Shore, is perfect for kids. The tropical children's garden features a gecko hedge maze, a tropical jungle gym, a treehouse in a rubber tree, and a 16-foot-tall Jack and the Bean Stalk Giant with a 33-foot wading pool below. Na Aina Kai is only open 3 days a week, so book before you leave for Hawaii to avoid disappointment.

Experiencing a Hands-On Learning Adventure (p. 192)   The **Kauai Museum,** located in Kapaa (© **808/823-8222**; www.kcdm.org), resulted from a grassroots community effort. The exhibits offer activities ranging from playing with Hawaiian musical instruments, to participating in virtual reality television, to hiding out in a "magic treehouse" and reading a book. (There's even a "baby area" for kids 4 and under.) There are also Keiki Camps (Children's Camps) where you can leave the kids all day. The kids will be taken on outings to the beach and other points of interest.

"tubing" the flumes and ditches of the old Lihue Plantation through **Kauai Backcountry Adventures** (© **888/270-0555** or 808/245-2506; www.kauaibackcountry. com). Passengers are taken in four-wheel-drive vehicles high into the mountains above Lihue and see vistas generally off-limits to the public. At the flumes, you will be outfitted with a giant tube, gloves, and headlamp (for the long passageways through the tunnels). All you do is jump in the water, and the gentle gravity-feed flow will carry you through forests, into tunnels, and finally to a mountain swimming hole, where a picnic lunch is served. The 3-hour tours are $92 and appropriate for anyone ages 5 to 95. Swimming is not necessary, since all you do is relax and drift downstream.

WATER-SKIING

Hawaii's only freshwater water-skiing is on the Wailua River. Ski boats launch from the boat ramp in Wailua River State Park, directly across from the marina. **Kauai Water Ski & Surf Co.,** Kinipopo Shopping Village, 4-356 Kuhio Hwy., Kapaa (© **800/344-7915** or 808/822-3574), rents equipment and offers lessons and guided tours. A half-hour trip costs $55; an hour-long trip costs $110.

WINDSURFING & KITESURFING

Anini Beach is one of the safest beaches for beginners to learn windsurfing. Lessons and equipment rental are available at **Anini Beach Windsurfing and Kitesurfing** (© **808/826-WIND** or 808/826-9463). Owner Foster Ducker has been teaching windsurfing for nearly a decade, he has special equipment to help beginners learn the sport. A 1-hour lesson is $50 and includes equipment and instruction. If you fall in love with the sport and want to keep going, he'll rent the equipment for $25 an hour or $50 for the rest of the day. For those experienced windsurfers who don't want to cart their equipment half way around the globe, he will rent windsurfing equipment for $25 an hour or $75 a day. Serious windsurfers should head to **Hanalei Bay** or **Tunnels Beach** on the North Shore.

For the really adventurous, Ducker also is a certified instructor in kitesurfing; he claims he can get people up and on the water in just one lesson. His introduction to kitesurfing is 5-hours long and costs $400 for one person and $600 for two.

3 Hiking & Camping

Kauai is an adventurer's delight. The island's greatest tropical beauty isn't easily accessed; you have to head out on foot and find it: More than 90% of Kauai is inaccessible by road. Trails range from a 10-minute nature loop from your car and back to check out Mother Nature without too much fuss, to several days of trekking requiring stamina and fitness. Those interested in seeing the backcountry—complete with virgin waterfalls, remote wilderness trails, and quiet meditative settings—should head for Waimea Canyon and Kokee Park or for the Na Pali Coast and the Kalalau Trail. Most trails are well marked and maintained, but occasionally, after a heavy rainy season, markers are down and the vegetation has taken over. Always ask about a trail before you go.

Camping on Kauai can be extreme (it's cold at 4,000 ft. in Kokee) or benign (by the sea). It can be wet, cold, and rainy, or hot, dry, and windy—often all on the same day. If you're heading for Kokee, bring rain gear, warm clothes, T-shirts, and shorts. (You will use everything.)

For more information on Kauai's hiking trails, contact the **State Division of Parks,** P.O. Box 1671, Lihue, HI 96766 (© **808/274-3446;** www.hawaii.gov/dlnr/dsp/kauai. html); the **State Division of Forestry and Wildlife,** P.O. Box 1671, Lihue, HI 96766 (© **808/274-3077;** www.dofaw.net); **Kauai County Parks and Recreation,** 4193 Hardy St., Lihue, HI 96766 (© **808/241-6670;** www.k12.hi.us/~pworks/parksand rec); or the **Kokee Lodge Manager,** P.O. Box 819, Waimea, HI 96796 (© **808/ 335-6061**).

Kayak Kauai Outbound (*, a mile past Hanalei Bridge on Highway 560 in Hanalei (© **800/437-3507** or 808/826-9844; fax 808/822-0577; www.kayakkauai.com), is the

---

Tips   A Warning about Flash Floods

When it rains on Kauai, the waterfalls rage and rivers and streams overflow, causing flash floods on roads and trails. If you're hiking, avoid dry streambeds, which flood quickly and wash out to sea. Before going hiking, camping, or sailing, especially in the rainy season (Nov–Mar), check the weather forecast by calling © **808/245-6001.**

---

premier all-around outfitter on the island. It's staffed by local experts who keep track of weather forecasts and sea and trail conditions; they have a lot of pertinent information that hikers, campers, and other backcountry adventurers need to know. Plus they have guided hiking tours starting at $81 per person. If you don't plan to bring your own gear, you can rent it here or at **Pedal 'n Paddle,** in Hanalei (© **808/826-9069**). If you want to buy camping equipment, head for **Ace Island Hardware,** at Princeville Shopping Center (© **808/826-6980**).

GUIDED HIKES   You can join a guided hike with the Kauai chapter of the **Sierra Club,** P.O. Box 3412, Lihue, HI 96766 (© **808/246-8748;** www.hi.sierraclub.org), which offers four to seven different hikes every month. The hikes vary from an easy family moonlit beach hike, to a moderate 4-mile trip up some 1,100 feet, to 8-mile-plus treks for serious hikers only. The club also does guided hikes of Kokee State Park (see below), usually on weekends. Because there's no staffed office, the best way to contact the chapter is to check the website; outings are usually listed 3 to 6 months in advance, with complete descriptions of the hike, the hike leader's phone number, and what to wear and bring. You can also check the daily newspaper, the *Garden Island,* for a list of hikes in the Community Calendar section. Generally, the club asks for a donation of $5 per person per hike for non-members, $1 for members. It also does service work (clearing trails, picking up trash) on the hikes, so you may spend an hour doing service work, then 2 to 3 hours hiking. Last year, the club took three service-work trips along the Na Pali Coast trail to help maintain it.

During the summer, **Kokee Natural History Museum** (© **808/335-9975**) offers **"Wonder Walks,"** a series of guided hikes throughout Kokee State Park for a donation. This is a great way to learn more about the unusual flora and fauna in this high mountain area and to meet new people. Space is limited, so you have to call in your reservation. Hikers are advised to eat lunch before the hike and to bring light rain gear, water, snacks, sunscreen, protective clothing, and hiking boots. The hike leaves promptly at 12:30pm.

Hawaiian Wildlife Tours ✦ (© **808/639-2968;** cberg@pixi.com) is environmental education in action. Biologist Dr. Carl Berg will take you out into the woods and down to the shoreline to see Kauai's native and vanishing species, from forest birds and flora to hoary bats, monk seals, and green sea turtles. His personalized tours last from 1 hour to a week and are tailored around the season and weather, your physical abilities, and what you want to see. He leads tours to Hanalei taro fields to see wetland birds, to Crater Hill to see nene geese, to Mahaulepu to see wildflowers in the sand dunes, to Kilauea Lighthouse to see oceanic birds, and much more. Rates are $45 per couple, per hour.

Kauai Hiking Trails

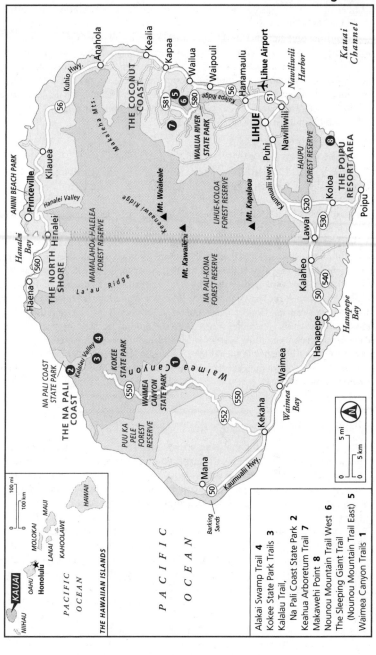

Alakai Swamp Trail **4**
Kokee State Park Trails **3**
Kalalau Trail,
    Na Pali Coast State Park **2**
Keahua Arboretum Trail **7**
Makawehi Point **8**
Nounou Mountain Trail West **6**
The Sleeping Giant Trail
    (Nounou Mountain Trail East) **5**
Waimea Canyon Trails **1**

Other options for guided hikes include **Princeville Ranch Hiking Adventures** (© **808/826-7669;** www.kauai-hiking.com), which offers various hikes on 2,000 acres of private property, such as a 3-hour hike to a waterfall (plus another hour spent swimming) for $79; and **Kauai Nature Adventures** (© **888/233-8365** or 808/ 742-8305; www.kauainaturetours.com), which offers a geological-history excursion, a tour of Kauai's environments from the mountains to the ocean, and a Mahaulepu coast hike. All Kauai Nature Adventures are led by scientists and cost $87 for adults and $54 for children ages 7 to 12, plus a host of other tours ranging in price up to $97 for adults and $64 for children.

THE POIPU RESORT AREA
MAKAWEHI POINT *

Like a ship's prow, Makawehi Point juts out to sea on the east side of Keoneloa Beach (known locally as Shipwreck Beach), which lies in front of the Grand Hyatt Poipu. This 50-foot-high sand-dune bluff attracts a variety of people: pole fishers, whale-watchers, those who just like the panoramic views of the Pacific, and daredevils who test their courage by leaping off the cliff into the waves (don't try it).

The trail head begins on the east end of Shipwreck Beach, past the Hyatt. It's an easy 10-minute walk up to Makawehi Point; after you take in the big picture, keep going uphill along the ridge of the sand dunes (said to contain ancient Hawaiian burial sites), past the coves frequented by green sea turtles and endangered Hawaiian monk seals, through the coastal pine forest, and past World War II bunkers to the very top. Now you can see Haupu Ridge and its 2,297-foot peak, the famously craggy ridgeline that eerily resembles Queen Victoria's profile and, in the distance, Mahaulepu Beach, one of the best looking in Hawaii. Inland, three red craters dimple the green fields; the one in the middle, the biggest, Puu Huni Huni, is said to have been the last volcano to erupt on Kauai—but it was so long ago that nobody here can remember when.

Moments Zipping through the Forest

The latest adventure on Kauai is an activity called *zipline*. From a high perch, participants (known as "zippers"), outfitted in harnesses and helmets, attach themselves to a cable, which is suspended above the ground from one point to another a hundred or so feet away. Ignoring gravity, the zippers, attached only by a cable, zoom through the air, above tree tops, at speeds of 35 mph from one end of the cable to the other. It's an adrenaline rush you will not forget. One of our favorite zipline tours is done by **Outfitters Kauai** *, 2827A Poipu Rd., Poipu (© **888/742-9887** or 808/742-9667; www.outfitterskauai.com). Their **Kipu Falls Zipline Trek** starts with a ¼-mile hike through the jungle to a steep valley with a 150-foot waterfall. You climb up one side of the valley, attach yourself to the cable some 50 feet above the earth, and step off the platform. Hollering with ear-to-ear grins is the result of "zipping" along the cable over the forest canopy, rivers, and waterfalls. Even first time zippers run as quick as their legs will carry them back up the trail to do it all over again. If you get your fill of zipping, there are hikes, a swimming hole, and rope swings to fill up the 3-hour adventure. Cost is $94 for adults and $75 for children ages 10 to 14.

Kauai Cabins & Campgrounds

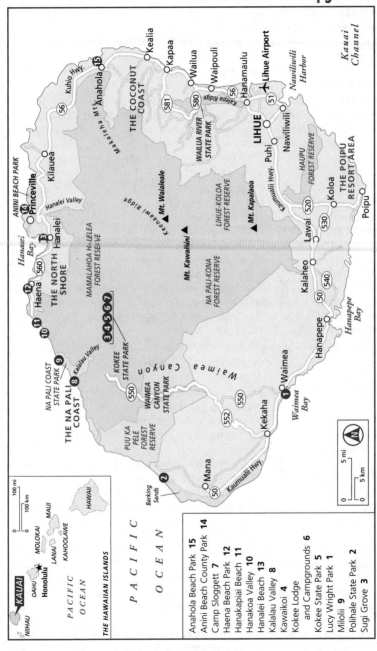

THE HAWAIIAN ISLANDS

NIIHAU

KAUAI

OAHU
Honolulu

MOLOKAI

LANAI

MAUI

KAHOOLAWE

HAWAII

PACIFIC OCEAN

Anahola Beach Park **15**
Anini Beach County Park **14**
Camp Sloggett **7**
Haena Beach Park **12**
Hanakapiai Beach **11**
Hanakoa Valley **10**
Hanalei Beach **13**
Kalalau Valley **8**
Kawaikoi **4**
Kokee Lodge
  and Campgrounds **6**
Kokee State Park **5**
Lucy Wright Park **1**
Milolii **9**
Polihale State Park **2**
Sugi Grove **3**

WESTERN KAUAI
WAIMEA CANYON TRAILS

On a wet island like Kauai, a dry hike is hard to find. But in the desert-dry gulch of Waimea Canyon, known as the Grand Canyon of the Pacific (once you get here, you'll see why—it's pretty spectacular), you're not likely to slip and slide in the muck as you go.

CANYON TRAIL   You want to hike Hawaii's Grand Canyon, but you don't think you have time? Well, then, take the Canyon Trail to the east rim for a breathtaking view into the 3,000-foot-deep canyon. Park your car at the top of Halemanu Valley Road (located between mile markers 14 and 15 on Waimea Canyon Rd., about a mile down from the museum). Walk down the not very clearly marked trail on the 3.5-mile round-trip, which takes 2 to 3 hours and leads to Waipoo Falls (as does the hike below) and back. We suggest going in the afternoon, when the light is best.

HIKE TO WAIPOO FALLS   The 3-hour round-trip hike to Waipoo Falls is one of Kauai's best hikes. The two-tiered, 800-foot waterfall that splashes into a natural pool is worth every step it takes to get here. To find the trail, drive up Kokee Road (Hwy. 550) to the Puu Hina Hina Outlook; a quarter mile past the lookout, near a NASA satellite tracking station on the right, a two-lane dirt road leads to the Waipoo Falls trail head. From here, the trail winds gently through a jungle dotted with wild yellow orchids and flame-red torch ginger before it leads you out onto a descending ridgeback that juts deep into the canyon. At the end of the promontory, take a left and push on through the jungle to the falls; reward yourself with a refreshing splash in the pool.

KOKEE STATE PARK

At the end of Highway 550, which leads through Waimea Canyon to its summit, lies a 4,640-acre state park of high-mountain forest wilderness (3,600 ft.–4,000 ft. above sea level). The rainforest, bogs, and breathtaking views of the Na Pali Coast and Waimea Canyon are the draws at Kokee. This is the place for hiking—among the 45 miles of maintained trails are some of the best hikes in Hawaii. Official trail maps of all the park's trails are for sale for 50¢ at the **Kokee Natural History Museum** (© **808/335-9975**).

A few words of advice: Always check current trail conditions. Up-to-date trail information is available on a bulletin board at the Kokee Natural History Museum. Stay on established trails; it's easy to get lost here. Get off the trail well before dark. Carry water and rain gear—even if it's perfectly sunny when you set out—and wear sunscreen.

For complete coverage of the state park, see p. 196.

AWAAWAPUHI TRAIL   This 3.25-mile hike (6.5 miles round-trip) takes about 3 hours each way and is considered strenuous by most, but it offers a million-dollar view. Look for the trail head at the left of the parking lot, at mile marker 17, between the museum and Kalalau Lookout. The well-marked and maintained trail now sports quarter-mile markers, and you can pick up a free plant guide for the trail at the museum. The trail drops about 1,600 feet through native forests to a thin precipice right at the very edge of the Na Pali cliffs for a dramatic and dizzying view of the tropical valleys and blue Pacific 2,500 feet below. It's not recommended for anyone with vertigo (although a railing will keep you from a major slip and fall). Go early, before clouds obscure the view, or go late in the day; the chiaroscuro sunsets are something to behold.

The Awaawapuhi can be a straight out-and-back trail or a loop that connects with the **Nualolo Trail** (3.75 miles), which provides awesome views and leads back to the main road between the ranger's house and the Kokee cabins, about a mile and a half from where you started. So you can hike the remaining 1.5 miles along the road or hitch a ride if you decide to do the entire loop but can't make it all the way.

HALEMANU-KOKEE TRAIL This trail takes you on a pleasant, easy-to-moderate 2.5-mile round-trip walk through a native koa and ohia forest inhabited by native birds. The trail head is near mile marker 15; pick up the Faye Trail, which leads to this one. The Halemanu–Kokee Trail links Kokee Valley to Halemanu Valley (hence the name); along the way, you'll see a plum orchard, valleys, and ridges.

PIHEA TRAIL This is the park's flattest trail, but it's still a pretty strenuous 7.5-mile round-trip. A new boardwalk on a third of the trail makes it easier, especially when it's wet. The trail begins at the end of Highway 550 at Puu o Kila Lookout, which overlooks Kalalau Valley; it goes down at first, then flattens out as it traces the back ridge of the valley. Once it enters the rainforest, you'll see native plants and trees. It intersects with the Alakai Swamp Trail (below). If you combine both trails, figure on about 4 hours in and out.

ALAKAI SWAMP TRAIL ✿ If you want to see the "real" Hawaii, this is it—a big swamp that's home to rare birds and plants. The trail allows a rare glimpse into a wet, cloud-covered wilderness preserve where 460 inches of rainfall a year is common. This 7-mile hike used to take 5 hours of sloshing through the bog, with mud up to your knees. Now a boardwalk protects you from the shoe-grabbing mud. Come prepared for rain. (The silver lining is that there are no mosquitoes above 3,000 ft.)

The trail head is off Mohihi (Camp 10) Road, just beyond the Forest Reserve entrance sign and the Alakai Shelter picnic area. From the parking lot, the trail follows an old World War II–era four-wheel-drive road. Stick to the boardwalk; this is a fragile eco-area (not to mention the mud). At the end of the 3.5-mile slog, if you're lucky and the clouds part, you'll have a lovely view of Wainiha Valley and Hanalei from Kilohana Lookout.

CAMPGROUNDS & WILDERNESS CABINS IN KOKEE

CABINS & TENT CAMPGROUNDS Camping facilities include state campgrounds (one next to Kokee Lodge, and four more primitive backcountry sites), one private tent area, and the **Kokee Lodge,** which has 12 cabins for rent at very reasonable rates. At 4,000 feet, the nights are cold, particularly in winter. Because no open fires are permitted at Kokee, the best deal is the cabins. (See chapter 5 for details.) The **Kokee Lodge Restaurant** is open daily from 9am to 3:30pm for continental breakfast and lunch. Groceries and gas aren't available in Kokee, so stock up in advance, or you'll have to make the long trip down the mountain.

The **state campground** at Kokee allows tent camping only. Permits can be obtained from a state parks office on any island; on Kauai, it's at 3060 Eiwa St., Room 306, Lihue, HI 96766 (© **808/274-3444;** www.hawaii.gov/dlnr/dsp/fees.html). The permits are $5 per night; the time limit is 5 nights in a single 30-day period. Facilities include showers, drinking water, picnic tables, pavilion with tables, restrooms, barbecues, sinks for dishwashing, and electric lights.

Tent camping at **Camp Sloggett,** owned by the Kauai YWCA, 3094 Elua St., Lihue, HI 96766 (© **808/335-6060;** fax 808/245-5961; campingkauai.com), is available for $10 per person per night (children under 5 stay free). The sites are on

Hiking Safety

According to a survey done in 2000, 78% of the hikers in Hawaii were from out-of-state. At the same time, Hawaii's search-and-rescue teams are responding to more and more calls from injured, stranded, or missing hikers. The best thing you can do to avoid becoming a statistic is to get Na Ala Hele's (the State of Hawaii's Trail and Access Program) free brochure, **Hiking Safety in Hawaii** (from the State Department of Land and Natural Resources, Division of Forestry & Wildlife, 1151 Punchbowl St., Room 325, Honolulu, HI 96813; (Ⓒ) **808/587-0166**; or print it off the Web at www.hawaii trails.org). This free brochure could save your life. It has comprehensive lists of trail safety tips and equipment you'll need; describes what to do in an emergency; and contains other information you should know before you lace up your hiking boots.

If you are not an experienced hiker, consider hiking with a commercial operator (we list several in this chapter), or join a Sierra Club hike. If you have experience hiking, keep these tips in mind when venturing out in Hawaii:

- **Remember you are a guest** in Hawaii and treat the land (especially sacred cultural areas) with respect by following posted signage on the trail. Always start your hikes with clean (well-scrubbed) boots, so you don't unintentionally carry seeds into the island's fragile environment.
- **Practice courtesy** when on a multiple-usage trail. The signs will let you know who to yield to (hikers generally yield to horseback riders, and bikers yield to both hikers and horses).
- **Plan your hike** by informing others where you are going and when you should be back. Learn as much as you can about the hike (the conditions you will encounter and the degree of difficulty) before you set out.

1½ acres of open field, with a covered pit for fires and a barbecue area, plus volleyball and badminton nets. There's also a hostel-style accommodation at the **Weinberg Bunkhouse,** with bunk beds, separate toilets, showers, and kitchenettes ($20 per person). To get here, continue on the highway past park headquarters and take the first right after the Kokee Lodge. Follow the dirt road and look for the wooden CAMP SLOGGETT sign; turn right and follow the bumpy road past the state cabins into a large clearing.

BACKCOUNTRY CAMPING The more primitive backcountry campgrounds include **Sugi Grove** and **Kawaikoi,** located about 4 miles from park headquarters on the Camp 10 Road, an often muddy and steep four-wheel-drive road. Sugi Grove is located across the Kawaikoi Stream from the Kawaikoi campsite. The area is named for the sugi pines, which were planted in 1937 by the Civilian Conservation Corps. This is a shady campsite with a single picnic shelter, a pit toilet, a stream, and space for several tents. The Kawaikoi site is a 3-acre open grass field, surrounded by Kokee plum trees and forests of koa and ohia. Facilities include two picnic shelters, a composting

- **Hike with a partner.** Never go alone. Dress in layers to protect yourself from Hawaii's intense tropical sun, carry light rain gear, have a brightly colored jacket (not only for weather, but so that if you get lost, people will be able to spot you), and bring a hat, sunglasses, and sunscreen. If you are hiking, you should wear hiking boots with traction and ankle support.
- **Check the weather.** Call © 808/245-6001. The bright, sunny day can dissolve into wind and rain, and you don't want to be caught in a narrow gully or streambed where flash flooding is possible.
- **Carry water** (2 liters per person per day), a cellphone, and a daypack (holding a whistle, sunscreen, insect repellent, a small flashlight, food, and a basic first-aid kit). Don't drink untreated stream water; *leptospirosis* (a bacterial disease transmitted from animals to humans, which can be fatal) is present in some streams.
- **Stay on the trail** and stay together. Most hikers are injured wandering off the trail or trying to climb rocks.
- **Watch the time.** Being close to the equator, Hawaii does not have a very long twilight. Once the sun goes down, it's dark. Be sure to allow enough time to return from your hike, and always carry a flashlight.
- **If an emergency arises** (for example, if an injury or illness prevents someone from walking, bad weather hits, it's too dark to see, or you become lost or stranded), call 911 and ask for fire/rescue. Tell them what trail you are on and what happened. Make yourself visible with either bright clothing or a flashlight, and use the whistle. Stay calm and stay put. Keep as warm as you can by getting out of wind and rain and by layering clothing to maintain your body temperature.

toilet, and a stream that flows next to the camping area. There is no potable water—bring in your own or treat the stream water.

Permits are available from the **State Forestry and Wildlife Division,** 3060 Eiwa St., Room 306, Lihue, HI 96766 (© **808/274-3444;** www.hawaii.gov/dlnr/dsp/fees. html). There's no fee for the permits, but camping is limited to 3 nights. You can also request the *Kauai Recreation Map* (with illustrations of all roads; trails; and picnic, hunting, and camping areas) by mail; contact the Forestry and Wildlife Division at the number above to find out how.

BEACH CAMPING AT POLIHALE STATE PARK

Polihale holds the distinction of being the westernmost beach in the United States. The beach is spectacular—some 300-feet wide in summer, with rolling sand dunes (some as high as 100 ft.), and the islands of Niihau and Lehua just offshore. Bordered by a curtain of Na Pali Coast cliffs to the north, razor-sharp ridges and steep valleys to the east, and the blue Pacific to the south and west, this is one of the most dramatic camping areas in the state.

Tips **Safety Tip**

Be sure to see "Staying Healthy," in chapter 2, before you set out on your Kauai adventures. It includes useful information on hiking, camping, and ocean safety, plus how to avoid seasickness and sunburn, and what to do should you get stung by a jellyfish.

The campgrounds for tent camping are located at the south end of the beach, affording privacy from daytime beach activities. There's great swimming in summer (even then, be on the lookout for waves and rip currents—there are no lifeguards), some surfing (the rides are usually short), and fishing. The camping is on sand, although there are some kiawe trees for shade. (*Warning:* Kiawe trees drop long thorns, so make sure you have protective footwear.) Facilities include restrooms, showers, picnic tables, barbecues, and a spigot for drinking water. You can purchase supplies about 15 miles away in Waimea.

Permits, which are $5 per night, are available through the **State Parks Office,** 3060 Eiwa St., Lihue, HI 96766 (*©* **808/241-3444**). You're limited to 5 nights in any 30-day period. To reach the park from Lihue, take Highway 50 west to Barking Sands Pacific Missile Range. Bear right onto the paved road, which heads toward the mountains. There will be small signs directing you to Polihale; the second sign will point to a left turn onto a dirt road. Follow this for about 5 miles; at the fork in the road, the campgrounds are to the left and the beach park is to the right.

BEACH CAMPING AT LUCY WRIGHT PARK

If you want to camp on the west side but can't get a space at Polihale State Park, the county allows camping at the 4½-acre Lucy Wright Park, located just outside Waimea. Not the best beach park, it's okay for camping in a pinch. The park, located on the western side of the Waimea River, is where Captain Cook first came ashore in Hawaii in January 1778. The park is named after the first native Hawaiian schoolteacher at Waimea, Lucy Kapahu Aukai Wright (1873–1931). The beach here is full of flotsam and jetsam from the river, making it unappealing. On the other side of the Waimea River, across from Lucy Wright Park, is the 17¼-acre Russian Fort, with ruins of a Russian fort built in 1815. Facilities at Lucy Wright include the camping area, restrooms, a pavilion, picnic tables, and (cold) showers. You need a permit to camp at any of the county's seven beach parks. Permits are $3 per person, per night. You can stay at the county parks a maximum of 4 nights (or 12 nights if you go from one county park to another). To apply for the permit, contact Shani Saito in the Permits Division of Kauai County Parks and Recreation, 4193 Hardy St., Lihue, HI 96766 (*©* **808/241-6660;** www.kauai-hawaii.com/activities.php). To get to Lucy Wright Park, take Kaumualii Highway (Hwy. 50) to Waimea and turn left on Alawai Road, which leads to the park.

THE COCONUT COAST

THE SLEEPING GIANT TRAIL (NOUNOU MOUNTAIN TRAIL EAST)

This medium-to-difficult hike takes you up Nounou Mountain, known as Sleeping Giant (it really does look like a giant resting on his back), to a fabulous view. The clearly marked trail will gain 1,000 feet in altitude. (Be sure to stay on the trail.) The climb is steadily uphill (remember you are climbing a mountain), but the view at the top is well worth the constant incline. To get to the trail head, turn *mauka* (toward the mountain) off Kuhio Highway (Hwy. 56) onto Halcilio Road (between Wailua and Kapaa, just past mile marker 6); follow Haleilio Road for 1.25 miles to the parking area, at telephone pole no. 38. From here, signs posted by the State of Hawaii Division of Forestry and Wildlife lead you over the 1.75-mile trail, which ends at a picnic table and shelter. The panoramic view is breathtaking. Be sure to bring water—and a picnic, if you like.

NOUNOU MOUNTAIN TRAIL WEST

If you would like to venture up Sleeping Giant from the other side of Nounou Mountain, this trail joins up with the east trail. This trail is shorter than the eastern trail and you're in forest most of the time. To get to the trail head, take Kuhio Highway (Hwy. 56) to Wailua. Turn left onto Kuamoo Road (Hwy. 580) and continue to Kamalu Road (Hwy. 581), where you turn right. Make a left on Lokelani Street and drive to the end of the road, where there's a parking area and trail head. This trail meanders through forests of Norfolk pine, strawberry guava and, as you climb closer to the top, hala trees. About a quarter mile into the hike you will come to a fork with the Kuamoo Trail; veer left. Continue to climb and you will reach the picnic area and shelter.

KEAHUA ARBORETUM TRAIL

If you are looking for an easy hike for the entire family, this half-mile loop will take you just a half hour. It offers you a chance to swim in a cool mountain stream and maybe enjoy a picnic lunch. To get here, take Kuhio Highway (Hwy. 56) to Wailua. Turn left on Kuamoo Road (Hwy. 580) and continue past the University of Hawaii Agricultural Experimental Station to the Keahua Arboretum. The trail head is on the left just past the stream, across the street from the parking lot. This area gets nearly 100 inches of rain a year, and the colorful painted gum eucalyptus trees at the trail head couldn't be happier. Along the trail you'll see kukui trees (which the Hawaiians used as a light source), milo (popular among wood artists), hau, and ohia lehua. As you walk parallel to the stream, be on the lookout for a good swimming area. There are lots of picnic tables and shelters along the trail at which to stop and have lunch.

BEACH CAMPING AT ANAHOLA BEACH PARK

Local residents, who love this park and are here almost every day, say that this is the safest year-round swimming beach and great for small children. Tucked behind Kala Point, the narrow park has a shallow offshore reef that protects the sandy shoreline from the high surf visiting the area. Another plus is that board surfing is prohibited in this area. Surfers have to head to the north end of the beach to the sandbar where surfing is allowed. Tall ironwoods provide relief from the sun. Facilities include a camping area, a picnic area, barbecue grills, restrooms, and cold showers. A part-time lifeguard is on duty. When you camp here, don't leave your valuables unprotected. You must have a permit, which costs $3 per person, per night. You can stay at the county parks a maximum of 4 nights, or 12 nights if you are going from one county park to another. To apply for the permit, contact Shani Saito in the Permits Division of Kauai County Parks and Recreation, 4193 Hardy St., Lihue, HI 96766 (© **808/241-6660;** www.kauai-hawaii.com/activities.php#CAMPING). To get to Anahola Beach Park, take Kuhio Highway (Hwy. 56 north) to Anahola, turn right onto Anahola Road, and then turn right onto Manai Road.

THE NORTH SHORE

ANINI BEACH COUNTY PARK 🏕️🏕️

This 12-acre park is Kauai's safest beach for swimming and windsurfing. It's also one of the island's most beautiful: It sits on a blue lagoon at the foot of emerald cliffs, looking more like Tahiti than almost any other strand in the islands. One of Kauai's largest beach camping sites, it is very, very popular, especially on summer weekends, when local residents flock to the beach to camp. It's easy to see why: This 3-mile-long, gold-sand beach is shielded from the open ocean by the longest, widest fringing reef in Hawaii. With shallow water 4- to 5-feet deep, it's also the very best snorkeling spot on Kauai, even for beginners. On the northwest side, a channel in the reef runs out to the deep blue water with a 60-foot drop that attracts divers. Beachcombers love it, too: Seashells, cowries, and sometimes even rare Niihau shells can be found here. Anini has a park, a campground, picnic and barbecue facilities, a pavilion, outdoor showers, public telephones, and a boat-launch ramp. Princeville, with groceries and supplies, is about 4 miles away. You must have a permit, which costs $3 per person, per night. You can stay at the county parks a maximum of 4 nights, or 12 nights if you are going from one county park to another. To apply for the permit, contact: Shani Saito in the Permits Division of Kauai County Parks and Recreation, 4193 Hardy St., Lihue, HI 96766 (© **808/241-6660;** www.kauai-hawaii.com/activities.php#CAMPING). Follow Kuhio Highway (Hwy. 56) to Kilauea; take the second exit, called Kalihiwai Road (the first dead-ends at Kalihiwai Beach), and drive a half mile toward the sea; turn left on Anini Beach Road.

HANALEI BEACH 🏕️

Camping is allowed at this 2½-acre park on weekends and holidays only. Reserve in advance, as this is a very popular camping area. Gentle waves roll across the face of half-moon Hanalei Bay, running up to the wide, golden sand; sheer volcanic ridges laced by waterfalls rise to 4,000 feet on the other side, 3 miles inland. Is there any beach with a better location? Celebrated in song and hula and featured on travel posters, this beach owes its natural beauty to its age—it's an ancient sunken valley with post-erosional cliffs. Hanalei Bay indents the coast a full mile inland and runs 2 miles point to point, with coral reefs on either side and a patch of coral in the middle—plus a sunken ship that belonged to a king, so divers love it. Swimming is excellent year-round, especially in summer, when Hanalei Bay becomes a big, placid lake. The aquamarine water is also great for boogie boarding, surfing, fishing, windsurfing, canoe paddling, kayaking, and boating. (There's a boat ramp on the west bank of the Hanalei River.) The area known as **Black Pot,** near the pier, is particularly good for swimming, snorkeling, and surfing.

Facilities include a lifeguard, a pavilion, restrooms, picnic tables, and parking. This beach is always packed with both locals and visitors, but you can usually find your own place in the sun by strolling down the shore; the bay is big enough for everyone. You must have a permit, which costs $3 per person, per night. You can stay at the county parks a maximum of 4 nights, or 12 nights if you are going from one county park to another. To apply for the permit, contact Shani Saito in the Permits Division of Kauai County Parks and Recreation, 4193 Hardy St., Lihue, HI 96766 (© **808/241-6660;** www.kauai-hawaii.com/activities.php#CAMPING).

To get here, take Kuhio Highway (Hwy. 56), which becomes Highway 560 after Princeville. In Hanalei town, make a right on Aku Road just after Tahiti Nui, then turn right again on Weke Road, which dead-ends at the parking lot for the Black Pot section of the beach; the easiest beach access is on your left.

HAENA BEACH PARK

There are a lot of pluses and minuses to this county beach park (next door to Haena State Park, which does not allow camping). One plus is its beauty: The nearly 6-acre park is bordered by the ocean on one side and a dramatic mountain on the other. In fact, old-timers call this beach Maniniholo, after the local manini fish, which used to be caught in nets during summer. Across the highway from this park are the dry caves, also called Maniniholo. The caves, really a lava tube, run a few hundred feet into the mountain. The area is great for camping, flat and grassy with palm trees for shade. Now the minuses: This is not a good swimming beach because it faces the open ocean, and Kauai's North Shore can be windy and rainy. However, good swimming and snorkeling are available either a quarter mile east of the campground (about a 5-min. walk) at Tunnels Beach, where an offshore reef protects the bay; or at Kee Beach, about a mile west of the campground. Come prepared for wet weather.

Facilities include the camping area, restrooms, outside screened showers, a pavilion with tables, electric lights, a dishwashing sink, picnic tables, and grills; however, there are no lifeguards. The water here is safe to drink. Supplies can be picked up in Hanalei, 4 miles east. You will need a permit, which costs $3 per person, per night. You can stay at the county parks a maximum of 4 nights, or 12 nights if you are going from one county park to another. To apply for the permit, contact Shani Saito in the Permits Division of Kauai County Parks and Recreation, 4193 Hardy St., Lihue, HI 96766 (✆ **808/241-6660;** www.kauai-hawaii.com/activities.php#CAMPING). To get here, take Highway 56 from Lihue, which becomes Highway 560. Look for the park, 4 miles past Hanalei.

YMCA OF KAUAI—CAMP NAUE

Attention, campers, hikers, and backpackers: This is the ideal spot to stay before or after conquering the Na Pali Trail, or if you just want to spend a few days lounging on fabulous Haena Beach. This YMCA camp site, located on Kuhio Hwy., 4 miles west of Hanalei and 2 miles from the end of the road, sits right on the ocean, on 4 grassy acres ringed with ironwood and kumani trees and bordered by a sandy beach that offers excellent swimming and snorkeling in the summer (the ocean here turns really rough in the winter). Camp Naue has two bunkhouses overlooking the beach; each has four rooms with 10 to 12 beds, $12 per bunk. The facilities are coed, with separate bathrooms for men and women. There's no bedding here, so bring your sleeping bag and towels. Large groups frequently book the camp, but if there's room, the Y will squeeze you into the bunkhouse or offer tent space, at $12 per person. Also on the grounds is a beachfront pavilion, a campfire area with picnic tables. You can pick up basic supplies in Haena, but it's best to stock up on groceries and other necessities in Lihue or Hanalei. Remember this is the Y, not the Ritz; they only have one employee who handles all the bookings plus everything else related to the Y activities. The best way to find out if they have space available is to call (*do not* e-mail, *do not* send a letter), ✆ **808/246-9090.** The Y simply is not set up to answer mail. Instead, a few months before your trip, call and they will let you know if there is space in the camp site or if the bunk house will be available.

NA PALI COAST STATE PARK

Simply put, the Na Pali Coast is the most beautiful part of the Hawaiian Islands. Hanging valleys open like green-velvet accordions, and waterfalls tumble to the sea from the 4,120-foot-high cliffs; the experience is both exhilarating and humbling. Whether you hike in, fly over, or take a boat cruise past, be sure to see this park.

Established in 1984, Na Pali Coast State Park takes in a 22-mile stretch of fluted cliffs that wrap the northwestern shore of Kauai between Kee Beach and Polihale State Park. Volcanic in origin, carved by wind and sea, "the cliffs" (*na pali* in Hawaiian), which heaved out of the ocean floor 200 million years ago, stand as constant reminders of majesty and endurance. Four major valleys—Kalalau, Honopu, Awaawa-puhi, and Nualolo—crease the cliffs.

Unless you boat or fly in (see "Boating," on p. 163; or "Helicopter Rides over Waimea Canyon & the Na Pali Coast," on p. 197), the park is accessible only on foot—and it's not easy. An ancient footpath, the **Kalalau Trail,** winds through this remote, spectacular, 6,500-acre park, ultimately leading to Kalalau Valley. Of all the green valleys in Hawaii (and there are many), only Kalalau is a true wilderness—prob-ably the last wild valley in the islands. No road goes here, and none ever will. The remote valley is home to long-plumed tropical birds, golden monarch butterflies, and many of Kauai's 120 rare and endangered species of plants. The hike into the Kalalau Valley is grueling and takes most people 6 to 8 hours one-way.

Despite its inaccessibility, this journey into Hawaii's wilderness has become increas-ingly popular since the 1970s. Overrun with hikers, helicopters, and boaters, the Kalalau Valley was in grave danger of being loved to death. Strict rules about access have been adopted. The park is open to hikers and campers only on a limited basis, and you must have a permit (though you can hike the first 2 miles, to Hanakapiai Beach, without a permit). Permits are $10 per night and are issued in person at the **Kauai State Parks Office,** 3060 Eiwa St., Room 306, Lihue, HI 96766 (© **808/274-3444;** www.hawaii.gov/dlnr/dsp/fees.html). You can also request one by writing the **Kauai Division of State Parks,** at the address above. For more information, contact the **Hawaii State Department of Land and Natural Resources,** 1151 Punchbowl St., Room 130, Honolulu, HI 96813 (© **808/587-0320**).

HIKING THE KALALAU TRAIL &&

The trail head is at Kee Beach, at the end of Highway 560. Even if you only go as far as Hanakapiai, bring water.

THE FIRST 2 MILES: TO HANAKAPIAI BEACH   Do not attempt this hike unless you have adequate footwear (closed-toe shoes at least; hiking shoes are best), water, a sun visor, insect repellent, and adequate hiking clothes. (Shorts and T-shirt are fine; your bikini is not.) It's only 2 miles to Hanakapiai Beach, but the first mile is all uphill. This tough trail takes about 2 hours one-way and dissuades many, but every-one should attempt at least the first half mile, which gives a good hint of the startling beauty that lies ahead. Day hikers love this initial stretch, so it's usually crowded. The island of Niihau and Lehua Rock are often visible on the horizon. At mile marker 1, you'll have climbed from sea level to 400 feet; now it's all downhill to Hanakapiai Beach. Sandy in summer, the beach becomes rocky when winter waves scour the coast. There are strong currents and no lifeguards, so swim at your own risk. You can also hike another 2 miles inland from the beach to **Hanakapiai Falls,** a 120-foot cascade. Allow 3 hours for that one-way stretch.

THE REST OF THE WAY   Hiking the Kalalau is the most difficult and challeng-ing hike in Hawaii, and one you'll never forget. Even the Sierra Club rates the 22-mile round-trip into Kalalau Valley and back as "strenuous"—this is serious backpacking. Follow the footsteps of ancient Hawaiians along a cliff-side path that's a mere 10-inches wide in some places, with sheer 1,000-foot drops to the sea. One misstep, and it's *limu* (seaweed) time. Even the hardy and fit should allow at least 2 days to hike in and out. (See below for camping information.) Although the trail is usually in good shape, go in summer when it's dry; parts of it vanish in winter. When it rains, the trail becomes super-slippery, and flash floods can sweep you away.

A park ranger is now on-site full time at Kalalau Beach to greet visitors, provide information, oversee campsites, and keep trails and campgrounds in order.

CAMPING IN KALALAU VALLEY & ALONG THE NA PALI COAST

You must obtain a camping permit; see above for details. The camping season runs roughly from May or June to September (depending on the site). All campsites are booked almost a year in advance, so call or write well ahead of time. Stays are limited to 5 nights. Camping areas along the Kalalau Trail include **Hanakapiai Beach** (facilities are pit toilets, and water is from the stream), **Hanakoa Valley** (no facilities, water from the stream), **Milolii** (no facilities, water from the stream), and **Kalalau Valley** (composting toilets, several pit toilets, and water from the stream). To get a permit, contact the Division of State Parks, 3060 Eiwa St., Suite 306, Lihue, HI 96766 (© **808/274-3444;** www.kauai-hawaii.com/activities.php). Generally, the fee for a state park camping permit is $5 per campsite per night, but the Na Pali fee is $10 per campsite per night. You cannot stay more than 5 consecutive nights at one campsite. Keep your camping permit with you at all times.

4 Other Outdoor Pursuits

GOLF

You can rent clubs from **Activity Warehouse,** 788 Kuhio Hwy. (across from McDonald's), Kapaa (© **800/343-2087** or 808/822-4000; www.travelhawaii.com), where top-quality clubs go for $15 a day, not-so-top-quality for $10 a day. For last-minute and discount tee times, call **Stand-by Golf** (© **888/645-BOOK;** www.standbygolf.com) between 7am and 9pm. Stand-by offers discounted (up to 50% off greens fees), guaranteed tee times for same-day or next-day golfing.

In the listings below, the cart fee is included in the greens fee unless otherwise noted.

LIHUE & ENVIRONS

Kauai Lagoons Golf Courses Choose between two excellent Jack Nicklaus–designed courses: the **Mokihana Course** (formerly known as the Lagoons Course), for the recreational golfer; or the **Kauai Kiele Championship Course** ★, for the low handicapper. The 6,942-yard, par-72 Mokihana is a links-style course with a bunker that's a little less severe than Kiele's; emphasis is on the short game. The Kiele is a mixture of tournament-quality challenge and high-traffic playability; it winds up with one of Hawaii's most difficult holes, a 431-yard, par-4 played straightaway to an island green.

Facilities include a driving range, lockers, showers, a restaurant, a snack bar, a pro shop, practice greens, a clubhouse, and club and shoe rental; transportation from the airport is provided.

Kalapaki Beach, Lihue (less than a mile from Lihue Airport). © **800/634-6400** or 808/241-5061. www.kauailagoonsgolf.com. From the airport, make a left on Kapule Hwy. (Hwy. 51) and look for the sign on your left. Greens fees at Mokihana Course: $120 ($75 for guests of the Kauai Marriott; $85 for guests of other hotels and condos on Kauai); at the Kiele Course: $170 ($130 for Marriott guests; $145 for guests of other hotels and condos on Kauai).

Puakea Golf Course   This former Grove Farm sugar plantation just opened up 18 holes in 2003 to rave reviews. The course was in the middle of construction when Hurricane Iniki slammed into it in 1992, rearranging the greens from what golf designer Robin Nelson had originally planned. The first 9 (actually the first 10) holes finally opened in 1997 to many kudos; *Sports Illustrated* named it 1 of the 10 best 9-hole golf courses in the U.S. The final 8 holes were finished last year and now are giving golfers something to think about. The course opens with a fairly standard first couple of holes, and just when you think you have nothing to worry about, you get to the third tee. Now you see the evidence of Nelson's work and the time he spent playing the first 10 holes numerous times. He offers golfers this advice on number three: "The fairway is really wide, and the difficulty of your second shot is really affected by which side of it you're on, because you've got to angle your shot over a lake. Hit your tee shot to the right and you've got a good shot, hit it to the left and it's almost impossible."

Facilities include lockers, showers, a pro shop, practice greens, a clubhouse, and club and shoe rental.

4150 Nuhou St., Lihue. © **866/773-5554** or 808/245-8756. www.puakeagolf.com. From the airport, take a left onto Kapule Hwy (Hwy. 51 south). Take another left at the stop sign onto Rice St. (Hwy. 51 south), which becomes Nawiliwili Rd. (or Hwy. 58). Turn left at Borders on Pikake St., then turn left on Nuhou St. Golf course is at 4150 Nuhou St. Greens fees: $125; twilight fees after 3pm $65.

Wailua Municipal Golf Course   The oldest course on Kauai (in fact the oldest course outside of Oahu in Hawaii), this municipal course was built in 1920 with just 6 holes. Another 3 holes were added; then the 9-hole course was reshaped in 1962, and 9 more holes were added after that. The result is a challenging and popular course. The local residents love this course and book up the tee times. You can book tee times up to a week in advance, and we suggest you do that or risk getting very late times or no time at all. The 6,631-yard, par-72 course gets tough from the 1st hole, where you face a par 5 that not only doglegs to the right, but makes you drive into the wind (generally blowing off the ocean from left to right). If you hit too far to the left, it's into the drink. If you hit too far to the right, better make sure the ball will stick. But regulars here agree that the 1st hole is nothing compared with the par-3 17th hole. There, you are once again shooting into the wind coming off the ocean, past the numerous bunkers surrounding the green, and up to the seemingly teeny-tiny, skinny hot dog–shaped green. Good luck. Facilities include pro shop, lockers, practice putting green, driving range, and golf cart rental. There is no restaurant, but a lunch wagon is stationed by the practice putting green.

3–5350 Kuhio Hwy., Lihue 96766. © **808/241-6666.** Take Kapule Hwy. (Hwy. 51) north from the airport, which becomes Kuhio Hwy. (Hwy. 56). Just after the 4-mile marker, the course is located on the ocean side of the highway. Green fees: $32 weekdays, $44 weekends. Twilight rates (after 2pm): $16 weekdays, $22 weekends. Cart rental fee $16.

THE POIPU RESORT AREA

Kiahuna Golf Club   This par-70, 6,353-yard Robert Trent Jones, Jr.–designed course plays around four large archaeological sites, ranging from an ancient Hawaiian temple to the remains of a Portuguese home and crypt built in the early 1800s. This Scottish-style course has rolling terrain, undulating greens, 70 sand bunkers, and near-constant winds. The third hole, a par-3 185-yarder, goes over Waikomo Stream. At any given time, about half the players on the course are Kauai residents, the other half visitors. Facilities include a driving range, practice greens, and a snack bar.

Kauai Golf Courses

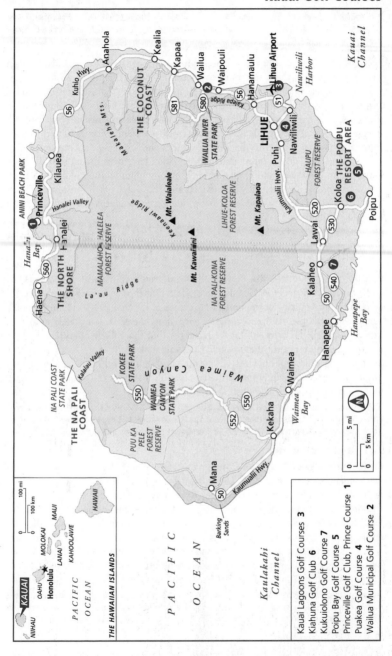

Kauai Lagoons Golf Courses **3**
Kiahuna Golf Club **6**
Kukuiolono Golf Course **7**
Poipu Bay Golf Course **5**
Princeville Golf Club, Prince Course **1**
Puakea Golf Course **4**
Wailua Municipal Golf Course **2**

2545 Kiahuna Plantation Dr. (adjacent to Poipu Resort area), Koloa. ☎ 808/742-9595. www.kiahunagolf.com. Take Hwy. 50 to Hwy. 520, bear left into Poipu at the fork in the road, and turn left onto Kiahuna Plantation Dr. Greens fees: $90, twilight rates $50 (times for twilight rates may vary throughout the year).

Kukuiolono Golf Course *(Finds*   This is a fun 9-hole course in a spectacular location with scenic views of the entire south coast. You can't beat the price—$8 for the day, whether you play 9 holes or 90. The course is in Kukuiolono Park, a beautiful wooded area donated by the family of Walter McBryde. In fact, you'll see McBryde's grave on the course, along with some other oddities like wild chickens, ancient Hawaiian rock structures, and Japanese gardens. Of course, there are plenty of trees to keep you on your game. When you get to the second tee box, check out the coconut tree dotted with yellow, pink, orange, and white golf balls that have been driven into the bark. Don't laugh—your next shot might add to the decor! This course shouldn't give you many problems—it's excellently maintained and relatively straightforward, with few fairway hazards. Facilities include a driving range, practice greens, club rental, a snack bar, and a clubhouse.

Kukuiolono Park, Kalaheo. ☎ 808/332-9151. Take Hwy. 50 into the town of Kalaheo; turn left on Papaluna Rd., drive up the hill for nearly a mile, and watch for the sign on your right; the entrance has huge iron gates and stone pillars—you can't miss it. Greens fees: $8 for the day; optional cart rental is $7 for 9 holes.

Poipu Bay Golf Course *(★★*   This 6,959-yard, par-72 course with a links-style layout is the home of the PGA Grand Slam of Golf. Designed by Robert Trent Jones, Jr., this challenging course features undulating greens and water hazards on 8 of the holes. The par-4 16th hole has the coastline weaving along the entire left side. You can take the safe route to the right and maybe make par (but more likely bogey), or you can try to take it tight against the ocean and possibly make it in two. The most striking (and most disrespectful) hole is the 201-yard, par-3 on the 17th, which has a tee built on an ancient Hawaiian stone formation. Facilities include a restaurant, a locker room, a pro shop, a driving range, and putting greens.

2250 Ainako St. (across from the Grand Hyatt Kauai), Koloa. ☎ 808/742-8711. www.kauai-hyatt.com. Take Hwy. 50 to Hwy. 520; bear left into Poipu at the fork in the road; turn right on Ainako St. Greens fees: $185 ($125 Grand Hyatt guest); $120 afternoon play noon–3pm ($110 Hyatt Regency guest); $65 twilight rate after 3pm.

THE NORTH SHORE
Princeville Golf Club, Prince Course *(★★*   Here's your chance to play one of the best golf courses in Hawaii. This Robert Trent Jones, Jr.–designed devil of a course sits on 390 acres molded to create ocean views from every hole. Some holes have a waterfall backdrop to the greens, others shoot into the hillside, and the famous par-4 12th has a long tee shot off a cliff to a narrow, jungle-lined fairway 100 feet below. This is the most challenging course on Kauai; accuracy is key here. Most of the time, if you miss the fairway, your ball's in the drink. "The average vacation golfer may find the Prince Course intimidating, but they don't mind because it's so beautiful," Jones says. Facilities include a restaurant, a health club and spa, lockers, a clubhouse, a golf shop, and a driving range.

Princeville. ☎ 800/826-1105 or 808/826-5070. www.princeville.com/play/prince_desc.html. Take Hwy. 56 to mile marker 27; the course is on your right. Greens fees: $175 ($150 for Princeville resort guests and $130 for Princeville Hotel guests) for the Prince Course; $125 ($110 for Princeville resort guests and $105 for Princeville Hotel guests) for the Makai Course.

ALL-TERRAIN-VEHICLE (ATV) TOURS
For those who may not have the stamina to go hiking or bicycling or who don't really enjoy horseback riding, now there is a new way to explore Kauai's wilderness:

All-Terrain-Vehicle (ATV) tours. Each person is given one of these four-wheel-drive vehicles resembling an oversized motorcycle. Don't think this is for the weak, either. Wrestling with an ATV and learning how to steer, shift gears, maneuver over ruts in the dirt, and charge up and down hills takes some instruction and practice. That's partially why we recommend **Kipu Ranch Adventures** (© **808/246-9288;** www.kipu tours.com)—they emphasize safety. They start out with a lesson on flat ground, making sure everyone on the tour feels comfortable maneuvering and shifting gears on the 300cc or 350cc Hondas. Off you go on the tour. After about 10 to 15 minutes of pretty easy riding, they take you to a hill, a very steep hill that has all kinds of ruts and bumps. Patiently, they teach each person how to ride down hills and over ruts and bumps. Everyone practices, until the instructors give the okay to proceed. Once you have passed this torturous hill test, the rest of the 3-hour tour is a breeze. The second reason we recommend this company is that they are the only operator on a 3,000-acre private property never before opened to the public. Here's your chance to see a part of Kauai that even local residents have not seen. Extending from the Huleia River to the top of the Haupu Mountains, this property has been the filming site for numerous movies *(Jurassic Park, Raiders of the Lost Ark, Outbreak, Six Days and Seven Nights).* The tour provides helmets, safety glasses, snacks, juice, water, fruit, and a stop over a swimming hole with a swinging rope. For those who would rather leave the driving to someone else (or who are ages 6–15), they have a "mule," a four-wheel-drive Kawasaki that holds up to three passengers. Cost for the ATV tour is $105; the mule is $105 for adults, $70 for children 6 to 15, and $88 for seniors over 65.

BIKING

There are a couple of great places on Kauai for two-wheeling: the **Poipu area,** which has wide, flat roads and several dirt-cane roads (especially around Mahaulepu); and the cane road (a dirt road used for hauling sugar cane) between **Kealia Beach** and **Anahola,** north of Kapaa.

The following places rent mountain bikes, from a low of $10 a day for cruisers to $15 to $20 a day for mountain bikes (with big discounts for multiple-day rentals): **Outfitters Kauai,** 2827A Poipu Rd. (look for the small five-shop mall before the road forks to Poipu/Spouting Horn), Poipu (© **808/742-9667;** www.outfitterskauai.com); and **Kauai Cycle and Tour,** 1379 Kuhio Hwy., Kapaa (© **808/821-2115;** www.bike hawaii.com/kauaicycle). For a great selection of high-quality mountain bikes at reasonable prices, it's worth the drive to **Pedal 'n Paddle,** in Hanalei (© **808/826-9069;** www.pedalnpaddle.com), which has not only high-grade Kona mountain bikes with Shimano components but also bikes with front-end suspension systems. Rentals start at $10 a day or $30 a week and include helmet, bike lock, and car rack. The shop even has kids' 20-inch BMX bikes. The knowledgeable folks here are more than happy to provide you with free maps and tell you about the best biking spots on the island.

GUIDED BIKE TOURS **Outfitters Kauai** ❧ (© **808/742-9667;** www.outfitters kauai.com) offers a fabulous downhill bike ride from Waimea Canyon to the ocean. The 12-mile trip (mostly coasting) begins at 6am, when the van leaves the shop in Poipu and heads up to the canyon. By the time you've eaten the fresh-baked muffins and enjoyed the coffee, you're at the top of the canyon, just as the sun is rising over the rim—it's a remarkable moment. The tour makes a couple of stops on the way down for short, scenic nature hikes. You'll be back at the shop around 10am. The sunset trip follows the same route. Both tours cost $90 per adult; $70 per child 12 to 14.

BIRDING

Kauai provides some of Hawaii's last sanctuaries for endangered native birds and oceanic birds, such as the albatross. If you didn't bring your binoculars, you can rent some at **Activity Warehouse,** 788 Kuhio Hwy. (across from McDonald's), Kapaa (© **800/343-2087** or 808/822-4000; www.travelhawaii.com), where rentals start at 99¢ a day.

At **Kokee State Park,** a 4,345-acre wilderness forest at the end of Highway 550 in southwest Kauai, you have an excellent chance of seeing some of Hawaii's endangered native birds. You might spot the apapane, a red bird with black wings and a curved black bill; or the iwi, a red bird with black wings, orange legs, and a salmon-colored bill. Other frequently seen native birds are the honeycreeper, which sings like a canary; the amakihi, a plain, olive-green bird with a long, straight bill; and the anianiau, a tiny yellow bird with a thin, slightly curved bill. The most common native bird at Kokee is the moa, or red jungle fowl, brought as domestic stock by ancient Polynesians. Ordinarily shy, they're quite tame in this environment. David Kuhn leads custom hikes, pointing out Hawaii's rarest birds on his **Terran Tours** (© **808/335-3313**), which range from a half day to 3 days and feature endemic and endangered species.

Kilauea Point National Wildlife Refuge ©, a mile north of Kilauea on the North Shore (© **808/828-0168**), is a 200-acre headland habitat that juts above the surf and includes cliffs, two rocky wave-lashed bays, and a tiny islet that serves as a jumping-off spot for seabirds. You can easily spot red-footed boobies, which nest in trees, and wedge-tailed shearwaters, which burrow in nests along the cliffs. You may also see the great frigate bird, the Laysan albatross, the red-tailed tropic bird, and the endangered nene. Native plants and the Kilauea Point Lighthouse are highlights as well. The refuge is open from 10am to 4pm daily (closed on Thanksgiving, Christmas, and New Year's Day); admission is $3. To get here, turn right off Kuhio Highway (Hwy. 56) at Kilauea, just after mile marker 23; follow Kilauea Road to the refuge entrance.

Peaceful Hanalei Valley is home to Hawaii's endangered Koloa duck, gallinule, coot, and stilt. The **Hanalei National Wildlife Refuge** (© **808/828-1413;** pacific islands.fws.gov/wnwr/khanaleinwr.html) also provides a safe habitat for migratory shorebirds and waterfowl. It's not open to the public, but an interpretive overlook along the highway serves as an impressive vantage point. Along Ohiki Road, which begins at the west end of the Hanalei River Bridge, you'll often see white cattle egrets hunting crayfish in streams.

HORSEBACK RIDING

Only in Kauai can you ride a horse across the wide-open pastures of a working ranch under volcanic peaks and rein up near a waterfall pool. No wonder Kauai's *paniolo* (cowboys) smile and sing so much. Near the Poipu area, **CJM Country Stables,** 1731 Kelaukia St. (2 miles beyond the Hyatt Regency Kauai), Koloa (© **808/742-6096;** www.cjmstables.com), offers both 2- and 3-hour escorted Hidden Valley beach rides. You'll trot over Hidden Valley ranch land, past secluded beaches and bays, along the Haupu Ridge, across sugar cane fields, and to Mahaulepu Beach; it's worth your time and money just to get out to this seldom-seen part of Kauai. The "Secret Beach and Breakfast Ride" costs $85 and includes breakfast. The 2-hour "Hidden Beach Ride" is $90. There's also a 3½-hour swim/beach/picnic ride for $115.

Princeville Ranch Stables, Highway 56 (just after the Princeville Airport), Hanalei (© **808/826-6777;** www.princevilleranch.com), has a variety of outings. The

1½-hour country ride takes in views of the Hanalei Mountains and the vista of Anini Beach ($65), while the 3-hour adventure meanders along the bluffs of the North Shore to Anini Beach, where you tie off your horse and take a short stroll to the beach ($110). The 4-hour "Waterfall Picnic Ride" crosses ranch land, takes you on a short (but steep) hike to swimming pools at the base of waterfalls, and then feeds you a picnic lunch for $120. Riders must be in good physical shape, and don't forget to put your swimsuit on under your jeans. The Princeville Ranch Stables also offers other adventures, ranging from the less strenuous wagon rides to a cattle-drive ride.

TENNIS

The **Kauai County Parks and Recreation Department,** 4444 Rice St., Suite 150, Lihue (© **808/241-6670**), has a list of the nine county tennis courts around the island, all of which are free and open to the public. Private courts that are open to the public include the **Princeville Tennis Club,** Princeville Hotel (© **808/826-3620;** www.princeville.com), which has six courts available for $15 per person ($12 for guests) for 90 minutes. On the south side, try **Hyatt Regency Kauai Resort and Spa,** Poipu Resort (© **808/742-1234;** www.kauai-hyatt.com), which has four courts, available for $30 an hour; and **Klahuna Swim and Tennis Club,** Poipu Road (just past the Poipu Shopping Village on the left), Poipu Resort (© **808/742-9533**), which has 10 courts renting for $10 per person per hour.

8

Exploring Kauai

Yes, Kauai has the best beaches in Hawaii, but don't forget the rest of this beautiful island. Get out and explore what makes Kauai the "Garden Isle." Walk back in history in the capital of Lihue. Make time to see Kauai's incredible botanical world of manicured gardens, the geological wonders of Waimea Canyon, the incredible carved cliffs of the Na Pali Coast, and the enchanted rainforests of the wettest place on earth. Book a helicopter flight, take a back-roads tour in a four-wheel-drive vehicle, make a pilgrimage to a Hindu temple located on a sacred Hawaiian site, drop the kids off at a children's museum, or sign up for an expedition to Kauai's famous movie sites. There's a lot more to Kauai than its gorgeous beaches, so get out there and discover why visitors become enchanted with this magical island.

1 Lihue & Environs

Grove Farm Homestead Museum   You can experience a day in the life of an 1860s sugar planter on a visit to Grove Farm Homestead, which shows how good life was (for some, anyway) when sugar was king. This is Hawaii's best remaining example of a sugar-plantation homestead. Founded in 1864 by George N. Wilcox, a Hanalei missionary's son, Grove Farm was one of the earliest of Hawaii's 86 sugar plantations. A self-made millionaire, Wilcox died a bachelor in 1933, at age 94. His estate looks much like it did when he lived here, complete with period furniture, plantation artifacts, and Hawaiiana.

4050 Nawiliwili Rd. (Hwy. 58) at Pikaka St. (2 miles from Waapa Rd.), Lihue. ✆ **808/245-3202.** www.hawaiiweb. com/kauai/html/sites/grove_farm_homestead.html. Requested donation $5 adults, $2 children under 12. Tours offered Mon and Wed–Thurs at 10am and 1pm; reservations required.

Touring Off the Beaten Path

If you are itching to get off the beaten path and see the "hidden" Kauai, **Four-Wheel-Drive Backroad Adventure** ⭐, 1702 Haleukana St., Lihue, HI 96766 (✆ **800/452-1113** or 808/245-8809; www.alohakauaitours.com), has a full-day, four-wheel-drive tour that starts in Waimea Canyon and goes up to Kokee Park, then on to Koloa and the Kilohana Crater. The tour, done in a four-wheel-drive van, not only stops at Kauai's well-known scenic spots but travels on sugar cane roads (on private property), taking you to places most people who live on Kauai have never seen. The guides are well versed in everything from native plants to Hawaiian history. Bring plenty of film for your camera. The tour costs $125 adults, $90 children 5 to 12.

Kauai Attractions

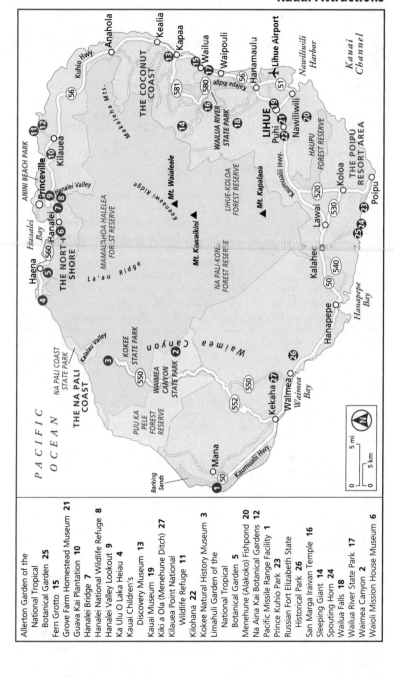

Allerton Garden of the
National Tropical
Botanical Garden **25**
Fern Grotto **15**
Grove Farm Homestead Museum **21**
Guava Kai Plantation **10**
Hanalei Bridge **7**
Hanalei National Wildlife Refuge **8**
Hanalei Valley Lookout **9**
Ka Ulu O Laka Heiau **4**
Kauai Children's
Discovery Museum **13**
Kauai Museum **19**
Kiki a Ola (Menehune Ditch) **27**
Kilauea Point National
Wildlife Refuge **11**
Kilohana **22**
Kokee Natural History Museum **3**
Limahuli Garden of the
National Tropical
Botanical Garden **5**
Menehune (Alakoko) Fishpond **20**
Na Aina Kai Botanical Gardens **12**
Pacific Missile Range Facility **1**
Prince Kuhio Park **23**
Russian Fort Elizabeth State
Historical Park **26**
San Marga Iraivan Temple **16**
Sleeping Giant **14**
Spouting Horn **24**
Wailua Falls **18**
Wailua River State Park **17**
Waimea Canyon **2**
Waioli Mission House Museum **6**

Kauai Museum *(★) (Kids)* The history of Kauai is kept safe in an imposing Greco-Roman building that once served as the town library. This great little museum is worth a stop before you set out to explore the island. It contains a wealth of historical artifacts and information tracing the island's history, from the beginning of time through Contact (when Capt. James Cook "discovered" Kauai in 1778), the monarchy period, the plantation era, and the present. You'll hear tales of the *menehune* (the mythical, elflike people who were said to build massive stone works in a single night) and see old poi pounders and idols, relics of sugar planters and *paniolo,* a nice seashell collection, old Hawaiian quilts, feather leis, a replica of a plantation worker's home, and much more—even a model of Cook's ship, the HMS *Resolution,* riding anchor in Waimea Bay. Vintage photographs by W. J. Senda, a Japanese immigrant, show old Kauai, while a contemporary video, shot from a helicopter, captures the island's natural beauty.

4428 Rice St., Lihue. © **808/245-6931.** Admission $5 adults, $4 seniors, $3 students 13–17, $1 children 6–12. Mon–Fri 9am–4pm; Sat 10am–4pm. First Sat of every month is "Family Day," when admission is free.

Kilohana There may have been a depression raging in the rest of the U.S., but on Kauai, sugar was king, and sugar plantation owner Gaylord Parke Wilcox was incredibly wealthy. In 1935, Wilcox built a plantation home to show off his prosperity. Designed by British architect Mark Potter, the 16,000-square-foot Tudor-style mansion, costing $200,000 at the time (some $3–$5 million in today's dollars) is still recognized as the most prestigious home on the island. You can tour the incredible home today, free. Housed in the structure are Gaylord's Restaurant, which is in the original dining room, and several small shops featuring art galleries and specialty boutiques. The living room still has furniture from Wilcox's period, and the same art on the walls. You can walk the manicured grounds by yourself or take a 20-minute **Carriage Ride** ($12 adults, $6 children 12 and under). A longer, 1-hour historical **Horse-Drawn Sugar Cane Tour** is offered in an 18-passenger "candy red" wagon (with padded bench seating) pulled by Clydesdale horses ($29 adults, $15 children 12 and under).

Kaumualii Hwy. (Hwy. 50), Lihue, HI 96766. © **808/245-5608** for Kilohana, 808/246-9529 for Carriage Ride and horse-drawn Sugar Cane Tour. www.kilohanakauai.com. Kilohana open daily 9:30am–9:30pm. Carriage Ride daily 11am–6pm. Sugar Cane Tour Mon, Tues, Thurs 11am. From Lihue, take Kaumualii Hwy. (Hwy. 50) for 2 miles, past Puhi, on the mountain side of the highway.

Menehune (Alekoko) Fishpond Just outside Lihue and Nawiliwili Harbor, on the Huleia River, lies a mystery that still can't be explained: the handiwork of the *menehune* (see "Discovering the Legendary 'Little People,'" below). The pond, called Alekoko ("rippling blood") and today known as the Menehune Fishpond, was an aquaculture feat built hundreds of years ago. The builders of this 2,700-foot-long stone wall (that cuts off a bend in the river) were believed to be the mythical people who inhabited Kauai before the Polynesians arrived. The fishpond is located in the Huleia National Wildlife Refuge, 238 acres of river valley that is a habitat for endangered Hawaiian water birds (ae'o or Hawaiian stilt, 'alae Ke'oke'o or Hawaiian coot, 'alae 'ula or Hawaiian gallinule, and Koloa maoli or Hawaii duck). Although you can see the fishpond and the refuge from the road, the area is not open to the public. Small boats, kayaks, jet skis, windsurfers, and water-skiers use the river.

Hulemalu Rd., Niumalu. From Lihue, take Rice St. to Nawiliwili Harbor. Turn left on Niumalu Rd. and right on Hulemalu Rd. Up the hill is a lookout where you have a view of the pond, Huleia Stream, and Huleia National Wildlife Reserve.

Wailua Falls For those looking for a short trip out of Lihue to see cascading waterfalls but who don't want to hike into the wilderness, this is your best bet. In fact, the

Fun Fact **Discovering the Legendary "Little People"**

Like many places in the world, including Ireland with its leprechauns, Hawaii has stories about "little people." According to ancient Hawaiian legend, among Kauai's earliest settlers were the *menehune,* a race of small people who worked at night to accomplish magnificent feats. However, archaeologists say the *menehune* may not be legendary people but in fact non-Polynesian people who once lived on Kauai. These people, believed to be from the Marquesas Islands, arrived in Hawaii between 0 and 350 A.D. When the Polynesians ventured from Tahiti to Hawaii between 600 and 1100 A.D., they fought the *"menehune"* already living in Hawaii. Some scholars claim the Polynesians were more aggressive and warlike than the Marquesans, and in a series of wars the Tahitians drove the Marquesans north through the island chain to Kauai.

Anthropologists point out that the Tahitian word *manahune,* which means a lower class or a slave, was used to describe the racial hierarchy, not the physical stature of the people already living in Hawaii. In other words, *"manahune"* (or *"menehune"*) was used to mean small in the Tahitians' strict caste system, not small in size.

In any case, everyone agrees that these people performed incredible feats, especially stonework that has stood for centuries. One example by these rock builders, who were able to construct elaborate edifices without using mortar, is the **Menehune Ditch** (Kiki a Ola), along the Waimea River. Only a 2-foot-high portion of the wall can be seen today; the rest of the marvelous stonework is buried under the roadbed. To get here from Hwy. 50, go inland on Menehune Road in Waimea; a plaque marks the spot about 1½ miles up.

Another example lies above Nawiliwili Harbor. The **Menehune Fishpond**—which at one time extended 25 miles—is said to have been built in just 1 night, with two rows of thousands of *menehune* passing stones hand to hand. The *menehune* were promised that no one would watch them work, but one person did. When the *menehune* discovered the spy, they stopped working immediately, leaving two gaps in the wall. From Nawiliwili Harbor, take Hulemalu Road above Huleia Stream. Look for the HAWAII CONVENTION AND VISITORS BUREAU marker at a turnoff in the road, which leads to the legendary fishpond. Kayakers can paddle up Huleia Stream to see it up close.

journey here, about a 4-mile drive outside of town, takes you through rolling hills past former sugar cane fields and across a valley, with majestic mountains in the background. From the Wailua Falls parking lot you can look down at two waterfalls cascading some 80 feet into a large pool. Legend claims that the *alii* (royalty) came to these waterfalls and dived from the cliff into the pool below to show the common people that monarchs were not mere men. Don't try this today.

Maalo Rd. (Hwy. 583), Wailua. From Lihue, take Kaumualii Hwy. (Hwy. 50) north, and turn left on Maalo Rd (Hwy. 583). After 4 miles, look for the parking area for Wailua Falls on the right.

2 The Poipu Resort Area

No Hawaii resort has a better entrance: On Maluhia Road, eucalyptus trees planted in 1911 as a windbreak for sugar cane fields now form a monumental **tree tunnel.** The leafy-green, cool tunnel starts at Kaumualii Highway; you'll emerge at the golden-red beach. The **Poipu Beach Resort Foundation** (© 808/742-4444; www.koloaheritage trail.info) produces a free brochure called the *Koloa Heritage Trail,* which is a 10-mile walk, bike ride, or drive that has some 14 historical stops and markers describing the history and culture of this area. The Historic Trail begins at **Spouting Horn** (see below) and finishes at the Koloa Mission Church in Koloa town. The trail is a great idea, but a few of the sites are either no longer there (like site number 10 on Hapa Road, where the pre-contact evidence of ancient Hawaiians is no longer), changed beyond what they once were (site number 13, the Yamamoto Store and Koloa Hotel, now gone), or difficult to get to (like site number 9, Pu'uwanawana Volcanic Cone, which you can see in the distance from the highway, but is located on fenced private property).

Allerton Garden of the National Tropical Botanical Garden ⋇   Discover an extraordinary collection of tropical fruit and spice trees, rare Hawaiian plants, and hundreds of varieties of flowers at the 186-acre preserve known as **Lawai Gardens,** said to be the largest collection of rare and endangered plants in the world. Adjacent **McBryde Garden,** a royal home site of Queen Emma in the 1860s, is known for its formal gardens, a delicious kind of colonial decadence. The garden contains fountains, streams, waterfalls, and European statuary. Endangered green sea turtles can be seen here. (Their home in the sea was wiped out years ago by Hurricane Iniki.) The tours are fascinating for green thumbs and novices alike.

Visitor Center, Lawai Rd. (across the street from Spouting Horn), Poipu. © 808/742-2623. www.ntbg.org. Admission $30. Guided 2½-hr. tours by reservation only, Mon–Sat at 9am, 10am, 1pm, and 2pm. Self-guided tours of McBryde Garden Mon–Sat 9am–4pm, $15 (trams into the valley leave once an hour on the ½ hour; last tram 2:30pm); guided tour Mon 9:30am, $30. Reserve a week in advance in peak months of July, Aug, and Sept.

Prince Kuhio Park   This small roadside park is the birthplace of Prince Jonah Kuhio Kalanianaole, the "People's Prince," whose March 26th birthday is a holiday in Hawaii. He opened the beaches of Waikiki to the public in 1918 and served as Hawaii's second territorial delegate to the U.S. Congress. What remains here are the foundations of the family home, a royal fishpond, and a shrine where tributes are still paid in flowers.

Lawai Rd., Koloa. Just after mile marker 4 on Poipu Rd., veer to the right of the fork in the road; the park is on the right side.

Spouting Horn ⋇ *Kids*   This natural phenomenon is second only to Yellowstone's Old Faithful. It's quite a sight—big waves hit Kauai's south shore with enough force to send a spout of funneled saltwater 10 feet or more up in the air; in winter, the water can get as high as six stories.

Spouting Horn is different from other blowholes in Hawaii, in that an additional hole blows air that sounds like a loud moaning. According to Hawaiian legend, this coastline was once guarded by a giant female lizard (Mo'o); she gobbled up any intruders. One day, along came Liko, who wanted to fish in this area. Mo'o rushed out to eat Liko. Quickly, Liko threw a spear right into the giant lizard's mouth. Mo'o then chased Liko into a lava tube. Liko escaped, but legend says Mo'o is still in the tube, and the moaning at Spouting Horn is her cry for help.

At Kukuiula Bay, beyond Prince Kuhio Park (see above).

3 Western Kauai

WAIMEA TOWN

If you'd like to take a self-guided tour of this historic town, stop at the **Waimea Library,** at mile marker 23 on Highway 50, to pick up a map and guide to the sites.

Hanapepe Swinging Bridge   The old plantation town of Hanapepe is a great place to stop for lunch and to wander through the shops. Founded by Chinese immigrants who worked in the plantations, Hanapepe is a great look at Kauai's past. While you are there be sure to walk across the suspended old wooden foot bridge. Originally built in 1911 and renovated after Hurricane Iniki in 1992, this bridge is a thoroughfare for people living on the other side of the Hanapepe River. The bridge swings, sways, and swoops as you cross from one side to the other. If people are crossing in different directions it becomes a Disneyland-like ride as the bridge bucks and bounces over the swirling muddy water of the river below.

Hanapepe Rd., look for the sign in the parking lot, Hanapepe.

Kiki a Ola (Menehune Ditch)   Ancient Hawaiians were expert rock builders, able to construct elaborate edifices without using mortar. They formed long lines and passed stones hand over hand, and lifted rocks weighing tons with ropes made from native plants. Their feats gave rise to fantastic tales of *menehune,* elflike people hired by Hawaiian kings to create massive stoneworks in a single night—reputedly for the payment of a single shrimp. (See "Discovering the Legendary 'Little People,'" above.) An excellent example of ancient Hawaiian construction is Kiki a Ola, the so-called Menehune Ditch, with cut and dressed stones that form an ancient aqueduct that still directs water to irrigate taro ponds. Historians credit the work to ancient Hawaiian engineers who applied their knowledge of hydraulics to accomplish flood control and irrigation. Only a 2-foot-high portion of the wall can be seen today; the rest of the marvelous stonework is buried under the roadbed.

From Hwy. 50, go inland on Menehune Rd.; a plaque marks the spot about 1½ miles up.

Russian Fort Elizabeth State Historical Park   Add the Russians to the list of those who tried to conquer Hawaii. In 1815, a German doctor tried to claim Kauai for Russia. He even supervised the construction of a fort in Waimea, but he and his

Keep Out: Pacific Missile Range Facility

At the end of Kaumualii Highway (Hwy. 50) lies the 42,000-square-mile **Pacific Missile Range Facility** (PMRF), which is technically run by the Navy. Lately it seems as if everyone on the base, from the military to federal agencies, works on "national defense." According to their website, PMRF "supports a variety of training exercises and developmental tests involving space, air, surface, and sub-surface units," such as missile and submarine tracking information. For years, the base shared its beaches with the people of Kauai, but 9/11 stopped all that. They still have a (very complex and convoluted) system whereby local residents gain clearance (through a long series of checks by the military and police department) to get a pass to the base's beaches, but it is impossible for visitors to do so. For more information, call © **808/335-4229** or go to www. pmrf.navy.mil/index.html.

handful of Russian companions were expelled by Kamehameha I a couple of years later. Now a state historic landmark, the Russian Fort Elizabeth (named for the wife of Russia's Czar Alexander I) is on the eastern headlands overlooking the harbor, across from Lucy Kapahu Aukai Wright Beach Park. The fort, built Hawaiian style with stacked lava rocks in the shape of a star, once bristled with cannons; it's now mostly in ruins. You can take a free, self-guided tour of the site. It affords a keen view of the west bank of the Waimea River, where Captain Cook landed, and of the island of Niihau across the channel.

Hwy. 50 (on the ocean side, just after mile marker 77), east of Waimea.

Sugar Plantation Tours   The only sugar tour in Hawaii, this 2-hour guided tour takes you into the fields and through the factory, viewing just how sugar goes from the soil to your dining room table. Along the way you learn the 165-plus-year history of sugar in Hawaii and all the trials and errors the industry went through to establish such a sweet crop in the middle of the Pacific. Also find out why this once powerful industry is now on the downswing.

Gay & Robinson Visitor Center and Museum, Hwy. 50 (on the ocean side, just after mile marker 22), east of Waimea. ℭ 808/335-2824. www.gandrtours-kauai.com. Tours 8:45am and 12:45pm, Mon–Fri. $30 adults, $21 for kids age 17 and under.

THE GRAND CANYON OF THE PACIFIC: WAIMEA CANYON ☺☺☺

The great gaping gulch known as Waimea Canyon is quite a sight. This valley, known for its reddish lava beds, reminds everyone who sees it of the Grand Canyon. Kauai's version is bursting with ever-changing color, just like its namesake, but it's smaller—only a mile wide, 3,567 feet deep, and 12 miles long. A massive earthquake sent a number of streams into the single river that ultimately carved this picturesque canyon. Today, the Waimea River—a silver thread of water in the gorge that's sometimes a trickle, often a torrent, but always there—keeps cutting the canyon deeper and wider, and nobody can say what the result will be 100 million years from now.

You can stop by the road and look at the canyon, hike down into it, or swoop through it in a helicopter. For more information, see "Hiking & Camping," in chapter 7, and "Helicopter Rides over Waimea Canyon & the Na Pali Coast," below.

THE DRIVE THROUGH WAIMEA CANYON & UP TO KOKEE

By car, there are two ways to visit Waimea Canyon and Kokee State Park, 20 miles from Waimea. From the coastal road (Hwy. 50), you can turn up Waimea Canyon Drive (Hwy. 550) at Waimea town; or you can pass through Waimea and turn up Kokee Road (Hwy. 55) at Kekaha. The climb is very steep from Kekaha, but Waimea Canyon Drive, the rim road, is narrower and rougher. A few miles up, the two merge into Kokee Road.

The first good vantage point is **Waimea Canyon Lookout,** located between mile markers 10 and 11 on Waimea Canyon Road. From here, it's another 6 miles to Kokee. There are a few more lookout points along the way that also offer spectacular views, such as **Puu Hina Hina Lookout,** between mile markers 13 and 14, at 3,336 feet; be sure to pull over and spend a few minutes pondering this natural wonder. (The giant white object that looks like a golf ball and defaces the natural landscape is a radar station left over from the Cold War.)

KOKEE STATE PARK

It's only 16 miles from Waimea to Kokee, but the park is a whole different world because it is 4,345 acres of rainforest. You'll enter a new climate zone, where the breeze has a bite and trees look quite continental. You're in a cloud forest on the edge of the Alakai Swamp, the largest swamp in Hawaii, on the summit plateau of Kauai. Days are cool and wet, with intermittent bright sunshine, not unlike Seattle on a good day. Bring your sweater and, if you're staying over, be sure you know how to light a fire. (Overnight lows dip into the 40s [single digits Celsius].)

The forest is full of native plants, such as mokihana berry, ohia lehua, and iliau (similar to Maui's silversword), as well as imports like Australia's eucalyptus and California's redwood. Pigs, goats, and black-tailed deer thrive in the forest, but the moa, or Polynesian jungle fowl, is the cock of the walk.

Right next to Kokee Lodge (which lies on the only road through the park, about a mile before it ends) is the **Kokee Natural History Museum** ✸ (𝄯 **808/335-9975;** www.kokee.org), open daily from 10am to 4pm (free admission). This is the best place to learn about the forest and Alakai Swamp before you set off hiking in the wild. The museum shop has great trail information and local books and maps, including the official park trail map. We recommend getting the *Pocket Guide on Native Plants on the Nature Trail for Kokee State Park* and the *Road Guide to Kokee and Waimea Canyon State Park*.

A **nature walk** is the best introduction to this rainforest; it starts behind the museum at the rare Hawaiian koa tree. This easy, self-guided walk of about a quarter mile takes about 20 minutes if you stop and look at all the plants identified along the way.

Two miles above Kokee Lodge is **Kalalau Lookout** ✸, the spectacular climax of your drive through Waimea Canyon and Kokee. When you stand at the lookout, below you is a work in progress that began at least 5 million years ago. It's hard to stop looking; the view is breathtaking, especially when light and cloud shadows play across the red-and-orange cliffs.

There's lots more to see and do up here: Anglers fly-fish for rainbow trout, and hikers tackle the 45 trails that lace the Alakai Swamp. (See "Watersports" and "Hiking & Camping," in chapter 7.) That's a lot of ground to cover, so you might want to plan on staying over. If pitching a tent is too rustic for you, the wonderful **cabins** set in a grove of redwoods are one of the best lodging bargains in the islands (see chapter 5.). The restaurant at **Kokee Lodge** is open for continental breakfast and lunch daily from 9am to 3:30pm.

For advance information, contact the **State Division of Parks,** P.O. Box 1671, Lihue, HI 96766 (𝄯 **808/335-5871;** www.hawaii.gov/dlnr/dsp/kauai.html); and the **Kokee Lodge Manager,** P.O. Box 819, Waimea, HI 96796 (𝄯 **808/335-6061**). The park is open daily year-round. The best time to go is early in the morning, to see the panoramic view of Kalalau Valley from the lookout at 4,000 feet, before clouds obscure the valley and peaks.

HELICOPTER RIDES OVER WAIMEA CANYON & THE NA PALI COAST ✸✸✸

Don't leave Kauai without seeing it from a helicopter. It's expensive but worth the splurge. You can take home memories of the thrilling ride up and over the Kalalau Valley on Kauai's wild North Shore and into the 5,200-foot vertical temple of Mount Waialeale, the most sacred place on the island and the wettest spot on earth. (And in some cases, you can even take home a video of your ride.) All flights leave from Lihue Airport.

Air Kauai Helicopters ✸   Since 1988, Chuck DiPiazza has been flying visitors over Kauai without incident. He flies custom-designed huge-windowed A STAR helicopters

Moments **Taking to the Skies—It's More
Than Just a Helicopter Ride**

The light on the floor-to-ceiling windshield sparkles dazzlingly. Only the sound of traditional Hawaiian music wafts through the noise-canceling headset as I relax into the plush, comfy seat. Staring at the ground, I notice that it begins to move away, almost like magic, as the helicopter effortlessly rises straight up.

Defying gravity, the high-tech aircraft smoothly glides through the air, like some kind of modern magic carpet. There really is nothing else that can compare to the helicopter's serene motion of floating. It's not a rocking sensation like being on a boat, nor the high-speed forward velocity of an airplane, but a gentle drifting.

Helicopter rides over Kauai are more than just a "ride," but a tour of the island. In fact, the only way to truly see a large percentage of the island is to sail the skies in a helicopter.

"On Kauai, a helicopter is really the only way to see two-thirds of the island because of the remote nature of the terrain," says Casey Riemer, of Jack Harter Helicopters. "You just can't see it any other way."

One of the first questions Hawaii's helicopter tour operators always get asked is, "How safe is flying in a helicopter?" To which most of them respond that statistically, it is more dangerous driving in your car than it is flying in Hawaii's helicopter tours.

"Hawaii's (helicopter tour's) safety record is quite frankly phenomenal," states Riemer. In the past decade, Hawaii has only seen a handful of helicopter accidents despite the hundreds of thousands of hours that helicopters are in the sky touring the state.

In addition, the industry not only meets federal safety standards, but most helicopter companies go beyond federal requirements to ensure the safest ride possible.

Safety, as well as the entire helicopter touring industry, is a pricey business. Helicopters are expensive aircraft (costing from $1 million to nearly $2 million), maintenance is very costly (several parts must be replaced every so many flight hours), and the number of personnel necessary for the air-touring

(37% larger than most helicopters), with high-back leather seats. The pilot sits on the left side of the helicopter instead of in the usual position on the right, which not only allows passengers better views, but more legroom. ***Another plus:*** All his helicopters have BOSE Acoustic Noise Canceling Stereo Headsets, which helps in these noisy birds. If possible, ask for Captain Chuck; his commentaries are informative and down to earth, and he welcomes questions. He also loves to show off his multi-CD disk player, combining the "right" music with the tour.

3651 Ahukini Rd., Lihue, HI 96766. (℗) **800/972-4666** or 808/246-4666. www.airkauai.com. The 60-min. tour is $253, but mention Frommer's and they will discount it to $190.

business (from the pilot to the mechanics to the dispatchers to the ground personnel to the people who book you) is immense.

The cost of a helicopter tour varies, see below. Yes, it is expensive, but worth every penny for an experience you will remember for a lifetime.

However, don't choose a helicopter tour company based on price alone. Remember that you get what you pay for, and if you are going to pay a few hundred dollars, you might as well get your money's worth. (Cheaper is not necessarily better.)

There are ways to save money. Check the Internet. Generally if you book 7 days in advance on the Internet, you can get 10% to 15% off. One company has an Internet discount as high as 37%.

This is one time that you might want to do the investigative work into the tour yourself—if you go to a booking agency, they may just book the helicopter company that gives them the best commission (and may not have the "right" tour for you). Also beware of timeshare presentations offering greatly discounted rates for helicopter tours only if you first sit through a lengthy presentation.

Tour operators all agree that you should book early in your trip, just in case weather cancels your tour. You will then still have several days remaining in your trip to re-book.

If a tour operator is unable to fly due to weather, then you are not charged for your trip. Some operators tell stories about taking off and then deciding that the trip will not be comfortable for their passengers, so they return them to base without charging them.

However, if you cannot make your flight, you must cancel 24 hours in advance or you could be charged for the flight.

There really is no such thing as a perfect time to fly. Conditions change. On Kauai, the east end of the island gets light early, but the Na Pali Coast, on the west side, gets light later in the day. And yes, helicopters fly when it is cloudy, because it nearly always is cloudy somewhere on the island. *But remember:* With a helicopter, it is possible to fly over the rainbow.

Blue Hawaiian ✦✦✦   Blue Hawaiian has been the Cadillac of helicopter tour companies on Maui and the Big Island for more than a decade, and recently they have expanded their operations to Kauai. I strongly recommend that you try to book with them first. Their operation is first-class, and they use state-of-the-art equipment: American Eurocopter ECO-Star, which reduces noise in the helicopter by 50% and allows 23% more interior room. Plus the craft has individual Business Class–style seats, two-way communication with the pilot, and expansive glass for incredible views. The 50-minute flights journey first to Hanapepe Valley, then continue on to Mana Waiapuna, commonly referred to as "Jurassic Park Falls." Next it's up the Olokele Canyon, then on to the Waimea Canyon, the famed "Grand Canyon of the Pacific."

Most of the flight will continue along the Na Pali Coast, before heading out to the Bali Hai Cliffs, and the pristine blue waters of Hanalei Bay and the Princeville Resort area. If the weather gods are on your side, then you'll get to see the highest point on Kauai: Mt. Waialeale, the wettest spot on earth, with an average rainfall of 450 to 500 inches annually. Your flight will take you right into the center of the crater with its 5,000-foot walls towering above and its 3,000-foot waterfalls surrounding you, something you will remember forever. ₃

3501 Rice St., Lihue. ℂ **800/745-2583** or 808/245-5800. www.bluehawaiian.com. 50-min. tour $210 ($179 if you book online). Harbor Mall staging area; take off from the Lihue Airport.

Heli USA Airways   If you are staying on the North Shore and don't want to drive into Lihue or farther, Heli USA flies out of the Princeville Airport. Operating an A STAR helicopter, they offer three different types of trips: a 35-minute tour of the mountains and valleys of the North Shore and a bit of the Na Pali Coast for $109; a 45-minute tour which goes further down the Na Pali Coast than the 35-minute trip and includes Waimea Canyon for $169; and a 60-minute tour of the entire island for $199.

Princeville Airport. ℂ **866/936-1234** or 808/826-6591. www.heliuse.com. Tours: $109–$199.

Island Helicopters ⊕   Curt Lofstedt has been flying helicopter tours of Kauai for nearly 3 decades. He personally selects and trains professional pilots with an eye not only to their flying skills but also to their ability to share the magic of Kauai. All flights are in either the four-passenger Bell Jet Ranger III or the six-passenger Aerospatiale A STAR, with extra-large windows and stereo headsets to hear the pilot's personal narration.

Lihue Airport. ℂ **800/829-5999** or 808/245-8588. www.islandhelicopters.com. 55-min. island tour $250. Mention Frommer's and receive 37% off.

Jack Harter ⊕   The pioneer of helicopter flights on Kauai, Jack was the guy who started the sightseeing-via-helicopter trend. On the 60-minute tour, he flies a four-passenger Bell Jet Ranger Model 204 (with "scenic view" windows), a six-seater A STAR, or a Eurocopter AS350BA A STAR. The 90-minute tour (in the Bell Jet Ranger only) hovers over the sights a bit longer than the 60-minute flight, so you can get a good look, but we found the shorter tour sufficient.

4231 Ahukini Rd., Lihue. ℂ **888/245-2001** or 808/245-3774. www.helicopters-kauai.com. 60-min. tour $199; 90-min. tour $269. (Book on the Internet and save up to 15%.)

Niihau Helicopter   This the only helicopter company offering tours of Niihau, the "Forbidden Island." The half-day tours, on an Agusta 109A twin-engine helicopter, include an aerial tour over the island. The helicopter then lands on Niihau at a beach (the island is generally closed to the public), where you can spend a few hours swimming, snorkeling, beachcombing, or just relaxing and sun-bathing. Lunch and refreshments are included. You leave from Port Allen Air Strip.

P.O. Box 690086, Makaweli, HI 96769. ℂ **877/441-3500** or 808/335-3500. www.hawaiian.net/~niihauisland/heli. html. Half-day tours, with lunch and a stop at a Niihau beach, $325.

Ohana Helicopter Tours   Hawaiian-born pilot Bogart Kealoha delights in showing his island his way—aboard one of his four-passenger Bell Jet Rangers or his six-passenger Aerospatiale A STAR helicopter. You're linked to a customized audio entertainment system through individual headsets with narration, as you swoop over and through 12-mile-long Waimea Canyon on a memorable sightseeing flight that includes the valleys and waterfalls of the Na Pali Coast.

Anchor Cove Shopping Center, 3416 Rice St., Lihue. ✆ 800/222-6989 or 808/245-3996. www.ohanahelicopters. com. 50- to 55-min. tour $185; 65- to 70-min. tour $240.

Safari Helicopters   This family-owned and -run company also flies custom-designed, huge windowed A STAR helicopters (37% larger than most helicopters) with high-back leather seats. Here, too, the pilot is on the left side of the helicopter (instead of the usual position on the right), which not only allows you better views, but more legroom.

3225 Akahi, Lihue, HI 96766. ✆ 800/326-3356 or 808/246-0136, www.safariair.com. 60-min. tour $209 ($139 on the Web).

Will Squyres Helicopter Tours   The 60-minute flight starts in Lihue and takes you through Waimea Canyon, along the Na Pali Coast, and over Waialeale Crater and the two sets of waterfalls that appeared in *Fantasy Island*. Will's A STAR six-passenger copter has side-by-side seats (nobody sits backward and everybody gets a window seat) and enlarged windows. A veteran pilot, Will has flown several thousand hours over Kauai since 1984 and knows the island, its ever-changing weather conditions, and his copters.

3222 Kuhio Hwy., Lihue. ✆ 888/245-4354 or 808/245-8881. www.helicopters-hawaii.com. 60-min. Grand Tour of Kauai $208.

4 The Coconut Coast

The **Kauai Historical Society** (✆ 808/245-3373) leads a 90-minute **Kapaa History Tour** on Tues, Thurs, and Sat at 10am led by trained interpretive guides. You'll walk back at least 125 years to a time when King Kalakaua came to Kauai seeking to make a fortune in sugar, when pineapple was king, and learn about the various ethnic groups that make Kapaa what it is today. Cost is $15 for adults and $5 for children under 12; be sure to make reservations in advance.

Fern Grotto   This is one of Kauai's oldest (since 1946) and most popular tourist attractions. Several times daily a 157-passenger motorized barge takes people up and down the river on a 90-minute, 2½-mile, river trip to a natural amphitheater filled with ferns. A steady flow of water from a plantation-created reservoir above the cavern keeps them happy and growing. The drought of the past few years, coupled with the closing of the plantation, and thus cutting off the supply of water, made the place dry up. But the Hawaii Tourism Authority and Kauai County are spending $440,000 to refurbish the Fern Grotto. The grotto is the source of many Hawaiian legends and a popular site for weddings. The Smith family has had a monopoly on the tours since a circuit court judge evicted the Waialeale Boat Tours from the river in August 2004—because the company had not paid rent for use of the state-owned marina and Fern Grotto State Park for more than 4 years (and owed more than $100,000).

Smith's Motor Boats. Wailua Marina, at the mouth of the Wailua River; turn off Kuhio Hwy. (Hwy. 56) into Wailua Marine State Park. ✆ 808/821-6892. www.smithskauai.com. Daily 9am–3:30pm. Admission $16 adults, $8 children 2–12; reservations recommended.

WAILUA RIVER STATE PARK

Ancients called the Wailua River "the river of the great sacred spirit." Seven temples once stood along this 20-mile river, which is fed by 5,148-foot Mount Waialeale, the wettest spot on earth. You can go up Hawaii's biggest navigable river by boat or kayak (see "Boating" and "Kayaking," in chapter 7), or drive Kuamoo Road (Hwy. 580,

Moments Make a Pilgrimage to a Hindu Temple

Believe it or not, a sacred Hindu temple is being carved out of rocks from India on the banks of the Wailua River. The **San Marga Iraivan Temple** is being built to last "a thousand years or more," on the 458-acre site of the Saiva Siddhanta Church monastery. In the making for years now and not expected to be completed until 2010, the Chola-style temple is the result of a vision by the late Satguru Sivaya Subramuniyaswami, known to his followers as Gurudeva, the founder of the church and its monastery. He specifically selected this site in 1970, recognizing that the Hawaiians also felt the spiritual power of this place. The Hawaiians called it *pihanakalani,* "where heaven touches the earth."

The concrete foundation is 68×168 square feet and 3 feet thick, designed not to crack under the weight of the 3.2-million-pound temple dedicated to the Hindu god Shiva. The granite for the temple is being hand-quarried by some 70 stonemasons in India, then shipped to Kauai for final shaping and fitting on the site. The center of the temple will hold a 700-pound crystal, known as the Sivalingam, now displayed at the monastery's smaller temple on the grounds.

Hindu pilgrims come from around the globe to study and meditate at the monastery. The public is welcome to the monastery temple, open daily from 9am to noon. There also is a weekly guided tour of the grounds that includes the San Marga Iraivan Temple. The weekly tour time varies depending on the retreat schedule at the monastery. For information, call *©* **808/822-3012,** ext. 198, or go to www.saivasiddhanta.com.

A few suggestions if you plan to visit: Carry an umbrella (it's very rainy here), and wear what the Hindus call "modest clothing" (certainly no shorts, short dresses, T-shirts, or tank tops); Hindu dress is ideal. Also, even though this is a monastery, there are lots of people around, so don't leave valuables in your car.

To get there, turn *mauka* (left, inland) off Kuhio Highway (Hwy. 56) at the lights, just after crossing the bridge, onto Kuamoo Road (between Coco Palms Hotel and the Wailua River). Continue up the hill, for just over 4 miles. A quarter mile past the 4-mile marker, turn left on Kaholalele Road and go 1 block to the end of the road. The Information Center is at 107 Kaholalele. Park on Temple Lane. Enter the open pavilion, where a guide will escort you through the monastery. You can also visit the Sacred Rudraksha Forest at 7345 Kuamoo Road for meditation, open 6am to 6pm; or the Nepalese Ganesha Shrine and Bangalore Gallery, which are located at 107 Kaholalele Rd.

sometimes called the King's Highway), which goes inland along the north side of the river from Kuhio Highway (Hwy. 56)—from the northbound lane, turn left at the stoplight just before the ruins of Coco Palms Resort. Kuamoo Road goes past the *heiau* (temple) and historical sites to Opaekaa Falls and Keahua Arboretum, a State Division of Forestry attempt to reforest the watershed with native plants.

The entire district from the river mouth to the summit of Waialeale was once royal land. This sacred, historical site was believed to be founded by Puna, a Tahitian priest who, according to legend, arrived in one of the first double-hulled voyaging canoes to come to Hawaii, established a beachhead, and declared Kauai his kingdom. All of Kauai's *alii* (royalty) are believed to be descended from Puna. Here, in this royal settlement, are the remains of seven temples, including a sacrificial *heiau*, a planetarium (a simple array of rocks in a celestial pattern), the royal birthing stones, and a stone bell to announce a royal birth. (You can still ring the bell—many people have—but make sure you have an announcement to make when it stops ringing.)

There's a nice overlook view of 40-foot **Opaekaa Falls** *★★* 1½ miles up Highway 580. This is probably the best-looking drive-up waterfall on Kauai. With the scenic peaks of the Makaleha Mountains in the background and a restored Hawaiian village on the riverbanks, these falls are what the tourist bureau folks call an "eye-popping" photo op.

Near Opaekaa Falls overlook is **Poliahu Heiau,** the large lava-rock temple of Kauai's last king, Kaumualii, who died on Oahu in 1824 after being abducted by King Kamehameha II. If you stop here, you'll notice two signs. The first, an official 1928 bronze territorial plaque, says that the royal *heiau* was built by *menehune,* who it explains parenthetically are "Hawaiian dwarves or brownies." A more recent, hand-painted sign warns visitors not to climb on the rocks, which are sacred to the Hawaiian people.

SLEEPING GIANT

If you squint your eyes just so as you pass the 1,241-foot-high Nounou Ridge, which makes a dramatic backdrop for the coastal villages of Wailua and Waipouli, you can see the fabled Sleeping Giant. On Kuhio Highway, just after mile marker 7, around the mini-mall complex of Waipouli Town Center, look *mauka* (inland) and you may see what appears to be the legendary giant named Puni who, as the story goes, fell asleep after a great feast. If you don't see him at first, visualize him this way: His head is Wailua and his feet are Kapaa. For details on an easy hike to the top of the Sleeping Giant, see "The Sleeping Giant Trail," p. 178.

5 Paradise Found: The North Shore *★★★*

ON THE ROAD TO HANALEI

The first place everyone should go on Kauai is Hanalei. The drive along **Kuhio Highway** (Hwy. 56, which becomes Hwy. 560 after Princeville to the end of the road) displays Kauai's grandeur at its absolute best. Just before Kilauea, the air and the sea change, the light falls in a different way, and the last signs of development are behind you. Now there are roadside fruit stands, a little stone church in Kilauea, two roadside waterfalls, and a long, stiltlike bridge over the Kalihiwai Stream and its green river valley.

If you don't know a guava from a mango, stop in Kilauea at the cool, shady **Guava Kai Plantation,** at the end of Kuawa Road (© 808/828-6121), for a refreshing, free treat. After you take a walk through the orchards and see what a guava looks like on the tree, you can sample the juice of this exotic pink tropical fruit (which also makes a great jam or jelly—sold here, too). For other sweet treats along the way, check out "Fruity Smoothies & Other Exotic Treats" on p. 210. The plantation is open daily from 9am to 5pm.

Birders might want to stop off at **Kilauea Point National Wildlife Refuge,** a mile north of Kilauea, and the **Hanalei National Wildlife Refuge,** along Ohiki Road, at the west end of the Hanalei River Bridge. (For details, see "Birding," in chapter 7.) In the Hanalei Refuge, along a dirt road on a levee, you can see the **Hariguchi Rice Mill,** now a historic treasure.

Now the coastal highway heads due west, and the showy ridgelines of Mount Namahana create a grand amphitheater. The two-lane coastal highway rolls through pastures of grazing cattle and past a tiny airport and the luxurious Princeville Hotel.

Five miles past Kilauea, just past the Princeville Shopping Center, is **Hanalei Valley Lookout.** Big enough for a dozen cars, this lookout attracts crowds of people who peer over the edge into the 917-acre Hanalei River Valley. So many shades of green: Rice green, taro green, and green streams lace a patchwork of green ponds that back up to green-velvet Bali Hai cliffs. Pause to catch your first sight of taro growing in irrigated ponds; maybe you'll see an endangered Hawaiian black-necked stilt. Don't be put off by the crowds; this is definitely worth a look.

Farther along, a hairpin turn offers another scenic look at Hanalei town, and then you cross the **Hanalei Bridge.** The Pratt truss steel bridge, pre-fabbed in New York City, was erected in 1912; it's now on the National Registry of Historic Landmarks. If it ever goes out, the nature of Hanalei will change forever; currently, this rusty, one-lane bridge (which must violate all kinds of Department of Transportation safety regulations) isn't big enough for a tour bus to cross.

You'll drive slowly past the **Hanalei River banks** and Bill Mowry's **Hanalei Buffalo Ranch,** where 200 American bison roam in the tropical sun; you may even see buffalo grazing in the pastures on your right. The herd is often thinned to make buffalo patties. (You wondered why there was a Buffalo Burger on the Ono Family Restaurant menu, didn't you?)

Just past Tahiti Nui, turn right on Aku Road before Ching Young Village, then take a right on Weke Road. **Hanalei Beach Park,** one of Hawaii's most gorgeous, is a half-block ahead on your left. Swimming is excellent here year-round, especially in summer, when Hanalei Bay becomes a big, placid lake. For details, see "Beaches" in chapter 7.

If this exquisite 2-mile-long beach doesn't meet your expectations, head down the highway, where the next 7 miles of coast yield some of Kauai's other spectacular beaches, including **Lumahai Beach** of *South Pacific* movie fame, as well as **Tunnels**

Tips **Bridge Etiquette: Showing Aloha on Kauai's One-Lane Bridges**

Unlike the aggressive drivers you see on the mainland, Hawaii's drivers are much more laid-back and courteous. Hanalei has a series of one-lane bridges where it is not only proper etiquette to be courteous, but it also is the law. When you approach a one-lane bridge, slow down and *yield* if a vehicle, approaching in the opposite direction, is either on the bridge or just about to enter the bridge. (This is not a contest of chicken.) If you are in a long line of vehicles approaching the bridge, don't just join the train crossing the bridge. The local "rule of thumb" is about seven to eight cars over the bridge, then yield and give the cars waiting on the other side of the bridge a chance to come across. Of course, not everyone will adhere to these rules, but then, not everyone visiting Hawaii truly feels the spirit of aloha.

Fun Fact Hollywood Loves Kauai

More than 50 major Hollywood productions have been shot on Kauai since the studios discovered the island's spectacular natural beauty. Here are just a few:

- The lush, tropical mountain waterfall and awe-inspiring peaks seen in the *Jurassic Park* films (1993, 1997, and 2001) were not filmed on an island off Costa Rica, but on Kauai at Manawaiopu Falls, Mount Waialeale, and other scenic areas.
- Kauai's verdant rainforests formed a fantastic backdrop for Harrison Ford in both *Raiders of the Lost Ark* (1983) and *Indiana Jones and the Temple of Doom* (1984).
- A pilot and his passenger are forced to land on the classical tropical island, believed to be in French Polynesia, in *Six Days, Seven Nights* (1998); actually, Ivan Reitman filmed Harrison Ford and Anne Heche for 11 weeks on Kauai's spectacular shores.
- Mitzi Gaynor sang "I'm Gonna Wash That Man Right Outta My Hair" on Lumahai Beach in *South Pacific* (1958).
- Jessica Lange, Jeff Bridges, and Charles Grodin tangled with Hollywood's most famous gorilla in Honopu Valley, in the remake of *King Kong* (1976).
- Elvis Presley married costar Joan Blackman near the Wailua River in *Blue Hawaii* (1961).
- Beautiful Kee Beach, on the North Shore, masqueraded as Australia in the mini-series *The Thornbirds* (1983), starring Richard Chamberlain and Rachel Ward.
- Kauai appeared as the backdrop for *Outbreak*, the 1994 thriller about the spread of a deadly virus on a remote tropical island, starring Dustin Hoffman. Hoffman also appeared with Robin Williams and Julia Roberts in *Hook* (1991), in which Kauai appeared as Never-Never Land.
- James Caan, Nicholas Cage, Sarah Jessica Parker, and Pat Morita shared laughs on Kauai (which appeared as itself) in *Honeymoon in Vegas* (1992).

If you are a film buff, you can get more movie trivia about Kauai and the movies in Chris Cook's book, *The Kauai Movie Book*, published by Mutual Publishing, Honolulu. Or log onto www.filmkauai.com, the Kauai Film Commission's website, which has lots of facts about films on the Garden Isle. You can also visit these and other Kauai locations that made it to the silver screen, plus locations from such TV classics as *Fantasy Island* and *Gilligan's Island*, with **Hawaii Movie Tours** (📞 **800/628-8432** or 808/822-1192; www.hawaiimovietour.com). Tickets are $95 for adults and $76 for children 11 and under; lunch is included.

Beach (p. 162), where the 1960s puka-shell necklace craze began, and **Haena Beach Park** (p. 162), a fabulous place to kick back and enjoy the waves, particularly in summer. Once you've found your beach, stick around until sundown, then head back to one of the North Shore's restaurants for a mai tai and a fresh seafood dinner. (See chapter 6.) Another perfect day in paradise.

ATTRACTIONS ALONG THE WAY

Ka Ulu O Laka Heiau   On a knoll above the boulders of Kee Beach (p. 162) stands a sacred altar of rocks, often draped with flower leis and ti-leaf offerings. The altar is dedicated to Laka, the goddess of hula. It may seem like a primal relic from the days of idols, but it's very much in use today. Often, dancers (men and women) of Hawaii's hula *halau* (schools) climb the cliff, bearing small gifts of flowers. In Hawaiian myths, Lohiau, a handsome chief, danced here before the fire goddess Pele; their passion became *Haena*, which means "the heat." Sometimes, in a revival of the old Hawaiian ways (once banned by missionaries), a mother of a newborn will deposit the umbilical cord of her infant at this sacred shrine. The site is filled with what Hawaiians call *mana*, or power.

From the west side of Kee Beach, take the footpath across the big rocks almost to the point; then climb the steep grassy hill.

Limahuli Garden of the National Tropical Botanical Garden 🕏   Out on

Kauai's far North Shore, beyond Hanalei and the last wooden bridge, there's a mighty cleft in the coastal range where ancestral Hawaiians lived in what can only be called paradise. Carved by a waterfall stream known as Limahuli, the lush valley sits at the foot of steepled cliffs that Hollywood portrayed as Bali Hai in the film classic *South Pacific*. This small, almost secret garden is ecotourism at its best. It appeals not just to green thumbs but to all who love Hawaii's great outdoors. Here botanists hope to save Kauai's endangered native plants. You can take the self-tour to view the plants, which are identified in Hawaiian and English. From taro to sugar cane, the mostly Polynesian imports tell the story of the people who cultivated the plants for food, medicine, clothing, shelter, and decoration. In addition, Limahuli's stream is sanctuary to the last five species of Hawaiian freshwater fish.

Visitor Center, ½ mile past mile marker 9 on Kuhio Hwy. (Hwy. 560), Haena. ℂ **808/826-1053.** Fax 808/826-1394. www.ntbg.org. Admission $10 self-guided, $15 guided; free for children 12 and under. Open Tues–Fri and Sun 10am–4pm. Advance reservations required for 2½-hr. guided tours. During peak seasons of July, Aug, and Sept, book at least a week ahead.

Na Aina Kai Botanical Gardens 🕏🕏🕏 *(Finds* Do not miss this incredible, magical

garden on some 240 acres sprinkled with about 70 life-size (some larger than life-size) whimsical bronze statues. Hidden off the beaten path of the North Shore, and only recently opened, this is the place for both avid gardeners as well as people who think they don't like botanical gardens. These gardens have everything: waterfalls, pools, arbors, topiaries, colonnades, gazebos, a maze you will never forget, a lagoon with spouting fountains, a Japanese teahouse, and an enchanting path along a bubbling stream to the ocean. The imaginary, fairy-tale creativity that has gone into these grounds will be one of your fondest memories of Kauai. A host of different tours is available, from 1½ ($25) to 5-hours ($70) long, ranging from casual, guided strolls, to a ride in the covered CarTram, to treks from one end of the gardens to the ocean. A tropical children's garden is the latest edition: it features a gecko hedge maze, a tropical jungle gym, a treehouse in a rubber tree, and a 16-foot tall Jack and the Bean Stalk Giant with a 33-foot wading pool below. Na Aina Kai is only open 3 days a week; book a tour before you leave for Hawaii to avoid being disappointed.

4101 Wailapa Rd. (P.O. Box 1134), Kilauea, HI 96754. ℂ **808/828-0525.** Fax 808/828-0815. www.naainakai.com. Open Tues–Thurs 8am–5pm. Tours vary. Advance reservations strongly recommended. From Lihue, drive north past mile marker 21 and turn right on Wailapa Rd. At the road's end, drive through the iron gates. From Princeville, drive south 6½ miles and take the 2nd left past mile marker 22 on Wailapa Rd. At the road's end, drive through the iron gates.

Waioli Mission House Museum   If you're lucky and time your visit just right, you can see this 150-year-old mission house, which serves today as a living museum. It's a real treasure. Others in Honolulu are easier to see, but the Waioli Mission House retains its sense of place and most of its furnishings, so you can really get a clear picture of what life was like for the New England missionaries who came to Kauai to convert the "heathens" to Christianity.

Most mission houses are small, dark Boston cottages that violate the tropical sense of place. This two-story, wood-frame house, built in 1836 by Abner and Lucy Wilcox of New Bedford, Massachusetts, is an excellent example of hybrid architecture. The house features lanais on both stories, and a cookhouse in a separate building. It has a lava-rock chimney, ohia-wood floors, and Hawaiian koa furniture.

Kuhio Hwy. (Hwy. 560), just behind the green Waioli Huia Church, Hanalei. © **808/245-3202**. Free admission (donations gratefully accepted). Tours: Mon and Wed–Thurs, 10am and 1pm. Reservations required.

THE END OF THE ROAD

The real Hawaii begins where the road stops. This is especially true on Kauai—for at the end of Highway 56, the spectacular **Na Pali Coast** begins. To explore it, you have to set out on foot, by boat, or by helicopter. For details on experiencing this region, see "Hiking & Camping" and "Boating," in chapter 7, and "Helicopter Rides over Waimea Canyon & the Na Pali Coast," earlier in this chapter.

9

Shopping

Shopping is a pleasure on this island. Where else can you browse vintage Hawaiiana practically in a cane field, buy exquisite home accessories in an old stone building built in 1942, and get a virtual agricultural tour of the island through city-sponsored green markets that move from town to town throughout the week, like a movable feast? At Kauai's small, tasteful boutiques, you can satisfy your shopping ya-yas in concentrated spurts around the island. This is a bonanza for the boutique shopper—particularly one who appreciates the thrill of the hunt.

"Downtown" Kapaa continues to flourish, and Hanalei, touristy as it is, is still a shopping destination. (Ola's and Yellowfish make up for the hurricane of trinkets and trash in Hanalei.) Kilauea,

with Kong Lung Store and the fabulous Lotus Gallery, is the style center of the island. The Kauai Heritage Center of Hawaiian Culture & the Arts makes it possible for visitors to escape the usual imitations, tourist traps, and clichés in favor of authentic encounters with the real thing: Hawaiian arts, Hawaiian cultural practices, and Hawaiian elders and artists. What else can you expect on Kauai? Anticipate great shops in Hanalei, a few art galleries and boutiques, and a handful of shopping centers—not much to distract you from an afternoon of hiking or snorkeling. The gift items and treasures you'll find in east and north Kauai, however, may be among your best Hawaiian finds.

1 Green Markets & Fruit Stands

The county of Kauai sponsors regular weekly **Sunshine Markets** throughout the island, featuring fresh Kauai **Sunrise papayas** (sweeter, juicier, and redder than most), herbs and vegetables used in ethnic cuisines, exotic fruit such as rambutan and atemoya, and the most exciting development in pineapple agriculture, the low-acid white pineapple called **Sugarloaf,** rarer these days but still spottily available. These markets, which sell the full range of fresh local produce and flowers at rock-bottom prices, present the perfect opportunity to see what's best and what's in season. Farmers sell their bounty from the backs of trucks or at tables set up under tarps. Mangoes during the summer, lettuces all year, fleshy bananas and juicy papayas, the full range of Filipino vegetables (wing beans, long beans, exotic squashes, and melons), and an ever-changing rainbow of edibles are all on offer.

The biggest market is at **Kapaa New Town Park,** in the middle of Kapaa town, on Wednesday at 3pm. The Sunshine Market in **Lihue,** held on Friday at 3pm at the Vidinha Stadium Parking Lot, is close in size and extremely popular. The schedules for the other markets: **Koloa Ball Park,** Monday at noon; **Kalaheo Neighborhood Center,** Tuesday at 3:30pm; **Hanapepe Park,** Thursday at 3pm; **Kilauea Neighborhood Center,** Thursday at 4:30pm; and **Kekaha Neighborhood Center,** Saturday at 9am.

For more information on Sunshine Markets, call © **808/241-6390.** Especially at the Koloa Market, which draws hundreds of shoppers, go early and shop briskly.

Those who miss the Sunshine Markets can shop instead at the privately run **Sunnyside Farmers Market** (© 808/822-0494), on Kuhio Highway in the middle of Kapaa, Monday through Saturday from 7am to 7:30pm and Sunday from 10am to 6pm. You'll find several varieties of papayas (grown by the same farmer they've used for 20 years), mangoes, lilikoi (passion fruit), Sugarloaf pineapples, locally grown organic lettuces, Maui onions, purple Molokai sweet potatoes, Molokai watermelons, and exotic seasonal fruits such as soursop and rambutan. Fruit preserves, gourmet breads, Taro Ko chips, and Kauai macadamia-nut cookies are among the made-on-Kauai products that are shipped and carried all over the United States. The expanded **Dori's Garden Cafe** adjoining the market serves sandwiches, soups, salads, and smoothies—everything from fresh juices to Lappert's ice cream.

On the North Shore, Kilauea is the agricultural heart of the island, with two weekly green markets: the county-sponsored **Sunshine Market,** Thursday at 4:30pm at the Kilauea Neighborhood Center; and the private Kilauea Quality Farmers Association (mostly organic growers) **Farmers Market,** Saturday from 11:30am to 1:30pm behind the Kilauea Post Office. Everything in the markets' wide-ranging selection is grown or made on Kauai, from rambutan and long beans to sweet potatoes, corn, lettuce, and salsas and chutneys. The markets are a dramatic, colorful tableau of how farming activity and enterprises are growing by leaps and bounds in Kilauea.

Also on the North Shore, about a quarter mile past Hanalei in an area called Waipa, the **Hawaiian Farmers of Hanalei**—anywhere from a dozen to 25 farmers—gather along the main road with their budget-friendly, just-picked produce. This market is held every Tuesday at 2pm. You'll find unbelievably priced papayas (in some seasons, several for a dollar, ready to eat), organic vegetables, inexpensive tropical flowers, avocados and mangoes in season, and, when available, fresh seafood. The best of the best, in season, are rose apples, mountain apples, and the orange-colored papaya lilikoi.

On the south shore, we're hearing great things about the two adorable fruit stands in Lawai, where you can find inexpensive bananas (sometimes $1.25 a hand!), papayas, and avocados along an old country road. The fruit are cheerfully displayed, and sometimes the honor system is used—leave the money if no one is there. This is country style nonpareil. (From Kaumualii Hwy., turn at the corner where Mustard's Last Stand is—Lauoho Rd.—then take the first right.) In Kauai jargon, directions would be: "Go to that old road where the old post office was, near Matsuura Store, the old manju place. . . ."

Closer to the resorts, in Poipu on Koloa Bypass Road, with a view across asparagus fields and the chiseled ridges of Haupu Mountain, the **Poipu Southshore Market** sells produce (some of it from Haupu Growers) daily from 10am to 6pm. Haupu Growers is the major supplier of Kauai asparagus, and this is where you'll find it. Asparagus season begins in October.

2 Lihue & Environs

DOWNTOWN LIHUE

The gift shop of the **Kauai Museum,** 4428 Rice St. (© **808/245-6931**), is your best bet for made-on-Kauai arts and crafts, from Niihau-shell leis to woodwork, *lauhala* and coconut products, and more. The master of *lauhala* weaving, Esther Makuaole, weaves regularly in the gallery on Monday and Wednesday from 9am to 1:30pm.

Fruity Smoothies & Other Exotic Treats

Fruit stands have sprouted on this island, and smoothies are gaining ground as the milkshake of the new millennium. New crops of exotic trees imported from Southeast Asia are maturing on Kauai, creating anticipation among residents and fruitful ideas for the smoothie world. "Everyone's waiting for the mangosteens and durians," comments Joe Halasey who, with his wife, Cynthia, runs **Banana Joe's** (© 808/828-1092), the granddaddy of Kauai's roadside fruit-and-smoothie stands. "They take about 12 years to start bearing, so there are a lot of maturing trees. We're all waiting for the fruit. Rambutans (with a hairy, red exterior and a translucent, litchilike flesh) are good for the farmers here because they're available, and they're a winter fruit. In the summer, mangoes and litchis are always in high demand."

Banana Joe's has been a Kilauea landmark since it opened in 1986 at 52719 Kuhio Hwy., between mile markers 23 and 24 heading north, on the *mauka* (mountain) side of the street. Sapodilla, star apple (round, purple, and sweet, like a creamy Concord grape), macadamia nuts, Anahola Granola, and homemade breads—like banana and mango-coconut—are among Banana Joe's attractions. The Halaseys have expanded their selection of organic vegetables and exude a quiet aloha from their roadside oasis.

Mangosteen, reputedly the favorite fruit of Queen Victoria, has a creamy, custardy flesh of ambrosial sweetness. When mangosteens start appearing at Hawaii fruit stands, they will no doubt be in high demand, like mangoes and litchis during their summer season. In the meantime, Banana Joe has a hit on his hands with Sugarloaf, the white, nonacidic, ultra-sweet, organically grown pineapple popularized on the Big Island. Whether made into

About a mile north of the Lihue Airport, on Highway 56 (Kuhio Hwy.), **Kauai Fruit & Flower** is a great stop for flowers like the rare Kauai maile in season, cut flowers for shipping, coconut drums the owner makes himself, Hawaiian gourds *(ipu)*, and Kauai fruit such as papayas and pineapples. Other products include *lauhala* gift items, teas, Kauai honey, Kauai salad dressings, jams and jellies, and custom-made gift baskets.

In the **Kukui Grove Center**, at Kaumualii Highway (Hwy. 50) and Old Nawiliwili Road, is the **Kauai Products Store** (© 808/246-6753). It's a font of local handicrafts (about 60% of whom are Kauai artists) and a respectable showcase for made-on-the-island products, such as soaps, paintings, clothing, coffee, Kukui guava jams, fabrics, and Niihau-shell leis. The Hawaiian quilts are made in the Philippines but designed by Kauai families. You'll find everything from a $10,750 bronze sculpture to bamboo chairs to a koa ukulele by Raymond Rapozo in Kealia, who does stunning work. Beware of the macadamia-nut fudge, found only at Kauai Products Store: It's rich, sweet, and irresistible.

For a great selection in alohawear—shirts, dresses, pareu—and lots of souvenirs to take to the folks back home, stop by **Hilo Hattie,** 3252 Kuhio Hwy. (Hwy. 50) and Ahukini Road (© 808/245-3404). Their selection of Hawaii-related gift items is immense: food, books, CDs, mugs, key chains, T-shirts, and more. They even offer free hotel pickup from Poipu and Kapaa. If you are on a budget, go to the **Kauai** smoothies or frostees (frozen fruit put through the Champion juicer), or just sold plain, fresh, and whole, the Sugarloaf is pineapple at its best. For litchi lovers, who must wait for their summer appearance, new varieties such as Kaimana and Brewster are adding to the pleasures of the season. In addition to fresh fruit, fruit smoothies, and frostees, Banana Joe's sells organic greens, tropical-fruit salsas, jams and jellies, drinking coconuts (young coconuts containing delicious drinking water), gift items, and baked goods such as papaya-banana bread. Its top-selling smoothies are papaya, banana, and pineapple.

Mango Mama's, 4660 Hookui St. (© **808/828-1020**), is another favorite on the Kilauea roadside. Recently expanded, it's now a full-service cafe serving espresso, smoothies, fresh-squeezed juices, sandwiches, bagels, coffee, coffee smoothies, and fresh fruit. The Kauai Breeze (fresh mango, pineapple, passion fruit, and guava) is a big winner here.

On the Coconut Coast, just before you reach the center of Kapaa town heading north on Kuhio Highway, keep an eye out to the left for **Sunnyside Farmers Market,** 4-1345 Kuhio Hwy. (© **808/822-0494** or 808/822-1154; see above). Here you can always find realistically priced Sunrise papayas, pineapples, local bananas, tomatoes, and other Kauai produce. You can also get pre-inspected Sunrise papayas for travel out of state, local apple bananas, coconuts, mangoes in season, and pineapples from Maui and Kauai.

Near the Lihue Airport, Pammie Chock at **Kauai Fruit & Flower** (© **808/ 245-1814;** see below) makes a pineapple–passion fruit smoothie that gets our vote as the best on the island.

Humane Society Thrift Shop, Lihue Center, 3-3100 Kuhio Hwy. (© **808/245-7387**), where a great selection of "vintage" aloha shirts starts at $5. All the money raised goes to help the Kauai Humane Society continue their excellent work on the island. If you want wooden or coconut buttons for your vintage aloha shirt, stop by **Kapaa Stitchery,** 3-3551 Kuhio Hwy. (© **808/245-2281**), and buy a few buttons; you can have an authentic aloha shirt for a quarter of what you would spend in retail stores. Quilters will be in heaven at the Kapaa Stitchery, where they will find a huge selection of Hawaiian quilts, quilting supplies, needlework designs, and lots of fabric.

Another good souvenir store is **Red Dirt Shirt,** 3-3229 Kuhio Hwy. (© **808/246-0224**), with other outlets in Waimea and Kapaa (see box on p. 215). Here you'll find zillions of the famous "red dirt" T-shirts in a variety of styles and designs (and sizes all the way to XXXXL).

If you are looking for something more artsy, **Two Frogs Hugging,** just down Kuhio Highway from Hilo Hattie and Red Dirt Shirt (© **808/246-8777**), is a great place to wander about marveling at their collection of Indonesian arts, crafts, furniture, pottery, and accessories.

If you just need necessities like suntan lotion, film, or a cheap pair of slippers, head for **K-Mart,** 4303 Nawiliwili, Lihue (© **808/245-7742**). If you need laundry done (and don't want to waste a minute of your vacation doing it), drop it off at **Plaza**

Tips **Photo Opportunity: Hang Ten without Getting Wet**

Here's your opportunity to take a photo of your trip to Kauai which will astound and amaze your friends—you on a surfboard. Oh, you don't surf; can't even swim? No problem. Drive down to Hawaiian Trading Post, at the intersection of Koloa Road and Kaumualii Highway. On the side of their building (facing the parking lot) is a fake backdrop with a surfboard and a huge wave (fashioned from plaster) that looks amazingly like the real thing. Bring your own camera (and bathing suit) and snap away.

Laundry, in the Hanamaulu Plaza Shopping Center, Kuhio Highway (Hwy. 56) and Hanamaulu Road (*C* **808/246-9057**), which offers a full wash, dry, and fold service for just 95¢ a pound.

KILOHANA PLANTATION

Kilohana, the 35-acre Tudor-style estate that sprawls across the landscape in Puhi, on Highway 50 between Lihue and Poipu, is an architectural marvel that houses a sprinkling of galleries and shops. At the **Country Store,** on the ground level, you'll find island and American crafts of decent quality, koa accessories, pottery, and Hawaii-themed gift items. On the other side of Gaylord's, the **Kilohana** and **Kahn galleries** offer a mix of crafts and two-dimensional art, from originals to affordable prints, at all levels of taste.

3 The Poipu Resort Area

Expect mostly touristy shops in Poipu, the island's resort mecca; here you'll find T-shirts, souvenirs, black pearls, jewelry, and the usual quota of tired marine art and trite hand-painted silks.

There are exceptions. The formerly characterless **Poipu Shopping Village,** at 2360 Kiahuna Plantation Dr., is shaping up into a serious shopping stop. **Hale Mana** has a glorious collection of hard-to-find gift items of excellent taste: fabulous incense sticks from Provence (lavender, amber, vanilla), antique picture frames, lacquer boxes, beaded bags, unique candles, sterling-silver chopsticks, sake sets, pillows, masks, Hawaiian handmade paper, and jewelry by Kauai artist Adove. The staggering selection also includes dramatic acrylic jewelry that looks like elk horn, one-of-a-kind jewelry and purses by Maya, gemlike sake cups, cotton yukata, silk kimonos, snuff bottles, and diaphanous silk dresses that you won't find elsewhere in Hawaii. Also in Poipu Shopping Village, the tiny **Bamboo Lace** boutique lures the fashionistas; its resortwear and accessories can segue from Hawaii to the south of France in one easy heartbeat. Across the courtyard, **Sand People** is great for understated resortwear (such as Tencel Jeans) and Indonesian coconut picture frames. Don't miss out on **Sand Kids,** with its adorable kids' clothes, books, gifts, T-shirts, and jewelry, plus cute stuffed "sea creatures" (like mermaids). It's one of the best places to get sunglasses for kids. The newly renovated **Overboard** rides the wave of popularity in alohawear and surf stuff, plus great swimwear, linens, a selection of Tommy Bahama clothing and accessories, and other island-style merchandise. Take a break from all the shopping at **Puka Dog,** serving up a range of island hot dogs (even veggie ones).

The shopping is surprisingly good at the **Hyatt Regency Kauai,** with the footwear mecca **Sandal Tree, Water Wear Hawaii** for swim stuff, **Kauai Kids** for the under-age, and **Reyn's,** an institution in Hawaii for alohawear. My favorite store here (and it's worth the drive) is the **Kohala Bay Collections,** filled with resort casual clothing with top names like Tommy Bahama, Toes on the Nose, Jams World, and M Mac, all at very wallet-pleasing prices.

Across the street from Poipu Beach, on Hoone Road, **Nukumoi Surf Shop** is a pleasant surprise: It has an excellent selection of sunglasses, swimwear, surf equipment, and watersports regalia, and not just for the under-20 crowd.

In neighboring **Old Koloa Town,** you'll find everything from **Lappert's Ice Cream** and **Island Soap and Candle Works** (where you can watch them make soap and candles), to **Crazy Shirts** and **Sueoka Store** on Koloa's main drag, Koloa Road. Walk the long block for gifts, souvenirs, sunwear, groceries, soaps and bath products, and everyday necessities. You might want to stop in at **Hula Moon,** 5426 Koloa Rd.

Niihau Shell Lei: The Island's Most Prized Artwork

Because Kauai is so close to Niihau (the "Forbidden Island" is just offshore, where the public is prohibited), it's the best place in the state to buy the exquisite art form, Niihau-shell leis. Nothing can match the craftsmanship and the tiny shells in this highly sought-after and highly prized jewelry. Niihau is in the best position to catch the very tiny and very rare shells that roll up from the deep onto the windward shores after a big storm (generally Nov–Mar). When the tiny shells are spotted on a beach, everyone (men, women, and children) on Niihau drops what they are doing and races down to the beach to begin the backbreaking work of collecting these exceptional shells.

The shells are then sorted according to size and color, and only the best are kept. Some 80% of the shells are thrown out because they are chipped, cracked, discolored, or flawed in some way that renders them imperfect. The best shells are the teeny, tiny ones. The best colors (the shells can be white, yellow, blue, red, or gold) are white or the rare gold.

The shells can be crafted into anything, but leis and necklaces are the most popular items. A necklace may take anywhere from hours to years to complete. Each shell is strung with very small and very intricate knots. The patterns sometimes mimic flower leis, and the length can range from a single-strand choker to a multi-strand, 36-inch (or longer) necklace. No two leis are alike. The leis are not cheap; they range from several hundred to several thousand dollars, depending on the length, the shells used, and the intricate work involved.

You can find Niihau shell leis at numerous locations on Kauai. One of our two favorite places is **Hawaiian Trading Post,** Koloa Road and Kaumualii Highway, in Lawai (© **808/332-7404**), which carries a range of items from junky souvenirs to excellent Niihau leis. (You have to ask for them to bring out the "good stuff" from the back.) Our other favorite place to buy the leis is at **www.hawaiian.net/~niihauisland/leis1.htm**, which is owned and operated by Niihau residents. (You can buy direct, so to speak.)

(© **808/742-6741**), which has a unique selection of gifts, especially hand-painted tiles with sayings like "I'd Rather Be On Kauai," or "Please Remove Your Shoes." If you are looking for a beach bag or Hawaiian-print hats, dresses, or T-shirts, **Paradise Clothing,** 5402 Koloa Rd. (© **808/742-1371**), has a great selection. Another great place for island-style clothes is **Progressive Expressions,** in Koloa town (© **808/742-6041**), which also has every kind of surfboard and surf accessory, as well as a great selection of sunscreens. For more stylish fashions, go to **Jungle Girl,** 5424 Koloa Rd. (© **808/742-9649**), which markets their clothes, jewelry, shoes, and artwork as "island funk and flash."

On Poipu Road, between Koloa and Poipu, there are two exceptional places you cannot miss: Kebanu Gallery and Pohaku T's. The two could not be more different, but each is worth stopping for. **Pohaku T's,** 3430 Poipu Rd (© **808/742-7500**), only sells clothing, artwork, T-shirts, and other whimsical things designed and produced by Kauai artists. All the products either have a great sense of humor or promote awareness of Hawaii's cultural and environmental issues. Prices are excellent. Next door is the very upscale **Kebanu Gallery,** 3440 Poipu Rd. (© **808/742-2727**), an oasis of quality in a sea of tourist schlock. Here you'll find beautifully carved wooden bowls, exquisite raku and glass vases, unique pottery, a range of melodious wood chimes, and unusual pieces for the discriminating buyer. They are not cheap, but the quality is worth the price. Even if you aren't looking to buy, this is a beautiful place to wander through.

Further down Poipu Road, in the tiny Poipu Plaza, nestled next to **Sea Sport Divers** and **Outfitters Kauai,** is the **Kukuiula Store**—a shop for everything from produce and sushi to paper products, sunscreen, beverages, and groceries. Occasionally, when fishermen drop by, the store offers fresh sliced sashimi and poke, quite delicious and popular with sunset picnickers and nearby condo residents. In Kalaheo, condo dwellers and locals flock to the solitary, nondescript building that is **Medeiros Farms,** 4365 Papalina Rd. (© **808/332-8211**), for everything they raise and make: chicken, range-fed beef, eggs, Italian pork, and Portuguese sausages. The meats are hailed across the island, and the prices are good. Medeiros Farms chicken is so good it's mentioned on some of the upscale menus on the island. Up the street is **The Bread Box,** 4447 Papalina Rd. (© **808/332-9000**), for just-baked breads (a deal at $3.25), gooey macadamia nut rolls ($1.50), a huge variety of muffins (poppy seed, blueberry, honey oat, among others), and wonderfully light and flaky croissants (only $1).

You can take paradise home with you—well, at least the outrageously beautiful flowers. The best place to order flowers to be sent home is **Tropical Flowers by Charles,** 3465 Lawailoa Lane, Koloa (© **800/699-7984** or 808/332-7984; www. a-tropical-flower.com). Not only is Charles a flower genius (who grows a range of tropical flowers, including some very rare and unusual varieties), but his hardy blooms and his skill at packing means that your little bit of Kauai will live for a long, long time. For all this, at extremely reasonable prices, we highly recommend Charles.

4 Western Kauai

HANAPEPE

This West Kauai hamlet is becoming a haven for artists, but finding them requires some vigilance. The center of town is off Highway 50; turn right on Hanapepe Road just after Eleele if you're driving from Lihue. First, you'll smell the chips at the sumptuous lavender **Taro Ko Chips Factory** ⊛, located in an old green plantation house at 3940 Hanapepe Rd. Cooked in a tiny, modest kitchen at the east end of town, these

Ultimate Kauai Souvenir: The Red Dirt Shirt

If you are looking for an inexpensive, easy-to-pack souvenir of your trip to Kauai or gifts for all the friends and relatives back home, check out the Red Dirt Shirt. Every T-shirt is hand-dyed and unique. The shirts were the result of a bad situation turned into a positive one. The "legend" is that **Paradise Sportswear,** in Waimea (© **808/335-5670;** www.dirtshirt.com), lost the roof of their warehouse during Hurricane Iniki in 1992. After the storm passed, employees returned to the building to find all their T-shirts covered with Kauai's red soil. Before throwing out their entire inventory as "too soiled to sell," someone had an idea—sell the shirts as a Kauai "Red Dirt Shirt." The grunge look was just starting to be popular. Unbelievable as it is, people took to these "dirt" shirts. Fast-forward a dozen years and the shirts have numerous outlets on Kauai.

There's also an interesting story behind how these T-shirts are dyed. Paradise Sportswear is a true community effort. They employ families who, due to family or disability challenges, prefer to work from home. Their employees take ordinary white T-shirts home and dye the shirts in vats with red dirt collected from valleys on Kauai where centuries of erosion have concentrated red iron oxide into the dirt. It's this red iron oxide that is used in the tinting agent, along with some other organic compounds to the dye solution, that ensure that your dirt shirt will keep its red-dirt color.

The best prices on the Red Dirt Shirts can be found at the factory by the Port Allen Small Boat Harbor, open daily 9am to noon and 1 to 4pm. You can watch the silk-screening process or purchase a few shirts from the retail shop, which has everything from T-shirts for infants to XXXXL. The deals are on the factory seconds and discontinued designs.

famous taro chips are handmade by the farmers who grow the taro in a nearby valley. Despite their breakable nature, these chips make great gifts to go. To really impress them back home, get the authentic Hawaiian *li hing mui*–flavored chips.

Our very favorite Hanapepe store is the **Banana Patch Studio,** 3865 Hanapepe Rd. (© **808/335-5944;** www.bananapatchstudio.com). For the best prices on the island for tropical plates and cups, hand-painted tiles, artwork, handmade soaps, pillows with tropical designs, and jewelry, this is the place. Plus, they will pack and ship for you anywhere. Farther along, Hanapepe Road is lined with gift shops and galleries, including **Koa Wood Gallery,** with its koa furniture, koa photo albums, and Norfolk pine bowls; and the corny but cherubic **Aloha Angels,** where everything is angel-themed or angel-related. The **Kauai Village Gallery** offers abstract and surreal paintings by Kauai artist Lew Shortridge, while nearby **Kauai Fine Arts** offers an odd mix that works: antique maps and prints of Hawaii, authentic Polynesian *tapa* (bark cloth), rare wiliwili seed leis, old Matson liner menus, and a few pieces of contemporary island art. Down the street, the **Kim Starr Gallery,** showing only Kim Starr's oil paintings, pastels, drawings, and limited-edition graphics, is a strong positive note in Hanapepe's art community. Taking a cue from Maui's Lahaina, where every Friday night is Art Night, Hanapepe's gallery owners and artists recently instituted the **Friday Night Art Walk** from 6 to 9pm. Gallery owners take turns hosting this informal event along Hanapepe Road.

WAIMEA

Neighboring Waimea is filled with more edibles than art. Kauai's favorite native super-market, **Big Save,** serves as the one-stop shop for area residents and passersby heading for the uplands of Kokee State Park, some 4,000 feet above this sea-level village. For more hard-to-find delicious gourmet items, try the **Ishihara Store,** where they have marinated meals, freshly made poke, and a range of prepared picnic items. A cheerful distraction for lovers of Hawaiian collectibles is **Collectibles and Fine Junque,** on Highway 50, next to the fire station on the way to Waimea Canyon. This is where you'll discover what it's like to be the proverbial bull in a china shop. (Even a knapsack makes it hard to get through the aisles.) Heaps of vintage linens, choice aloha shirts and muumuus, rare glassware (and junque, too), books, ceramics, authentic 1950s cotton chenille bedspreads, and a back room full of bargain-priced secondhand goodies always capture our attention. You never know what you'll find in this tiny corner of Waimea.

Be sure to stop in **Aunty Lilikoi Passion Fruit Products,** 9633 Kaumualii Hwy. in Waimea (*©* 866-LILIKOI or 808/338-1296; www.auntylilikoi.com), where they have wonderful products—from jelly to mustard to butter to soap—all made from lilikoi. They will even ship your purchase home for you.

Up in Kokee State Park, the gift shop of the **Kokee Natural History Museum** (*©* 808/335-9975) is *the* stop for botanical, geographical, historical, and nature-related books and gifts, not only on Kauai, but on all the islands. Audubon bird books, hiking maps, and practically every book on Kauai ever written line the shelves.

5 The Coconut Coast

As you make your way from Lihue to the North Shore, you'll pass **Bambulei** (*©* 808/823-8641), bordering the cane field in Wailua next to Caffè Coco. Bambulei houses a charming collection of 1930s and 1940s treasures—everything from Peking lacquerware to exquisite vintage aloha shirts to lamps, quilts, jewelry, parrot figurines, and zany salt and pepper shakers. If it's not vintage, it will look vintage, and it's bound to be fabulous. Vintage muumuus are often in perfect condition, and dresses go for $20 to $2,000.

Wood-turner **Robert Hamada** (*©* 808/822-3229) works in his studio at the foot of the Sleeping Giant, quietly producing museum-quality works with unique textures and grains. His skill, his lathe, and his more than 60 years of experience have brought luminous life to the kou, milo, *kauila,* camphor, mango, and native woods he logs himself.

WAILUA

The Kinipopo Shopping Village, on Kuhio Highway just past Wailea Beach, is more of a mini-mall than a "shopping village," but a few places here are worth a stop. Entering **The Tin Can Mailman** (*©* 808/822-3009) is like stepping into the past. It's filled with old things Hawaiian, like out-of-print books on Hawaii, rare artifacts, kitschy items from the 1940s, and artwork. **Kauai Water Ski and Surf Co.** (*©* 808/822-3574) has everything you could possibly need for playing in the water, from swimwear to equipment (fins, mask, snorkel, and so on), all for sale and for rent.

KAPAA

Moving toward Kapaa on Highway 56 (Kuhio Hwy.), don't get your shopping hopes up; until you hit Kapaa town, quality goods are slim in this neck of the woods. The

Coconut Marketplace features the ubiquitous Elephant Walk gift shop, **Gifts of Kauai,** and various other underwhelming souvenir and clothing shops sprinkled among the sunglass huts. Our favorite shop here is the unassuming **Overboard,** a small but tasteful boutique with great aloha shirts by Kahala, Tommy Bahama, Duke Kahanamoku, and other top labels for men and women. Also check out **Ship Store Gallery** (© 808/822-7758) for an unusual collection of nautical artwork, antiques, and contemporary Japanese art.

Nearby, set back from the main road across from Foodland supermarket, **Marta's Boat** is one of the island's more appealing boutiques for children and women. The shop is a tangle of accessories, toys, chic clothing, and unusual gift items.

Among the green-and-white wooden storefronts of nearby **Kauai Village,** you'll find everything from **Wyland Galleries'** trite marine art to Yin Chiao Chinese cold pills and organic produce at **Papayas Natural Foods.** Although its prepared foods are way overpriced, Papayas carries the full range of health-food products and is your only choice in the area for vitamins, health foods to go, health-conscious cosmetics, and bulk food items. Also in the same shopping mall is **Life's Treasures** (© 808/823-0042), a potpourri of interesting items ranging from crystals to jewelry, including aromatherapy, gemstones, cards, books, and CDs. If you are interested in Hawaiian arts and crafts, stop by **Kauai's Heritage Center of Hawaiian Culture & the Arts** (© 808/821-2070), which not only has a retail shop with authentic Hawaiian artwork, but also offers exhibits, demonstrations, and lectures on Hawaiian culture and art. You can sign up for workshops ranging from lei-making and hula to language and legends.

Less than a mile away, on the main road, the **Waipouli Variety Store** is Kapaa's version of Maui's fabled Hasegawa General Store—a tangle of fishing supplies, T-shirts, thongs, beach towels, and souvenirs. Fishermen love this store as much as cookie lovers swear by nearby **Popo's Cookies,** the *ne plus ultra* of store-bought cookies on the island. Popo's chocolate-chip, macadamia-nut, chocolate–macadamia nut, chocolate-coconut, almond, peanut butter, and other varieties of butter-rich cookies are among the most sought-after food items to leave the island.

And Kapaa town is full of surprises. On the main strip, across from Sunnyside Market, you'll find the recently expanded **Kela's Glass Gallery** (© 808/822-4527), the island's showiest showplace for handmade glass in all sizes, shapes, and prices, with the most impressive selection in Hawaii. The gallery is owned and operated by Larry Barton, who loves to display more than 50 artists specializing in glass. Go nuts over the vases and studio glass pieces, functional and nonfunctional. The gallery also has a great collection of hand-carved and hand-painted wooden flowers. Continue on to **Hula Girl** (© 808/822-1950), where the wonderful and the dreamy prevail, with aloha shirts (very pricey), vintage-looking luggage covered with decals of old Hawaii, Patrice Pendarvis prints, zoris, sandals, sunglasses, and shells. Next is **South China Sea Trading Company** (© 808/823-8655), a treasure trove of Indonesian furniture, vases, artwork, wind chimes, and baskets. You'll find everything from little carved turtles for $1.95 to a bamboo four-poster bed; from mosquito netting to carved doors; from inexpensive bead necklaces to a coconut inlaid armoire for $2,500. We love the fragrance of rush and reed; the amber tones of Indonesian, Vietnamese, and Philippine crafts; the coconut rice paddles and kitchen accessories; and the sumptuous Indonesian silk sarongs of high quality and reasonable prices.

Down the street, **Earth Beads** (© 808/822-0766), on the main drag (Hwy. 56), sells beads, jewelry, gemstones, and crafts materials, along with a small selection of gifts and accessories. Across the street is the town's favorite fashion stop, **Island Hemp & Cotton** (© 808/821-0225), where Hawaii's most stylish selection of this miracle fabric is sold: gorgeous silk-hemp dresses, linen-hemp sportswear, hemp aloha shirts, Tencel clothing, T-shirts, and wide-ranging, attractive, and comfortable clothing and accessories that have shed the hippie image. It's also a great store for gift items, from Balinese leather goods to handmade paper, jewelry, luxury soaps, and natural-fiber clothing for men and women. A few doors to the north, **Orchid Alley** gets our vote for most adorable nursery on the island. A narrow alcove opens into a greenhouse of phalaenopsis, oncidiums, dendrobiums, and dozens of brilliant orchid varieties for shipping or carryout.

6 The North Shore

Kauai's North Shore is the premier shopping destination on the island. Stylish, sophisticated galleries and shops, such as **Kong Lung,** in a 1942 Kilauea stone building (the last to be built on the Kilauea Plantation) off Highway 56 on Kilauea Road (© 808/828-1822), have launched these former hippie villages into top-drawer shopping spots. Save your time, energy and, most of all, discretionary funds for this end of the island. Kong Lung, through all its changes, including pricier merchandise in every category, remains a showcase of design, style, and quality, with merchandise from top-of-the-line dinnerware and bath products to aloha shirts, jewelry, ceramics, women's wear, stationery, and personal and home accessories. The book selection is fabulous, and the home accessories—sake sets, tea sets, lacquer bowls, handblown glass, pottery—are unequaled in Hawaii. The items are expensive, but browsing here is a joy. For those on a budget, the **Shared Blessings Thrift Shop** in Kilauea, across the street from the Shell Station, offers a range of great gifts and vintage used clothing.

Directly behind Kong Lung is **Lotus Gallery** (© 808/828-9898), a showstopper for lovers of antiques and designer jewelry. Good juju abounds here. The serenity and beauty will envelop you from the moment you remove your shoes and step through the door onto the bamboo floor. The gallery contains gems, crystals, Tibetan art, antiques and sari clothing from India, 12th-century Indian bronzes, temple bells, Oriental rugs, and pearl bracelets—items from $30 to $50,000. Owners Kamalia (jewelry designer) and Tsajon Von Lixfeld (gemologist) have a staggering sense of design and discovery that brings to the gallery such things as Brazilian amethyst crystal (immense and complex); emeralds; a fine, 100-strand lapis necklace ($4,000); and Kamalia's 18-karat pieces with clean, elegant lines and gemstones that soothe and elevate.

Also behind Kong Lung is **Island Soap and Candle Works** (© 808/828-1955; www.handmade-soap.com), which has been making traditional soaps for more than 2 decades. What started as a mom-and-pop operation in 1984, today is still the only soap and candle factory in Hawaii, with two locations on Kauai and a third on Oahu. You can stop by to watch them hand-pour the soap and, depending on which soap they are making that day, see them add coconut, olive, palm, macadamia, or kukui nut oils, as well as herbs and essential oils, to each bar. There is a small retail shop on the property.

In Hanalei, at **Ola's,** by the Hanalei River on the Kuhio Highway (Hwy. 560) after the bridge and before the main part of Hanalei town (© 808/826-6937), Sharon and

Doug Britt, an award-winning artist, have amassed a head-turning assortment of American and island crafts, including Doug's paintings and the one-of-a-kind furniture that he makes out of found objects, driftwood, and used materials. Britt's works—armoires, tables, lamps, bookshelves—often serve as the display surfaces for others' work, so look carefully. Lundberg Studio handblown glass, exquisite jewelry, intricately wrought pewter switch plates, sensational handblown goblets, and many other fine works fill this tasteful, seductive shop. Be on the lookout for the wonderful koa jewel boxes by local woodworker Tony Lydgate.

From health foods to groceries to Bakelite jewelry, the **Ching Young Village Shopping Center,** in the heart of Hanalei, covers a lot of bases. It's more funky than fashionable, but Hanalei, until recently, has never been about fashion. People take their time here, and there are always clusters of folks lingering at the few tables outdoors, where tables of Kauai papayas beckon from the entrance of **Hanalei Health and Natural Foods.** Next door, **Hot Rocket** is ablaze with aloha shirts, T-shirts, Reyn Spooner and Jams sportswear, flamingo china, backpacks, pareu, swimwear, and, for collectors, one of the finest collections of Bakelite accessories you're likely to see in the islands. **Savage Pearls** features a terrific collection of Tahitian black pearls, with everything from loose pearls to elegant settings to custom designs (they even repair jewelry).

Next door to Ching Young Village is **On The Road to Hanalei** (© **808/826-7360**), which is definitely worth your time to wander around in and check out the unusual T-shirts (great gifts to take home because they don't take up much suitcase space), scarves, pareu, jewelry, and other unique gifts.

Across the street in the **Hanalei Center,** the standout boutique is the **Yellowfish Trading Company** ✿ (© **808/826-1227**), where owner Gritt Benton's impeccable eye and zeal for collecting are reflected in the 1920s-to-1950s collectibles: menus, hula-girl nodders, hula lamps, rattan and koa furniture, vases, bark-cloth fabric, retro pottery and lamp bases, must-have vintage textiles, and wonderful finds in books and aloha shirts.

10

Kauai After Dark

Kauai is known for lots of things: the most beautiful beaches in the state, the magnificent Na Pali Cliffs jutting into the ocean, the incredible rainforests, and the wide panoramas of the Waimea Canyon, but it is not known for a vibrant nightlife. This is a rural island, where work stops when the sun goes down and people go to bed early. There are a few nightlife options, but you pretty much have to search them out and be ready to blend into the island-style options.

1 Lihue

The former plantation community and now county seat, Lihue is a place where local residents live and work. For action after sunset, music, dancing, and bars, the hotels and resorts are the primary players. There are a few local places, but generally all is quiet in Lihue after dark.

The **Kauai Marriott Resort & Beach Club,** 3610 Rice St., Nawiliwili (© **808/ 246-9599**), has a host of nightlife activities. **Kukui's Restaurant** has a sunset hula show on Saturday and a torch-lighting ceremony on Monday and Thursday. **Duke's Canoe Club's Barefoot Bar** offers traditional and contemporary Hawaiian music nightly. On "Tropical Friday," tropical drinks start at $4 from 4 to 6pm, when live music stirs up the joint.

On the other side of Lihue, the **Radisson Kauai Beach Resort,** 4331 Kauai Beach Dr. (© **808/245-1955;** www.radissonkauai.com), has a nightly torch-lighting ceremony and hula show in the central courtyard. Musical fans will love their dinner theater, which currently is showing Rogers and Hammerstein's *South Pacific* every Monday and Wednesday nights. The 3-hour dinner show includes a dinner buffet, a cocktail, and the show for $68 for adults and $50 for children age 12 and under.

If you are looking for a neighborhood bar, **Rob's Good Time Grill,** in the Rice Shopping Center (© **808/246-0311**), is a terrific place to have a beer, shoot some pool, watch the big-screen TV, and display your talent at karaoke. This down-home bar is not fancy, with its Formica tables, but the crowd is friendly and it's a great place to meet local folks.

If you are up for a movie, the **Kukui Grove Cinemas,** in the Kukui Grove Shopping Center, 4368 Kukui Grove St. (© **808/245-5055**), features the latest films at prices a lot cheaper than those in New York City.

For arts and culture, local residents flock to the plays put on by the nonprofessional group the **Kauai Community Players.** Call © **808/245-7700** (www.kauaicommunity players.org) to find out what the latest production is and where it will be performed. It's not Broadway (or off-Broadway), but it is energetic community theater at its best.

⸜Moments⸝ It Begins with Sunset . . .

A must-do on your Kauai vacation—take the time every day to stop and enjoy the sunset. You can watch the big yellow ball descend slowly into the blue waters of the Pacific anywhere, from Poipu to Polihale State Park to Kee Beach to the entire Na Pali Coast. Some insist on viewing the sunset with a locally made tropical mai tai. The entire day can be built around the sunset—shopping for the mai tai ingredients, checking the angle of the sun, and swimming with the knowledge that your big, salty thirst will soon be quenched with a tall, homemade mai tai on one of the world's best beaches. When the sun is low, mix the tropical drink with fresh lime juice, fresh lemon juice, fresh orange juice, passion-orange-guava juice, and fresh grapefruit juice, if possible. Pour this concoction on ice in tall, frosty glasses, and then add Meyer's rum, in which Tahitian vanilla beans have been soaking for days. (Add cinnamon if desired, or soak a cinnamon stick with the rum and vanilla beans.) A dash of Angostura bitters, a few drops of Southern Comfort as a float, a sprig of mint, a garnish of fresh lime, and voila!—you have a tropical, homemade mai tai, a cross between planter's punch and the classic Trader Vic's mai tai. As the sun sets, lift your glass and savor the moment, the setting, and the first sip—not a bad way to end the day.

In Hawaii, the mai tai is more than a libation. It's a festive, happy ritual that signals holiday, vacation, or a time of play, not work. Computers and mai tais don't mix. Mai tais and hammocks do. Mai tais and sunsets go hand in hand.

2 Poipu Resort Area

The south shore, with its sunset view and miles of white-sand beaches, is a great place for nightlife. At the far end of Poipu, **Stevenson's Library** at the **Hyatt Regency Kauai Resort & Spa,** 1571 Poipu Rd., Koloa (© 808/742-1234; www.kauai-hyatt.com), is the place for an elegant after-dinner drink with live jazz nightly from 8 to 11pm. Dress in casual resortwear (no tank tops or flip-flops) for this wood-lined bar with comfy, overstuffed chairs. You can be mesmerized by the fish in the big saltwater aquarium, or engage in activities like pool, billiards, or chess. For those so inclined, tickle the ivories on the grand piano.

Also in Poipu, **Keoki's Paradise,** in the Poipu Shopping Village, 2360 Kiahuna Plantation Dr. (© 808/742-7534), offers live music Thursday and Friday evenings from 8:30 to 10pm. The cafe menu is available from 11am to 11:30pm. Hawaiian, reggae, and contemporary music draw the 21-and-over dancing crowd. No cover.

The **Poipu Shopping Village** offers free hula performances every Monday and Thursday at 5pm in the outdoor courtyard.

Down the street at **Sheraton Kauai Resort,** 2440 Hoonani Rd. (© 808/742-1661), **The Point,** on the water, is the Poipu hotspot, featuring live music Wednesday to Saturday with dancing to a range of different artists from contemporary Hawaiian to good ol' rock and roll.

3 West Side

For a romantic evening that will linger in your memory as the highlight of your trip, **Capt. Andy's Sailing Adventure** (© 800/535-0830 or 808/335-6833; www.napali. com) has a **Na Pali Sunset Dinner,** a 4-hour cruise along the Na Pali Coast, $95 for adults and $70 for kids age 2 to 12. Your evening will include commentary on the history and legends of this coast, great views of the island from out at sea (turtles are frequently spotted), live music, and a sumptuous buffet dinner, catered by Mark's Place and Gaylord's Restaurant, offering Kauai garden salad served with sunrise papaya seed dressing, a ginger-sesame marinated Kauai tomato, green bean and red onion salad, Teriyaki chicken topped with diced pineapple, Pulehu beef with sautéed mushrooms and onions in garlic sauce, Kaffir lime and lemon rice pilaf, and pineapple bars for dessert. It's best enjoyed during the calm summer months, May to September, but they do have cruises during the winter as well.

In the old plantation community of Hanapepe, every Friday is **Hanapepe Art Night** from 5 to 9pm. Each art night is unique. Participating galleries take turns being the weekly "host gallery" offering original performances or demonstrations, which set the theme for that art night. All the galleries are lit up and decked out, giving the town a special atmosphere. Enjoy a stroll down the streets of quaint, historic Hanapepe town and meet the local artists. Also in Hanapepe on Friday night, the **Hanapepe Café,** 3830 Hanapepe Rd. (© **808/335-5011**), is open for dinner from 6 to 9pm and has live music.

4 Coconut Coast

The Coconut Coast towns of Wailua, Waipouli, and Kapaa offer sunset torch-lighting ceremonies, music, and other evening entertainment, but the real action is in the Coconut Marketplace after dark. Starting at 5pm, the **Coconut Marketplace,** 4-484 Kuhio Hwy. (© **808/822-3641**), features a daily free hula show performed by local residents ranging from the hula troop of tiny dancers who still don't have their permanent teeth, to lithe young women and men gracefully performing this ancient Hawaiian art, to grandmothers who have been dancing for decades.

For a change of pace, the **Blossoming Lotus Restaurant**, 4504 Kukui St, in Kapaa (© **808/822-7678;** www.blossominglotus.com), has nightly entertainment and music ranging from relaxing instrumentals to exotic Middle Eastern to belly dancing.

The **Hukilau Lanai Restaurant,** in the Kauai Coast Resort, located *makai* (oceanside) of the Coconut Marketplace (© **808/822-0600**), features live music Sunday, Tuesday, and Friday 6:30 to 9:30pm.

Also in the Coconut Marketplace are the **Plantation Cinema 1 and 2** for film buffs looking for a good movie. (To find out what is playing, call © **808/821-2324.**) Down the highway, the **Aloha Beach Resort** (formerly the Holiday Inn Sunspree), 3-5920 Kuhio Hwy. (© **808/823-6000;** www.alohabeachresortkauai.com), features a variety of music on Friday night, at **Kuhio's,** from 10pm to 2am, with no cover charge.

At the end of Kapaa, look for the **Shack,** 4-1639 Kuhio Hwy. (© **808/823-0200**), a family-style restaurant featuring burgers, sandwiches, and salads, which has music every night ranging from local bands to CDs being spun by disc jockeys.

If you are just looking for a place to have a drink and wind down, there are a couple of bars visited by local residents: **Pau Hana Bar and Grill,** Kauai Village Shopping Center (© **808/821-2900**); and the **Lizard Lounge,** in the Waipouli Center

Watch for the Green Flash

If you have been on the island for a few days, you'll notice that people seem to gather outside and watch the sunset. After the sun has set, several people may call out, "Green flash!"

No they haven't had too many mai tais or piña coladas. They are referring to a real, honest-to-God phenomenon that happens after sunset—there is a "green flash" of light.

The romantic version of the story is that the green flash happens when the sun kisses the ocean good night. (Honeymooners love this version.) The scientific version is not quite as dreamy; it goes something like this: Light bends as it goes around the curve of the earth. When the sun dips beneath the horizon, it is at the far end of the spectrum. So this refraction of the sun's light, coupled with the atmosphere at the extreme angle of the sunset on the horizon, causes only the color green to been seen in the color spectrum just before the light disappears.

Here's how to view the green flash: First, the day has to be clear, with no clouds or haze on the horizon. Keep checking the sun as it drops. (Try not to look directly into the sun; just glance at it to assess its position.) If the conditions are ideal, just as the sun drops into the blue waters a "flash" or laserlike beam of green will shoot out for an instant. That's the flash. May it be with you on your vacation.

(© 808/821-2205). Neither is glamorous; they are down-home, neighborhood bars with reasonably priced drinks in a relaxing atmosphere.

5 The North Shore

Kilauea generally rolls up the sidewalks at night, with the exception of the **Lighthouse Bistro** (© 808/828-0480) in the Kong Lung Center, which has live music (from Flamingo guitar to Hawaiian music) during dinner from Wednesday to Sunday.

Hanalei has some action, primarily at **Sushi & Blues,** in Ching Young Village (© 808/826-4105). Reggae, rhythm and blues, rock, and good music by local groups draw dancers and revelers Wednesday, Thursday, and Sunday from 8:30pm on. The format changes often there, so call ahead to see who's playing.

Across the street, **Hanalei Gourmet,** in the Old Hanalei Schoolhouse, 5-5161 Kuhio Hwy. (© 808/826-2524), has live music every night. Down the road, **Tahiti Nui** (© 808/826-6277) is a great place to "experience" old Hawaii. Stop by for an exotic drink, and "talk story" with the owner, Louise Marston, who actually is from Tahiti. The restaurant/bar is family-friendly and someone always seems to drop in and sing and play music, just like they used to do in the "old days."

Every week, **Ki Hoalu, Slack Key Guitar Music of Hawaii** (© 808/826-1469; www.alohaplentyhawaii.com/shows01.htm) performs at the Hanalei Community Center, usually Fridays at 4pm and Sundays at 3pm. In addition to old-style slack-key guitar, they also feature stories and legends of Hawaii. Cost is $10 for adults and $8 for children.

Just down the road, Princeville has several nightlife spots. **Hanalei Bay Resort,** 5380 Honoiki St. (© **808/826-6522;** www.hanaleibayresort.com), is a music lover's gem, with a Sunday Jazz Jam in its **Happy Talk Lounge** from 3 to 7pm and again on Saturday from 6:30 to 9:30pm. Al Jarreau and Quincy Jones are among those who have stopped by the Sunday Jazz Jam, and the evening crowd has had its share of well-known Hawaiian jammers. On Saturday evenings, Kenny Emerson, a fabulous guitar and steel-guitar player, performs with Michelle Edwards; if you're lucky, they'll play "Hula Blues" and other 1920s to 1940s hits.

Over at the **Princeville Resort Kauai,** 5520 Kahaku Rd. (© **808/826-9644;** www. princeville.com), in the main lobby, the **Living Room** (filled with comfy, overstuffed furniture) has a range of nightlife activities, like a Hawaiian ceremony of chanting, dancing, and an entertaining talk on Hawaiian culture, from 6:30pm on Tuesday, Thursday, and Sunday, and other island-related entertainment from 7 to 11pm the rest of the week.

As close as you can get to a neighborhood pub is **The Landing Pad,** located in the old Princeville Airport, 5-3541 Kuhio Hwy. (© **808/826-9561**). Open from 8pm on, Wednesday through Sunday. They feature a range of music from reggae to salsa (with salsa dance lessons even) to rock 'n' roll.

Appendix:
Hawaii in Depth

Today, other tropical islands are closing in on the 50th state's position as the world's premier beach destination. But Hawaii isn't just another pretty place in the sun. There's an undeniable quality ingrained in the local culture and lifestyle—the quick smiles to strangers, the feeling of family, the automatic extension of courtesy and tolerance. It's the aloha spirit.

1 History 101

Paddling outrigger canoes, the first ancestors of today's Hawaiians followed the stars and birds across a trackless sea to Hawaii, which they called "the land of raging fire." Those first settlers were part of the great Polynesian migration that settled the vast triangle of islands stretching from New Zealand in the southwest to Easter Island in the east to Hawaii in the north. No one is sure exactly when they came to Hawaii from Tahiti and the Marquesas Islands, some 2,500 miles to the south, but a dog-bone fish hook found at the southernmost tip of the Big Island has been carbon-dated to A.D. 700.

An entire Hawaiian culture arose from these settlers. Each island became a separate kingdom. The inhabitants built temples, fish ponds, and aqueducts to irrigate taro plantations. Sailors became farmers and fishermen. The *alii* (high-ranking chiefs) created a caste system and established taboos. Ritual human sacrifices were common.

THE "FATAL CATASTROPHE" No ancient Hawaiian ever imagined a *haole* (a white person; literally, one with "no breath") would ever appear on one of these "floating islands." But then one day, in 1779, just such a person sailed into Waimea Bay on Kauai, where he was welcomed as the god Lono.

The man was 50-year-old Captain James Cook, already famous in Britain for "discovering" much of the South Pacific. Now on his third great voyage of exploration, Cook had set sail from Tahiti northward across uncharted waters to find the mythical Northwest Passage that was said to link the Pacific and Atlantic oceans. On his way, Cook stumbled upon the Hawaiian Islands quite by chance. He named them the Sandwich Islands, for the Earl of Sandwich, first lord of the admiralty, who had bankrolled the expedition.

Overnight, Stone-Age Hawaii entered the age of iron. Gifts were presented and objects traded: nails for fresh water, pigs, and the affections of Hawaiian women. The sailors brought syphilis, measles, and other diseases to which the Hawaiians had no natural immunity, thereby unwittingly wreaking havoc on the native population.

After his unsuccessful attempt to find the Northwest Passage, Cook returned to Kealakekua Bay on the Big Island, where a fight broke out over an alleged theft, and the great navigator was killed by a blow to the head. After this "fatal catastrophe," the British survivors sailed home. But Hawaii was now on the sea charts. French, Russian, American, and other traders on the fur route between Canada's Hudson Bay Company and China anchored in Hawaii to get fresh water. More trade—and more disastrous liaisons—ensued.

Two more sea captains left indelible marks on the islands: The first was American John Kendrick, who, in 1791, stripped Hawaii of its sandalwood and sailed to China. The second captain was Englishman George Vancouver, who, in 1793, left cows and sheep, which spread out to the high-tide lines. King Kamehameha I sent to Mexico and Spain for cowboys to round up the wild livestock, thus beginning the islands' *paniolo* (Hawaiian cowboy) tradition.

The tightly woven Hawaiian society, enforced by royalty and religious edicts, began to unravel after the death in 1819 of King Kamehameha I, who had used guns seized from a British ship to unite the islands under his rule. One of his successors, Queen Kaahumanu, abolished the old taboos, thus opening the door for religion of another form.

STAYING TO DO WELL In April 1820, God-fearing missionaries arrived from New England, bent on converting the pagans. Intent on instilling their brand of rock-ribbed Christianity on the islands, the missionaries clothed the natives, banned them from dancing the hula, and nearly dismantled their ancient culture. They tried to keep the whalers and sailors out of the bawdy houses, where a flood of whiskey quenched fleet-sized thirsts, and the virtue of native women was never safe. They taught reading and writing, created the 12-letter Hawaiian alphabet, started a printing press, and began recording the islands' history, until then only an oral account in remembered chants.

Children of the missionaries became the islands' business leaders and politicians. They married Hawaiians and stayed on in the islands, causing one wag to remark that the missionaries "came to do good and stayed to do well." In 1848, King Kamehameha III proclaimed the Great Mahele (division), which enabled commoners and, eventually, foreigners to own crown land. In two generations, more than 80% of all private land was in *haole* hands. Sugar planters imported waves of immigrants to work the fields as contract laborers. The first Chinese came in 1852, followed by Portuguese in 1878, and Japanese in 1885.

King David Kalakaua was elected to the throne in 1874. This popular "Merrie Monarch" built Iolani Palace in 1882, threw extravagant parties, and lifted the prohibitions on the hula and other native arts. For this, he was much loved. He also gave Pearl Harbor to the United States; it became the westernmost bastion of the U.S. Navy. In 1891, King Kalakaua visited chilly San Francisco, caught a cold, and died in the royal suite of the Sheraton Palace. His sister, Queen Liliuokalani, assumed the throne.

A SAD FAREWELL On January 17, 1893, a group of American sugar planters and missionary descendants, with the support of gun-toting U.S. Marines, imprisoned Queen Liliuokalani in her own palace, where she penned the sorrowful lyric "Aloha Oe," Hawaii's song of farewell. The monarchy was dead.

A new republic was established, controlled by Sanford Dole, a powerful sugarcane planter. In 1898, through annexation, Hawaii became an American territory ruled by Dole. His fellow sugarcane planters, known as the Big Five, controlled banking, shipping, hardware, and every other facet of economic life on the islands.

Oahu's central Ewa Plain soon filled with row crops. The Dole family planted pineapple on its vast acreage. Planters imported more contract laborers from Puerto Rico (1900), Korea (1903), and the Philippines (1907–31). Most of the new immigrants stayed on to establish families and become a part of the islands.

Meanwhile, the native Hawaiians became a landless minority.

For nearly a century on Hawaii, sugar was king, generously subsidized by the U.S. government. The sugar planters dominated the territory's economy, shaped its social fabric, and kept the islands in a colonial-plantation era with bosses and field hands. But the workers eventually struck for higher wages and improved working conditions, and the planters found themselves unable to compete with cheap third-world labor costs.

THE TOURISTS ARRIVE Tourism proper began in the 1860s. Kilauea volcano was one of the world's prime attractions for adventure travelers, who rode on horseback 29 miles from Hilo to peer into the boiling hellfire. In 1865, a grass version of Volcano House was built on the Halemaumau Crater rim to shelter visitors; it was Hawaii's first tourist hotel. But tourism really got off the ground with the demise of the plantation era.

In 1901, W. C. Peacock built the elegant Beaux Arts Moana Hotel on Waikiki Beach, and W. C. Weedon convinced Honolulu businessmen to bankroll his plan to advertise Hawaii in San Francisco. Armed with a stereopticon and tinted photos of Waikiki, Weedon sailed off, in 1902, for 6 months of lecture tours to introduce "those remarkable people and the beautiful lands of Hawaii." He drew packed houses. A tourism-promotion bureau was formed, in 1903, and about 2,000 visitors came to Hawaii that year.

Steamships were Hawaii's tourism lifeline. It took 4½ days to sail from San Francisco to Honolulu. Streamers, leis, and pomp welcomed each Matson liner at downtown's Aloha Tower. Well-heeled visitors brought trunks, servants, even their Rolls-Royces, and stayed for months. Hawaii amused the idle rich with personal tours, floral parades, and shows spotlighting that naughty dance, the hula.

Beginning in 1935, and running for the next 40 years, Webley Edwards' weekly live radio show, "Hawaii Calls," planted the sounds of Waikiki—surf, sliding steel guitar, sweet Hawaiian harmonies, drumbeats—in the hearts of millions of listeners in the United States, Australia, and Canada.

By 1936, visitors could fly to Honolulu from San Francisco on the *Hawaii Clipper*, a seven-passenger Pan American Martin M-130 flying boat, for $360 one-way. The flight took 21 hours, 33 minutes. Modern tourism was born, with five flying boats providing daily service. The 1941 visitor count was a brisk 31,846 through December 6.

WORLD WAR II & ITS AFTERMATH On December 7, 1941, Japanese Zeros came out of the rising sun to bomb American warships based at Pearl Harbor. This was the "day of infamy" that plunged the United States into World War II.

The aftermath of the attack brought immediate changes to the islands. Martial law was declared, stripping the Big Five cartel of its absolute power in a single day. Feared to be spies, Japanese Americans and German Americans were interned in Hawaii as well as in California. Hawaii was "blacked out" at night, Waikiki Beach was strung with barbed wire, and Aloha Tower was painted in camouflage. Only young men bound for the Pacific came to Hawaii during the war years. Many came back to graves in a cemetery called Punchbowl.

The postwar years saw the beginnings of Hawaii's faux culture. Harry Yee invented the Blue Hawaii cocktail and dropped in a tiny Japanese parasol. Vic Bergeron created the mai tai, a rum and fresh-lime-juice drink, and opened Trader Vic's, America's first theme restaurant that featured the art, decor, and food of Polynesia. Arthur Godfrey picked up a ukulele and began singing *hapa-haole* tunes on early TV shows. Burt Lancaster and Deborah Kerr made love in the surf at Hanauma Bay in 1954's *From Here to Eternity*. In 1955, Henry J. Kaiser built the Hilton Hawaiian Village, and the 11-story high-rise Princess Kaiulani Hotel opened on a site where the real princess once played. Hawaii greeted 109,000 visitors that year.

STATEHOOD In 1959, Hawaii became the 50th of the United States. That year also saw the arrival of the first jet airliners, which brought 250,000 tourists to the fledgling state. The personal touch that had defined aloha gave way to the sheer force of numbers. Waikiki's room count virtually doubled in 2 years, from 16,000 units, in 1969, to 31,000, in 1971; more followed before city fathers finally clamped a growth lid on the world's most famous resort. By 1980, annual arrivals had reached four million.

In the early 1980s, the Japanese began traveling overseas in record numbers, and they brought lots of yen to spend. Their effect on sales in Hawaii was phenomenal: European boutiques opened branches in Honolulu, and duty-free shopping became the main supporter of Honolulu International Airport. Japanese investors competed for the chance to own or build part of Hawaii. Hotels sold so fast and at such unbelievable prices that heads began to spin with dollar signs.

In 1986, Hawaii's visitor count passed five million. Just 2 years later, it went over six million. Expensive fantasy megaresorts bloomed on the neighbor islands like giant artificial flowers, swelling the luxury market with ever-swankier accommodations.

The highest visitor count ever recorded was 6.9 million in 1990, but the bubble burst, in early 1991, with the Gulf War and worldwide recessions. In 1992, Hurricane Iniki devastated Kauai, which is only now staggering back to its feet. Airfare wars sent Americans to Mexico and the Caribbean. Overbuilt with luxury hotels, Hawaii slashed its room rates, giving middle-class consumers access to high-end digs at affordable prices—a trend that continues as Hawaii struggles to stay atop the tourism heap.

2 Hawaii Today

A CULTURAL RENAISSANCE A conch shell sounds, a young man in a bright feather cape chants, torch lights flicker at sunset on Waikiki Beach, and hula dancers begin telling their graceful centuries-old stories. It's a cultural scene out of the past come to life once again—for Hawaii is enjoying a renaissance of hula, chant, and other aspects of its ancient culture.

The biggest, longest, and most elaborate celebrations of Hawaiian culture are the Aloha Festivals, which encompass more than 500 cultural events from August through October. "Our goal is to teach and share our culture," says Gloriann Akau, who manages the Big Island's Aloha Festivals. "In 1946, after the war, Hawaiians needed an identity. We were lost and needed to regroup. When we started to celebrate our culture, we began to feel proud. We have a wonderful culture that had been buried for a number of years. This brought it out again. Self-esteem is more important than making a lot of money."

In 1985, native Hawaiian educator, author, and *kupuna* George Kanahele started integrating Hawaiian values into hotels like the Big Island's Mauna Lani and Maui's Kaanapali Beach Hotel. (A *kupuna* is a respected elder with leadership qualities.) "You have the responsibility to preserve and enhance the Hawaiian culture, not because it's going to make money for you, but because it's the right thing to do," Kanahele said. "Ultimately, the only thing unique about Hawaii is its

Hawaiianness. Hawaiianness is our competitive edge."

From general managers to maids, resort employees went through hours of Hawaiian cultural training. They held focus groups to discuss the meaning of *aloha*—the Hawaiian concept of unconditional love—and applied it to their work and their lives. Now many hotels have joined the movement and instituted Hawaiian programs. No longer content with teaching hula as a joke, resorts now employ a real *kumu hula* (hula teacher) to instruct visitors, and have a *kupuna* take guests on treks to visit *heiau* (temples) and ancient petroglyph sites.

3 Life & Language

Plantations brought so many different people to Hawaii that the state is now a rainbow of ethnic groups. Living here are Caucasians, African Americans, American Indians, Eskimos, Japanese, Chinese, Filipinos, Koreans, Tahitians, Vietnamese, Hawaiians, Samoans, Tongans, and other Asian and Pacific islanders. Add a few Canadians, Dutch, English, French, Germans, Irish, Italians, Portuguese, Scottish, Puerto Ricans, and Spaniards. Everyone's a minority here.

THE HAWAIIAN LANGUAGE

Almost everyone here speaks English, so except for pronouncing the names of places, you should have no trouble communicating in Hawaii.

But many folks in Hawaii now speak Hawaiian as well, for the ancient language is making a comeback. All visitors will hear the words *aloha* and *mahalo* (thank you). If you've just arrived, you're a *malihini*. Someone who's been here a long time is a *kamaaina*. When you finish a job or your meal, you are *pau* (over). On Friday, it's *pau hana*, work over. You put *pupu* (Hawaii's version of hors d'oeuvres) in your mouth when you go *pau hana*.

The Hawaiian alphabet, created by the New England missionaries, has only 12 letters: the five regular vowels (a, e, i, o, and u) and seven consonants (h, k, l, m, n, p, and w). The vowels are pronounced in the Roman fashion, that is, *ah, ay, ee, oh,* and *oo* (as in "too")—not *ay, ee, eye, oh,* and *you*, as in English. For example, *huhu* is pronounced *who-who*. Most vowels are sounded separately, though some are pronounced together, as in Kalakaua: *Kahlah-cow-ah.*

WHAT *HAOLE* MEANS When Hawaiians first saw Western visitors, they called the pale-skinned, frail men *haole,* because they looked so out of breath. In Hawaiian, *ha* means *breath,* and *ole* means an absence of what precedes it. In other words, a lifeless-looking person. Today, the term *haole* is generally a synonym for Caucasian or foreigner and is used casually without any intended disrespect. However, if uttered by an angry stranger who adds certain adjectives (like "stupid"), the term can be construed as a mild racial slur.

SOME HAWAIIAN WORDS Here are some basic Hawaiian words that you'll often hear in Hawaii and see throughout this book. For a more complete list of Hawaiian words, point your Web browser to **www.geocities.com/~olelo/hltable ofcontents.html** or **www.hisurf.com/ hawaiian/dictionary.html**.

akamai   smart

alii   Hawaiian royalty

aloha   greeting or farewell

halau   school

hale   house or building

heiau   Hawaiian temple or place of worship

hui   club, assembly

kahuna   priest or expert

kamaaina   old-timer

kapa   tapa, bark cloth

kapu   taboo, forbidden

keiki   child

lanai   porch or veranda

lomilomi   massage

mahalo   thank you

makai   a direction, toward the sea

malihini   stranger, newcomer

mana   spirit power

mauka   a direction, toward the mountains

muumuu   loose-fitting gown or dress

nene   official state bird, a goose

ono   delicious

pali   cliff

paniolo   Hawaiian cowboy(s)

wiki   quick

PIDGIN: 'EH FO'REAL, BRAH

If you venture beyond the tourist areas, you might hear another local tongue: pidgin English. A conglomeration of slang and words from the Hawaiian language, pidgin developed as a method sugar planters used to communicate with their Chinese laborers in the 1800s.

"Broke da mouth" (tastes really good) is the favorite pidgin phrase and one you might hear; "'Eh fo'real, brah" means "It's true, brother." You could be invited to hear an elder "talk story" (relating myths and memories) or to enjoy local treats like "shave ice" (a tropical snow cone) and "crack seed" (highly seasoned preserved fruit). But since pidgin is really the province of the locals, your visit to Hawaii is likely to pass without your hearing much pidgin at all.

4 A Taste of Hawaii

TRIED & TRUE: HAWAII REGIONAL CUISINE

Hawaii's tried-and-true baseline remains Hawaii Regional Cuisine (HRC), established in the mid-1980s in a culinary revolution that catapulted Hawaii into the global epicurean arena. The international training, creative vigor, fresh ingredients, and cross-cultural menus of the 12 original HRC chefs have made the islands a dining destination applauded and emulated nationwide. (In a tip of the toque to island tradition, *ahi*—a word ubiquitous in Hawaii—has replaced *tuna* on many chic New York menus.) And other options have proliferated at all levels of the local dining spectrum: Waves of new Asian residents have transplanted the traditions of their homelands to the fertile soil of Hawaii, resulting in unforgettable taste treats true to their Thai, Vietnamese, Japanese, Chinese, and Indo-Pacific roots. When combined with the bountiful, fresh harvests from sea and land for which Hawaii is known, these ethnic and culinary traditions take on renewed vigor

and a cross-cultural, uniquely Hawaiian quality.

Hawaii Regional Cuisine has evolved as Hawaii's singular cooking style, what some say is this country's current gastronomic, as well as geographic, frontier. It highlights the fresh seafood and produce of Hawaii's rich waters and volcanic soil, the cultural traditions of Hawaii's ethnic groups, and the skills of well-trained chefs who broke ranks with their European predecessors to forge new ground in the 50th state.

Fresh ingredients are foremost here. Farmers and fishermen work together to provide steady supplies of just-harvested seafood, seaweed, fern shoots, vine-ripened tomatoes, goat cheese, lamb, herbs, taro, gourmet lettuces, and countless harvests from land and sea. These ingredients wind up in myriad forms on ever-changing menus, prepared in Asian and Western culinary styles. Exotic fruits introduced by recent Southeast Asian emigrants—such as sapodilla, soursop, and rambutan—are beginning to appear regularly in Chinatown markets. Aquacultural seafood, from seaweed to salmon to lobster, is a staple on many menus. Additionally, fresh-fruit sauces (mango, litchi, papaya, pineapple, guava), ginger-sesame-wasabi flavorings, corn cakes with sake sauces, tamarind and fish sauces, coconut-chile accents, tropical-fruit vinaigrettes, and other local and newly arrived seasonings from Southeast Asia and the Pacific impart unique qualities to the preparations.

Here's a sampling of what you can expect to find on a Hawaii Regional menu: seared Hawaiian fish with lilikoi shrimp butter; taro-crab cakes; Pahoa corn cakes; Molokai sweet-potato or breadfruit vichyssoise; Ka'u orange sauce and Kahua Ranch lamb; fern shoots from Waipio Valley; Maui onion soup and Hawaiian bouillabaisse, with fresh snapper, Kona crab, and fresh aquacultural shrimp; blackened ahi summer rolls; herb-crusted onaga; and gourmet Waimanalo greens, picked that day. You may also encounter locally made cheeses, squash and taro risottos, Polynesian imu-baked foods, and guava-smoked meats. If there's pasta or risotto or rack of lamb on the menu, it could be *nori* (red algae) linguine with *opihi* (limpet) sauce, or risotto with local seafood served in taro cups, or rack of lamb in cabernet and *hoisin* sauce (fermented soybean, garlic, and spices). Watch for ponzu sauce, too; it's lemony and zesty, a welcome new staple on local menus.

PLATE LUNCHES & MORE: LOCAL FOOD

At the other end of the spectrum is the vast and endearing world of "local food." By that, we mean plate lunches and poke, shave ice and saimin, bento lunches and manapua—cultural hybrids all.

Reflecting a polyglot population of many styles and ethnicities, Hawaii's idiosyncratic dining scene is eminently inclusive. Consider Surfer Chic: Barefoot in the sand, in a swimsuit, you chow down on a **plate lunch** ordered from a lunch wagon, consisting of fried mahimahi, "two scoops rice," macaroni salad, and a few leaves of green, typically julienned cabbage. (Generally, teriyaki beef and shoyu chicken are options.) Heavy gravy is often the condiment of choice, accompanied by a soft drink in a paper cup. Like **saimin**—the local version of noodles in broth topped with scrambled eggs, green onions, and, sometimes, pork—the plate lunch is Hawaii's version of high camp.

Because this is Hawaii, at least a few licks of *poi*—cooked, pounded taro (the traditional Hawaiian staple crop)—and other examples of indigenous cuisine are a must. Other **native foods** include those from before and after Western contact, such as *laulau* (pork, chicken, or fish steamed in ti leaves), *kalua* pork (pork cooked in a Polynesian underground oven known here as an *imu*), *lomi* salmon (salted salmon with tomatoes and green onions), squid *luau* (cooked in coconut milk and taro tops), *poke* (cubed raw fish seasoned with onions and seaweed and the occasional sprinkling of roasted *kukui* nuts), *haupia* (creamy coconut pudding), and *kulolo* (steamed pudding of coconut, brown sugar, and taro).

Bento, another popular quick meal available throughout Hawaii, is a compact, boxed assortment of picnic fare usually consisting of neatly arranged sections of rice, pickled vegetables, and fried chicken, beef, or pork. Increasingly, however, the bento is becoming more health-conscious, as in macrobiotic bento lunches or vegetarian brown-rice bentos. A derivative of the modest lunch box for Japanese immigrants who once labored in the sugar and pineapple fields, bentos are dispensed everywhere, from department stores to corner delis and supermarkets.

Also from the plantations come **manapua,** a bready, doughy sphere filled with tasty fillings of sweetened pork or sweet beans. In the old days, the Chinese "manapua man" would make his rounds with bamboo containers balanced on a rod over his shoulders. Today you'll find white or whole-wheat manapua containing chicken, vegetables, curry, and other savory fillings.

The daintier Chinese delicacy **dim sum** is made of translucent wrappers filled with fresh seafood, pork hash, and vegetables, served for breakfast and lunch in Chinatown restaurants. The Hong Kong–style dumplings are ordered fresh and hot from bamboo steamers from invariably brusque servers who move their carts from table to table. Much like hailing a taxi in Manhattan, you have to be quick and loud for dim sum.

For dessert or a snack, particularly on Oahu's north shore, the prevailing choice is **shave ice,** the island version of a snow cone. Particularly on hot, humid days, long lines of shave-ice lovers gather for the rainbow-colored cones heaped with finely shaved ice and topped with sweet tropical syrups. (The sweet-sour *li hing mui* flavor is a current rage.) The fast-melting mounds, which require prompt, efficient consumption, are quite the local summer ritual for sweet tooths.

AHI, ONO & OPAKAPAKA: A HAWAIIAN SEAFOOD PRIMER

The seafood in Hawaii has been described as the best in the world. In Janice Wald Henderson's pivotal book *The New Cuisine of Hawaii,* acclaimed chef Nobuyuki Matsuhisa (chef/owner of Matsuhisa in Beverly Hills and Nobu in Manhattan and London) writes, "As a chef who specializes in fresh seafood, I am in awe of the quality of Hawaii's fish; it is unparalleled anywhere else in the world." And why not? Without a doubt, the islands' surrounding waters, including the waters of the remote northwestern Hawaiian Islands, and a growing aquaculture industry contribute to the high quality of the seafood here.

The reputable restaurants in Hawaii buy fresh fish daily at predawn auctions or from local fishermen. Some chefs even catch their ingredients themselves. "Still wiggling" or "just off the hook" are the ultimate terms for freshness in Hawaii. The fish can then be grilled over *kiawe* (mesquite) or prepared in innumerable other ways.

Although most menus include the Western description for the fresh fish used, most often the local nomenclature is listed, turning dinner for the uninitiated into a confusing, quasi-foreign experience. To help familiarize you with the menu language of Hawaii, here's a basic glossary of island fish:

ahi   yellowfin or bigeye tuna, important for its use in sashimi and poke at sushi bars and in Hawaii Regional Cuisine

aku   skipjack tuna, heavily used by local families in home cooking and poke

ehu   red snapper, delicate and sumptuous, yet lesser known than opakapaka

hapuupuu   grouper, a sea bass whose use is expanding from ethnic to nonethnic restaurants

hebi   spearfish, mildly flavored, and frequently featured as the "catch of the day" in upscale restaurants

kajiki   Pacific blue marlin, also called *au,* with a firm flesh and high fat content that make it a plausible substitute for tuna in some raw fish dishes and as a grilled item on menus

kumu   goatfish, a luxury item on Chinese and upscale menus, served *en papillote* or steamed whole, Oriental style, with sesame oil, scallions, ginger, and garlic

mahimahi   dolphin fish (the game fish, not the mammal) or dorado, a classic sweet, white-fleshed fish requiring vigilance among purists, because it's often disguised as fresh when it's actually "fresh-frozen"—a big difference

monchong   bigscale or sickle pomfret, an exotic, tasty fish, scarce but gaining a higher profile on Hawaiian Island menus

nairagi   striped marlin, also called *au;* good as sashimi and in poke, and often substituted for ahi in raw-fish products

onaga   ruby snapper, a luxury fish, versatile, moist, and flaky

ono   wahoo, firmer and drier than the snappers, often served grilled and in sandwiches

opah   moonfish, rich and fatty, and versatile—cooked, raw, smoked, and broiled

opakapaka   pink snapper, light, flaky, and luxurious, suited for sashimi,

poaching, sautéing, and baking; the best-known upscale fish

papio   jack trevally, light, firm, and flavorful, and favored in island cookery

shutome   broadbill swordfish, of beeflike texture and rich flavor

tombo   albacore tuna, with a high fat content, suitable for grilling and sautéing

uhu   parrotfish, most often encountered steamed, Chinese-style

uku   gray snapper of clear, pale-pink flesh, delicately flavored and moist

ulua   large jack trevally, firm-fleshed and versatile

5 The Natural World: An Environmental Guide to the Islands

The first Hawaiian Islands were born of violent volcanic eruptions that took place deep beneath the ocean's surface, about 70 million years ago—more than 200 million years after the major continental land masses had been formed. As soon as the islands emerged, Mother Nature's fury began to carve beauty from barren rock. Untiring volcanoes spewed forth rivers of fire that cooled into stone. Severe tropical storms, some with hurricane-force winds, battered and blasted the cooling lava rock into a series of shapes. Ferocious earthquakes flattened, shattered, and reshaped the islands into precipitous valleys, jagged cliffs, and recumbent flatlands. Monstrous surf and gigantic tidal waves rearranged and polished the lands above and below the reaches of the tide.

It took millions of years for nature to shape the familiar form of Diamond Head on Oahu, Maui's majestic peak of Haleakala, the waterfalls of Molokai's northern side, the reefs of Hulopoe Bay on Lanai, and the lush rainforests of the Big Island. The result is an island chain like no other—a tropical landscape rich

in unique flora and fauna, surrounded by a vibrant underwater world.

THE ISLAND LANDSCAPES

OAHU   Oahu is the third-largest island in Hawaii (behind the Big Island and Maui). As the home of Honolulu, it's also the most urban island, with a population of nearly 900,000. Oahu is defined by two mountain ranges: the Waianae Ridge in the west, and the jagged Koolau in the east, which form a backdrop for Honolulu. These ranges divide the island into three different environments. The windward (eastern) side is lush with greenery, ferns, tropical plants, and waterfalls. On the leeward (western) side, the area between the Waianae Range and the ocean is drier, with sparse vegetation, little rainfall, and an arid landscape. Between the two mountain ranges lies the central Ewa Valley; it's moderate in temperature and vibrant with tropical plants, agricultural fields, and trees.

HAWAII, THE BIG ISLAND   By far the largest island at some 4,034 square miles (and still growing), the Big Island is twice the size of all the other islands combined. Here you'll find every type of climate zone existing in Hawaii. It's not uncommon for there to be 12 feet of snow on the two largest mountain peaks, 13,796-foot Mauna Kea and 13,680-foot Mauna Loa. These mountains are the tallest in the state; what's more, when measured from their true base on the ocean floor, they reach 32,000 feet, making them the tallest mountains in the world. The 4,077-foot Kilauea volcano has been continuously erupting since January 3, 1983, and has added more than 600 acres of new land to the Big Island since then. Just a few miles from the barely cooled barren lava lies a pristine rainforest. On the southern end of the island is an arid desert. The rest of the island contains tropical terrain; white-, black-, and even green-sand beaches; windswept grasslands; and productive farming and ranching areas growing tropical fruits, macadamia nuts, coffee, and ornamental flowers.

MAUI When two volcanoes—Mauna Kahalawai, a 5,277-foot ancient volcano in the West Maui Mountains, and 10,000-foot Haleakala—flowed together a million or so years ago, the event created a "Valley Isle" with a range of climates from arid desert to tropical rainforest. This 728-square-mile island is the only place in the world where you can drive from sea level to 10,000 feet in just 38 miles, passing from tropical beaches through sugar and pineapple plantations and rolling grassy hills up past the timber line to the lunarlike surface of the top of Haleakala. In addition to 33 miles of public beaches on the south and west shores, Maui is home to the arid lands of Kihei, the swampy bogs of the West Maui Mountains, the rainforest of Hana, and the desert of Kaupo.

MOLOKAI Roughly the shape and size of Manhattan, Molokai is 37 miles long and 10 miles wide, with a "thumb" protruding out of the North Shore. The North Shore begins on the west, with miles of white-sand beaches that fringe a desertlike landscape. The thumb—the Kalaupapa Peninsula—is cut off by a fence of cliffs, some 2,000 feet tall, that line the remainder of the north side. Molokai can be divided into two areas: the dry west end; and the rainy, tropical east and north ends. Its highest point is Mount Kamakou, at 4,970 feet.

LANAI This small, kidney bean–shaped island—only 13-miles wide by 17-miles long—rises sharply out of the ocean, with cliffs on the west side that rise to a high point of 3,370 feet. Lanai slopes down to sea level on the east and south sides. The only town, Lanai City, sits in the clouds at 1,600 feet. The island's peak is covered with Norfolk pines and is usually shrouded in clouds, while the arid beaches survive on minimal rainfall. One area in particular stands out: the Garden of the Gods, just 7 miles from Lanai City, where oddly strewn boulders lie in the amber- and ocher-colored dirt and bizarre stone formations dot the landscape. The ancient Hawaiians formed romantic legends explaining this enigma, but modern-day scientists still debate its origins.

KAUAI This compact island, 25-miles long by 33-miles wide, has Mount Waialeale, the island's highest point at nearly 5,000 feet and the earth's wettest spot, with more than 400 inches of rain annually. Just west of Mount Waialeale is the barren landscape of Waimea Canyon, dubbed "the Grand Canyon of the Pacific"—the result of the once 10,000-foot-tall Olokele shield volcano, which collapsed and formed a *caldera* (crater) some 3,600 feet deep and 14 miles across. Peaks and craters aren't Kauai's only distinctive landscape features, though: Miles of white-sand beaches rim most of the island, with majestic 2,700-foot cliffs—the spectacular Na Pali Coast—completing the circle. Lush tropical jungle inhabits the north side of the island, while balmy, palm tree–lined beaches are located in the south.

SEA LIFE

Approximately 680 species of fish are known to inhabit the waters around the Hawaiian Islands. Of those, approximately 450 species stay close to the reef and inshore areas.

CORAL   The reefs surrounding Hawaii are made up of various coral and algae. The living coral grows through sunlight that feeds a specialized alga, which in turn allows the development of the coral's calcareous skeleton. The reef, which takes thousands of years to develop, attracts and supports fish and crustaceans, which use it for food and habitat. Mother Nature can batter the reef with a strong storm or large waves, but humans—through seemingly innocuous acts such as touching the coral—have proven far more destructive.

The corals most frequently seen in Hawaii are hard, rocklike formations named for their familiar shapes: antler, cauliflower, finger, plate, and razor coral. Wire coral looks like a randomly bent wire growing straight out of the reef. Some coral appears soft, such as tube coral; it can be found in the ceilings of caves. Black coral, which resembles winter-bare trees or shrubs, is found at depths of more than 100 feet.

REEF FISH   Of the approximately 450 types of reef fish here, about 27% are native to Hawaii and are found nowhere else in the world. During the millions of years it took for the islands to sprout up from the sea, ocean currents—mainly from Southeast Asia—carried thousands of marine animals and plants to Hawaii's reef; of those, approximately 100 species not only adapted, but also thrived.

Some species are much bigger and more plentiful than their Pacific cousins, and many developed unique characteristics. Some, like the lemon or milletseed butterflyfish, developed specialized schooling and feeding behaviors. Hawaii's native fish are often surprisingly common: You can see the saddleback wrasse, for example, on virtually any snorkeling excursion or dive in Hawaiian waters.

GAME FISH   Hawaii is known around the globe as *the* place for big-game fish—marlin, swordfish, and tuna—but its waters are also great for catching other offshore fish like mahimahi, rainbow runner, and wahoo; coastal fish like barracuda and scad; bottom fish like snappers, sea bass, and amberjack; and inshore fish like trevally and bonefish.

Six kinds of **billfish** are found in the offshore waters around the islands: Pacific blue marlin, black marlin, sailfish, broadbill swordfish, striped marlin, and shortbill spearfish. Hawaii billfish range in size from the 20-pound shortbill spearfish and striped marlin to the 1,805-pound Pacific blue marlin, the largest marlin ever caught with rod and reel in the world.

Tuna ranges in size from small (a pound or less) mackerel tuna used as bait (Hawaiians call them *oioi*) to 250-pound yellowfin ahi tuna. Other local species of tuna are bigeye, albacore, kawakawa, and skipjack.

Other types of fish, also excellent for eating, include **mahimahi** (also known as dolphin fish or dorado), in the 20- to 70-pound range; **rainbow runner,** from 15 to 30 pounds; and **wahoo** (*ono*), from 15 to 80 pounds. Shoreline fishermen are always on the lookout for **trevally** (the state record for a giant trevally is 191 lb.), **bonefish, ladyfish, threadfin, leatherfish,** and **goatfish.** Bottom fishermen pursue a range of **snapper**—red, pink, gray, and others—as well as **sea bass** (the state record is a whopping 563 lb.) and **amberjack** (which weigh up to 100 lb.).

WHALES   Humpback whales are the popular visitors who come to Hawaii to mate and calve every year, beginning in November and staying until spring (Apr or so), when they return to their summer home in Alaska. On every island, you can take winter whale-watching cruises that will let you observe these magnificent leviathans close up. You can also spot their signature spouts from shore as they expel water in the distance. Humpbacks can grow up to 45 feet long, so when they breach (propel their entire body out of the water) or even wave a fluke, you can see it for miles.

Humpbacks are among the biggest whales found in Hawaiian waters, but other whales—such as pilot, sperm, false killer, melon-headed, pygmy killer, and beaked—can be seen year-round, especially in the calm waters off the Big Island's Kona Coast. These whales usually travel in pods of 20 to 40 animals and are very social, interacting with one another on the surface.

SHARKS Yes, there *are* sharks in Hawaii, but you more than likely won't see one unless you're specifically looking. About 40 different species of sharks inhabit the waters surrounding Hawaii, ranging from the totally harmless whale shark (at 60 ft., the world's largest fish), which has no teeth and is so docile that it frequently lets divers ride on its back; to the not-so-docile, infamous, and extremely uncommon great white shark. The most common sharks seen in Hawaii are white-tip reef sharks, gray reef sharks (about 5-ft. long), and black-tip reef sharks (about 6-ft. long).

HAWAII'S ECOSYSTEM PROBLEMS

Officials at Hawaii Volcanoes National Park on the Big Island saw a potential problem a few decades ago with people taking a few rocks home with them as souvenirs. To prevent this problem from escalating, the park rangers created a legend that the fiery volcano goddess, Pele, did not like people taking anything (rocks, chunks of lava) from her home, and bad luck would befall anyone disobeying her wishes. There used to be a display case in the park's visitor center filled with letters from people who had taken rocks from the volcano, relating stories of all the bad luck that followed. Most of the letters begged Pele's forgiveness and instructed the rangers to please return the rock to the exact location that was its original home.

Index

See also Accommodations and Restaurant indexes, below.

ACCOMMODATIONS

Restaurants

THE NEW TRAVELOCITY GUARANTEE

EVERYTHING YOU BOOK WILL BE RIGHT, OR WE'LL WORK WITH OUR TRAVEL PARTNERS TO MAKE IT RIGHT, RIGHT AWAY.

To drive home the point, we're going to use the word "right" in every single sentence.

Let's get right to it. Right to the meat! Only Travelocity guarantees everything about your booking will be right, or we'll work with our travel partners to make it right, right away. Right on!

Here's a picture taken smack dab right in the middle of Antigua, where the guarantee also covers you.

The guarantee covers all but one of the items pictured to the right.

For example, what if the ocean view you booked actually looks out at a downright ugly parking lot? You'd be right to call – we're there for you. And no one in their right mind would be pleased to learn the rental car place has closed and left them stranded. Call Travelocity and we'll help get you back on the right track.

Now, you may be thinking, "Yeah, right, I'm so sure." That's OK; you have the right to remain skeptical. That is until we mention help is always right around the corner. Call us right off the bat, knowing that our customer service reps are there for you 24/7. Righting wrongs. Left and right.

Now if you're guessing there are some things we can't control, like the weather, well you're right. But we can help you with most things – to get all the details in righting,* visit **travelocity.com/guarantee**.

*Sorry, spelling things right is one of the few things not covered under the guarantee.

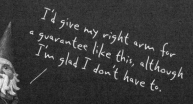

I'd give my right arm for a guarantee like this, although I'm glad I don't have to.

travelocity
You'll never roam alone.

IF YOU BOOK IT, IT SHOULD BE THERE.

Only Travelocity guarantees it will be, or we'll work
with our travel partners to make it right, right away.
So if you're missing a balcony or anything else you
booked, just call us 24/7. **1-888-TRAVELOCITY.**

travelocity
You'll never roam alone.